McALMON

and the

LOST GENERATION

McALMON

and the

LOST GENERATION

A SELF-PORTRAIT

EDITED WITH A COMMENTARY BY ROBERT E. KNOLL

UNIVERSITY OF NEBRASKA PRESS
LINCOLN AND LONDON

For Virginia, again

Contents

A picture section follows page 216.

McALMON

and the

LOST GENERATION

Prologue

In 1926 a Paris avant-garde magazine introduced to the French the work of four young American writers: E. E. Cummings, Ernest Hemingway, Robert McAlmon, and William Carlos Williams.[1] Three of these names belong to the literary history of the twentieth century. But what became of Robert McAlmon?

When Robert McAlmon died in the deserts of the American Southwest in February 1956, he and his avant-garde friends had been out of touch for years. Back in the twenties "the Crowd" —this was how McAlmon referred to them—had all been geniuses together; now in the fifties some were known to a far larger world than that of Greenwich Village, Bloomsbury, and the Left Bank. Hemingway was living his legendary life in Cuba, Malcolm Cowley had become a prominent man of letters in New York, Robert M. Coates was respected as an art critic and anthologized as a writer, Katherine Anne Porter and Kay Boyle ranked among the best storytellers of their generation, Samuel Putnam had distinguished himself as a translator, William Carlos Williams was prescribed reading in college poetry courses, and E. E. Cummings had delivered the Charles Eliot Norton lectures at Harvard. Three of McAlmon's most celebrated friends—James Joyce, Marsden Hartley, and Gertrude Stein—were dead, but their work remained triumphantly alive. Three others, for all their brilliance, had come to disaster. Ezra Pound, charged with treason, was confined in a Washington mental hospital; Hart

3

Crane and Harry Crosby had killed themselves more than twenty years before. But their names were not forgotten. They were fixtures in the history of the lost generation and the Roaring Decade.

As for McAlmon, his isolation, unlike Ezra Pound's, had been self-imposed; and his passing, unlike that of Crane and Crosby, had been neither dramatic nor appropriately timed. Indeed after his long years of obscurity, death was almost redundant.

Why, of all "the Crowd," had McAlmon been the one to drop out of sight? His stories and novels had been praised by astute critics, but more than that he was a personality and a power. Almost from the moment of his entrance into the literary life of the twenties, he had been at the center of things. The Contact Publishing Company which he founded and operated in Paris was the leading expatriate press of the day, a showcase for new and experimental writers. At a time when the old established publishing houses of America and England were slow to accept their work, Contact proved an effective pump-primer; many of McAlmon's authors got contracts with such firms as Scribner's, Macmillan, and Harper's. Some of the writers who appeared in Contact Editions were not worthy of much attention —Ezra Pound has suggested that McAlmon published a number of Paris geniuses simply to show them up [2]—and the Contact list was not large, but it carried titles by an extraordinarily influential group of authors. The contributors to McAlmon's *Contact Collection of Contemporary Writers* (1925) included Djuna Barnes, Bryher, Mary Butts, H.D., Norman Douglas, Havelock Ellis, Ford Madox Ford, Wallace Gould, Marsden Hartley, Ernest Hemingway, John Herrmann, James Joyce, Mina Loy, Ezra Pound, Dorothy Richardson, May Sinclair, Edith Sitwell, and William Carlos Williams.

Hemingway was the biggest name on his list (although this might have been disputed by Gertrude Stein, whose *Making of Americans* McAlmon published at her own behest), and bringing out Hemingway's first book was his most memorable publishing achievement. But the books he printed went unsold because he could not get them distributed in the United States, which was their natural market. McAlmon lost money, and outside his own circle he received little or no credit for having secured important new writers a hearing. The tides of taste were changing, helped along by McAlmon and others like him who encouraged the avant-garde in their break with conventional forms, and perhaps if he had hung on a few more years his publishing venture might have succeeded. But the stock-market crash, the depression, and the ominous international situation dispersed the expatriate colony, and by the mid-thirties "the Crowd" had gone home to America. Except for McAlmon: he went his way, and it took him off the literary scene.

If his friends asked *What became of McAlmon?* a younger generation may well ask *Who was McAlmon?* While there is no easy answer, certainly McAlmon was, above all, a man of his time. His life reflects all the obvious characteristics of the lost generation—rootlessness, disenchantment, an uncommon bravura and energy. In some ways he is more representative of the twenties than its accepted spokesmen. Unlike Scott Fitzgerald, he attained no early, glossy success. The *Saturday Evening Post* and the movies were not interested in him, nor he in them. The writing that recorded his observations and doings was uncomplicated by Hollywood glamour. Unlike Harry Crosby, whom Malcolm Cowley sees as the incarnation of the Jazz Age, his origins were not exalted. His uncle was not J. P. Morgan, nor had he gone to Harvard, nor was he listed in the Social Register. McAlmon was the normal, lost-generation expatriate—the "abnormal norm," one might say—and the title that he gave his last book, *Not Alone Lost,* was acknowledgment of his typicalness.

Like so many others he had been born in the Middle West, had rebelled against the provincialism of the life, had grown skeptical of the values preached by his father, a Presbyterian minister. As with the others, his college years had been interrupted by the war; he had served in the army, gone back to college for a few restless months, and then migrated to the Greenwich Village of Edna St. Vincent Millay and Maxwell Bodenheim, to the London of T. S. Eliot and Wyndham Lewis, to the Paris of James Joyce and Gertrude Stein. When the opportunity presented itself, he founded his publishing company and set out to print those books which might not otherwise have appeared. But publishing books was not enough: he wandered from city to city, from culture to culture, apparently without a plan, writing and drinking his only consistent activities. "I prefer Europe, if you mean France, to America," he wrote in 1928, "because there is less interference with private life here." [3] He acknowledged being uneasy when away from "the Crowd" too far or too long, but he stayed on in Europe when the expatriate party was over. Caught in Occupied France after the German invasion of 1940, he finally made his way back to the United States and lived out his remaining years in the Southwest, separated from his celebrated friends by time and distance.

The words *friend* and *friends* occur often in connection with Robert McAlmon. A dominant factor in his life—perhaps second only to his compulsion to write—was his personal magnetism. From first to last, and despite a belligerence that became more marked as he grew older, people were drawn to him, and he made friends as easily with James Joyce (who christened his first collection of stories) as with Kiki of Montparnasse. Even after he had lived in obscurity for twenty years, Kay Boyle, Williams, Katherine Anne Porter, Ezra Pound, and others still spoke of him affectionately.

Yet in spite of his wide circle of famous friends, in spite of his record as a writer and publisher, McAlmon has been almost entirely overlooked by literary historians of the twenties. In the published reminiscences of the period—and there were a number *—it is true that his name turns up again and again. But

* Richard Aldington, Margaret Anderson, Sherwood Anderson, George Antheil, Sylvia Beach, Gertrude Beasley, Konrad Bercovici, Lord Berners, George Biddle, Maxwell Bodenheim, Mary Butts, Emanuel Carnevali, Malcolm Cowley, E. E. Cummings, Marguerite D'Alvarez, Norman Douglas, John Gould Fletcher, Ford Madox Ford, Donald Friede, Peggy Guggenheim, Nina Hamnett, Ben Hecht, Sisley Huddleston, Matthew Josephson, Alfred Kreymborg, Grace Hegger Lewis, Wyndham Lewis, Harold Loeb, Mabel Dodge Luhan, Lady Diana Manners, Harriet Monroe, Grace Moore, Gorham Munson, Samuel Putnam, Siegfried Sassoon, Clement Shorter, George E. Slocombe, Gertrude Stein, Leo Stein, Michael Strange, J. W. N. Sullivan, Mark Van Doren, Carl Van Vechten, Glenway Wescott, William Carlos Williams, and McAlmon himself were some of the people who wrote memoirs.

still he is the man at the edge of the picture. The references to him are nearly all casual or oblique, as though the authors assume that of course we know him too.

In the context of McAlmon's own writing, however, these random remarks are unexpectedly illuminating. The memoirists comment on McAlmon; McAlmon comments on them; and their conjoined observations shed light on McAlmon, his friends, and their milieu. "He doesn't exclude anything from his world and is like Walt Whitman in his completeness but differs from Whitman in that he doesn't argue with his readers," one of "the Crowd" wrote of McAlmon. "He doesn't explain either. He doesn't apologize." [4] Always sharply aware of his own identity, he put down only what he had seen for himself. Even his fiction was autobiographical. Whatever names he gave his heroes, each was a projection of himself.

All his life McAlmon worked on what he thought of as a "transcontinental novel"—a kind of epic which was to embody the ideas and qualities of a cosmopolitan people. Pieces of it lie scattered in forgotten magazines and faddish books. He never collected them. When they are brought together what they reveal is not the picture of a people—this would have required a far greater degree of objectivity than was attainable by one so bound up in himself—but a valid image of a real man. We see a young scamp in the harvest fields, a post-adolescent in Bohemia, a Paris expatriate, a deracinated wanderer, a lost and exiled spirit returning in imagination to the Dakota plains of his boyhood. And always in the background we perceive the landscape of a most fecund and exuberant period in American letters, catch glimpses—ironic but uncynical—of the makers and shakers, the dilettantes and pretenders of the twenties. From the assembled fragments of that incomplete and blemished biography-novel which McAlmon spent his life writing, there emerges a self-portrait which is also the portrait of an era and a generation.

PART I

ALL-AMERICAN
BOYHOOD
1896-1919

Comments on the persons mentioned in Part I will be found in the Biographical Repertory, beginning on page 367.

1. The Plains

Robert McAlmon's spiritual biography begins in the Bible-belt villages of the Middle West. His father was a nomadic Presbyterian minister, and shortly after McAlmon's birth in 1896—he was the tenth and last child—the family moved from Clifton, Kansas, to eastern South Dakota where for the next fourteen years they lived in a succession of small towns and villages. When McAlmon came to write of his childhood in "this wild and dreary plains state," he did so with an objectivity unblurred by nostalgic overtones. He had been endowed from the beginning with a "sceptical nature," and he had no patience with the "attitudinized insistence upon starry-eyed innocence and idealism and sentimentality of not only the child but of the 'sensitive roughneck'" which, in his view, marred so much of the work of his contemporaries. His aim was to present a straightforward account of the way things were and the way things happened. He admired candor, above all. In his sketches there are no dramatic moments of revelation or initiation, no transmogrifying insights. They are plain, simple narratives of a young boy's perplexing experiences. The boy, whether called Bennie or Horace or Grant, is McAlmon himself.[1]

The Jack Rabbit Drive

It was agreed upon by members of the community that the thousands of jack rabbits throughout the countryside must be exterminated, in part at least. Their burrowings and nibblings destroyed too much grain and property. So for two weeks the day set for a drive was given wide publicity.

Horace slipped out of the house through the kitchen, stopping there to sneak cookies from under Linda's eyes. At the moment, however, she was feeling in good humor, and her black face, already gleaming with perspiration, gleamed more with a tender smiling at his six-year-old guile, and she gave him six cookies, whereupon he went joyfully into the back yard to look hopefully about. Maybe Freddie was around to be played with. He didn't like Freddie much but he was better than nobody. Horace felt uncomfortable because his mother had put a new suit on him, and made him wear an overcoat, and if Billie Anderson saw him with his yellow hair slicked back Billie might call him "mamma's boy" and that would mean another fight, because he and Billie were supposed to have a great scrap someday to show which was the best fighter in town of their age.

It was somewhat sheepishly that he began to play with Sally Porter a few minutes later. She was more fun to be with than Freddie, if she only weren't a girl. She dared do anything, and wasn't nearly so scared of going blocks from home if she could without her mother seeing and calling her back to play on the Porter's front lawn. Horace didn't want to play there because every boy in the neighborhood could see, and Sally might want to play doll-house, which Horace didn't mind if Billie Anderson wasn't apt to know about it. The Porter horse, that was to run in the County Fair races, was picketed on the lawn too, and he'd stepped on Horace's bare foot one day when Horace was petting him. That was no fun, you can bet. The horse didn't mean to maybe, but Horace didn't want that to happen again.

As playing on the lawn was no fun at all Horace and Sally were out in back of the barn, almost without thinking to get there. It was the alley they were supposed not to play in too, because the nigger washerwoman's kids played there, since their ma's shack sat on top of the alley. Mrs. Darian told Horace there wasn't any harm in his playing with the colored children, but Mrs. Porter wouldn't let Sally. They had not been there long, however, before Horace got scared, remembering that he'd killed one of those niggers' chickens by hitting it on the head with a stone he'd thrown; except he hadn't really killed it. He had only stunned it, because when he and the nigger kids, all scared of what their mas would say, buried the rooster in the manure pile, it began to flop and finally got up and ran away, dizzy in the head. Maybe Mrs. Lincoln, the nigger woman, wasn't mad at him though, because she had sent him an egg no bigger than a robin's that one of her hens had laid, but he didn't know. Maybe she'd just sent it to please his mother for whom she did washing.

"We gotta go somewhere else and play because I'm not going to have them darkie kids butting in on us. I have an idea anyway. Billie Anderson says you can get a cent a bottle for beer bottles from the bartender at the saloon."

"Why you awful boy, Horace. If we did that we'd just get the hide licked off us and you know it," Sally said, pretending great horror. "Why mamma is always giving it to papa because he goes in there and if she heard I did that! And she would because someone would tell her."

"Aw rats, don't be a fraidy cat."

"You know I ain't no fraidy cat."

"Maybe you ain't, but Freddie is. I ast him yesterday to look for beer bottles with me and he wouldn't, and he cried and ran home and we scrapped, and he was going to tell on me, but I didn't care. I told him 'Tattle-tale, tattle-tale,
                    Hanging to the bull's tail—' "

"You are the naughtiest boy," Sally said with triumphant righteousness, and so daring Horace, encouraged him to the scandalous conclusion of the ditty. Sally believed it her duty to act shocked and refuse to speak to Horace for a few seconds, but the strain of that soon told on her, and being sure that no older person had heard Horace, she relaxed to curiosity.

"Where do you suppose we can find some beer bottles?" she asked. "We could hide them and collect a lot and then maybe get in the back door of the saloon and Mr. Murphy wouldn't tell on us."

After an hour's search in the alleys Sally had found one bottle that might be a beer bottle, or even a whiskey bottle, and Horace had found three bottles that he was sure were beer bottles, as he was sure Sally's was only a pop bottle. So the two went around to the alley behind the main street until they came to the backshed entrance to the saloon. They were afraid to go in, but after a consultation decided they'd better go in together and both get lickings if they were caught.

"The men will take it more like a joke if you're there," Horace sagely informed Sally. "They always think girls don't know nothing."

Sidling up to the bar inside Sally looked discreetly wide-eyed and innocent as she piped up, "I'se got some beer bottles, Mr. Man. P'ease give me some pennies for them." Horace was too scared to notice much that Sally was putting on baby accents.

"Well, I'll be—" Murphy, the bartender, started to say, but checked his profanity. "You kids will get paddled if your families hear you're coming in here. You'd better beat it quick. You'll get me in trouble too if they hear I let you in."

"We want candy." Horace broke in, feeling more at ease as he sensed that Murphy was a companion in guilt. "Just this once, buy these bottles." His heart was going at a terrific pace and he felt uncomfortable because of many strange men about the bar who had laughed raucously at him and Sally.

"Here's a nickel. Now quick and beat it, kiddies," Murphy said and handed Horace the money.

"Don't I get none too?" lisped Sally.

"Divide that, you two kids. You'll founder yourself on all day suckers or cheap chocolates if I give you more," Murphy explained good naturedly, leaning over to pat Sally's tow head, and to tweak at one of her braids. He relented, however, and slipped her a nickel too, so she and Horace went happily out of the saloon, in their glee carelessly going through the front door, when they quickly remembered and were scared.

"O golly, Sally. I'll bet yer pa can see us because his office is right across the street."

"It ain't papa I care about knowing. He wouldn't lick me and he wouldn't dare tell mamma on me either, because she'd say that was his blood coming out in me. That's what she always says when she licks me."

The children now felt completely involved in guilt and decided it wasn't any use resisting temptation any more that afternoon, so they bought some all day suckers, and gum, and chocolates. They walked down the main street and soon came to the edge of the town where Daly's pasture was. It was a warm autumn afternoon, but too chilly to sit on the bank of the pond long, and few minnows were to be seen in the muddy water. A few cows were grazing on the dry grass in the pasture, but the children saw that they didn't come too near.

"I wonder which gives the most milk, the papa or the mamma cow," Horace queried, remembering the cow his father had sold because she went dry.

"It ought to be the papa cow because that's how cows support themselves, and the papa ought to always support the family, but mamma says it ain't so with us, cause papa drinks up everything he makes. I like pap better though. He isn't cranky every minute of the day."

This problem did not interest Horace much. He was full of candy, and drowsy in the sun except that it was cold on his pants when he sat on the ground. As his mind wandered he remembered that his brother Ralph had spoken of a jack-rabbit drive at the breakfast table. That had excited Horace, but his mother told him of course he couldn't watch anything so brutal.

"I tell you, Sally," Horace said, "there's a jack-rabbit drive to end up at the corner down the road. Let's run down there and see if there's any sign of it."

Since ten o'clock in the morning groups of men and boys had been occupied with the jack-rabbit drive. On every side for miles from town, farmers, farm boys, and all the countless dogs of the countryside had been scouring the land to scare up rabbits. The clamor of guns firing, dogs barking, men shouting and beating with clubs, and horses trampling about was calculated to terrify all the rabbits who came within the range of the two semicircles of inclosing rabbit hunters.

It was by now four o'clock in the afternoon and evening chill was coming into the air. Going to the corner fence Horace knew of, Sally and he soon began to discern noises of the drive off in the distance. Now and then there was an echo or re-echo of a gunshot. Faintly, as though imagined, the resonance of a shot would sound, though neither Sally or Horace could verify any one report as the noises were becoming more clear and decisive, or their expectant senses made them alert.

"I saw Dingo, pa's half-breed hunter dog, tear up a rabbit's burrow once, and he just ripped that rabbit all to pieces," Sally said. "That made pa mad because it showed that Dingo was no good as a hunter to tear game to pieces. That rabbit squealed once when Dingo grabbed it but it just squealed once."

"Ralph said he bet all the rabbit burrows in the country would be dug open, there are so many dogs," Horace volunteered. "I've never seen a jack rabbit. Only them pet rabbits I had when I was a baby two years ago. Gosh, I was mad at mamma for making me wear skirts a whole year after Billie had been wearing pants, but it wasn't as bad as Freddie having to wear long hair up till just last month. His mamma wants to make a girlboy out of him."

Fifteen minutes passed, with sounds of the drive coming clearly to them, and again seeming to grow dimmer, until finally the resonance of noises became continually louder. The distinguishable bark of dogs could be heard: the baying of hounds, the yipe of fox terriers, the excited joyful bark of mongrels, and the general hysteria of all the dogs' excitement. It was infrequently that a gun was fired.

Suddenly there was a rush of men from across the fields on every side, and they were shouting at each other.

"Here you are, boys; here you are." "Get in on every side." "Get your clubs ready. Knock them out as fast as they come hurtling against the fence." "They'll be here in thousands inside of three minutes." "Kill 'em at one blow."

From the village men, women, and children too had begun to arrive for the end-up of the drive, the sounds of which had echoed through the town for the last half-hour. A share of even the women from the village carried clubs, or limbs of trees, and all the men and boys in the drive were so armed. The hullabaloo grew greater, with cursings, leaping about, and rabbit-threatening gesticulations in mock display of what they'd do to the rabbits.

The rabbits began coming. Tearing along, panic-struck huge white jack rabbits catapulted across the prairie towards the fence corner. Men on horses, men on foot, and dogs with lapping slobbery tongues circled in on them. The rabbits hurled themselves on at leaps of twenty, thirty, or even forty feet in the case of the huge-sized jacks. Shrilly, above the pandemonium a shriek of rabbit pain sounded now and then as some dog captured a jack and ripped it to bits.

Horace and Sally, standing near the front of the spectators, watched feverishly. Rabbits smashed into the impenetrable fence to be beaten on the head by men or boys jumping about. Before struck, terror was making the rabbits squeal. A continuous ripping, tearing sound, punctuated by the thump, thump, thump of clubs against the light-boned heads of the rabbits, went on.

At one moment Horace saw a rabbit caught by a great lean greyhound. Within a second another dog had caught the same rabbit by another portion of its body. Horace heard the squeal of that rabbit, saw the look of rodent terror in its eyes; and—dizzy within himself—heard the rip of the body. A stunned feeling held him, watching as though hypnotized. He was biting his lips and twitching his face nervously, unaware of himself or of his reactions to what he was seeing. It didn't seem that what he was seeing was actual. The jack rabbits looked so powerful and electric as they came across the prairie, and so limp, like damp besmudged cotton, as they lay torn upon the ground with the yellow of their hides, and the red of their interiors, showing.

Shortly the thing was done with. Heaped in piles against the fence were more than a thousand rabbit bodies. Their dull, glazed, half-open eyes, Horace noticed. He lingered, half wondering if they might not move again. Surely something more was going to happen after all this excitement.

"What happens to rabbits when they're dead?" Horace wondered, dazedly curious, to Sally, having heard of death before, but never having realized what it might mean.

"Huh, listen to the kid. Say sonny, them jacks is dead, and dead they'll stay and not be destroying crops on us farmers," a heavy-set man said with rough good nature to Horace, who shrank within himself from the obscenity, to him, of the man's manner. Yet his wonder made him speak in mechanical bewilderment.

"But they were alive just a few minutes ago."

"Sure kid, but they ain't now. We saw to that."

Horace didn't know how to think, and maybe he was afraid but not in a way he could cry about, or that he could ask his mother about. What if something began chasing people like the rabbits had been chased?

Sally was ready to go home, though she was still looking fascinatedly at the pile of rabbits. Horace had a moment of aversion to her because she leaned over and touched one, and didn't seem to feel sorry for it. A farm boy picked up a little mutilated rabbit and handed it to her. "Here, girlie," he told her, patting her head, "take this home to your mamma and have her cook it for you. It's nicer than chicken."

Sally took the rabbit and started to follow Horace, who had walked ahead of her. She caught up to him.

"You aren't going to take that rabbit home, are you? You couldn't eat it, could you?"

"Why not? Mamma feeds us rabbits lots of times."

"But it's dead," Horace explained.

"Every meat you eat is. That's what happens to all the cows that get shipped out of the stock yard every week."

Horace's mind was stalled. He couldn't think. He changed the topic. "I'll bet them rabbits were stronger than you or me. I'll bet we couldn't have held one without its kicking away because a man I saw grab a live one could hardly hold it."

Sally, becoming conscious that Horace walked away from her because she was carrying the rabbit, threw it aside with a quick gesture and said, "Nasty dead thing."

"It isn't its fault it's nasty," Horace said.

"I think it's awful. The poor rabbits."

"I don't know whether it's awful or not. People said it was a good thing to get rid of them."

When Horace and Sally got back to their houses they separated. Horace went through the kitchen, not even noticing Linda. In the sitting room he avoided speaking to his mother and, taking up a picture book, buried himself in the big easy chair. There was much he wanted to know but he didn't want his mother to know he had seen the jack-rabbit drive.

Continually his mind reverted to the rabbits, how their white furry flesh had been torn, their squeals, the fear in their eyes. As he sat trying to think his mind was filled, not with definite pictures of rabbits, but with a flood of nervous images of rabbit carnage that made him shudder and want to shut the thought out. But he didn't try to look at his book. He even felt impatient with his mother when she began talking to him and so prevented him from thinking about the rabbits. He liked to think that as he shuddered he was trying to shut out the white ripping and squealing image.

Through dinnertime Horace was very quiet, and his mother asked him if he didn't feel very well.

"Rats, sick," his brother Ralph said. "Don't baby him. He's probably been up to something and keeps quiet not to give himself away."

"Nonsense, Ralph," his mother answered. "I can see that the boy is pale, and his eyes have a feverish look. Don't think I don't know children better than my own son knows them. Think of your wanting to let him see the rabbit drive. At his age what would you have thought? He's been hearing about that brutal affair I'm sure."

Soon after dinner Horace was sent up to bed, where, after saying his prayers, he was left, and ducked his head under the covers as soon as his mother was out of the room and he was alone in darkness. He began to tell himself a long story about a rabbit drive, except that the rabbit drive would come later on in the story. He kept delaying it, wanting a very exciting situation to work up to. Gradually, however, sleep overtook him, in spite of his fear in the dark, out of which anything might come. Suppose a great jack rabbit leaped right on him through the open window. He wouldn't know what to do then. He lay still, except that at imagined sounds he peeked from under the covers. At one moment he was sure there was something standing at the foot of his bed, but he knew he'd get scolded and teased if he called out, or ran downstairs, and he would have to say of course he didn't believe in boogie mans. He wondered if Sally was scared in the dark too, if she really was, but maybe she wouldn't say so any more than he would.

He was standing way out in the dark fields, and everywhere rabbits were nibbling about him, so many that he could not walk without stepping on them. They nibbled at his feet too, trying to eat him up. And one came running terrifically to leap at him; and after him many others came, running straight at him to knock him down and cover his face and body with their cottony bodies. They would smother him like the two princes smothered by their uncle. He couldn't move and they kept coming. Awaking, he moaned, and then, knowing it was a dream, kept quiet with his fear. Looking out from under his covers he saw the moon shining through the window, so that he could see there was no one, only his coat, at the foot of his bed. Half of his room was almost in day lightness, but back there in the corner, or in the closet—

He wanted to cry, almost, but nobody he wanted would hear him, and if there was somebody back in the corner and they heard him they'd know he was afraid. He must not cry, so as to be able to speak if they came over to get him. He must tell them that they dare not touch him; that he wasn't scared.

At last he went to sleep again.

(See Bibliographical Note, page 360.)

Wisdom Garnered by Day

Bennie ran from the kitchen, having chucked several cookies in his pocket. If his Cousin Bessie saw him she said nothing as usual, for he well knew she still viewed him as a visitor and also as a little boy to be pampered, for, goodness knows, he had heard her declare, Uncle John could be severe and disciplinary enough for the entire clan. In the orchard he stopped to pick up several huge yellow apples, for Abie and Naps. The apples no longer looked bigger than pumpkins to his eyes as they had on the day of his arrival. By now they and all of Uncle's farming possessions had become very usual to him, and the apples, of which he had at first eaten too many, tasted flat and were not very juicy. The Greens still liked them though.

Abraham and Napoleon were fun to play with even if they were nigger kids, and there wasn't anybody else his age, and all of the older boys were doing farm work. Besides, Abie and Naps didn't try to hog the whole show like Felix and Cousin Harry.

They even let Bennie do most of the suggesting of what to do, except that they knew more about country life and what places were fun to visit than did he. As he ran across the cow pasture he eyed askance Abraham, the ancient bull. Cousin Bessie had named him that because he was the patriarchal father of so many and tyrannized his flock mercilessly, she claimed, and Bennie reflected how much he had learned in three weeks on the farm, and mainly from Abie and Naps. The others never told him anything much, or they didn't tell the truth or they told him fairy stories. He would still believe that fib of Cousin Bessie's about Father Abraham looking for higher land if it hadn't been for Abie's enlightening explanation about how very tiny calves indeed grow up inside their mammas until they are big enough to get borned.

Abie and Naps were sitting outside their mammy's kitchen, both of their faces sticky from corn pone and syrup, or black-jack 'lasses, of which Bennie immediately had some, for Mammy Green never worried about ruining a boy's appetite for his meals because of gorging done between times. She was waddling, black, fat, and glistening, about her makeshift kitchen, but from that shack emerged very wonderful food at times, if Pap Marston had bothered to work to earn a few dollars for food supplies. In any case Mammy Green managed to do washings or to get gifts from the members of the white community about, and she and Pap Marston did together manage always to have a few chickens about the yard, and there were several razorback hogs grunting and rooting about piles of refuse, lazily because of the heat.

When Bennie had asked Cousin Bessie why Pap Marston's name wasn't the same as Mammy Green's and Abie's and Naps' he didn't get the answer he wanted. Instead Cousin Bessie explained that Pap Marston was quite old, having been a slave who had escaped from the South years ago. Mammy Green, it appeared, had been married to Mr. Green long ago and he might return some day, but now nobody knew where he was and nobody looked peaked with worry about the matter.

A mother sow lay in the dust not far off and her litter of six dozed or nozzled at her udders. She grunted with complaining content and submitted herself to her youngsters even when they prevented her from oozing herself as deeply into the dust as she wished. Generally the litter snoozed in the heat and dust as it was mid-afternoon and sweltering. She was a horrible looking sow, Bennie thought, and did not quite believe that she was thin only because she was a razorback. Her babies were horrible looking too, and he thought of the fat pink-nosed porkers which Uncle John had in his clean, well-kept pig pens. "They's a diffrunt breed, dat's all. You cain't know how dem hogs eat and nebber get real fat, but dey's well streaked with lean meat and dat's what's good eatin'," Naps explained, and added that there was another old sow who was going to drop young 'uns that afternoon. Upon this information Bennie, Naps, and Abie went to sit on the pigsty fence to watch proceedings, and Bennie learned a great deal more about the facts of animal nature. For well over an hour he was watching the sow become a parent of eight piglets. By that time he felt replete with information and rather disappointed and bored with the whole display, but it was a hot afternoon and he did not know what to suggest, although he did feel restless and wanted to get away from Mammy Green's shack. She was very easy-going, but she had the habit of telling stories to Aunt Mary and Bennie's mother days when she helped them with their cooking, canning of fruit, or laundering. She laughed and thought Bennie "jes' up to everything, so's Abie and Napoleon don't know wot he's going to ask or want to do next." To Bennie's dismay, however, his mother did not always respond to Mammy Green's amused attitude. She became austere and gave him scoldings, or whippings, although she threatened the whippings more and gave them less than she had at home. She was being far less strict with him this summer, rather placidly agreeing with her sister that little harm could come to him in this quiet countryside.

Finally the three decided to go into the meadows which were knee-deep with clover and alfalfa, so that a cutting was sure to take place within a few days. There was an undercurrent humming and chanting of insect and bird life, and a variety of colored butterflies, blue, yellow, orange, purple, with designs embroidered upon their frail wings and bodies, floated about in the clear pure atmosphere. Across from the meadows the wheat, barley, corn, and oat fields were beginning to turn golden, but their stalks still contained juices to make them resilient as they swayed in the breeze, the wheat field seemingly endless, stretching so far out that it was cut off only by the horizon. Abie and Naps spoke of future delights, if Bennie only dared. In the corn fields were the vines of watermelons and cantaloupe, and within a week or so the melons would be ripe, and they might swipe them but they'd have to be very careful not to get caught. Bennie said that it was wicked to steal, but Abie and Naps didn't sense much conviction in his assertion, because they knew that he was like themselves, not at all deterred from doing something naughty if only there was a fair chance of not being detected by their elders, and Bennie wasn't afraid that Mammy Green or Paps Marston would tell about their taking a watermelon or so. He knew that joke about a nigger in the melon patch, and how a colored man can't resist a chicken coop. He felt very pleased about the Green outfit. They might be easy-going, shiftless, good-for-nothing coons, like Cousin Dave said, but they were mighty easy to be about with.

Seated upon a bridge, the three watched minnows and sizable fish, suckers, shiners, bullheads, pass in the clear waters of the brook beneath them. At last they decided they could build up a dam a little way down where the stream narrowed, and this they proceeded to do, leaving a very small space through which the water could flow, and their hopes were realized. They did trap five fish, three suckers, one shiner, and a bullhead, who stuck or horned Bennie when he clutched at it too carelessly. He knew that in such hot weather the fish were not very good eating, but had they been he wouldn't have dared bring them to his aunt. Upon the thought he became aware that he had been wading up to his knees in the water, and his shoes and pants were soaked. There wasn't much chance his mother wouldn't notice that, but he comforted himself with the idea that he might slip through the kitchen and get on his overalls, go barefoot, and claim that he was going to help Uncle John and the others with the chores. He couldn't milk, but he could mix up the bran mash, and fork out hay to the horses.

Napoleon suddenly recalled that he knew where there was a hive of wild bees and he bet a million that it was chock full of honey. It was in the dead trunk of an old oak tree. "No sah, I won't git stung," he was positive, "an' anyway, what's an old bee sting or two?"

Naps' recklessness infected Bennie, and upon coming to the tree it appeared that most of the bees must be away, collecting pollen, they decided. They dug into the tree, and ran away. Soon they returned. "Yas, sah, it is shuah full of honey. Dat white stuff, wid dem maggoty things crawling in it. Dem's young bees."

Bennie looked most dubiously at what Naps said was honey. He had expected to come upon well-filled cones of waxen cells filled with a light gold substance, such as the honey he had eaten with pancakes, biscuits, corn pone, and cream. Abie explained that such honey was made by tame bees who kept house better than the wild ones, and also, it was men who made the wood frames and started the waxen cells which contained the tame honey. "Dis year honey has got a sweeter taste. It's wild wid flavor like a wild duck has got more game taste dan a tame one." Naps dug his finger into the white mass, removed the maggots, and ate the honey. He didn't get stung.

Bennie tried to copy his example, but he decidedly did not like the looks of the maggoty things in the so-called honey. He was dubious about the nigger boys' natural information, as he had been a few times before. Nevertheless, he tasted the mess, and then wiped the rest of it on the grass, or he started to, for immediately he was up running and yelling in pain and panic. The bees were stinging him all right, a whole swarm following after him. Abie and Naps, however, took off their shirts and helped shoo them away, and after a good run the bees were no longer following Bennie. "You shuah shuddn't a stuck yer finger right in de honey where perhaps de queen bee is. You shud a done like me, a stuck yer finger where it was all honey and maggots and de bees not working dere no moah. Dat's all right. Jest wait. I'll fix you so's you won't know you's been stung."

Abie calmly removed a plug of tobacco from his pocket and took a chaw, as did Naps. Bennie didn't want to try any new experiments at the moment and felt most sceptical about honey, bees, and the nigger boys' information. Nevertheless, he let Abie and Naps smear him with bits of chawed tobacco and juice, and listened to their explanation that it would shuah draw out the bee-stings. In any case there the stings were and Bennie reflected that he might utilize them. When he returned home he would wail as in great pain and tell about having been stung by the bees, and possibly Cousin Bessie, Aunt Mary, or even mother would pity his sufferings and forget to ask where he had been and what he had been up to all afternoon. Unfortunately the bee-stings did cease to pain and he had forgotten them by the time he did return home so that all of his planned guile came to naught.

The day was cooling, sweet and clean and clear, and the odors of clover, grains, and of the apple orchard at the end of the meadows infiltrated the atmosphere. They went to sit on the empty stanchion where Father Abraham was kept during days when neighbors' cows came to visit him. Generally, however, during the summer months, he was at pasture with Uncle John's herd of cattle. Now the herd was down in the marshes, some of them knee-deep in the mud and water, amongst the water lilies and water weeds, nibbling, or just standing, chewing their cuds. A cowy smell came from the herd, a smell admixed with that of marshes, cow manure, and alive cowhide. The three boys discussed odors; the odor of a cow stable when the cows are being milked and huge pails of white foaming milk are poured steamingly into separators. "It's de bes' place to git warm in de winter time, I tell you," Abie explained, and upon Bennie's questionings told of the winter in this section of Canada. Bennie couldn't believe him really, feeling and sensing the peaceful calm and gentleness of the air and scenery about now. Upon reflection, however, he recalled that it was so with the seasons back in Dakota. He had simply been too young to notice, and at home there was always the warm stove fires, warm overcoats, mittens, and a sleigh ride to school. He was sure he wouldn't like to be here in the wintertime, because perhaps it would be as lonely and bleak as it was for poor Draguy Andorovitch in that creaky farmhouse eight miles from nowhere, and with his Polack papa and mamma so poor that they hadn't money for proper warm clothes and fuels, let alone to repair the leaks and cracks in the house.

As evening's vague and gentle twilight came on, Bennie began to feel dimly nostalgic—what he knew by the word homesick. He rejected the emotion because he had learned that it was sissy-like to be homesick. He thought of Stephanie and Liz and Amalia, and even of Sam and Eugene in spite of the fact that they tried to older-brother and boss him and make him run their errands. He thought more of his playmate friends, however, and of being in a city rather than in the country, now that Abie's tales made him think of how lonely it would be here in the cold weather. Here if the snow was six feet deep he couldn't manage to get across the meadows to Abie and Naps because they'd be snowed in, and he'd have no one to play with. He was mighty glad that they weren't staying here till winter then.

Still a quiet mood came upon him and it didn't seem to matter where he was or what he was doing. For the moment he was desireless, feeling that he never wanted to do anything but just sit in the air. Not eat, not sleep, not move, but just sit and have Abie and Naps tell him stories about life and ghosts— hants, they called them. He didn't believe their ghost stories by a long shot, but they gave him the shivers, and indeed he did not intend to visit the haunted house any night, but he felt safe because he knew Abie and Naps wouldn't dare visit it either. They were just talking big now. He wasn't any more afraid of that haunted house or of the dark than they were, but suppose some bad man stayed there and was the ghost and you had to run, you might stumble in the dark. And bump your nose and get a nosebleed and be caught out telling fibs by your mother.

It had come suppertime and Bennie did not want to be late and have his mother discover that he'd been playing with the nigger kids again. She might not let him run off by himself the next time, if she could help it. He promised Abie, who was eleven, that he would try and get brother Felix and Cousin Harry to take him to the evangelical meeting at the negro church that night, just to see if pure spirits did come to possess people, to cleanse and purify them, making black people as white as snow with purity, Abie swore. Naps, who was only eight, wasn't allowed to go to the meeting either because Pap Marston didn't believe in dat kind ob religion, and also knew that Uncle John did not approve. Pap Marston believed in keeping in with Mistah Rossmere. Bennie suspected his mother would refuse to let him go, but it was religion and it was going to church, as he would tell her, but he was doubtful that his argument would win her over.

He got home to find the women busy in the kitchen and gratefully realized that they were too busy to bother about him.

His shoes and pants had dried and he rubbed the shoes with a brush, washed his face, and looked as guiltless as possible. At supper the very cleanliness of his face and hands should have warned his parent that he had been disobedient, but evidently she was too tired by the heat of the day to bother.

No, indeed, his mother said after supper, she would not permit any seven-year-old boy to stay up all hours of the night listening to a group of colored people going through their hysterical rites. She was very fond of many colored people, found them faithful and loyal servants, good nurses and gentle and generous companions, but their ways were not many generations removed from the primitive and the jungle. He was too young to understand. Their way of looking up to God was right and just for them, but decidedly no, the question was ended. Off to bed Bennie was to take himself at once and no whimpering nonsense about his not being allowed the freedom of other children. Well she knew that she had often been censured for allowing her children entirely too much freedom, and a noisy wild crew of young Indians they were, as children, and not properly respectful towards their parents when they were older. Married and settled down some of them might improve, but as yet they were all enough to make a nervous wreck of a woman who hadn't the constitution of a draft horse.

Bennie was soon off to bed after a whispered conference with brother Felix, who was twelve and also keen upon going to the evangelical meeting. Bennie's mother came into his room above the woodshed to see that he was properly asleep, and he heard her say that this country air and plenty of exercise was doing the boy a world of good. He went to sleep at once these evenings.

When she was gone downstairs, as he knew by the clatter of her heels on the steps, he saw from his window that Felix and Harry had harnessed the horse and were waiting in the shadow of the old maple tree. Taking off his nightgown—for his mother might have turned back the covers—he crawled out the window, down the woodshed roof, and soon was off with Felix and Harry.

When they were a quarter of a mile from the negro church or shack they had to drive at a walk as so many buggies were ahead of and behind them. In one buggy was a coal-black woman with a white starched cape, and upon her head was a huge white-brimmed affair, not a hat. It was starched and protruded a foot into the heavens, while the lower portion fitted her brow and skull. Felix surmised that she was a nun of some kind. Harry explained that she was supposed to hold communion with spirits on a higher plane than most mortals. She was, other colored people said, The Exalted Sistah. When they drove into the churchyard Bennie went near her, timidly, as he felt timid with a spirit of awe, afraid of what his mother would do if she found out he'd come to the meeting, and awe at the reverential atmosphere and mien of the various colored people about. The Exalted Sistah seemed not of this world. Her manner was distant and a faraway look was in her eyes. She spoke in a low deep voice, somehow consoling, but also warning that she was not of the common people and not to be addressed trivially. She called all people "brothah" or "sistah," and towards the minister, who also was very black, her manner was that as of one equal to another. She called him "youah reverend sah." Her manner certainly awed Bennie, who wondered if she meant to keep ordinary people from addressing her.

Felix and Harry did not go into the church because now surrounded by colored people they felt shy, as intruders, although they had been able to joke about their meetings earlier in the day when about with white people entirely. A few other white farmers and people from the near-by town stayed out in the ground about the church-shack also. They were all curious, and Bennie particularly was drawn to the entry door to listen, after the singing, chanting, praying, and preaching had been going on for some time.

The very black minister was preaching, and at first his manner of delivery was not unlike that of white ministers Bennie had seen and heard. The colored man, however, became more vehement, predicting brimstone and hell fire and pitchforks, at first, but finally his imagination flowered. Bennie did not understand much that he said, as he spoke so often of "de sin ob carnality" and "de blighting searing ruination which come from de obsession which is dat ob most ob my congregation."

Bennie had heard Billie Sunday and other evangelists preach, but finally the negro left them all in the shade with his oratory, or rather, as Bennie saw it, his delivery. Suddenly, after a passionate burst of preaching he asked for repenters to come to the altar and confess their sins, and there was a rush of some twenty colored people down the sawdust aisle. Some of the women started screaming their sins and repentance. They beat their breasts, tore at their hair, and prayed to God, confessing many sins. They quieted down as though hypnotized when the preacher prayed, and when all of the congregation started singing hymns the air was electrified with fervor and rhythm and mellow shouting voices making a grand chorus of a hackneyed hymn.

Bennie was less afraid now, but he was feverish with curiosity. Still this singing was not unlike that he had heard in church as he was used to it. He crept into the church and sat down beside a huge black woman who looked a comfortable mammy to him. He sat near the back entrance, however, and saw that it was Eliza, who had done washings for his aunt, who sat beside him. He was not afraid of her because always she had pampered him, giving him sugared candy, and one day she had actually given him a penny. He looked at her timidly, expecting to be recognized, but she paid no attention to him. Her eyes were on the pulpit, and she appeared to have much more whites to her eyes than usual. A strained tense look was on her face, and Bennie began to be frightened, wishing that he had not sat beside her, that he had not come into the church.

Soon the minister got up and began his harangue again. His prayers built up to a sonorous crescendo, a ringing timbre in their tones, as he pointed his empassioned finger down at the faces of those in the audience. One time he pointed directly at Bennie, unless it was at Mammy Eliza. Bennie felt too uneasy to move, but he wanted to get outside. The minister talked passionately now about the sins of man, and exhorted all people to "git down on yoah knees and crawl like de low creatures you is, an' wid wailin' an' weepin' crawl to de Lawd befoah you is all smitten by de fires ob His wrath."

How wicked everybody is and only God is good, Bennie was feeling—hopelessly—and there was holiness all about him. White fervor was a vapor in the air, pressing down upon all present. Suddenly as the preacher was shouting Bennie was terrified so that the blood halted frozen within him, and he could not move. Mammy Eliza had made a strange heavy breathing whistling sound as of agonized strangulation. He turned to see blood dripping from her lips which she had bitten with her gleaming white teeth. Her eyes rolled back and back, white into her head. Her bosom heaved mightily. She trembled all over, ash-colored instead of gleaming ebony black. Her forehead was covered with drops of sweat. "Oooooh, Lawd Jesus," she moaned and shrieked, "ah'm heah, ah's youah's, ah's comin' to youah altah and throne. Git ready to receive me. I's comin' to youah blessed arms."

It was as though a mighty unseen force lifted her high out of her seat. She crushed stumblingly past Bennie and swept blindly up the aisle down the sawdust trail to the pulpit box before which she threw herself in a long, stumbling, face-down swoop. Her hands tore at her powerful bosoms as though she would rend them from her breast. Her hands ran with mad animal hysteria through her black kinky-wire hair that she had torn loose. She held it above her head, an exalted expression upon her face, and then bore the mass of it over her face as she bent back and forth, moaning, writhing, and screaming.

At first, for a century which was actually a moment, Bennie could not move. His heart had evaporated to a cold vapor of fright within him. At last he was able to slip off his chair and go quietly until near the door, through which he bolted with a rush.

"Ha, ha, ha, look at Bennie," he heard as he got out into the yard amongst the white men and their horses and buggies. He saw vaguely that Harry and the older men were laughing at and teasing him. "I tell you, Bennie, those nigger wenches are hot when they're getting religion, and when they're not too. You'd better look out that one doesn't take after converting you," a hired man from Uncle John's farm said.

Bennie felt sick and dazed. He wondered if Eliza had been struck so that the devil was being driven out of her, she seemed so in agony with her writhings.

Felix came up to him and took his hand, saying, "Come on, we'll go home. Don't let them tease you." Bennie was not even surprised that Felix was gentle rather than teasing older-brother to him. Dimly he realized that Felix, too, was frightened. When

Harry and the hired man started to joke at Bennie, Felix turned on them savagely. "Oh, shut your gabs for a while. You can see how pale the kid is. You were scared yourself and you weren't sitting by that bedtick of a black woman. You didn't dare go in the church and Bennie did."

None of them talked much while driving back to the farmhouse. Bennie's fear, indefinable to himself, rather a dumbfoundment of unknown forces in life than a sharp terror, was not so keen as it had been. He was now, instead, smoldering with resentment at Harry, the hired man, and all who had laughed at him. Their raucous vulgarity of mirth angered him and he wished he were big enough to strike at them as they laughed, not because of himself but because they laughed at what was so obviously and passionately real to the colored people.

He wanted to be back home in the city with his family, left alone to himself by them, left to play with his neighboring playmates. Towards Felix he felt not unfriendly, comforted rather, but the presence of Felix's arm about his shoulder, protectively, bothered him. He felt cold emotionally about everybody, and smothered by the physical and would-be comforting contact. There were many questions he wanted answered, but he could not understand enough to ask them and knew surely that could he question he would not be answered. He didn't believe that older people could answer the questions in him themselves.

When he was back in bed he went almost immediately to sleep, it being a late hour for him and he was exhausted by the day's playing and emotion.

The next day he could not quickly enough get to the Greens to tell Abie and Naps that he had been to the evangelical meeting, but his report of the experience was a sceptical one, endeavoring to convince the colored boys that he was not taken in by that sort of thing, not he.

(See Bibliographical Note, page 360.)

Potato Picking

"If I let you go to Mr. Schultz's farm you must be back for Sunday. He would let you pick potatoes that day I am sure, and four days of such food as he gives his workmen will make one of your mother's meals look good to you," Bessie Donley told Grant.

Grant felt impatient with his mother. She knew he was janitor of the Episcopalian church and had to clean it Sundays as well as ring the church bell. He had been selling papers and magazines for the last year to make money; he had done many odd jobs. She might know he understood that if he was to have proper clothes and spending money he must make it himself. Why, when he "loaned" her money, must she take the attitude that she was granting his boyish whim when he went to work for the money involved? If she didn't know that picking potatoes gave a fellow a backache and was no fun she might better learn so. He had no patience with her attitude that he must go to Sunday School and Christian Endeavor either, since many of his playmates never bothered. She refused to realize that at twelve years old a boy knows more about what having to make a living means than she wanted to admit. Not bothering to promise her to be back for Sunday, he went to the front yard.

Who was that woman at the front gate? It looked like one of those gypsy women, of the lot camping across the road under the willows. Going to the front door, Grant called, "Ma, there's a woman coming up to the house. A gypsy."

She was blowsy skinned and her hair was coarse and disheveled. Grant stood as she was talking to his mother.

"Yes, Missus, I had to run away. You will help me, lady, won't you? He's threatening to kill me, and the bairn, and it's only six months," the woman explained. She had a strange accent. Scotch, she said to Mrs. Donley, and Grant pretended not to be listening. She had married in Scotland and come with the man and his mother to travel in a camp wagon through America. Her husband took to beating her when they were only a week married. He drank and was uncontrollable when drunk. Would the lady let her stay in her house that night? Yes, and have something stolen from her, Grant thought. No good came of believing gypsy women like that one. He had better go and see that his pet, club-footed pig wasn't rooting around near their wagons. The woman wanted to get out to her sister in California, nearly two thousand miles away. Mother was saying that of course she would put her up for the night, and call the sheriff if any ruffianly husband came storming at her gate to demand that a terrified wife be given back for him to have his drunken brutal will with. The woman was kissing mother's hand.

"It's a bonnie lad you have," the woman said, and her accent made Grant think she meant he was skinny. She ought to have sense enough not to say that when she was asking a favor of his mother.

"Don't be silly," Bessie told her son. "The woman is no gypsy, I know. She comes from the Scotch highlands near where my father was born. She's frightened and sick. It is those ruffianly men, and her mother-in-law is a reprobate, too, I'm sure. The girl would be terrified, naturally, coming from a simple, godly home, to traipse all over America with such a crew. *Bony* is the Scotch pronunciation of *bonnie*. She was being nice about you."

Nevertheless Grant did not like the woman and her wild windblown look, black hair, dark eyes. She was a scold and probably pestered the life out of her husband so he drank. Why didn't she get on the train and just go to California and leave him? Then he thought and was sorry for her, because of course she had no money for railway fare. Scotland must have taken a long time to come from, across the sea, and everybody would think she was a gypsy and a thief because she went around in a covered wagon.

Grant went to bed early to be up early and join the other boys going to Schultz's farm for potato picking.

2

Grumpy with sleep, Grant met Gould Lamar and Ellsworth Cummings in the Schultz backyard. The wagon was leaving at once, to be at the farm before seven o'clock. By the time it was half a mile out of town, the boys felt fine and bragged about how many potatoes they would pick. No one of the three boys paid any attention to Sloppy May, who was the high school superintendent's son, but nobody liked him. He picked his nose and chewed his fingernails and told dirty stories.

"I hope the potato hills are full," Grant said, "except he's paying us kids by the row rather than by the bushel. I know he's paying the older men by the bushel and we pick just as fast. They think they can get by with anything on us because we're young and I bet we do more work than most of the hoboes he gets."

They passed the hobo jungle soon. About twenty men were hanging about, sitting on ties thrown by the railroad track. Heaps of cans, some new, others rusted with last or several seasons' rust upon them, were off to the side. A big tin of coffee was boiling over the fire built in a hole in the ground. The men looked without interest at the boys and the Schultz wagon. It was well known that Schultz furnished lousy grub, and hired kids when he could get them because he had to pay them less and made them work more by making them think he was doing them a favor to employ them at all.

"It'd be swell being a hobo," Ellsworth commented. "Just nothing to do but loll around and go wherever you want to and when it's the best season to be there. You can always pick up meals somewhere and sleep in haystacks or barns."

Grant reflected that Ellsworth was a putty-nosed mamma's boy, never knowing much about anything and always getting caught if he did anything his mamma had told him not to. "You and I'll take rows next to each other," Grant whispered to Gould, "and if one is quicker than the other let's wait for the other to catch up. Potato picking isn't a fire we got to put out right away, I guess."

Later Grant was disgusted. Gould could not pick potatoes for sour apples and a fellow couldn't earn anything waiting for him to catch up. Sloppy May made a fellow work hard to keep up with him so he couldn't think himself too damned smart for being the quickest. Why couldn't he take a row other than one just next to Grant? He bet Sloppy pretended to know a lot more

than he did, because kids don't know for sure all the rot that
Sloppy was talking. Grant fretted in the heat and dust, not being
able to think his own ideas so long as Sloppy picked potatoes
alongside of him, and kept talking. His back ached. The sun was
scorching on his dust-grimed, sweating body. His neck was sunburned. It wasn't fun picking potatoes, but he could stick it if
the others could.

Sloppy May would have to grab the wash basin first and not
even throw away his dirty water after using. Grant did not want
to use the same basin right after Sloppy, and the towel was black
with dirt, because you get covered with dust picking potatoes
when the wind is blowing. Later the food tasted good, though.
"I guess he can afford to feed us well," even Ellsworth agreed.
"He makes a pile of money every year with his produce and he's
got two hundred acres of onions planted, too. We can have a job
picking onions after this job, if we want to. We ought to make
him pay us a man's wage though. It's the work we do and not our
ages that should bring the pay. We shouldn't let him kid us,
because maybe too our working so hard stunts our growth for
life. You never get a chance till you're grown up."

Grant saw that Gould Lamar looked pale, and Gould wasn't
strong since that fool doctor cut out his appendix six months
back. He wished Sloppy May would wipe his nose and not eat
as though he were at a trough. He wasn't the only one who had
been doing a little work and had a backache.

It was going to be good to have some sleep this night, Gould,
Ellsworth, and Grant agreed. They climbed up to the haymow
with their horse blankets, and hid behind a pile of hay, hoping
that Sloppy May would not find them. They talked in whispers
until they knew he had located himself, and maybe he would go
to sleep quickly. It was a sure bet he snored something terrible,
along with his other bad habits.

The city, what would the city mean? Would Gould someday
be an attorney like his father, and go into politics? Grant guessed
Gould would stay in this one-horse burg and go into his father's
office, because Gould didn't have any ambition or desire to change
his life. Ellsworth said he wanted to live in the city. What was

the matter with Gould that he could stand to think of living all his life in this town?

"Are you asleep?" Gould whispered, lying nearby in the hay.

"I'm not," Ellsworth answered. "I don't feel a bit sleepy like you'd have thought the way our backs ached from picking those damned potatoes. Let's take it light tomorrow. My shirt's as wet as if I'd swum in it."

"I can't sleep either," Grant answered. "Listen to Sloppy snore. He's like a pig anyway."

"It's kind of chilly. You wouldn't have thought it, hot as it was today," Gould said. "And dusty. I felt sick in the morning, but we'll get toughened up. The third day's the worst, they say, and after that you just kind of go along."

"Let's put our blankets together and cuddle up to keep each other warm," Ellsworth suggested. "We don't want to let no draft in and the hay is down a guy's neck too. Let's put one blanket under us, and the three of us can crawl under the other two."

"There is going to be all the hoboes in the country about this burg soon, if they aren't starting now," Grant said. "Those guys never stay more'n half a day on a job. Us kids stay longer and work more. We ought to make old man Schultz pay us more than he does. Being kids doesn't mean we do less work."

They were cuddled together. Grant was in the middle and felt no draft coming from the sides but his feet were chilly and a draft came from below. Wisps of hay worked their way down his neck and back. He felt itchy and wanted to toss about, but maybe the other fellows were sleepy and he didn't want to toss and have them cranky. He felt Gould's breath on his face and Ellsworth's on his back and neck. A warmth from the other two made him feel too smotherily warm, if only his feet were not in a draft. But he began to feel drowsy.

"Damn draft. Wish I had the middle place," Ellsworth muttered, putting his arm over Grant's shoulder and snuggling closer. Gould snuggled closer from the other side too, whispering, "You got all the luck. This is heaps of fun though, ain't it? Wished that Sloppy was a decent guy and I'd get him to sleep on the other side of me to keep the draft out."

It was eight o'clock Saturday night when Grant came up the path to his house. He knew he was all tanned but he felt a millionaire with six dollars on him. He would beat it down to the drugstore as soon as he had kissed his mother and could get away. He didn't want her to catch him charging things—ice cream and soda pops—on her account. He whistled, and whistled again. Then he called, "Porkie, Porkie," but his pet club-footed pig did not come squealing. Grant's heart sank. Those Scotch gypsies. He looked across the road. They were still there.

"Mother, mother," he said excitedly as he went into the house, "Where's Porkie? He doesn't come when I call. Them damn gypsies have stolen him, I bet, and maybe they have butchered him already." He was trying not to cry but he blamed his mother very much. She had promised to look after Porkie and see that he wasn't stolen or didn't wander off while Grant was away. He wished you could take pet pigs on jobs with you the way you can dogs, and Porkie was funnier than a dog. He didn't like mud, either.

"He was rooting around the yard not long ago," Bessie said, feeling guilty. "He must be around. I'll help you look for him."

Grant, hot with excitement, ran out into the barn, the chicken coop, and back to the cow pasture, but there was no answer to his call. He went running to the gypsy wagons.

"Have you seen a small pig around?" he asked a red-faced old woman who sat darning socks in one of the wagons, and he noticed that the wagons were packed, ready to drive on elsewhere. He was frightened. He could not say he must look into their wagon and see if Porkie was there. "Nae, laddie," the old woman answered. "You're a bonnie laddie. We wouldn't be taking a piggie on ye."

Grant ran down the road calling, and suddenly stopped in an eagerness of expectancy. He heard squealing, and it came from the empty barn belonging to the house next his. He ran to its door and opened it. There was Porkie, tied by his hind club-foot, and squealing with delight at seeing Grant, who ran to hug, pet, and release him quickly. Porkie was too heavy for him to carry now, but he came hobbling at a great pace, to keep up with Grant, who ran quickly, happy now, but not wanting that damned old drunken Scotch wife-beater to come along and pretend that Porkie was his pig.

"There you are," Mrs. Donley said later. "I told you the man was a reprobate. It's the young husband who tried to steal

Porkie on you. The womenfolk are good honest Scotch women, but he hasn't a scruple in his lowdown nature. If I only had the money I would give the poor girl fare out to California, though she is foolish enough to say she wants to stay with the man even if he does beat her. It's men like that who seem to get the strongest hold on some women."

"I'm not going potato picking Monday if those people are still camping anywhere in this neighborhood," Grant said with morose decision, wondering if Porkie would really be safe locked up in the grain bin in the barn. He wondered if he might not smuggle Porkie to his bedroom for just this one or two nights. It was a sure thing, and Grant knew it, that Porkie would have to go to the butchers or be butchered by his older brothers before long, certainly before winter. But Porkie was still his pet and he didn't want no Scotch gypsies stealing him. If there was any money to be made from Porkie it should be his, except of course if Porkie was butchered at home and eaten by the family there wouldn't be any money paid. But anyway, he didn't want Porkie stolen by no-good people he didn't know and who never did any work so far as anybody knew.

(See Bibliographical Note, page 360.)

2. The Middle West and California

Like many another country boy, Robert McAlmon looked to the city to resolve his adolescent discontents. City life, he thought, would be quicker paced and less confining. But when the family moved to Minneapolis, he was let down. His classes at East High were dull and so was the work he found to do outside school hours. During the four-year interval between graduating from high school and entering the University of Minnesota, McAlmon thrashed around indecisively. He worked in a flour mill, at an advertising agency, on a surveying crew. Already interested in writing he got a job as a cub reporter, but threw it up when he saw that the city editor, in assigning him to sob stories, exploited his youthful sympathies. Even as an adolescent he refused to be bound by convention and the dictates of prudence: life was to be 'lived, he thought, not anatomized, bought, and sold. Footloose, he revisited the little towns of his childhood. He could not stay put.

In his fictionized account of these years McAlmon drew on his brothers' experiences as well as his own. Summers George and Will McAlmon (the latter a Minnesota football star) went on muscle-building, money-making forays into the harvest fields of the upper Midwest. They brought back good stories.

Blithe Insecurities

Squat Herr Max, Dr. Friedman, the Croatian chemist, chewed at his sandwich and grunted speech through hunks of food. He was morose with distaste for Dinkie Fahnestock, whose manner was impudent. Herr Max was too intent upon original research work to have his laboratory used as a catch-all department for employing the dissolute relatives of firm executives. His inset eyes glinted. "Herr Gott, dey dink I am a garbage department, vot?"

"Well, pop, they pull their line on someone else after Saturday," Grant Conkling said breezily. "I asked Boutwell for a raise and he said I could quit if I wasn't satisfied. I quit. I can't, or won't, live on $12 a week when I'm not learning anything. I did the tests after the first week, doing Dinkie's work with him getting triple my salary. That's for six months. Boutwell told my sister over the phone he plans great things for me, but I don't like the old fart."

"You iss young, Grant. You iss a goot poy. Vy should you pe a pizness man? Schwein-chops. You pe pright, und ven you ist older more you get you vork vor de brain."

"That's me."

"Dere iss all de high monkey-monks of de chief's relatives vor de big jobs. Some day I qvit too. Ven more letters telling me vere I go." Pop Friedman's eyes were calculating, but they had a kind twinkle. He was grumpily silent when Dinkie Fahnestock came cockily into the laboratory. Pop knew Dinkie was only half there, and didn't bother to be cranky with him. Grant rinsed out testing bottles and prepared for flour tests. "I go out on pizness," Herr Max told Grant. "You know vot you tell boss, if he comes."

Dinkie Fahnestock was busy-mannered to conceal his awareness that he'd spent long over the firm-granted lunch hour.

"You'll get the can tied to your tail someday," Grant told

him. "Boutwell doesn't like you. Your uncle can't get you out of many more scrapes."

Dinkie stood before the mirror, primping his small black mustache. He turned a freely vain smile on Grant, showing tiny but perfect teeth. His slight, graceful body moved with dapper briskness which was too haberdashery calculated to be quite elegant. "I had luck today. I ran into a broad who kept me once, when the old man lost his money. She's nuts on me yet; says she's starting a high-class house and if I stick around she'll keep me in money."

"Hell, don't lie," Grant scoffed. "Yesterday you went into the dope business with another broad. What's the use?" Grant was sure that Dinkie had a mania for lying, and always about underworld connections: whores, white-slavers, procurers, pimps, gangsters, broads, wrens, thieves, pickpockets. Maybe his tales had a basis of fact; he had abnormality in him. His pale, oval face with its luminous, blue-veined skin was an aristocrat weakling's. His pretty mouth gave him away.

"And I have an idea." Dinkie was chipper. "There's a fortune in the bootblack business. This broad will equip a parlor for me and all the bootblacks will be classy girls. Men will like that idea: girls kneeling to them. The joint will coin money and the broads will have to split earnings with us for the chance we give them to pick up customers."

"What will your wife say?"

"She won't know about it. I must have money. They won't raise my salary because they think I go on tears if I have money. My wife's classy, isn't she?"

"Yes," Grant said briefly, thinking how ridiculous Dinkie's mother and sister were not to accept his wife. They would keep up a pretense of social standing when the father was a town-bounder and their wealthy relatives cut them generally. Dinkie's wife had been a telephone operator, but his sister wasn't anything just now, and with no looks so that marriage would be forthcoming to re-establish her class.

"I head for Duluth Saturday. To hell with the sawdust flour company," Grant divulged.

"You'd better stay. Boutwell is keen about you. He doesn't think you mean to quit. You could get a lot out of the old boy.

He sees you're pretty but you're too stand-offish." Dinkie would be insinuatingly flippant. "I guess I'll quit before I get fired," he brooded. "I know some broads who can line up opium. We'll make piles."

"You damn fool, quit lying. You'll get jugged for shooting off your mouth someday."

"I know the ropes."

"Do your wheat-weighing tests," Grant said.

"No, you do. To learn how." Dinkie was ingratiating.

"Why should I learn when I'm leaving? But I'll do them for you," Grant said, and was soon weighing samples of wheat and flour on the finely adjusted scales. He saw that Dinkie was restless, with the twitchiness of a defective or a dopehead. Dinkie took up the ether bottle and rubbed ether on his face. "Great stuff," he breathed. "This isn't the right kind, but it's great in the right form. Makes you joy all for joy."

"I wish you had sense," Grant said. "It's not your fault, though. Your parents should have been careful, but they didn't have sense either. Ever see your dad now?"

"No, he avoids me if he has money, and I avoid him if I have any. We understand the ropes."

Grant laughed. "His days are over. Do you think he has paresis, or is it just lack of drink and decent food that's shocked the old boozehound to shivers? You ought to be scared. Sometimes your laugh gives me the willies. You should see a doctor. That damned family of yours did you wrong."

Dinkie was grave and then became restive. "I know the way I can make the gold come in. I could be a high-class pimp, and my wife would never know."

"Don't talk rot. You're not that hot. Why don't you try the stage? You have looks and the public would never know you belonged to the down and out branch of your family. If you had sense I'd suggest our getting to Europe together, but I'd have to look after you when you got into scrapes."

"Don't give me hell just as you're leaving." Dinkie laughed nervously. "Nobody ever thinks I can do anything, and I've stuck this job a year."

"I'm not giving you hell. Why stick here? They call our jobs laboratory work but we're bottle-washers. It's none of my business, but I think you're being watched by dicks who think you're in with that oriental rug stealing gang."

"Who said I was?" Dinkie was startled.

"It doesn't matter. But you talk too much to clerks in the office. You don't think a lot of stoop-shouldered clerks hear you talk of broads and dope without squealing? They'd like something on a relative of Boutwell. They don't know you like to lie."

"I can't live on nothing."

"I gave you the tip. You haven't sense enough to be a crook. Suppose you were had up, and I or Pop were called as witnesses. We couldn't stand up against the cross-examining of a hardboiled attorney. I wouldn't perjure myself, and I'd get caught saying things I wanted to be quiet about. The court wouldn't think that half what you say is romantic lies."

"But you're going Saturday." Dinkie was triumphant.

"Hell, you're hopeless. Friedman stays. He wouldn't squeal but he's not quick-minded. I hope they don't catch you, but stop shooting off your gab."

"They can't get me."

"You spieled a line about rugs sometime back, to others besides Pop and me, probably. Pop knows you're featherbrained, but he isn't going to be a conspirator because you're a damn fool."

Dinkie's weak face was fretful. His brooding black eyes were evasive, and he ran his tongue over his small, pretty mouth. Grant felt sorrow for the bird-witted being, but concluded his mind never stayed on track long enough for any comment to hurt him.

"It's a great day in the pit, I bet," Dinkie said. "Wheat has fallen three points, and there's hell to pay."

"I'm going to the gallery to look on. If the boss comes in say I'm in the can or on an errand," Grant said, and went out of the laboratory and down five flights to the gallery room. Messengers hurried through the pit room, to and from offices. Men lifted hands giving bids, while others consulted messages, gave directions to messengers, and walked among tables running various samples of grain through their hands. Grant wondered if he might be a grain buyer later. It had excitement, but he didn't like the faces of men he saw below.

Two hours later Dinkie and Grant left the office. A steady

stream of people were going down in express elevators, pouring through hallways, whirling through constantly revolving doors, and walking quickly down the street. Every corner had its group of people waiting for streetcars. It was past five and dusk drifted over the spring evening. Fifth Street was brilliant flaring, yellow. A bright coldness was in the air. Grant and Dinkie walked quickly, without conversation until Grant reached out his hand to say goodbye.

"Old man Boutwell saw me in the pit and talked. When I said I meant my quitting he was angry, and asked if I didn't think the firm knew best, as they promote men rapidly. I swore and said it looked more to me that they made hacks of everybody, and I didn't want to be like a man in the concern from president on down. He got red and told me I didn't know when big things were planned for me, and finally said for me to get my salary and I needn't come back."

"Hell, Grant, I'm sorry. Boutwell's mad as a goat. You were his great pet, everybody in the office said. Some thought he wanted to adopt you."

"Yes indeed. He might permit bright boys to have temperament since he has temper himself. He's kept others on dinkie jobs for years, if they were damn fools enough to stay. Who's he to try to discipline anyone into being a worm?"

"Well, drop up and see me when you come back after the summer," Dinkie said, and went on, worried because his wife had given him hell over the phone during the afternoon. She threatened to leave him.

At the dinner table Grant said he was going to Duluth the next day.

"Can't you ever keep a job?" his older sister scolded. "Have you no ambition? Other boys your age—"

"Dry up," Grant said. "I'm not your problem. When I indicate I have any admiration for the way you manage your existence you might start advising, but wait till I do."

"Somebody has to bother about your problems or you'll come to a pretty pass."

"You've come to a damned nagging one already. Sit inside your pants. You won't be involved in whatever I become."

"Boutwell was planning to advance you. The first man of influence who takes an interest in you—"

"Lay off. I haven't been on newspapers and hanging around town the last few years without knowing something. Talk your purpose and ambition to somebody else. I see the employees who stick with that firm and wouldn't be like one of them for any money; and Boutwell's no sort I want to emulate. Where does that old fart get the idea that he's one to direct a young man's destiny?"

"You needn't brag that you act like a gangster."

"I'd be in a hell of a shape if I was an innocent young boy. At fifty I might be a bookkeeper with an extra office coat," Grant said and left the table to go downtown. At breakfast the next morning his mother told him he hadn't money enough to get to Duluth.

"I have ten bucks. That will get me there with six dollars left and I'll get a job on a boat, or head for the country and do farm work."

"I don't like having you mingle with those rough, vicious types you'll meet."

"I know what I'm meeting, Mother, and if I can't take care of myself it's hard luck, but that's how it is."

"You won't get so much more than others in the world, Grant," his mother reproved him. "You are too high and mighty in your ideas."

"It's not me who said the humble inherit the earth. They can have most of the damned place for all I care. Why fuss about my going to Duluth? It's not the end of the world."

"Write me often then," his mother said as she kissed him goodbye. "And be a good boy, and go to church whenever you get a chance."

Grant laughed, sorry that his mother clung to him in so worried a manner. "Mother, don't be silly. You know I want my life to be as much as it can be. I'll be good if I am because things are finer that way, not because of tosh preachers' talk."

At the station Grant was about to mount the train when he saw Dinkie Fahnestock. "I called up your house to say goodbye," Dinkie said. "Your sister said you were taking this train so I ran down to say goodbye. I knew how you felt and wish I were going along."

Gratitude pulsed in Grant. "I'm glad you came, Dinkie. The family gently insinuate I'll never amount to anything. It's foolish but I'm feeling melancholy and cut adrift. Why is it so damned much worse to be a drifter than to submit to being a lousy clerk?"

"Don't I know? But I wanted to say you can wire me for money if you strike hard luck. I'll send some, somehow, from one of my broads. You won't be pimping. I won't say where I get it, or you just think it's part of my salary."

Grant laughed, squeezing Dinkie's hand. "Thanks, that is fine of you, Dinkie. I'll drop you a letter. But behave. I'd hate to see you in a mess."

Grant got on the train feeling very fondly towards Dinkie. He wasn't a rotter. He was just unbalanced, and had had too much money as a kid. As the train pulled out Grant saw Dinkie waiting on the platform. He looked slight and forlorn, but soon he straightened up and walked snappily away, visualizing himself, no doubt, as a man of wealth and fashion, and of exquisite ability to attract the ladies. Grant buried himself in a book as the landscape was too usual to interest him. Looking out of the window now and then he wondered. Farmlands about were not fertile, and all the inhabitants couldn't be business or professional men. How do people live, and why do most of them want to? It takes little, though, with most people asking for little and getting less.

2

The shipping and employment office was thronged with men ostensibly wanting jobs. Others loitered about the door and along the street. Grant was self-conscious and shy among these types, who were floaters inured to the grim aspects of existence.

"You want a job as porter, huh?" the burly, red-faced man at the desk asked Grant. "You kids who want vacation jobs aren't dependable. If I line you up work, will you stick?"

"I'm broke. I have to," Grant said, and added, "Are we the only ones not dependable?"

"There may be a job on a private yacht. Stick around and see me once or twice a day. I have to give the job to the man that's on the spot, but most of these birds don't want work," the man admitted. Grant felt a security as the man evidently favored him, or was kindly. Grant tried not to feel young and lost. He could not explain that he had seen tough life, cub reporting, and hoboing last harvest season. His slightness didn't mean lack of resistance. There was toughness here though, he didn't know much about.

"It's a bad year," the employment agent confided. "Look at the number of men hanging around."

"I want to get to Europe in the fall, if I can," Grant answered. "I'd like a job for a few months, and then I'd try shipping aboard a cattle boat even."

"That listens well. It's damned hard work; long hours, bad food, and plenty of crap."

"Others stand it. I could, too."

"Why do you want to get to Europe? I used to think it would be swell there. It's hell being stranded in a foreign port. I was in Marseilles once. That's a tough town, but the birds there ain't no tougher than the mugs in this burg. Watch your step. Some of them have you spotted already. Watch what money you have on you."

"That's safe. I have little."

The employment agent felt chummy. "You had trouble at home, what?"

"No, I hated office work and quit. I've earned my own living for several years, mainly. I stayed at home but paid board."

"There's lots of kids had better stick home. I wish I had when I had the chance. Bumming's no lark. Things ain't much better one place than another."

"Yes, but there is movement and variety," Grant said, feeling despondent only because he looked too much like a young boy and used to money. In the afternoon he went to the shipping office again. More men were about, isolated, or in groups, chewing tobacco, smoking, shooting craps, and carrying on conversations full of obscenities.

"Hell kid, ain't you lined up yet?" a ragged man asked Grant at the head of the stairs. "I thought you'd get a job right away.

That employment guy likes you young swells and lets us regulars
starve if he don't have to use us."

"Say cull, slip me a jit, can't juh. I ain't had nothing to eat
for two days," another man said.

Grant was uncomfortable and wished he looked rougher.
"Hell, do you think I'd want a job if I could take on charity
cases?" he said gruffly.

"Well, stick around and be chummy. We're in the same
jam," the first man said. Grant ignored him, sure that he was one
who would never take work and who begged off newcomers.
There was no call for a porter, everything was slack, Grant was
told at the desk. Already he was treated indifferently. He was
sure shipping was bad this season and the agent was bored telling
men there were no jobs. At the door Grant stood for a time. A
half-witted looking man with mossy teeth and a misshapen-egg
head spoke to him.

"Did that guy ask for a fee to get you a job? Don't let him
stick you."

"I know," Grant answered, not distrusting the speaker, but
not wanting to talk to him.

"You probably are hard up. You probably don't know how
to make your money last. I know where you can get soup that's
a meal, and all the bread you want, for a jitney. I'll show you,
but I ain't eat myself for days."

"Here's a dime," Grant said. "Give me the address of the
place. I'll find it."

"Where you sleeping?"

"A cheap hotel."

"That's too expensive. Why don't you stay at the Civic lodging house? There's room for fifteen hundred there; rooms, or a
cot, at five cents a throw."

Grant was antagonistic to the idea, though the Civic house
was probably cleaner than his hotel.

"You come from good folks, I kin see," the stranger probed.

Grant wanted him away, despising him for his inferior's wish
to attach himself to somebody he believed of better class. He
wasn't tough, only a hanger-on. Grant walked away. The man
strolled along.

"If you git hard up, let me know. When it's six I ask for

money on the street. You'd get it quicker though, because they'd believe your hard luck story."

"No, no, I shan't need your help," Grant said quickly. "I go in here to telephone," he added to get away. A fear began to settle in him. He didn't know whether a deeply burning resentment was stronger. He should pity the masses, wasn't he one of them? He felt rage that the man back there made him so consciously alien. Would a period of hardship make him feel one of their kind? At that, their lives were not so dull as an office clerk's. They had freedom of movement. He tried to keep panic out of him, as he could walk into the country and get a farm job if need be.

By six o'clock a misty chill was on the city, and fog obscured the high portion of the town. Boats in harbor looked deserted. Grant thought of going aboard some boat and striking the captain for a job. The wind chilled him. He saw a lighted restaurant and recklessness had him. Why should he be careful of a miserable $2? He entered and ordered food. A warm abandonment was in him. Life seemed free. Nothing mattered much. He might as well be one of the floating horde of unemployed for a while, as an experience. Soon he was in bed and felt protected by warm coverings.

The next day Grant felt more at ease among the job-seekers. He was infected by the spirit of loiterers, who week in and out waited for a chance job. It was only with the approach of night that desolation and fear struck into him. The employment agent was curt to him now. He was no novelty. "Nothing doing, kid. Stick around. I got yuh in mind."

The violet-eyed man who had first spoken to him yesterday ignored him. He was relieved. The man was a heavy drinker, with a weak, shifty face. The atmosphere in the office was smoke-ridden; the floor covered with tobacco juice, unclean spittoons, and cigarette butts.

"Dis is a hell of a year," one man said. "You'd tink a guy wuz askin' a favor fer a chance to earn his bread."

"I could get money from my old man," a youth with the violet-eyed derelict boasted. "De old man's wort' a pile o' kale, but I had a helluva fight wit' him, but dat's a year ago. He'd come tru' and be glad to hear from me now."

Grant disbelieved the speaker, sure that he was going to pull a fellow-rich-man's-son line. Outside Grant saw a young man whose face was vaguely familiar. He went down the dock and stood by an anchor post to look across the great lake. A private yacht steamed by, with no other ship in motion visible. Grant began to daydream, imagining himself a yacht owner, and planning places to go.

"You're wanting a job too, I see," the young man who had looked familiar spoke. Grant turned, jolted out of his daydream.

"Yes, and it's a bad season. I've never done it before and don't know the ropes. I wanted to get to Buffalo, or New York, to ship to Europe."

The newcomer was well-dressed, and good-looking in an advertisement way. "I had a fine job on a private yacht, last year. Might get the same job again, too. The agent says the owner may do the Thousand Isles this summer."

"You're from Minneapolis. I remember your face, from the university campus, maybe."

"Yes, are you at college there?"

"No, I live near the campus. I had a pledge pin stuck on me my last year in high school and when I didn't like the gang in the fraternity I stayed out a year to break my pledge."

"What house was it?"

"I hadn't better say, under the circumstances."

"I suppose a better house rushed you. We don't know which are best when we're in high school, do we?"

"No," Grant said, knowing there would be a long conversation on fraternities now. "None of them strike me as worth a damn. I wish they didn't exist because they cost too much money if a man tries to keep up with the wealthy fellows. It's hell being a barb though, because all college would mean to me would be the social side. One learns little that isn't catalogued."

"I had a swell night before I came here. A gang of us went to Harry's and got drunk on highballs. It was some party."

The word "highball" had a luxurious sound to Grant. It must be better than mere whiskey. He had been shy of entering speakeasies if he could have gotten in. He pretended now to know all about drinking parties. "Yes, you don't get a fuzzy throat after highballs."

"Do you know—" the older boy started to quiz Grant about various people in Minneapolis. Grant knew some of the people mentioned.

"You're older than I am. Everybody you mention is," Grant said. "You know how underclassmen aren't noticed much by older men in high school. Last year I worked down town and saw only fellows working in the same building as I did. I don't want to go to college though. I don't like the hazing stuff they do to freshmen."

"It's good for you. You have to have it, and after the first year you're able to razz freshmen yourself."

"I suppose so, but some of the upperclassmen are carps," Grant said. He felt some comfort in the presence of this fellow, but he didn't like him. He talked names, and assumed an older patronizing attitude. "I guess I'll go and eat," Grant said after a time.

"Come to a place I know. We can have a drink."

Grant went, afraid he didn't have money for a drink and food too. He ate a sandwich. The highball was only whiskey and soda. It had no kick and left him nearly broke. He wanted to get away from the other man.

Grant went up to the five-story Civic lodging house. The attendant said he could have a cot for five cents and finally gave him fifty cents for two jack-knives. He was led up four flights of stairs. It was eleven o'clock. Dim lights burned in the corridors. There were two floors of small wired cages in which were cots, a wash basin, a chair, and a mirror. On the fifth floor the attendant opened the door to a great sleeping-room. Five rows of cots stretched across the space, dimly discernible. Grant saw figures seated on various cots, undressing, and in one group, talking.

"Ah," a voice snarled. "Fer Christ's sake can de chatter. Whatcha suppose we're here for if not to sleep?"

Seating himself upon the cot Grant undressed and got under the blanket. Snores sounded through the room, and gurglings and sighs. He thought the cot next his empty but a deep groan informed him it was occupied. The man was on his back, motionless. In the corner of the room a dim splotch of moonlight shone on ten or twelve cots, but the room otherwise was dark. There was no whispering or conversation. These men did not know and probably did mistrust each other. Poverty does not breed an atmosphere of comradeship. Rather it makes men sullen and wolfishly resentful or suspicious. Grant put his shoes, coat, and trousers under his pillow, and fell asleep more quickly than he expected with such a variety of snores in the place. Some were hoggish. Others were sighs, or groans, or garglings. Now and then a voice cried out as in pain, anger, or fear. At one time a man let out a shout and struck savagely at something in a dream. "Wot de hell's eating yuh, cull?" the man next him asked, angry at being awakened. Grant woke twice during the night. The first time the room was heavy with silence, but for a lull of snoring only. Far out on the lake a foghorn sounded, deeply menacing as a full-throated bull bellowing. It moaned a primitive, long-drawn-out sob. Grant wanted to dress quickly and go out but it was cold and he could not wander the streets all night. When he awoke the second time dawn was coming. He felt tired and lay nursing the warmth of his body. After an hour of half-sleep he went to the large room where twenty men were washing. There was little talk among them, and what there was was sullen and filthy. Quickly Grant finished his toilet and went outside. He bought a half-dozen buns, sawdust dry. That night he slept again in the Civic lodging house. The next day he had not a cent and nothing to pawn. He slept in an empty freight car. Three other men crept into the car during the night, and he was glad of their presence. A feeling of kinship was in him now. By the morning light it was dim, misty, and cuttingly cold. He saw that one of the men was the one he had given a dime three days before.

"When do we eat?" he joked.

"You ain't used to not, I guess," the man commiserated, without humor or irony in his cringing nature.

"I'll get used. Here's a bun if it does you any good. I recklessly ate four yesterday. Got six with my last nickel. Masticate your food. You have to, those buns. They're made of mud and wood-shavings."

Outside Grant went to a watering tank and splashed icy water on his face and sticky eyes to waken himself. He started to walk but it seemed ages before he could move other than rheumatically. There was no sign of a job at the shipping office, and tomorrow would be Sunday. No regulars touched him for

money now. They knew he was broke. He felt no aversion or
fear of any of them. After all, what do toughness and viciousness
mean? These men drank, begged, slept where they could, but
few of them could be thieves or holdup men or they wouldn't
be so down and out.

Again that night Grant slept in the freight car. In the morning he was up at five o'clock. Duluth was dismal. The streets
were deserted. The over-shadowing cliff of the upper town
threatened grimly. On the top of it was the "swell" residential
district. Grant stood looking down the railway track. A fellow
bum came along.

"What direction is Minneapolis?" Grant asked.

"That direction. You ain't walking?"

Grant said no, and wondered if the fellow knew that was
just what he thought of doing. Why not? It was Sunday and he
could be in the country rather than in Duluth all day with nothing to eat. He couldn't beg on the streets. He waited for the
other man to disappear, and started down the tracks.

3

At first his body hunched up towards his shoulders. The
tendons in his legs would not give. He tried to walk fast but he
felt stiff and chilled. Then he had forgotten about physical discomfort and was swinging along at a fine pace. Duluth was two
miles behind and he did not feel hungry. He'd heard that one
does not after the third day of not eating. The sun was high; the
air clear and vital; he loved his body, and thought it foolish he
had felt weak among those unemployed Great Lake toughs who
couldn't bring any variety of imagination to their livings. The
world grew large and full within his vision. He was free, young,
and healthy, with years of wandering ahead of him, and always
the possibility of settling down to some kind of employment if
he ever had to or felt differently, but he wouldn't submit to the
idea that life is much the same everywhere. He thought of pio-
neers, adventurers, engineers, painters, writers; and his imagination created exciting and amusing experiences for him of which
he was always the central figure. After two hours he bathed his
feet in a cold stream and dipped his head under water. After
the sun shed clear warmth upon his wet hair, and he tingled with

vitality, being beautiful within a reckless imagination. Walking
he decided to stop at some farmhouse and ask for food, but he
delayed. To ask for food would make him shy and take him out
of his created world into contact with something humdrum. It
was one o'clock and he had walked fifteen miles when he asked
a man before a farmhouse for something to eat.

"The missus is away and I don't tamper with her kitchen,"
the man answered, not being unkind, just not wanting to bother.
"The woman in the house back there will take care of you."

At the next house a slovenly woman came to the open door.
Two dirty children played on the kitchen floor, one was in her
arms, and another in her belly.

"I'll do what I can for you," she said apathetically, and put
a bowlful of milk and a loaf of soggy bread before him. The milk
tasted sour, but he devoured the heavy bread and drank the milk.
Thanking her he started off again. It was eight o'clock evening
before he stopped again at a large farmhouse. Two sheep dogs
barked at him, but not savagely. A woman called them back.

"Could I sleep in your barn tonight?" Grant asked, seeing
that the woman was tidy and American born, surely. He decided
to invent a tale. "I'm walking to Minneapolis on a bet, and said
I would not spend any money or sleep in a bed until I got there."

"Come into the kitchen and I'll get you a basin to clean up,"
the woman said. "Where are you from and how far have you
walked today?"

"From Duluth."

"What does your mother think? You're from a good home,
I see."

"She doesn't know. I told her I was seeing friends in Minneapolis."

"You're just in time for supper. We eat late Sundays and as
you're a clean boy you will eat with us."

Grant rubbed his face till it glowed more vividly than the
sun and wind had already made it glow. He was grateful for his
young-boy look now.

Soon he was at the table with the farmer, his wife, and son.
"And our guest tells me his folks are church people. I'm right
glad to hear that," the woman said. "We are strict church-going

people ourselves. Have some more potatoes. You must be hungry and a growing boy needs plenty of food."

After supper the farmer said Grant could sleep in the extra bed, but he remembered having said his bet was that he would sleep in no beds and asked to stay in the haymow, blaming himself for having lied more than was necessary.

"I'm glad you keep your word," the wife said. "I wouldn't want to be thought lacking in hospitality to the son of Christian people though."

In the morning Grant was up early and had a huge breakfast of ham and eggs, pancakes, and coffee. Thanking his hosts he departed, having promised to write them from Minneapolis. By afternoon he had come to barren country, inhabited by poor "polack" farmers. At three he stopped at a village and got a meal by chopping wood for a woman who looked on lazily and seemed to think him amusing. She stopped him soon, saying the axe was too heavy for him; then she gave him fried eggs and cold meats and a salad from the icebox. It was again eight before he stopped at a farmhouse. Several people were collected around the back door. Two savage dogs came out at him and were called back reluctantly, but he asked the oldest man if he might have supper. The man said yes, in broken accents. "Mind de dogs. Dey are fierce, not pets."

This family was Polish. There was a mother and three younger women, daughters or in-laws. One was beautiful, with sleek, purplish hair and great dark eyes which had a glazed quality. Her face was eggshell smooth and expressionless. During the meal there was no conversation, but the people were not unfriendly, and they seemed not curious. "You want to sleep early?" the father asked, and told his son to take blankets and show Grant the haymow. He was soon asleep. It was seven morning before he awoke and climbed down from the mow. The dogs started to attack him but were called off.

"When you weren't here for breakfast we thought you had slipped away," the farmer said, and Grant believed they'd thought he had stolen something.

"No, I'm sorry I slept so heavily. Thanks for letting me stay. I'll go on now."

"Without your breakfast?" the man said almost crossly. "No boy, go to the womenfolk. They will feed you."

"I don't want to be a nuisance," Grant said, believing the farmer thought him a silly child. The farmer called to the women. They were cleaning up; one girl scrubbed the floor, and everything was spotless. Pots and pans shone where they hung against the rafters of the low-ceilinged room. The atmosphere was foreign. He wondered if the women spoke English. The night before they had talked in their language. He was given breakfast, and felt that the girl serving thought him a bother. It made him uncomfortable. Soon however he went on. He walked five miles. Agony was in his muscles. Holes in his socks made blisters on his feet, and his shoes bit into the achilles tendon. At three o'clock he went into a farmyard where haystacks stood beside a silo. A maternally full young woman with long, plaited, yellow hair was working in the kitchen. She jumped, affrighted, when he spoke behind her. An older woman came. He could not make either of them understand, and they were distrustful. At last he understood that their man was in town, and they didn't like serving strangers when he was not around. Grant started away but the younger woman called him back and gave him a huge sandwich. He asked if he could nap against one of the haystacks, and was told he could. After two hours he awoke, feeling energetic. Knowing that a town was five miles on he started there, planning to sleep in a barn if need be. The air, which was dampish, was clearer. He was coming into more fertile country, and Spring, the vitality of growing things, affected him. It was past seven before he realized he had long since passed the town. It didn't matter. He could sleep in a haystack. He began to lope, and settled into a longstrided run which he kept up for half an hour, triumphant because his wind and energy were sound. He felt as if he could walk on through the night. Then he could nap and walk on in the afternoon. Passing a red barn he saw a herd of Jersey cattle and that made him happy as he knew cows, and could talk registered stock to the owner. Going into the barn he found the dairyman, Mr. Clark.

"I'd like to get a night's lodging if I can," he said. "I know Jersey cattle. Maybe you know the Silver Ring herd in Iowa. I worked with their owner one summer when I was a kid."

Mr. Clark looked curiously at Grant. "Yes, I know that herd. It's broken up now, isn't it?"

"Yes, the owner went bankrupt, buying too many expensive cows, but he had some wonderful animals."

"You can help us milk, but be sure and milk clean. Where are you from?"

"Minneapolis. I went to Duluth to get a job but it is a bad shipping year. I went broke and am walking home, unless I can get a farm job before I get there," Grant said, believing it well to be honest to Mr. Clark who looked intelligent and reserved. Grant learned that he was a New England, college-bred man who'd gone into dairying because his health was bad in the city. After milking they went to the house where Mr. Clark introduced his wife.

"I would hire him if he were heavier. He knows cattle and he milks well; knows food rationing too, but we need a full-grown man this season of the year." Mr. Clark consulted his wife hesitatingly. She looked prim and austere, and surely made decisions for the outfit.

"Young boys ought not be wandering about the country," she said.

Grant felt repelled by her and angry. Who in hell was she to judge at once what any strange young boy ought to be doing? He might be an orphan, or have no home. He felt irritated hate for her. She was waspish, rigid, and it was she who had stopped Mr. Clark from hiring him. It was best. He wouldn't have liked to work with her hawk-eyeing him all the time, but he felt the injustice of her righteous and disapproving type.

In the morning Grant had breakfast and after helping with the chores started walking again. Mr. Clark slipped him a dollar, implying that his wife need know nothing of this. Walking along, Grant's imagination created tales of wandering and freedom, of exciting encounters and conquest. In the afternoon a truck went by, and the driver offered him a lift. It was with relief that Grant found he was driving the twenty-five miles into Minneapolis. There he boarded a streetcar and arrived home to find the family just through dinner.

"So you're back," his mother said. "I wondered if you wouldn't be when we didn't hear from you. Sit down and I'll give you your dinner. Henry didn't come home and I saved his strawberry shortcake for him but you can have it. I suppose you've discovered home is best after all."

"That may be but I'm going to South Dakota in a few days. I will get more money and experience that way than doing any kind of office job I can get now."

"You'll amount to a great deal with your low-life wanderings," his older sister said bitterly.

"You amount to nothing with your damned purposefulness. Someday, when you're a bright girl, bother about my existence and I might be interested," Grant retorted.

"You two are alike. The others don't quarrel every time they speak. Rhoda, it's your fault however. At thirty-four you might stop taunting a boy who isn't yet grown," Mrs. Conkling said, but with an air of knowing her comment was useless.

4

It rained the next day and was dull for a week but June opened brilliantly, with a flow of glowing days. Grant decided to depart. He sold some books, pawned a watch, collected old clothes from the garret to sell to the secondhand man, and his mother gave him $10, saying he might try to sell the old house back in Merrivale. Sticking most of the money into the bank, he was that night in an empty freight car consigned to Fargo. He crouched back in a dim corner to avoid prying trainmen. The train pulled out and by nine o'clock he was sleeping soundly, after the three-time beat of the wheels became comforting rather than bothersome to his senses. In the morning he caught another freight headed towards Merrivale. A brakeman discovered him but became chummy rather than putting him off.

"Be careful, I don't give a damn if you bum. I've done it myself, but don't try riding the bumpers. If you had an accident your family might try collecting from the train company."

"I'll stick in an empty freight car. Many hoboes out this season?"

"It's early. There'll be thousands in a couple of months, and we don't try to keep them off then. They're needed for harvesting

the crops anyway. Have a chaw of tobacco. Good for the health.
I'll sit and talk a while. I'm going to change my job soon. Been
too long on braking."

Grant dropped off at Merrivale to find the town seemed
tiny. His three years in the city had changed his idea of size in
towns. He wondered if he'd see anybody he knew. Walking down
Egan Avenue he saw Bill Jennings in front of his dad's shoe-
store, and shook hands with him. Bill was becoming such a man
as his father, lazy, with a bay window, and in front of the store
chewing at a cigar almost any time.

"If it ain't young Grant Conkling," Bill said, eyeing Grant.
"You were a kid last time I saw you. How's Pete? Making a name
for himself as a football player, isn't he? The old town's turned
out some good men." Bill put his head through the door to call
his brother, Lenard, who came out and went through an elaborate
program of recognition and reminiscence about the old football
days of Grant's brother in Merrivale. Grant collected information
about people in town. Dopie Stearns was a clerk in the Jew
haberdashery store; Chemo Wright had a job as town telegraph
agent; Stan Ellerson was away studying to be an optician; Ben
Stevens intended to be a dentist; Mike Connolly was at Kelly
Field in Texas, gone nuts over aviation; Joe Shaw and Frank
Sellers were at college, but not taking up any particular profession.

"I haven't kept track of who's got back to town," Lenard
said. "Bill and I take the business off the old man's hands so he
can tend his farms. The town's pepped up since you left. The
Chautauqua lake is filled, and stocked with fish, and it's a regular
city during summer months. Motor and rowboats, and all that
makes a swell resort."

Grant was not interested in the Jennings boys as they were
of an older generation, so he went down the street to look up
Gould Lamar. He was surprised that he wasn't sure which was
the Lamar house, as new houses were beside it, and it had been
repainted. As he stood wondering if a man could forget so
quickly, Gould came down the steps.

"Holy Jiminy, Grant, why didn't you write you were coming?
I saw you from the window and wondered who the new guy in
town was. We were both in short pants when you left town,"

Gould said. He was tall, weedy, with a face broken out in pimples. There was fuzz on his face and his voice was bass, except when it cracked.

Grant felt chagrined that he hadn't grown more, and that he had no use for a razor as yet. Still he wondered why Gould had to look messy because he was growing. All boys don't. "What have you been up to?" he asked.

"Not much. The old man said he wouldn't let me go away to college so long as I could get two years credit at the Normal School, and have more sense when I did leave home. I go to Wisconsin next year. I'll be a Junior and take law. Why don't you come along? You could earn your way through."

"Jump into the old man's boots, what? Do you like the idea?"

"It's as good as anything else. What will you do?"

"I stuck out of school, and I'm not keen on going to college. I worked for a lumber company; got canned. Tried cub reporting and quit, and I want to get to Europe; to see a little of the world before I decide anything much, anyway."

"Hell, Grant, a college degree is worth money to a fellow, dad says, and you'd have four years of not having to decide what to do."

"I know, but I'm restless. I know already I don't want to be a doctor, lawyer, journalist, or anything I can think of. I'll bum around a bit."

"Same old Grant. Always kicking, and I suppose you're a great highbrow with your newspaper work and all that bunk. I tell you, the old man says he'll pay me if I repaint the house and barn this summer. You do them with me. We can take our time and dad will pay for our meals at the City Restaurant. The family go out of town to visit my aunt. You can sleep with me."

"I'm on. When do we start?"

"In a couple of days, when the family's away. There's a dance on tonight. We'll call up Dot Thompson for you to take."

"She's just a kid."

"Wait and see. Some of the girls we thought babies are high-steppers now. Dot may be dated up, but she'll know of somebody else."

After dinner Grant went to get Beryl Baker as Dot was engaged. He had misgivings about Beryl, whom he remembered as tow-headed, freckled, and noisy. When she came downstairs, however, he saw she was grown. Grant admired her dress, and saw that her manner was subdued.

"It's all right, but I'm damn tired wearing my older sisters' hand-me-downs. The folks don't give me credit for ever wanting anything of my own. Mayme and Lillian make me tired. They never had much sense, and getting older gives them less. They're getting scared they might not marry."

"Isn't it hell?" Grant agreed. "Just because people get old sitting on their behinds while they rot in their belfries they think they can tell younger people how to live."

"I'm not going to the Normal and be a schoolteacher," Beryl said. "I don't talk of going East to school either. The folks can't afford it. When I finish my business course this girl heads to the city and Merrivale can be ancient history to me."

At the dance Grant was busy meeting old friends. Not many fellows were keen to dance with Beryl, though everybody was chummy with her. The belles were Helen Goff, Marie Stearns, and Genevieve Holden. Only the last two Grant liked. Helen Goff was pretty but languid and sarcastic. All of the girls dressed better than he recalled. Dress competition was keener because more closed-in than in the city, but the people knew each other with easier casual intimacy. Grant felt alien. He'd known them all three years back, but their habits and outlook were no longer the same as his.

"Grant, come and dance with me," Marie Stearns said, coming up as he felt completely cut out. "You look lonely. Don't you remember some of the water fights we used to have, and the snow battles?" Marie had a slender buoyancy which was exhilarating. Her dark-red hair and jaunty little head with its tilted nose, and her red-brown eyes, appealed to Grant much, as did her direct boyish manner and slangy wit. He blushed when she spoke, but felt at ease as soon as they began to dance. During the evening he danced with her three times, though Gould Lamar and Arkansaw, a southern boy visiting the town, were both rushing her. Marie, however, didn't take anybody's attention seriously. She was alert and chummy with everybody but not at all sexily coquettish. In the years before she had been a rowdy youngster, but her kid rowdiness was gone now.

He danced with Lela Bayne. He liked her. She had always talked to him seriously even when he was a little boy. "I remember when you used to perch on my veranda while I dried my hair," Lela said. "You were a grave youngster, but we had some great talks, didn't we? I feel as I did then, and should have had enough sense to know that my music wasn't much. Now with the talkies I've lost my job in the moving picture house. I've about decided to go in with mother and run the boarding house. It's almost a hotel now, and if we make it that, I'd have freedom."

Lela was slender, flat-bodied, and dashing. Her bosoms were delicately tender against Grant's chest. He guessed that she had relaxed more than was formerly her habit. The year's difference in their ages didn't seem so much now. He saw the sharp perfection of her profile, her keen blue eyes. Her soft white dress added to the delicate sensuality of her body which tingled electrically against his.

The orchestra played a waltz, deeply swaying and accented, so that soft jets of music, pulsations of ecstasy, threw the dancing pair into the joy of waltz sentimentality. Grant held Lela closely, and she responded. The room was about only as a quality of light and movement. His cheek was close to Lela's. A pain of holding her tenderly was in him.

"You're a pet, Grant," Lela said softly. "I thought I was going to get away from this damn town, but tonight you seem the only person who knows how I can feel about it. You always wanted to get away too."

Grant knew that Lela had thought Tom Warden would ask her to marry him, and as he was rich, she had thought that through him she would have escape. He had merely taken up with Martha Stearns, Marie's sister, however, and people said Lela had been jilted. Then Tom left town, and nobody knew what he was doing.

The dance was finished and Lela was away. Grant did not at once look for Beryl. He tingled with ecstasy and rebellion, knowing of the consent, the sweet admission, that had occurred between him and Lela. But the music was finished. The barrier of conventional pretense was up at once, for Lela was a *nice* girl, at least too bound to niceness not to think him a little boy, whatever she felt.

It was past one o'clock when Grant was in bed with Gould Lamar. "We can sleep till ten, and then we'll go to Sunday School," Gould said.

"Do you go to Sunday School?" Grant said in surprise. "Not for me."

"Mother insists, and it's good for a fellow."

"Doesn't that twaddle get on your nerves?"

"Why twaddle?"

"Our folks were brought up to pretend they care, but they know nobody knows, if they admit it."

"What are you talking about?" Gould said with plaintiveness in his maturing tones.

"Oh nothing. I suppose you haven't thought what you believe. There are too many earthquakes, degenerates, illiterates, and kinds of religion for me to bother about church ideas."

"You hadn't better let mother hear you say things like that, or she won't let me be around with you," Gould said, shocked.

"We won't talk religion. It's here and now for me. People aren't so wonderful they need to be preserved for eternity, and if they are it must be full of mobs of damned boring people by now."

"You'll get it in the neck someday for thinking things like that," Gould reproved.

"I won't live in tank towns where it's a sin to think." Grant felt antipathetic to Gould. What had happened to him, or what had not happened to Gould, that their outlooks were so different? He was foolishly conscious that Gould was lumpish and messy in his adolescence.

"You've been up against it too much, Grant," Gould said after a silence, but disapprovingly yet. "I'd feel rotten if I had to make my living of course."

Grant felt that Gould believed his own family superior because they had money so he had never been let to earn any money for himself.

"That isn't it. I feel blue often and hate jobs I have, but they're not what get me. I hope sex doesn't bother a man always as it does me now. The first few years are the most awful, I guess," Grant confided.

"You hear too much dirty talk." Gould was righteous.

"Hell," Grant swore. "That's it. If the thing is natural and also dirty where does God head in? It's the way people look at things which is dirty, not things themselves."

"You think you know too much, Grant. You didn't use to be so swell-headed. I guess what's good enough for other people is good enough for you."

"What other people, Gould? The Chinese, the niggers, the insane people, or who?" Grant said, and added quickly, "We'd better sleep. I feel dopey after not having slept well last night."

He wanted to talk and he had hoped that Gould would be thinking much the same sort of thing as himself. He wished now he were alone in bed. In spite of tiredness sleep would not come wholly to him. Half asleep at one time he heard the clock downstairs strum out three, and, awake, stifled with the violence of revolt in him, he lay. He hated the inert body of Gould beside him, and moved far to the side of the bed, preferring a draft on his back to possible contact with Gould's flesh. He tried to think his aversion an idea only, since he and Gould had slept together many times as children. The cold repellence did not go out of him, nevertheless. His blood and limbs tingled with sex desire also, as though millions of pinpoints were pricking him. Gradually sleep came, a drifting heavy vapor upon his conscious, and his last waking emotion was one of confused pity for Gould, who seemed to him not more than half alive.

5

Grant went nights to the pool-hall, leaving Gould to fuss with his wireless set. This night he watched Joe Shaw and Frank Sellers playing billiards. A mystification had Grant because he found he didn't like Joe Shaw now, and as youngsters they had thought themselves sworn to eternal devotion. Grant told himself that the past friendship had existed merely because they'd been promoted together ahead of their other mates twice, and they had confessed with painful gravity the phenomena of pubescence to each other. It had all seemed rarely fine and intimate then, but watching Joe, Grant believed he had more fondness for the amiable and easily swayed Frank Sellers.

Frank stopped playing and came over to stand by Grant while Joe played a game with attorney Scott. "He keeps in with those old geezers," Frank said sourly. "Have you noticed how Joe's even worse about guarding money and knowing people who can help him out than he used to be?"

"Have I noticed? I don't need to," Grant said drily. "Two summers ago he came to Minneapolis and stayed two weeks at our house. My brother slipped me money and I took him to shows and about town, and mother was fine to him, but he went away without thanking her or writing her a letter. That would not have bothered me, but when I found that his father had given him $100 to spend and he'd let me stand him everything for two weeks, I was riled. It kept me broke for a month after. I decided our friendship wasn't so damned good. Now he hasn't even invited me to his house for dinner. I know his mother doesn't have hospitable ideas, but I guess he's her kind of son."

"He doesn't get by so strong at Vermillion, except on his football, and everybody says he's a grandstand player and no good on teamwork," Frank criticized.

"To hell with his football. That bores me. Pete being pompous all over our house because he's captain of the Minnesota teams had given me a perfect earache when people talk football. What's been happening to you, Frank? To hell with Joe. He's past bad news for me, I suspect."

"It's this way," Frank grew very casual. "Some people think I act fast on the campus, but, Jesus, I used to think girls something to be afraid of. Now I'd have any of them and walk away and not think a thing about the consequence."

"Bah, what to hell you saying?" Grant was scornful. "Try that on Carrie, and she'd biff an ear off you, with her mit and with her mind. Who's been shoving that line on you? If they've kidded you for being a softie don't think you have to act tough to prove different. Who's Frank been bumming with that he gets his hardboiled line from?" Grant asked Joe Shaw as he came near.

"I don't know." Joe was very considered. "You know Frank. I'm glad you called him. He damn near queered himself with people on the U campus, and it gives our house a bad name too."

"Where do you guys get this calling me?" Frank said.

"Hell, Frank, I just mean your line doesn't take with me any more than it does with Grant. If he calls you what do your fraternity brothers think? You haven't only yourself to think of."

"I'm taking a walk down the street," Grant said, sorry to have given Joe a chance to attack the soft, impressionable Frank. Joe had more mind, of a sort, for memory, calculation, and independence, but Frank was impulsive and generous.

"Hello Grant, I just heard you were in town." Sylvester Graham spoke to Grant at the pool-hall door. Grant was surprised, as Sylvester had always been either patronizingly older or indifferent to him three years back. Grant saw that Sylvester was much better looking than he remembered. His head was beautifully formed and his brown skin and direct grey eyes were disconcerting. Well-dressed, he didn't give that conscious "dressed-up" feel that Joe and Frank seemed to have, particularly Joe, who struck Grant as being painfully aware of being a young man of standing now.

"I'm glad you're in town," Grant said, shaking hands, and recognizing in a flash that sympathy existed between him and Sylvester as it didn't between him and other fellows in town. Sylvester had either become less reserved, or found Grant less a mere kid. "I hadn't heard where you were and thought maybe you'd left town."

"I'm at the State University studying law. Wanted to go East but the folks couldn't afford it," Sylvester said.

"Do you see Sellers and Shaw there, much?"

"No, they're arts and science, and we belong to different houses. Let's take a walk. I don't want to start right away hanging around this damn pool-hall just because it's the town hangout."

"Sure. I rather agreed to meet Joe and Frank later."

"That so," Sylvester said. "You three were pretty thick as youngsters, weren't you?"

Grant chuckled. "You bet me, boy. Say thick as thieves and you hit some of our boyish pastimes too, but if you want me to know you don't hand them much, shoot. Joe particularly has been talking about not seeing too much of this or that fellow we used to bum around with, because his dad's only a railwayman, or a barber, or whatnot. Joe thinks he's the original crown prince, I take it, but his hick-town snobberies get on my nerves. How do you like college?"

"I wouldn't go, but I'm not keen on settling down to work yet," Sylvester said.

"Fay Neilson spoke of you the other night. She was romantic about you in high school, I gather, and not so keen about her husband."

"Yes, she thought she'd have a career as a singer, but they overtrained her voice. She didn't want to put up much fight, either."

"She's really beautiful, you know, if she'd lose the village belle manner, and look as if she was careless about being so. As I remember the way she used to sing she had more voice and manner than lots of musical comedy stars. I did theatrical reviews for the cheap shows sometimes when I was a cub, and thought I was stage-struck for a few months."

"How'd you like newspaper work? I think of doing it," Sylvester said.

"It was all right for a while, until I discovered they were using me on sob stuff. About old men, or paupers dying of consumption and neglected by Charity Institutions. When it filtered into my head how yellow the paper was and how tricky they wanted their dope, I got ashamed of how I'd become muckishly morbid. The City Editor knew how, for a while, to drag the tears into my copy. I quit anyway."

"I've tried writing stories," Sylvester confided.

"Yes," Grant exploded. "I took a short story course last year and the instructor told us to take a story of Hawthorne's, copy it three times, reproduce it nine, and then write a story of our own on the same plan. When I asked why not use the adding machine he looked blank. It infuriated me that my contempt didn't freeze his guts, so I walked out. It was a night class full of old maids of all sexes, thinking because they were hopeless every other way they'd better be writers."

"I wish you'd come to Vermillion," Sylvester said. "I might get you a job as secretary there. I had one. We could talk, and

I'd get hell if this was repeated, but there's nobody at my fraternity or at college I give a damn about."

"My mind is set on trying Europe, and I chuck what money I get into the bank so I can make it," Grant said. "I feel suicidally low sometimes, but tell myself it's adolescence and everybody gets that way. After an accident I saw I felt that way particularly, early this spring. Three autos collided, and four college students were killed. I knew some of them. One girl's head was snapped off against a lamp post, and I was sick. She was one of those people who clutch at something inside one, not pretty, but alive. I hadn't felt keen on her; just loved her being, with a warm, life-adoring, look on her face. The accident happened after a dance, and nobody was drunk either. It wouldn't make it less worse if they had been. You know how one could feel. What's everything about, anyway?"

"I know. But how will you support yourself in Europe?" Sylvester was cautious.

"We don't pass out by starvation easily. It's not Europe anyway; it's knowing something about other places in the world I want. Why can't a fellow get into some of these exploring expeditions? I'm fed up with the family line that one should settle into some lousy job in the home city."

"You aren't a joybird," Sylvester chuckled, "but you make me feel restless. I'm lazier than you are though. Half-persuaded I'd try bumming to Europe with you though."

"It'd be no good unless you did it on your own impulse, and you have a rich uncle to give you a start in this burg, if you can stick it. I couldn't. I don't care how lowdown in the economic scale I hit, so long as I feel interested. When I'm liking things, there isn't much gradation of high and low, and when I dislike people everybody is low down."

"We have to fit in somehow, Grant. We can't always beat the game."

"No, but who declares the game and its rules? You don't think we have to fit into the way of living most people we know do. We can bury ourselves and be part of the 100,000,000, just mud, but if it comes to that I'm ready to delay the day and raise hell to have something to look back on. I don't know anybody who can tell me what the right standards to live by are."

"It might be better for me to study science, geology, or engineering," Sylvester said. "A lawyer may never get anywhere."

"Oh hell, you'd get chances to travel maybe, as a geologist or engineer, but you might get stranded in some minor job. We don't have to stay placed ever if we don't want to though."

"We'll get more sense some day." Sylvester was sagacious.

"Yes, or less expectancy. Let's go back to the pool-hall and see if any of the fellows are game to line up a drink. I feel depressed."

Half an hour later eight young men were sauntering towards the Normal School grounds with the avowed purpose of looking over the assortment of girl students. As Swede Holthausen went by the Greek fruit-stand he knocked several oranges off the pile. Others stopped to pick them up. Red Reeves took half a dozen bags of peanuts from the roasting wagon outside the Paris store. As the group progressed, others joined it. "We ought to throw a barbecue at the lake while you're in town," Joe Shaw said to Grant. "Let's organize and pick our people."

"That sounds good," Sylvester agreed. "We'd roast weenies and let the girls bring along pies and cakes."

"Ya," Frank said sotto voice to Grant. "Joe's going to get somebody to organize a party for you to repay your entertaining him in the city."

"Hey, a fight," Red Reeves called joyfully.

"The devil," Joe swore. "What lowbrows are starting a fight now? Let's leave this gang. We can go and powwow in my barn. I haven't had a good talk with Grant since he turned up. How did we stop writing to each other, Grant?"

"It's easy getting out of touch with people you don't see," Grant said shortly.

"What's the fight?" Frank was curious.

"Hell," Joe answered, "Slim Spear took Bull Hanson's engineering job on the Sioux City run after Bull got canned for drunkenness. They want to beat each other up. That's all right when you're kids, but I'm off those roundhouse lowbrows. Red Reeves says he's coming to Vermillion next year too, and we can't stick around him. He'll think we want him around with us on the campus there."

"It won't be any but a cockfight anyway," Grant said. "If

talk doesn't do the trick they'll stop. They've been talking of having a fight since the year one. Frank, where's that bottle of whiskey you said you could get hold of? We need a drink."

Soon the four were seated in Joe Shaw's barn, Frank having procured a bottle of whiskey from his house. Each took turns at tipping the bottle to their lips. The harness room smelled of musty manure and old leather, as it had been unused for years. Cobwebs hung in the corners, and the workbench was covered with old woodshavings, rusty tools, dust, rope, a broken bridle, and various empty boxes. A dim light came from the low-candled electric globe.

"It isn't ingratitude, Frank," Grant said, "but this firewater is sure rot-gut. Here's how, though."

Frank, tall, broad but stoop-shouldered, and saggily collegiate in manner, leaned in grandly assumed old-soak manner against the wall. His round face with its soft babyish eyes already showed the effects of drink. Frank went under quickly. Joe Shaw, short-necked, solid, and careful, kept his tones down. Grant believed he held the whiskey in the bottle with his lips and actually drank nothing. The conversation was too elaborately good fellow, when the only two present who liked each other were Grant and Sylvester. Sylvester was little inclined to pretend sociability. He wasn't talkative anyway. "Don't get drunk, fellows," he advised. "The town will blame me if we get drunk and get caught raising hell." Grant knew that Sylvester just wanted to avoid listening to an argument between any of the others.

The room swerved slightly for Grant. Lights splintered in the offing. He decided he would not let himself go, drink whatever he might.

"Let's sing some college songs," Frank Sellers said, feeling the atmosphere not sociable.

"What do our songs mean to Grant? He's our guest," Joe said curtly.

"Oh what to hell, Joe, why crab everything?" Frank said cajolingly. "I guess Grant ain't throwing off on guys he's known as long as us. He'd pick up any song."

"Have a sip, Frank. We might raise our voices to the night air later," Sylvester said ironically.

"What gets me is what's come over Joe."

"Hell, Frank, you and Joe see too much of each other at school. Let's be sociable," Grant advised.

"You said it, see too much," Joe said nastily. "He has great ideas for entertaining guests."

"Bull," Grant exploded. "You've pulled that 'guest' line enough, Joe. I'm not your guest or Frank's. Oh yes, this is Frank's whiskey, and your barn, but I'd as soon be at the alley shack hangout. Don't lay on the guest business so heavy. I'm in town as a hobo, in overalls generally, to take in the harvest season."

Joe didn't answer, but took a sip from the bottle. This time Grant saw that he did take whiskey into his mouth and swallow. "It takes a good man to hold his drink and not get nasty," Joe said quietly.

"Right you are," Grant answered, "but you managed to get nasty at Frank without even taking a drink. It would be awful too if Red Reeves had come to sit in the barn with us. Of course he was fine a few years back when we wanted to go apple-stealing. He'd take the chances and we'd eat the apples, but he's not our class now. Say boy, because you have a reputation as a football player in a hick university and belong to a fraternity that's not so hot nationally you needn't high-hat the village boys."

Frank Sellers looked rather wobbly as he leaned against the wall. Sylvester suggested that he'd better sit down. "Shay, I can sthand my likker," Frank protested weakly, but he sat down and leaned his head on his hands.

"Are you going to be sick?" Joe was disgusted. "You always start puking and we don't want to get stunk out of the place."

"Lean your head against the bench," Sylvester said, placing Frank's head for him. Frank leaned back, head wagging, his mouth making grimaces of distaste. The whiskey they had was vile.

"This rot-gut's impossible, Joe. Can't you get some hot water, lemon, and sugar? It might be drinkable diluted. As it is it's enough to make a rhinoceros puke."

"Hell, you guys are never satisfied," Joe growled. "Why didn't we stick to the gang?"

"Don't put yourself out," Grant said. "Who suggested leaving them? They were too lowbrow for you. You suggested coming here. We'd better have gone to the alley shack."

"I'll get the water then, and get hell from mother if I'm caught," Joe said and banged out of the place.

"He'esh a damned bad sport, if he'esh my fraternity brother," Frank muttered.

"Do you remember, Frank," Grant asked. "When we used to swipe pies and cakes from the bakery, he always let the other guy do it? When he had money he'd say he was broke but when he was broke he let the other man spend money all right. I'm just remembering."

"Ballocks, what in hell, goddamn," Sylvester swore. "Let us three beat it and leave him the bottle. We can say Frank got sick and we took him home. He and Frank have grudges against each other and you're siding in with Frank."

"It's my grudge that's strong," Grant insisted. "We'll finish the bottle. I'm remembering the time Joe let Stan Stevens take the blame for swiping some picnickers' lunch. We'd all done it. This firewater has me in a state of mind to call him for his yellowness."

"Don't let's fight, Grant. What will you get out of it?" Sylvester placated.

"There won't be a fight. Joe and I used to be the original Damon and Pythias, and what our letters contained for about two years, just as we passed fourteen, would make damn good documentary reading. He gives me a pain when he starts this snooty line. Hell, Red Reeves has hung around with us for years without trying to be part of our high-class society. He gives a goddamn because Mrs. Shaw thinks she's an aristocrat. Red's a good rounder. He won't bore himself trying to hang out with the birds in Joe's lousy frat, and they're roughnecks themselves, generally."

"What's thash?" Frank said thickly.

"I'm not throwing off on you, Frank. Nationally your house isn't so hot that Joe need get hoity-toity, that's all I said. You're a softie but you're there when it comes to a showdown."

"Don't you get nasty too," Sylvester said. "I didn't think drink would affect you that way."

"Get nasty on Frank, me?" Grant said putting his arm about Frank's shoulder. "Hell, we were in fifty messes together as kids, from his peeing the bed at my house to my swearing about his mother when I didn't know she was there. I've always told Frank he was a damn fool. That proves I like you, doesn't it, Frank?"

"Joe's not liked at college, I know," Sylvester agreed. "Of course you and he were pals. Get what you want off your chest, but the party won't be much fun."

"There's no use. He gets now what I think and he'll be placatory as hell. I say, drink up quick when he comes and we'll clear out. You pretend sicker than you are, Frank. We'll take you home."

Joe came back with hot water but no glasses, and when asked about them said, "You didn't say anything about glasses."

"That's all right," Sylvester Graham said curtly. "We can drink it straight and chase it with hot water. There's only about a swallow each."

"I guess there's another round, fellows," Joe said later. "Come on. Down with it, and here's to you, Grant. It's good to see old Grant back, isn't it Frank? Hope you're in Minneapolis in August because I'm spending a week there before I go back to college."

Nobody played up to Joe's belated heartiness, and Grant wondered disgustedly if Joe thought him fool enough to ask him to stay with him if he was in Minneapolis. Frank dozed, and when Sylvester pulled him into a sitting position he mumbled.

"We'll take him home," Grant said, putting his arm about Frank to help him to his feet. Frank staggered and nearly fell face down. He swayed helplessly.

"I'll help you," Joe said with fake generosity.

"Two's enough," Sylvester said quickly. "He's near our house, and I'm turning in right after."

"So long, then," Joe said. "See you tomorrow at the pool-hall." The others went through a dark alley to the avenue. "How about it, Frank?" Grant asked. "You sick, or just playing possum?"

"Um-gum-um-hun," Frank gurgled and droned.

"He'd better throw up," Sylvester suggested. "Come on, Frank, snap out of it." Frank drooled and grunted.

"We'll take him into my barn and make him dish it,"

Sylvester said. "There's soap to wash with after. I think I'll snap up too."

"Me too," Grant agreed, and in the barn tried to make Frank use his finger. "He's stoney. I hate the job, but it's got to be done. Open your mouth, Frank, I got a feather, and for god's sake, look where you shoot."

Frank protested, gargling feebly, but at last the trick was done. Frank sat weakly on the bench, while Grant and Sylvester got rid of the poison in them, and cleaned up. They all looked grey-green and watery-eyed, but Frank could talk with fair coherence now. At his house he said he could get upstairs alone. "Shure, thash all right. Youch fellows' damn good sports. Joe'sh a shonofabitch. He'esh left me sleeping in the gutter to queer me with th'other guys. You'sh two real guys."

"Bye bye, Frank," the others said, and went downtown to get food and coffee.

"Why drink with those two?" Sylvester said. "Joe's a cheap climber, and Frank's a mushhead. If a man can't hold his drink he'd better lay off."

"Frank hasn't much control. God, there wasn't a third of a bottle of whiskey drank, all together. It was rotten stuff, but he had so little to pass out as he did."

"Drink's a way of finding out what a man has in him. A good drunk is a good man. You and I shouldn't have joined that gang tonight, but you suggested going back to the pool-hall. I thought I was boring you."

"No," Grant said. "I thought you knew I was for you. We'll know better now."

At the City Restaurant several people were being served. Two were travelling salesmen who had come in on the eleven o'clock train and they talked of poker. Flossie White, sometimes waitress and intermittent prostitute, chewed a sandwich as she let old man Perkins feel her up. Other men, drifters, sat before plates of beans, hash, or pie. Grant and Sylvester soon cleared out.

"Another time we won't mix Joe and Frank in our parties. It was my fault," Grant said. "I had a hangover idea that we were friends because of the kid days. I'm cured. Whatever I want of friends they haven't."

Sylvester took Grant's arm. "I'd ask you to dinner at our house, but mealtimes are about as amiable as a hyena feast sometimes. Mother's hardly on speaking terms with my sister Mary since she's turned against Catholicism."

Grant pressed Sylvester's hand beneath his arm. "Are you up against the religious mother thing too? And a scrappy older sister. Aren't families hell?"

At Sylvester's they shook hands goodbye. "I'm for you, Grant. I always did like you even if I was kind of snooty when you were a kid. Being at college I discovered the old home-town attitudes not so good. We get on fine together."

They shook hands again. "I'm glad Syl. We get each other."

"I'd ask you to stay with me tonight, but we'd get hell if we talked. The family would say we were keeping them awake."

"I know. We'll see tomorrow." They shook hands again.

Grant stood on the corner wondering if he wanted to go back to the restaurant for more coffee. No, it was grey and dull there. He wanted light and movement and the feeling of many people about; unknown people, so that he might expect things. The people back at the restaurant were types he knew and didn't like. He wanted the unknown quantities of city streets. The emptiness of this small town appalled him, as did the silence of deserted streets. He felt a warmth of ecstasy, however: Sylvester was fond of him. He wondered if Sylvester liked him as he liked Sylvester: but he feared too that Sylvester thought him foolish not to be planning to go to college, to fit in with people of their kind of class and condition. That conforming idea merely irritated Grant when expressed by most people, but he wanted Sylvester approving of him wholly.

6

There were plenty of farm jobs to be had. Grant worked at haying for a time, and then spent a month with an early harvesting crew, working from seven morning till six evening, but he got pay which he saved with the thought of getting to Europe. Then he took a job with Jerry Ryan, a young farmer whose sister kept house for him. Grant had misgivings as Ryan was not well financed, but he took the job. Jerry Ryan was worried-eyed, most earnest, and talkative.

"I wish you'd work by the month for me," Ryan said. "It'd pay less during harvest season but you're sure of a steady job."

"I'm not looking for a steady job. I'm not a farm hand; I'm a hobo following the seasons," Grant answered.

"But you're only a kid. I can't pay you a man's wage."

"No? I don't work for you then. I've been getting a man's wage."

"But a boy can't expect . . ." Ryan began.

"This boy gets a day's wage if he does a day's work. It'd be great if being young meant old people didn't impose on you."

"You're one of those kids gone socialist, I see," Ryan said.

"I'm doing just what you are, getting all I can for what work I do."

"You aren't a hobo. I remember your family when they lived in town. You don't realize how hard it is for a young farmer to get started."

"I'm sorry you're hard up," Grant said. "I am too. I'm not doing the harvest season for my health."

Much rain had fallen for two weeks before Ryan started reaping. The grain stalks were swollen and fluffy. Whether it was because the binding machine was out of order, or the stalks, the grain shocks were loose and readily became untied, so that it was hard to make a respectable looking shock. Ryan criticized Grant, though his shocks were quite as neat as those of two bums Ryan employed. "You're hardly heavy enough to stand the work. You should take less wages."

"Yes?" Grant was cross with heat and the prick of grain beards inside his shirt. "If I'm not doing as much as the others, can me."

"Well, you may harden up. I do think you might work for $4.00 a day, though. The older men think you're only a kid."

"I give a damn what they think. You're lucky if those bums don't quit after half a day. Some leave after they've had a meal and before they've done a stroke of work."

"Some farmers would work you from five morning till eight night," Ryan persisted.

"They'd deserve a gold medal if they got by with it. Help's too scarce this season for the farmers to do all the bossing."

Ryan decided he was getting nowhere. At noon he and Grant

went to the house to eat with Ryan's sister. "That's why I want you to work by the month, so I can say you are a regular," Ryan persuaded. "My sister won't have floaters at her table."

Grant said nothing. He'd have as soon eaten with the other men, and figured that Ryan thought he'd eat less in the presence of the sister. The hoboes raised a row if there weren't quantities of food. Grant chuckled, pleased at how hard-boiled he'd become. His face was in a condition so he needed to purchase a razor too.

Miss Ryan was pleasing to look at. Her grave face, with deep-set, melancholy eyes, her cameo-clear features and slight body, attracted him. She was going to the Normal School to be a teacher, and sullen, evidently, over having to keep house for her brother. She showed no readiness to get conversational as she and Ryan had grouches on each other. After four days Grant got tired of listening to Ryan bewail the bad fortune of a young farmer, so he quit, wanting to get in with a big threshing crew.

It was Saturday, market day, and Egan Avenue was crowded with Fords, wagons, trucks, and buggies. Stores were thronged with farm wives shopping, and groups of men hung around street corners. The seasonal migration of drifting labor was on in full force now. The hobo jungles down the railroad track were stampeded with floaters. Cooking fires were burning over the ashes of former years' cooking fires. Grant stood on post office corner ready to take work from the most likely looking farmer who needed help. Unshaven, sunburned, in well worn work clothes, he was more apt to be employed than when city pallor was on him.

"Cripes, what's a man to do? I bin in town every day for two weeks gittin' men. I thought, being ten miles out, they'd stay with me, but most of them eat my vittles, get a night's sleep, and when I look for 'em after breakfast, they're gone. Do you think of the thousands going through this town there are ten who want work? A half day, a day, and they want wages as if us farmers were millionaires. What's a man to do? And when we market our grain we git beat on all sides," Pete Robbins complained. He'd been talking so for years. Hoboes knew his wife was an old shrew. She served miserable food, sloppily, and the beds Peter furnished were lousy with bugs and hadn't had clean covers for years.

"Hello, Grant, I didn't recognize you," Marie Stearns hailed Grant as she tripped along. "I haven't seen you in ages."

"I look like all the other hoboes, don't I?" Grant said with pride. "Act like them too. No farmer need pull sob stuff on me, or I'll tell him my sob line. Them lousy swedes and dutchers think us hoboes will put up with rotten food and filthy beds. It's the richest ones who have the sloppiest kitchens too."

"I wish I were a boy," Marie said. "Do you think I could wear boy's clothes and get away with it?" Marie asked jauntily.

"Look here, Marie, you weren't giving yourself the once-over in store windows before you bumped into me without knowing you can't."

"Smarty."

"There's a dance on tonight. I suppose you're dated up, though."

"No, come and get me."

"But suppose I get offered a job today."

"If that's all you think of me . . ." Marie was pert.

"You're right. How does it happen you're not dated up?"

"I had my appendix out six weeks back, and mother says I can't dance for two months. She needn't think I'll sit around and act prissy forever, though."

"I'll get you then."

"I have to trip along," Marie said airily. "I'm glad you're coming along tonight. I want to talk about schools in Minneapolis. I've sworn at the family so much they say I don't have to go back to the convent, but can go to a private school to learn to act like a lady. I want to find some school were girls aren't deadheads." As Marie tripped away an ecstasy of elation was in Grant. Marie had zip. She made him happy with her openness of manner. She had electricity and buoyancy.

The one o'clock train came in, over an hour late. It was loaded so heavily with hoboes that it could not keep schedule. Train gangs didn't try to keep hoboes off the cars this season as farmers needed this wandering labor, shiftless as much of it was. Some were college boys, but most of them were regular drifters who knew the States from harvesting in the Middle West to hop and fruit picking in the South and West.

At lunchtime in the City Restaurant Grant had to wait

long for his plate of beans and hash. The restaurant was packed. Odors of food, human flesh and sweat, stable smell, and grain filled the atmosphere. Hoboes and farmers didn't bother much about bathing at this season. After lunch Grant leaned lazily against the outside wall of the restaurant. The freight train puffed slowly away. It had thirty cars attached, and still was covered with men so that space for an extra man would be hard to find. Already hoboes who had poured into the streets when the train pulled into town had mingled with others already in town.

"Ain't you Casper Conklin's youngest lad?" a voice said at Grant's elbow. He turned to recognize old man Ellis who had at one time been a renter on a farm owned by his father in the better days.

"I just came to town for the harvest," he told Mr. Ellis.

"Well now," Mr. Ellis was leisurely. "Ain't you the likely lad? You was a splinter when last I saw you. Molly will be right glad. She was always partial to your folks. And how are they all?"

"Fine. I suppose most of your family is married and settled by now?" Grant asked.

"Um," old man Ellis paused, not so sure about the settledness of his offspring. His boys were steppers among the farmer lads of the community, but none of them, any more than he, were first rate farmers. They were easy-going, liked larking parties, or hunting season came on just as crops needed attention. "You're looking for a job?" Ellis asked. "My crops ain't ready yet, but our neighbors and us get together and use the same threshing outfit. We'll fix you up out our way."

"Good, I'll come out."

"Sure, come out with me, and let Molly feed you with some of her cooking for a few days. The young ones will be right glad to see you. Ollie has just turned sixteen, and it seems there's a barn-dance out our way this night. You go to Herrmann's store and find the missus. We'll see that you are put to driving a hayrack. You're too slight for the heavy work. I have business across the street, but you find Molly."

Grant watched Ellis departing toward the town's one-time saloon where now they supposedly sold only soft drink. He was glad to have run into this amiable, rather shiftless, but hospitable family. He knew he could be their guest as long as he wished.

They insisted on petting the Conklings as gentle people. Grant
went to find Mrs. Ellis and was greeted with vociferous vivacity.
It was all he could do to keep from being piled into the wagon
and taken out as an exhibition for the Ellis brood. Molly Ellis,
tall, thin, olive-skinned, with snappy black eyes, and a manner
of competence which covered her impractical generosity, insisted
that she must send cards to her married sons and daughters,
telling them that Mrs. Conkling's youngest son was in town.
"Bertie and Sue speak of yer sister Laura that frequent," Molly
said. "She was a fine lady, with no airs about her. They'd be
writing her for the city styles, but I tell them she can't be bothering trying to make them stylish."

Grant felt a pang for the generous-hearted pathos of the
Ellis family, who since they had rented his father's farm sixteen
years back had been faithful to the idea of the Conklings as fine,
elegant, and aristocratic people. The whole family of fifteen were
goodhearted, irresponsible beings. Their father's shiftless Irish,
and their mother's misdirected, industrious French, in their
natures and moods, kept them from accumulating property.
Grant left Molly Ellis to call Marie Stearns on the phone.

"There's a big barn-dance at Baldwin's tonight. They're
christening the new barn. They'll have barrels of cider and
masses of food. Let's go there instead of the dinkie town dance."

"I'm on," Marie said eagerly. "I'm crazy to go to a real
barn-dance. Mom says I can't go to any dance, but I'll slip away.
Meet me in front of the post office at seven."

7

"Luck for me," Marie began to jabber as soon as she met
Grant. "Dad says I have him licked; says I'm an insolent baggage,
so he'll send me to the musical conservatory in Minneapolis to
get rid of me. I can get somewhere with music, maybe. Dad says
since Martha got back from Europe it's a waste spending money
to educate girls, but it's girls he's got. I get furious. I never lolled
around the way Martha does. Why don't they realize people are
made differently? Mother never had any zip, and I doubt that
dad had. Martha makes me laugh when she affects a French accent
after being there one year, and you'd howl. Arkansaw spoke

French to her but she didn't understand a word. I'll fool dad though. He knows I have a temper. I had to use it to get away tonight. He wasn't going to let me out the door and I threw a book at him."

A farmer going out that way gave Marie and Grant a ride to Baldwin's farm. In the back seat of the Ford they cuddled close together, Grant's arm on the back of the cushion until it slid over Marie's shoulder. She snuggled closer. "We won't fuss," she said. "I think it's cheap and gets one all upset, but let's be cozy."

Grant felt the fine contours of her shoulder beneath a thin dress. He caressed it. Spontaneously their lips met, and Marie's hand petted his face. "I feel reckless as anything tonight, Grant," she said. "I don't know why I feel wilder than other girls, or maybe they feel the same way, and we don't tell each other when we're together, feeling gay. But it's too deadly at home. Mother is whiney, and Martha is lazy, but afraid she's not going to have a good chance at marriage. I have to break the jinx some way. Tonight, you'd be shocked if you saw what a real rage I was in, I used language on dad that made him pale. He didn't know how I could swear. He told me I acted as though I were a chippy, and I got cold and asked him how he knew so much about how chippies acted. Then he tried to push me into my room to lock me in and I let go on him. I told him I would be a tough just to get away. Oh, he can't handle me. There isn't any harm in my going to a dance with you."

"Your father isn't strict with you though, is he?"

"Not usually, or not at all. I just want to swear when he and mother mew around."

Grant cuddled Marie, and they kissed again. "I like you; Jesus, I like you, Marie," he said, feeling an overpowering tenderness. He felt passion too, but he didn't kiss too passionately for fear the farmer ahead might turn and tease them.

"Wait," Marie said, straightening herself. "We'd get into something hardly realizing it, Grant. I don't fuss, and most boys get to talking about things, and their silly suggestions make me mad. I got to be careful with you. You start out sweet and affectionate like, and it all seems not to matter, but that's what gets us girls into trouble. Hell, I'd go crazy being fondled as Sylvester Graham fondles Martha when he calls on her. She must be made of wood. He's wonderful, I think."

Grant felt pained with a flooding emotion which numbed something in him. "Yes, Syl's fine," he said.

"I used to be shy with him, and still he treats me like a little girl. It riles me some, and I don't know how to talk to him. Except you, I can't stand boys my own age much. You seem older."

It was past nine when they arrived at Baldwin's barn. Marie, for a time, acted dignified because of shyness, but soon she was a spontaneous, impudent-mannered, girl-kid, again. Her ruby-lighted eyes flashed alertly interested glances about. She was completely direct and good-willed. Her warm, brown face was poised on a slender, perfect throat. Grant watched her zealously, getting a joy out of her exuberance. He and she both knew she made the farmer boys and girls at ease, when they might readily have found her stuck-up, and have felt resentful or lumpish and awkward. He loved her comradely capacities.

In the loft two long tables were loaded with food and drink. It was certain too that some of the men had whiskey, ready to offer whoever wanted strong drink. Loaves of pressed meat, a whole roast pig, still hot, salads, hams, cheese, sandwiches of all kinds, and various fruits were on the tables in quantities. Old man Baldwin might be tight as a business man, but as a host he spent.

The three-piece orchestra, violin, accordion, and piano, began to play. Its rhythm was such that dancers whirled madly to the quick swing of its waltz time, and soon their faces gleamed with perspiration and the effects of food and drink freely imbibed. However old the dancers were they generally finished the course, puff as they might.

Three Ellis boys greeted Grant heartily and offered food and drink to him and Marie. Grant soon danced off with her again, knowing that the Ellis boys weren't at ease dancing with her. She danced with so fleet a lightness that they felt cloddish. Marie said she didn't know how to act to make them treat her less as fragile and breakable. By midnight few people danced continually, and many couples had disappeared for intimate converse. The food tables looked struck by a cyclone. Old man

Baldwin had two more bottles of beer brought from the cellar. Mrs. Baldwin sprung three freezers of ice cream on the party, and more pies and cakes were laid upon the table. Neighboring farmers' wives had brought food along, knowing what a barn-dance means in the way of food consumption.

"Let's go downstairs and find a quiet place to sit," Grant suggested. He was tipsy, and Marie was gay, having had three bottles of beer, and sips of whiskey from the Ellis boys' bottle.

"I'm hot. We won't stay past three, will we? I can sneak in the window when I get home and say in the morning that I got in by one."

Downstairs they located themselves on a pile of gunnysacks in a dark stall. The smell of fresh grain and alfalfa hay was in the black air, and barrels of apples gave added pungency to the night. "It's wonderful here," Marie sighed, leaning against Grant. He pressed his lips to hers, and they caressed each other's cheeks. "We understand each other, don't we, Grant?" Marie said. "You look sad sometimes. I know how you feel." Their lips held each other, warmly loving. Grant pressed her body to his intensely. She responded. "Maybe we shouldn't, but I won't understand why."

Marie said warmly, "Don't tremble so, Grant. You make me want to do anything you wish, which we both wish. I would, too. I won't wait and grow old and ugly and marry and just fall into a habit. If that's the way life is, I won't play."

Grant had her lips again, and she took them away to run over his forehead and down his neck. "It's you who gets it in the neck, Marie," Grant whispered. "I don't want you to be in trouble."

"I don't care," Marie was reckless. "We ought to go ahead, Grant. We're young and feel beautiful, and I don't want to wonder what it is. I couldn't, or wouldn't with Arkansaw. I thought he had the wrong attitude towards girls; and Gould Lamar would be shocked if he thought I'd even think of such a thing. It's awful to think of growing old, just waiting to marry so it will be called all right. Nothing can be nice between old people. They get ugly and are ashamed of their bodies. I hate it, Grant. I'm not afraid. I hate to think of it. I can't think mother and father ever had any feeling about each other. People just marry for that. I won't, I won't. I'll go ahead and if I ever marry it won't be for that alone."

"Wait," Grant said suddenly, holding his lips to Marie's neck. "We have to get out of here. Be quiet. There are people in the next stall. Be careful. Let's go home. But you're too tired to walk. I'll get Ben Ellis to drive us back."

"We don't want to ask that boy to leave now when he can't have much fun generally. I'm not tired. Let's walk. I feel flying," Marie said.

Soon they were on the road towards town. A great moon was out and the road was light before them. They walked with Grant's arm about Marie. "Lean up against me if you get tired. My conscience bothers me for tiring you if your operation wound isn't all healed," he said.

The hooting of an owl sounded from a strip of woods. Further on a startled animal dashed into the brush along the way. The odor of clover hay assailed their nostrils. A sharp pulsation of tenderness for Marie throbbed deeply in Grant. He was suffused with a tormenting glow. His throat ached. He drew her closer to him and stopped to kiss her, flooded with impulse. She put her arms about his neck and held him close. "Nothing we feel is wrong, Marie. It can't be," Grant said. "But we don't know how to be careful, but maybe we won't feel so beautiful about things with anybody ever again."

"I don't want to be careful," Marie said.

"Tomorrow though, won't you be afraid?"

"No. Hold me tight. If you go away we'll probably never see each other again, too, but we like each other. We know how each other feels about things."

They went to a clearing in a grove by the roadside, at the edge of a clover hayfield. It was nearly an hour before they heard the sound of a buggy coming down the road. Grant heard a whistle. "I think that's Ben Ellis. His mother would send him after us if she thought we were walking home." They went to the road again, and it was Ben Ellis in the buggy.

"Why didn't you say you were going home? Mother was mad and said I was a drunken slouch to let you walk home. We thought you'd stay for the ice cream."

Twenty minutes later Grant was standing outside Marie's window. Ben Ellis had driven off, tactfully. Marie leaned out the window to kiss Grant goodbye. "I'm not afraid, and never will be, but we have to be careful," she whispered.

At last Grant walked away, but turned to hear Marie's high whisper sounding after him. She was impish now, and unready to remain sentimental. "Ta-ta, Grant. We'll go dancing again in spite of our sad farewell. You call me up. I'm sensible now, but I don't want you to go away so I never see you again."

"Sure, Marie, but why did you ruin that last effect by being sensible? I felt Romeo as hell, and now I have to go back to Ellises' feeling sensible too. But no, I'll imagine a lot. I'll call up. Monday I join a threshing crew, and I'll sleep all tomorrow. I'm going back and get pop-eyed drunk."

8

Grant slept till noon Sunday, and then drove with two Ellis boys to call on a married brother, four miles away. Their brother, Mike, sat lazily in his undershirt, picking at a fiddle. Pigs grunted and dug around the kitchen floor. A plump, blonde wife worked carelessly, throwing slops out of the door for the pigs to nose. Monday morning Grant started working with the threshing crew, except that, the machine being out of order, two hours were spent in idleness and cursing among the farmers and men. Grant was to drive a hayrack to the grain fields for shocks, and to the threshing machine for shock-feeding to the separator. Farmer Judson had six hundred acres of grain to thresh; Holthausen, Baldwin, and the Ellis fields were to follow.

Because of the forty men in the threshing crew, no one farm wife tried to feed the lot. A cooking camp was in Judson's backyard. Crewmen slept in barns, tents, on the ground, or went with the farmer whose regular employees they were. Most of the other workers were farmers' sons or regular hired men. This lot of farmers were so well organized that they could afford to discharge any drifter who was obviously a slacker.

At mealtimes huge tin basins of stew, hash, joints of meats, bowls of soup, cabbage, weenies, potatoes, pies, bread, and other heavy food were laid upon the long tables. Men forked food across each other, tipped over bowls and poured sloshy food upon their plates, and dipping their noses down, steadily shoveled food into their maws. After meals men dozed for about an hour.

During work hours Grant drove a team of black horses to

and from grain fields. Hearing much profanity his vocabulary grew rich as he swore at his horses. Chaff blew about the machines; the men were browned and dusty, with grit-blackened eyes. After twelve days' steady work, rain delayed proceeding somewhat for three days. The food, which was very good, was much criticized now that idle days made the men less ravenously hungry. "You'd think we wuz a pack o' hogs being fed from the swill barrel," a tall, distinguished, but rundown looking individual complained. He had been telling Grant of his fine family, and as he was, when working, a voracious eater, now, not hungry, he wanted to make Grant believe in his table manners.

Grant was four months working around the Ellises', for when threshing was over, corn husking season came on. Christmas vacation season came before he returned to Merrivale, intending now to return to Minneapolis. He hoped to see Sylvester Graham and Marie Stearns, both of whom had been out of town at school. Feeling much the farm laborer, careless of appearance, Grant hung about the pool-hall waiting for somebody he knew to heave in sight. He was in worn overalls, but browned and unshaven as he was he did not feel self-conscious for looking hayseedy. He felt clean, and clean-smelling with grain odors. After a time he saw with joy Sylvester Graham coming down the street with his cousin, Helen, who was very aloof. Grant started to speak to Sylvester until it struck him that Sylvester was not going to notice him.

Quickly Grant withheld himself, hoping he hadn't grown red or shown that he was bothered. He was amazed before he was hurt. He hadn't thought Sylvester would cut him because he was in working clothes. Going into the pool-hall he was greeted casually by Joe Shaw and Frank Sellers. He felt cut by them too, though he had himself been distant towards Joe since summer.

Joe and Frank didn't matter though. It was Sylvester's having cut him that made him think he was enraged. To hell with Sylvester. A damned hick snob. He left the pool-hall to go to his room over the City Restaurant. Quickly he shaved himself, bathed, threw away all his farm clothes, and dressed, anxious to be out of town. He had to wait for the eleven o'clock night train, however. He thought of Marie Stearns, and intended to call her on the phone. She'd see him off on the train. Still he condemned her for being a part of Merrivale, but again he thought tenderly of her.

As suddenly as his fury had come upon him it departed. What did it matter? His life wouldn't be led in little towns. He must be in cities, with a vibration about. Mobs of people passing, playhouses, a well stocked library, dance halls, cabarets, restaurants, all made him want a city quality.

"Grant," Sylvester Graham said, coming up to him. "I have been looking for you. I didn't recognize you a while back. You must be two inches taller and twenty pounds heavier than you were this summer, and I couldn't see beneath the ambush you'd grown. Helen was giving me hell as I came along the street. I thought you'd left town long ago, so when something about you looked familiar I was puzzled. Jesus, you looked as though you thought I'd meant to cut you."

"Hell, Syl, it's all right," Grant said, relief so intense in him he could hardly speak. "I'm glad you came up though. I go to Minneapolis tonight, and there's no telling if we'll ever meet again. I have five hundred bucks saved up, so I can get to Europe even if I don't get a job on a ship, and I will. I head to New York a couple of days after I get back to Minneapolis."

"I wish you'd come to Vermillion," Sylvester said.

"I want big cities; I want to see places, Syl. Let's go and see Marie Stearns. I don't care if I miss the night train if she is home."

"She was talking about you last night, Grant. She's darling. I used to call on Martha and didn't know Marie had grown up. She's back from the city looking like a million. I got to know her pretty well just after you saw her last," Sylvester talked. Grant knew he wanted to say something.

"I'll be darned glad to see her. She and I liked each other pretty well," Grant said.

"I know, Grant. She told me. She was scared and said you and I were the only people in town she'd let know. I had her see a doctor, and it was all right. She didn't know but that you'd gone away from town long ago."

"Oh the devil, I should have written her. I am a damn fool," Grant said.

"Oh it was all right. She knew there wasn't anything you could do. I wish you'd come to the university, Grant. I know you're independent-minded, but you're too young to head to Europe alone, yet."

"It's no use, Syl. If I went to college I'd quit on an impulse. You stick to your law course because it represents something to you, but college doesn't represent anything to me."

"You make me not like to look in the face of the future I seem to be in for. I'm not as restless as you are though."

"Oh stick at law, Syl. You'll get as much satisfaction out of living your way as I do mine; more, probably; but I can't plan and be cautious. That's why Marie and I understand each other. Maybe we'll get something we want someday. I'm glad you've found out she's somebody. It'll be a sad parting tonight, but I'll be damned happy in my misery that I have both you and Marie saying goodbye to me at the train. The end of nothing has come, but I feel as if everything were going to begin new and strange in my life. I can't go back to things. Except for mother I wouldn't even go to Minneapolis to say goodbye to the family. It isn't any place I intend to go, it's just cutting loose. I have to do it."

"Jesus, Grant, I wish I had something to say to you which was wisdom; to Marie too. I didn't think so, but you're both apt to get yourself into jams, and I'd hate it."

"Syl, don't you worry. Marie and I will get into jams and out of them. If you think Marie and I did what we did together, just carried away, you're wrong. We had a long time ago not believed that wrong. By god, now that you say things, I'm going to put the idea in Marie's head tonight, that she's to begin a campaign on her family to send her to New York and Europe, too. Marie's not meant for hickville. I love that child more for not letting me know she was scared afterwards, but I knew Marie wouldn't squeal."

(See Bibliographical Note, page 360.)

In 1917, the year that the United States declared war on Germany, the McAlmon family moved to California, and Robert, now twenty-one, transferred to the University of Southern California. In those days USC was raw and Methodist; one large wooden building held the whole institution. When he revisited the campus a few years later, McAlmon discovered "quantities of stone buildings. I wondered if the old sociologic professor and the instructors in so-called philosophy and the psychology of religions were still about. I had nearly been expelled from the school for writing and reading a paper in the latter class. The paper noted that of fifty great writers of the last half-century all had been completely or partially agnostic. A girl left the class room as I read; the professor was pale and wiped sweat from his brow; and a fraternity brother attempted to have me expelled from the University as a heretic." [1] *But despite this rather romantic view of himself, McAlmon's undergraduate activities were ortho-dox enough: he belonged to a literary society whose members read crepuscular poems to one another, and he danced with coeds in roadhouses late at night. He didn't study much—his teachers seemed to him pedants and poseurs and frightened ex-preachers.*

Like so many of his contemporaries, McAlmon left college to join the armed forces, but he never saw overseas service. Hoping to be sent to Europe, he enlisted in the infant air corps, and wound up instead at Rockwell Field, San Diego, working on a camp newspaper. Demobilized early in 1919, he spent a restless year back at USC: he edited an unsuccessful aviation magazine called The Ace, *worked as a manual laborer side by side with Negroes and Mexicans (he found them congenial), and picked up some money as a movie extra. All during these months he was trying his hand at fiction and poetry. In a kind of credo printed a year or so later, he declared that "One does not become an artist by going into the arts. One has some perception, some interpretation, some essential record that one must leave."* [2]

The "essential record" of this first postwar year can be read in "Three Generations of the Same." The society which McAlmon had observed in Southern California—a society which had neither roots nor direction—is appropriately mirrored in the story's plotless meandering.

Three Generations of the Same

Carl Thomas went up the walk to the pillared entrance of the large white house, and rang the bell. An elderly maid, looking austere, said she would announce him, and returned later to say that Mrs. Bougher would be down shortly. Carl wondered whether he'd get this tutoring job, and hoped if so that the youngster was not dull, or priggish. The patronizing manner of the maid disturbed him; that seemed a bad omen. However, when Mrs. Bougher came into the room he had an agreeable sensation. Her slender figure was neatly clad in a mouse brown tailored suit, and a beaverskin hat nestled over her dark, warm face, which in repose looked dissatisfied. When speaking, an alertness came upon her, and her brown eyes were keen. She spoke in a business-like manner.

"My boy won't go either to a public or a private school for any period of time, and as seventeen is a difficult age I thought I'd try a tutor, if I can find one that's a good companion for him, and can manage to make him work a little," she explained.

After discussion Mrs. Bougher said she'd send for Billy. "As far as I'm concerned you can have the position, but perhaps you'd better meet Billy so he and you can judge how you'll like each other." When the youth appeared, Carl saw a slender boy, dressed with adolescent elegance. His manner was direct. A look which was on his face as he came into the room disappeared as he talked, and he adopted a good-fellow manner.

"It'll be up to us to tackle Latin, mathematics, and the rest of the rigmarole," Carl said, in the background of his mind rather doubting the ability of both Billy and himself to concentrate on these subjects during Spring months. He questioned whether he, but five years older than Billy, and impatient with his college life, was to bring balance to Billy.

"Oh, you and I'll get on all right," Billy remarked, apparently sure that a tacit consent had passed between him and Carl regarding his mother's idea of tutoring him; a consent to accept her wish, but not to take the lessons too seriously.

The next afternoon when Carl arrived Billy received him in his den as a friend paying an afternoon call rather than as an instructor bent on duty. "Have a cigarette," he invited. "Beastly dull morning I've had. That's what's bad about not being at school, because there're no fellows around, and nothing much to take up the time."

"What happened at the schools you've been that you couldn't stand them?"

"Oh hell, I've always broken rules. They don't want to give a fellow fifteen minutes to himself, and I'd just walk out on them and go for a walk. Then when anything would be said to me I'd answer back. Usually I couldn't stand most of the fellows at school either; none of them game enough, and always afraid of breaking rules."

"Schools are pretty bad, but you'll regret it later on if you don't get a few things they offer in their curriculum. Have you any idea what you're going in for later on?"

"Not a blasted idea. Dad says I can take up anything I want so long as I take up something, or if I go into business with him. He suggested engineering, but that takes too long, and I don't want to spend much more time in school. I'd go into business with dad now, but he and I don't get on well all the time. He goes in for wildcat investments too—oil, you know. Used to be in the oil well business in Oklahoma, but now that those fields are drying up he's doing Texas. Dad's made three fortunes in ten years, and lost two, but he generally comes back; always has so far anyway. Hell though, I can't seem to get interested in business when I think ahead through a lifetime of it."

"Well, yes," Carl said, and having no suggestions, added, "perhaps we'd better start some algebra now."

"Just a minute though. I want to read you this letter from Green, the only guy I could stand at the last school. He was a good cartoonist too. I've thought maybe I'd try that myself; it's more fun than business. Listen, and you'll see how anyone feels at those damned schools: 'Billy, I guess you're the only friend I got, and the family are the same as usual, give me the devil.

You know that queer fellow, Jenkins—well, he tried to kill himself in the bathroom the other day and he's in the hospital now. I sure am going to run away from school and go somewhere. I wish you'd go somewhere with me. Maybe Mexico, or maybe we could get a job on a ship and try that for a year or so. Your old pal and friend for life, Green' . . . Ain't that the devil, a guy trying to kill himself because of that school. I'm sure glad I had guts enough not to stand it. Dad says all the stuff they cram into you doesn't help much after you're through. He says he wouldn't give ten cents for all the good college ever did him."

"Yes—but if you want to do something more than make money; if you'd like knowing people? . . . You might feel out of things some time if you haven't certain kinds of information," Carl suggested, and finally got Billy to attempt a little mathematics. Later, on taking up the history book he became more interested, as that permitted him to discuss life, and he had an anecdote or tale to relate for every historical one Carl told him. Departing that afternoon, however, Carl reflected that a good share of every day's two-hour period would be spent in attempting to lighten the dark emotional and mental states of the seventeen-year-old William, since his interest in studies could not be captured when morbidity was eating out his insides.

One day Mrs. Bougher came in to sit for a few minutes while lessons were going on, but she retired shortly, apparently satisfied. As Carl was leaving that day she stopped him, however, and said, "Billy's reading too much Russian literature, I think. You are not giving him those books to read, are you? They'd be bad for him with his temperament."

Carl laughed. "No, I haven't given him any books, but he's asked me about things to read. Possibly I've suggested Russian things, but he appears to like Service's Barroom Ballads best of anything yet."

"Of course it might be well for him to have all the pessimism in the world to look at, and then have done with it," Mrs. Bougher said, tiredly, and offered to take Carl wherever he was going, as she was driving downtown to shop. "I won't talk about Billy; I can't solve him, and if I could what's the use? He won't be coerced. We try giving him everything, but he gets so despondent. Possibly he ought to be made to make a living for himself.

We haven't always had money, and there may be 'do' in the blood that makes luxury hard on him." Speaking, Mrs. Bougher appeared for the moment interested, and vital, but after a moment she relapsed, and a look of boredom settled on her face, as she leaned back in the car and looked indifferently at what they were passing on the street.

The next day when Carl arrived Billy was taking a shower bath. He appeared soon, rubbing himself with a turkish towel, and glancing at himself in the long mirror. Not wishing to have it too evident that he was surveying his frame, he did not inflate his chest, or draw in his stomach as positively as Carl was sure he'd do were he alone. Then he sought in the wardrobe for a highly colored lounging robe and settled himself into an easy chair. "Let's go easy on the lessons today. It's too hot. In a half an hour I can get hold of the car and we'll take a ride in the canyons," he requested.

There was a tap on the door, so that Billy sprang up. "I'll bet that's grandma. I told her to come up and meet you today. She arrived last night from Oklahoma, and is curious about who is tutoring me." Calling that he would be only a minute, Billy completed dressing, and admitted Mrs. Tartran. As soon as she was introduced to Carl she spoke.

"Parley vouse française?"

Seeing that she was not understood, she said, "You speak French, don't you? Do talk it with me sometimes. I'm taking it up. One's got to keep one's mind occupied some way or the other."

Mrs. Tartran was wiry bodied, sharp faced with eyes that peered in keen curiosity everywhere, and always, when she was awake. Carl judged she must be past sixty, but she could have passed for forty easily. Later he discovered that she was never at rest. There was for her always a woman's club lecture, the theatre, a call, a shopping trip, a motor run, a tea, a political meeting, the chaperonage of a dance, or a moment's stopover conversation to occupy her time. She dressed smartly, wore broad-rimmed hats with brisk feathers stuck at sharp angles in them, and usually she tipped her hat a bit over her left eye.

"We ought to let the lessons go today," she commented after a moment. "I won't keep Billy from his work—not me—but this is my first day.—You know," she said a little later, "I'll have to take an interest in Billy's education. My daughter's too languid; too used to riches. Now me—I haven't always had money. Utter nonsense, that, utter nonsense, being a leisurely person simply because you have enough money to be lazy. Nonsense, tosh. She ought to have something to interest her mind—if she has a mind, which I doubt often even if she is my own daughter. Sh! . . . now . . . Sh! really I shouldn't be talking like this in front of you and Billy," she chattered briskly, cocking her head about jerkily, observing things in the room.

Off the three went in the automobile. When, on the outskirts of town, Billy sped the car up to sixty miles an hour not a word of discretion did Mrs. Tartran utter. If she was aware that the speed limit was being exceeded the knowledge put no dismay into her countenance. She leaned back for moments, but the passing of a bit of scenery made her sit erectly watching again.

"Wonderful country around here! Wonderful air this!" she sniffed, noting the foliage along the roadside. "I like the breeze going past me; makes me feel vital and resistant. Billy, we aren't going very fast, are we?"

Billy needed no encouragement to get all of the speed out of the car of which it was capable, and boasted back to her that he had driven it eighty miles an hour.

"Tosh that is, Billy. So heavy a car as this isn't capable of speed such as that. But anyway, you oughtn't to attempt it I'm sure, and if your father knew I permitted it when I was driving with you he'd be provoked." Her lukewarm admonition, however, did not prevent Billy's stepping on the accelerator and turning on the gas the first long stretch of country road they reached. Half a mile ahead was a smaller car going at a good speed. At once Billy began to sound the klaxon horn continuously, to warn the car to make way for him. The speedometer ran up to sixty-five, seventy, seventy-five. "Eighty miles an hour, granny," Billy shouted back exultantly. "Didn't I tell you? Oh, damn that fellow, why doesn't he get out of the way. He's not going to give us roadspace to pass him. The damned hog."

"We might have a collision, you know," Mrs. Tartran commented enthusiastically, but poised to collect herself. Billy sounded the klaxon frantically. The car ahead was gathering speed, its driver evidently intent on not being passed. However, at a little wider piece of roadway Billy drove his car near the embankment, and riding on two side wheels, shot past the other car, shouting as he went by, "You damned louse. What do you want to do, cause an accident?"

"Well I never," asserted Mrs. Tartran. "Does that man think he owns this road? Now out in Oklahoma I'd well see that he got taken in for that. . . . But you'd better slow down, Billy, we really are risking an accident you know." Mrs. Tartran looked eminently satisfied, as though in some way justice had been brought about and that, the other car being now far behind, she was vindicated. Billy, turning into a road going to the city, went at a pace not exceeding thirty miles an hour now. The exhilaration of speed by, Mrs. Tartran's mind sought other subjects to interest it. Suddenly out of the open air and clear sky she shot a question and answered it herself in the one direct shot of comment.

"Do you believe in the bible? . . . I don't. I can tell you I don't and nobody needs say to me that it's my duty to pretend I do. I was talking to a minister the other day—big church he's the head of too—and he told me that though the bible may be largely misinterpreted at the present time, it can be interpreted so that I would not disagree with its preachments. Huh! That's it, it's capable of too blamed many interpretations, so say I, and who listens can hear me."

Even while she was reclining in the seat of the car Mrs. Tartran's thin, fibrous body gave the impression of restlessness, her eyes bright with keen and curious abstraction. Walking, she continually made one think of a nervous bird, on the lookout for something to dart at and peck—particularly the bird known as the roadrunner, which has a slender turkey-long tail that bobs up and down, as does its head, while it runs, skips, and flutters along the roadside.

Billy's slight long body, which had been intense while he was speeding, relaxed now, but a shine in his brown eyes remained. "That's the way to ride, isn't it, granny? I can't stand riding slow when I'm out for fun."

Mrs. Tartran, however, was intent on other ideas and had her say. "Shucks, I don't believe in anything—not a thing—not me. Theosophy?—some of Rose's friends play around with that, but bosh! All bosh! I go to meetings, as I go to political meetings, or listen to the radicals talk about social reorganization just to keep my time and mind occupied, but don't you think I take any stock in that tosh. You won't find me worrying about religion, or the way people suffer, or the mistakes the administration is making—and it's making them, you can know. It's human, and silly in consequence. There's too much fuss about what should be, and too little doing, and just being," she rippled on.

"I've just been reading a book that says things like that, granny," Billy commented, "but he makes most of his characters shoot themselves. It made me glum as the devil when I was reading it, but riding like this makes me forget that sort of feeling."

"You must not read those morbid Russian books, Billy. What was the name of it? Give it me when we get home, and I'll see what I think of it. It can't affect me, I assure you."

From that day it was difficult to indulge in lessons, and Carl was not more anxious than Billy to bother. Mrs. Bougher was seldom at home to know whether the two were in Billy's den studying or not, and if she was, either she or Mrs. Tartran were ready to say that the day was too nice to expect anybody to study. As Mr. Bougher was away in Texas on oil business, Billy had the family car to himself a great deal. One day out of three Billy might be feeling calm, and ready to let things be casual; the other days he felt "completely fed up about it all" or recklessly desirous of adventure for the afternoon. Soon he began to introduce other people into his automobile drives, as he'd lately met some moving picture people.

"You know this Bob Goff that I met—he's a prince of a fellow," Billy explained to Carl one afternoon. "I want you two to meet. He has a wonderful den, and a collection of all sorts of things."

Carl met Bob Goff, who was ornately groomed, with brilliantined hair smoothed carefully upon a head tending to fleshiness in the back. He worked his smile extensively to show even and tiny cut white teeth. He was smooth with the suavity begot of tailoring establishments, and barber-shop treatments.

"Bob, show Carl that skull of a German you got when you were at the battlefront," Billy requested, wanting to make his friend appear impressive.

Goff took down a skull nonchalantly, saying, "There—not a bad one. Of course I got more than one Hun, but I couldn't take a trunkload full of skulls back with me, could I? But I've forgotten all that now—don't even know where my medals are."

Carl didn't answer him, to ask what medals he had, or to comment on the possession of the skull. A moment after, when Goff, standing near him, placed a hand upon his shoulder, saying, "This boy Billy of ours is quite a lad, isn't he? I'm going to see that he gets a big job in the movies and then he won't be wondering what to do with himself so often," Carl felt uncomfortable, and moved away, realizing, however, the attraction in Goff's show of sympathy, and companionable way of using his hands.

The three left Goff's studio soon, to go and pick up Dorothy Madden, of whom Billy had spoken. When they arrived at her bungalow she came out at the sound of the horn.

"I've just been making a cake; I do like to cook," she confided at once, throwing off an apron. She was a plump person of perhaps nineteen, with schoolgirlish manners, mildly coquettish but still simple. Her pretty face, punctuated with vamping brown eyes and puckering lips, was of a likeable flapper variety. She climbed into the car, in the front seat between Billy and Carl, saying that she liked the front row, and that Bob could have the luxury of the broad back seat to himself. Her plump white arms were bare; she placed one of them on the seat back of Billy as he was driving because sitting space was congested.

"Oh Billy, the thought of you saved me from being too wild last night. Bob came around with that Swede movie director and a girl, and we all went for an auto ride. Then the Swede suggested that just as a lark we go around to the church and get married. I was almost on the point of it—just silly, you know, Billy, and it was such a wonderful night and made me feel sentimental—but just at the door of the church I thought about you and what you'd think, and wouldn't go on. So nobody got married."

"But Dolly, you and I'll marry later on," Bob broke in, "and let Billy be our best man."

"I don't know about that. I think I'll wait for Billy, and you can be his best man," Dorothy chortled, patting Billy's shoulder. She had been observing Carl out of the side of her eye, a trifle reserved at first, but gradually her manner lost its restraint with him, when he suggested that she come to a university dance with him some night.

"Oh, that would be just too adorable. I'm just crazy about dancing, you know. I'll bet you're great at dancing too," she informed him with confiding intimacy, leaning towards him as she talked. He placed his arm discreetly back of the seat, and gradually let it slip down to rest across her shoulder. As she did not object, he let his hand cuddle over her shoulder.

"We'll be shocking Billy," she whispered, "and of course I don't really fuss, you know, but it's kind of nice to cuddle, isn't it? But I can't stand the way Bob acts if he gets started, so I'm always awfully careful when he's around. He's pretty fast, and I'm not that kind of a girl. I just like fun."

Billy looked with patronizing tolerance at Carl and Dorothy, seeming to say by his half smile that he understood all, but would seem not to see anything. However, he finally had to speak. "I didn't think you'd let somebody else cut me out so soon, Dorothy, but I don't mind as long as it's my teacher."

"Why Billy Bougher; I don't know what you mean. You know yourself how crowded it is with three in this front seat. But anyway, Billy, you just know how fond I am of you. Because you never get fresh, and I don't think you'll ever get so."

Seven days later when Carl arrived to tutor Billy, the boy was in a black funk. "Either Bob Goff is a damn fine fellow, or he's a rotten animal," Billy commented.

"What's happened, Billy?" Carl asked.

"Oh, I ain't saying anything. I don't squeal, but I just repeat either he's a damn fine person, or as rotten as they make them, and I know what I'm guessing too."

With inquiry Carl discovered that Billy had been working mornings for the last five days at a moving picture studio. He had said nothing about it because he wanted to be sure he'd get on. For three hours he would flash films on the screen for the directors to judge what cuts were necessary. However, upon being late three mornings in succession, he had been spoken to about tardiness, and on the fourth morning decided to quit with a two days' notice. What upset him, however, were things he saw around the studio, and the way Bob Goff talked about Dorothy. More particularly something had happened the night before, when he'd been out till four o'clock in the morning at a country club, drinking and dancing. He declared that it wasn't because he had been got to sign his name to the bill, which came to over one hundred dollars. "Dad is a good sport about things like that, and always says that a fellow who has money—or whose father has—is sure to get stuck," he commented. What disturbed him was the way he had been treated during the evening; indifferently for a long time, affectionately at moments when a bottle of champagne was wanted, patronizingly by Bob Goff's actress friends, and again too affectionately by Bob as they were going home. "He means too much or nothing but bleeding me, I'm thinking," Billy reflected.

The next day Billy was gloomier than ever. Life was too appalling for him to contemplate it. Nothing new had happened, but the café bill bothered him, and the family had just received word that Mr. Bougher would be back soon, and that also Billy's married sister was to arrive with her husband.

"That means hell, and scenes, because dad's lost a lot of money, and he'll be cross, and give us all hell most of the time," he mourned. He opened the drawer of his chiffonier, and taking out a pistol, balanced it in his hand with dark significance.

"There's an answer to everything I say, and I'll be knowing what my answer is pretty soon, or . . . ," he stated forebodingly.

Carl laughed forcedly. "Hell, Billy, buck up. What does it all matter—one damn thing or the other, and you know you're as good for seeing things through as anybody else. Take the hell your dad gives you, and let it slip off your back as soon as you get out of his hearing."

"But it's the wondering what to do with myself that gets me. I think of going away sometimes to Mexico, or just to be a hobo; and when dad says he doesn't care what I do so long as I do something, he makes me choose."

"He's not insisting too hard at the moment, is he? and if he is, see that through. See anything that happens through, and you'll find you come out."

With the arrival of Billy's father however, every day found Billy tormentedly unhappy, or defiantly reckless, except that one day he felt, for that day only, that his father was a sympathetic person because he'd been so good-natured at a dinner party Mrs.

Bougher had given the night before. "He even said he'd get me a new roadster to run about in," he said to confirm his father's goodness.

Billy's brother-in-law seemed to have no other occupation than smoking cigarettes, visiting various hotel lobbies to meet chorus girls, and dancing at night clubs. His vocabulary consisted of about two hundred words, apparently, but he was used to spending money in quantities. To understand that boredom is not mental, one need only watch him register ennui. His conversation was made up of relating how late he'd been up every night for the last five, how much he'd spent, drunk, danced, and what he thought the old man would think of it all.

Coming into the house one afternoon Carl sensed that something unusual had occurred. The maid's manner was consciously quiet with suppressed knowledge of privacies. When Carl came upon Billy, he found him silent, not brooding or sullen as usual, but quietly wondering. Before long he volunteered an explanation.

"Well, dad's lost most of his fortune again; this is the third time, and maybe the third time's out. I don't suppose it matters though. As granny said, we've not been too damned happy with all the money."

"Oil plunging means chances," Carl suggested. "It will probably come out all right for you. You might have to do some of the things you wanted to do for adventure."

They went down the stairs together. At the bottom of the stairs they halted, hearing an irritated voice speaking through the open door of the dining room. Carl saw Mr. Bougher standing there, listening to his wife. He was an erect, hard-muscled man, with a thin body, and a brown hardened skin. His long convex featured face, with cold grey eyes and look of nervous intensity, was that of a promoter's, indicative of a plunger temperament. Mrs. Bougher was speaking. She was not languid now, but flushed, and angry.

"You damn fool, Tom, you utter damn fool, to be letting us in for this. Haven't two times before taught you anything? Damnit, I say, now you listen to me, out of the three million dollars you said you had two months ago couldn't you have put aside enough not to bring this down upon us? It's all right for you—your game to play—you get your amusement in that way, but all I want to say is that you hustle around and retrieve some money. I have stood back of you always, and I will now. Sell the cars. Sell my jewels, if you must, though I'd better do so myself and salt down the money to keep you from losing it. Mortgage the house or sell it—but come back. I'm not going to have to explain poverty. Next time any money gets into this family's hands I'll see to it that some of it remains there, say what you will."

Mrs. Tartran came into view from behind the curtain of the next room. "Nonsense, Rose, nonsense, don't be hysterical. Explain! explain poverty to whom, I ask you? Who are these people you are to explain to? I can snap my finger in the face of the best of them. I could snap my fingers if I had on rags, if I had on nothing—even if I am a bit of a bonebag at my age. Tom takes chances; so do we all. What's all this fuss about—what is it? Tom, go to your room, not a word. You go to your room too, Rose. You've been arguing this same argument for ten minutes and getting nowhere, and you had it last night too. Spilt milk! and a good thing it is too! We'll all have something to think about now; some way to express ourselves, and we're not bowing our heads low to anybody or anything."

With these explosive comments Mrs. Tartran gave Mr. Bougher a push on his shoulder and headed him towards the door, to which he went grumbling, but not in bad nature. His string-muscled face worked in an effort to control irritation and disgust, but amusement showed through too. "It's the damned scolding that gets me; as though I didn't always come back. I've made good three times before; can't any of you have a little trust in me? It's not going to be up to anybody to fight this problem but myself. I'm the head of the family yet, and take the responsibilities," he explained, before going up the stairs. Then Mrs. Tartran pounced out into the hall and started to her room, when she saw Billy and Carl standing by the stairway.

"That's life, isn't it though? That's life," she jerked forth. "You might as well accept it too, is what I say. Now if I have to take in washings at my age to eat, well, what of it—I'm good for it. I haven't always had money by a long shot. It'd do that daughter of mine good to have to do ironing for my washings too."

Whereupon she went up the stairs decisively. A minute later she leaned over the bannister of the second floor, and called down, "Billy, phone out to the garage and tell the chauffeur to be at the house in ten minutes. I'm going downtown to dinner; can't stand this atmosphere of wrangling.—We haven't sold the cars yet, might as well use them," she finished and snapped her head back to go into her room and dress for going out.

Carl saw Billy only one time more, and soon after departed himself for Chicago. Some months later, curious as to Billy and Mrs. Tartran, he wrote Billy a letter, and received in reply:

"Well old man, I received your letter yesterday and was even more glad than surprised to get it. Yes, Carl, our paths seem to have parted for a while, maybe for good and maybe not, who knows? But I, for one, hope that it is not for long.

"You say you are interested in my state of mind, etc. Well, Carl, as you most likely know, one expresses one's present state of mind when writing a letter. But I will do my best to tell you of my last six months on this planet called earth.

"To begin with, dad got back a good deal of money, and I went east to school. Dad told me to go to New York and look until I found a school that I liked, and then settle down and stay there. I went east as per schedule but did not settle down as per schedule, but that comes later. My brother-in-law went east to look after me, as it were. Well, we stayed in New York taking in the sights. After a week I picked out the only school that we had visited. I arrived at the school on Monday afternoon, stayed until Tuesday A.M., and then ran away to N.Y. I can give no other reason for my running away than that I was not happy. We stayed in N.Y. five weeks after that, drunk most of the time. Took in all the cabarets and spent four thousand dollars. I also got a dose of clap that I just got over last month. The old man was pretty mad but I told him that boys would be boys and he was good about it. I can not begin to explain any of the different moods that I was in, but I was 'I don't give a damn,' worried, regretful, glad, happy, in the dumps, and all of it. I hope that you will understand.

"Then after I got home I fell desperately in love and am still struggling under the illusion. But as they all think, I think that I have the real thing this time.

"Then came the good era. I got a car of my own, and every-thing that goes with it. Then like a bolt out of the clear sky dad went broke. I lost my car and everything that goes with it. I had a natural gloomy mood for a while. But it was soon over and I settled down to make the best of things.

"But again in the last two weeks things have turned, or at least are turning now. Dad has made good again and all is looking fine again. How will it all turn out? Now that is enough about me. How about yourself? What are you doing? Please write me, Carl, as you are the only real friend that I have. From your old pal and pupil, Billy.

"P.S. we have had several minor and one fairly big earth-quakes lately but nothing serious happened. Nothing ever hap-pens in this old burg.

"P.S. Again: Granny says she wishes you were here so she could talk French with you. She says she can't be bothered any longer knowing whether dad's up or down financially."

Carl, at the time looking impatiently at his own present rather than at any past or future, shoved Billy's letter into his pocket, commenting to a person with him that most anxiety and personal unhappiness are trumped-up emotions, with no reality outside oneself.

(See Bibliographical Note, page 360.)

Abruptly, in the first months of 1920, McAlmon left USC (he was on probation anyway) and his job in a Federal court (some would have considered it good enough to hang on to), and caught a train east. He was bored with what he had seen of Los Angeles literary life—he thought it effete and affected—and he could find no intellectual community at all. But in Chicago, the word was, things were stirring—and especially on Cass Street where Harriet Monroe held forth. The year before, Miss Monroe had published a few of McAlmon's poems in Poetry; *since then he had been in correspondence with Emanuel Carnevali, a young poet who was currently—and momentarily—her associate editor. In the reckless Carnevali McAlmon could see some of that full-blooded acceptance of the world which he admired, but recogni-*

tion of a kindred spirit was not enough to keep him in Chicago once he realized that it housed only a sideshow, that the main attraction was in New York. Things were stirring in Chicago, but in Greenwich Village, he heard, the lid was clear off and the kettle boiling over.

POST-ADOLESCENCE
1920-1921

Comments on the persons mentioned in Part II will be found in the Biographical Repertory, beginning on page 367.

1. Greenwich Village

In 1920 Greenwich Village was the capital of the avant-garde in America. When McAlmon got there, he quickly singled out William Carlos Williams—or Williams singled him out—at a party given by Lola Ridge, an artist-poet whom he knew through his Chicago acquaintances. The gentle doctor was the first of his literary associates and remained all his life the most faithful, unselfish, and forgiving of his friends. With Williams holding the door, McAlmon entered the literary history of the twenties.

At the time of his literary debut, McAlmon as seen by Williams was "a coldly intense young man, with hard blue eyes, who . . . found a living posing in the nude for mixed classes at the Cooper Union. He had an ideal youth's figure—such a build as might have served for the original of Donatello's youthful Medici in armor in the niche of the Palazzo Vecchio. He got a dollar an hour, and was tough enough to take it for nine consecutive hours sometimes in various poses." [1] He was not tall, under six feet, and slightly built. His hair grew straight back from his forehead, his jaw was determined, his mouth straight and thin-lipped; he had a way of looking unblinkingly at the person he spoke to. When he chose to disagree, which was constantly and with anyone, McAlmon did so to the hilt in language which was pungent, vigorous, and uncompromising. All conventional restraints, artistic and social, were abhorrent to him, and although he was not so cantankerous in his Greenwich Village days as he later became, he was frequently involved in quarrels.

For a time McAlmon "lived . . . on a scow in New York harbor to make a go of it," Williams tells us; later he had a room in a boarding house on Fifteenth Street. As much at home in the Village as in Madison or Wentworth or Volga, South Dakota, he

107

worked at getting acquainted with his neighbors, the literary celebrities whom he had always wanted to know; [2] *and their portraits appear in the novella he was writing at the time. In* Post-Adolescence *McAlmon describes Greenwich Village life as he was living it. His characters are identifiable. The exquisite "Brander Ogden" is Marsden Hartley, already well known as a painter; "Vere St. Vitus" is Edna St. Vincent Millay; "Jim Boyle" is of course Williams; and "Nellie" is his wife Flossie. "O'Brian" is Kenneth Burke, the critic and literary theorist; "Dora" is probably Lola Ridge; and "Martha Wullus" is certainly Marianne Moore. "Gusta Rolph" is no doubt Mina Loy, the beautiful poetess whom Pound found all brains and no heart; "Reginald Crackye" may be Alfred Kreymborg, the poet and editor of contemporary verse anthologies; McAlmon himself is "Peter."*

Post-Adolescence *is filled with the "preoccupation with life" that McAlmon required of all his writing. Reviewing it in Ford Madox Ford's* transatlantic review *(1924), Williams characterized the book as a* journal intime. *"On the surface [it] sets out to depict many sorts of people encountered among the city streets. But the final impression, and the fact, is that here is only one person, a young man hounded in his own body by the realities of love and sex, which just at the close of adolescence are seen introspectively possessing him. These appearances come to him in the persons of his friends."* [3]

The Studio

Morning! The alarm. Hell's bell. Get up? No—just five minutes more, just a tossover—wonder, could he pretend sick today, no, it'd be him who'd lose the money—well, a few minutes more. . . . What! eight-thirty, Christ! He jumped out of bed. Have to get up when the alarm rang after this—getting a habit—have to quit smoking so many cigarettes—have to quit drinking so much coffee at night and eating at irregular hours—oh to hell with it all—he wouldn't have to quit anything; all oughts and musts and can'ts in existence anyway—who makes an ought that ought to be, who's so damn good at judging as all that if nature or some supposed God doesn't let us know in our impulses. Too many conventions in the world. . . . Morning's a heavy time. He needed to get outdoors. He washed in the cold running water. Nice tasting toothpaste, cold vital touch of water on face, over sticky sleepy eyes, fine on a leady head. Now for the cold outdoors. Too damned little ventilation in the room.

He went out and had hot milk and oatmeal with coffee; a delicious warm downflowing liquid that, coffee—everything made up of little warm or little cold sensations—or big hot, or cold ones. Huh! the exalted, the sublime—glad he was past the days of metaphysical yearnings in college, when he was worried about not being able to think beginning or end, or to discover decent purpose in nature. Bally college rot, that. It's enough to dig into the possibilities of oneself, and of today without a past or future. The time! . . . well, he didn't mind being late anyway.

There were no students yet at the studio when he arrived, but he undressed anyway, and took some exercise on the rings, chinning himself and trying to do a giant swing. That tired him. He wasn't feeling alert yet; takes a couple of hours after waking up to feel lively. He sat on the model stand. The looking glass faced him, reflecting his body. What was he posing for? None of the students would ever sketch or sculpture him well enough for it to matter. Nice lines he had after all, there around the belly particularly. It was nice being slender, but his belly might be getting a little too paunchy. He'd have to stand straighter, draw it up, take some exercises. Hated a paunchy belly. He ran his lips along his arms, his hands up and down his legs. Legs are graceful things; slender, deerlike, and how fine the skin is on the side of the foot, frogbelly fine with ethereal tiny pores and pearly white. That's the nicest skin on the body. He wondered if he could touch it with his mouth, and strained to do so, but was unsuccessful. He supposed a contortionist could. Wished there was a young girl in here with him, and undressed, but she'd have to be young and slender. He was tired of older women, too sophisticated, and not buoyant enough; wanted one with exuberance, not shy but capricious—what to hell anyway; why was his mind always dwelling on stuff like that, always looking forward to a climax, a change, a progression? Are these things? The mind grows in its ability to experience—experience what—not much that isn't tiresome—maybe his shortcoming not to have gone beyond that, but who has that's to be respected—persons dogmatizing their hopes into a faith—didn't matter though, whatever is or isn't one goes on somehow even if one is questioning and rebelling all the time.

Students began to come in. There was red-faced, shiny-eyed, overserious Green, with his dogged habit of plugging away every possible minute at his clay and doing the poorest sculpturing of them all. Not a flicker of light in his derived talk about "discipline of the will," "hard workers," and "big conceptions." Perhaps though his trained to acceptance attitudes were no worse than trained to rebellion ones. Both attitudes are full of mistakes, and boring. What does anyone know, and why should anyone pretend to know beyond the point where simple confronting facts assert their being? He was tired of people who try proving things.

Louie slouched in and fumbled about the room with his long arms dangling from his slumping shoulders that sank down towards his fat stomach. He said he'd make a new start on his figure. Who in the devil ever made him think he wanted to be a sculptor? His lazy good nature and weak amiability was amusing though. Pozbick there too, painstakingly imitating the Jewish painter he most admired. What is sculpturing? What is an art? Lovely lines, reeds whistling form melody in the wind, swaying; a field of lilies breezebending, pistiline flowers gesturing to the moon or to the sun; many longstalked gracile bodies in a marsh. (Damn those puttering students. He was tired holding his ankle on one knee, posing for them to putter and dabble away, and the best of them mattered how much?) Is sculpturing important then? If so maybe they mattered. The human body, wonderful alive, but in clay as they handled it—what could he think—why not sculpture waterfalls, the conception? Falling, surge-rushing, breath-taking madness of water, burbling, boiling, seething, cold granite swirling of green or blue or purple ocean water, and its wills on dark and highly colored days. What's the will of water, and what's its form?

He liked the idea of what he could conceive as sculptured better than anything any one of them could sculpture, or than what he could dabble with himself. Singing concepts. Polished stone, tinted, enameled pale blue, faint pink, shiny as a sun-basking snake's belly, polished slender stone, or gleaming pigeon-blood stone, fireglowing, passionately kissable stone, warm red, lyric bright, with a song going upwards fluidly, tinctured with brilliant tragic ecstasy. Say, the diamond on platinum hoofs of an ivory antelope in the sunlight glistening have clangored on tuned steel and a note soars high into the pitch of hypnotic silence. Sculpture that. Not the color; not the tone; the motion, color ringing, motion singing in space; domination of relationship inexplicably lovely. Body, of antelopes, of waterfalls, of people?— No, not body, creation! The impulse to break away, to annihilate, to create, to be free. The contour in mass, the potential germ to emerge matured, the grace out of protoplasm groping gelatin-ously.

He wished he sculptured, in stone, cold, freezing with the inhibition of conceptions. Life is a prison of yearnings, joy, and anguish that physical motion or intellectual will cannot attain expression of. He wanted lyric bronze that lilted upward jubilantly, meaning nothing and everything. What do men's bodies, or women's bodies, say of all the blood wishes, the soul craves, the mind thinks or strives to think? How are bodies sculptured in dead stone, white duplicates of pulp flesh, and where is the blush of madness, of shyness, the sensitive eyetwitching or nervous muscle-on-legs jerking from impatience to be off accomplishing some desire, and when accomplished what is accomplished? Ach! These people here sculpturing "his" body. Oh hell. What did they know of what he was thinking and feeling? But if people think they want to then they do want to, but why? Why not abstract, stone music, frozen, imperishable, of iced movement, a floe of rigid inarticulate sound and line of beauty riding the wavecrests of relativity:—a golden bird with agate eyes whistling a dirge; a long-legged bird with silver white throat, vermilion blood life-forceful beneath the glittering white feathers; agate eyes toward the sun, singing, graceful voice song-praying to the sun in color, so undulant, gracious, hard and cold, dentlessly flowing before and forever into infinite space. Mysticism submerged in conscious intellect; a pillar tip pointed signifying there is no end, diminishing gradually into the immeasurable and ascending therefore into the irrational, and sole abiding beauty.

Green spoke, interrupting Peter's rhapsodizing reveries that beneath his present-thinking mind he was doubting. "I don't like most of the pictures at the Granger exhibition. Too many cheap subjects."

"There isn't any such thing as a cheap subject. Things are. If the pictures are cheap the painters' minds made them so," Peter said, disgustedly, feeling antagonistic because his body was cramped with posing.

"I guess you're right," Green responded, "but . . ."

"No use talking to our model. He won't stand for anything not modern, Green," Louie joked.

"Balls on you," Peter exploded. "You don't know what I'll stand, and I won't try to tell you. Your mind and your clay is confused enough, I'd judge. One has a right to some selection though, even if you don't think so."

"Is that so?" said Louie, throwing a small piece of clay at Peter. "If you'd sit still a few minutes . . ."

"You would feel the need of smoking another cigarette. Don't kid the goldfish, old top. You're about as intent on your work as a streetcleaner. Tell me though, did you manage to make a date with that girl who's posing for you afternoons?"

"Not yet, but maybe I'll get to it. She acts willing enough, but how's one going to see her alone with this bunch of roughnecks hanging around all the time, I'm asking you? Green's the only one who works while she's posing."

"She wants too much attention. She talks almost as much as our present model," Poznick said curtly.

Peter felt anger at Poznick bilge up in him. Damned seventh street Jew, he thought. "Well, probably what both she and the present model say in talking will count as much as any work that's turned out of this classroom," he grunted, and after a pause when his irritation had subsided he chuckled and said in an aside to Louie, "Every once and a while my little trick of conversing to get extra rest is met with distrust and suspicion. Temperamentally I wasn't exactly meant for a model, I'd judge."

"Say boy, me neither. What do you do it for—going to school somewhere?"

"No, I'm through that. It's just less binding than a day in

and day out job at some office or on a newspaper. Some days I don't pose at all; and some days I don't eat too; but between not eating now and then and doing eight hours work a day I'll take the former."

The talk stopped. Peter wondered if he was being square trying to keep from posing. Suppose there was some one of the students who was wanting to work, and was a good workman. He'd have to be openminded, as long as he was pretending to pose. He didn't think much of any of them, but it takes a few thousand to find a good one; perhaps this class was of value. Oh to the dickens with them all. What's valuable? His own emotions were as valuable as anything in this room; he'd bet more on himself than on any one of them, and that was as far from being lost regarding any sense of value as he could get. Is it best to try and stay all openminded? One can go wild with the chaos of that attempt, and in trying to discover a basis. What is a basis, when one's own emotions and one's own mind do not respond? He'd have to stop thinking so much, but how, his mind would run on if only on futility, and bafflement. But still—things would come about as they would come about.

He couldn't solve anything at this moment but this moment.

In the afternoon Peter had an appointment to meet Jim Boyle. He sauntered about the streets to pass away time. Wondered how Jim would be today, harried as usual, and tired out, or maybe the clear spring weather had let him get more rested than usual as so many people wouldn't be ailing as had been the slushy days a week or so back. Funny mixture Jim was, Italian, Irish, Welsh, Yankee, and he thought there was a little Jewish blood in him too. No wonder he was up in the air most of the time, with a feminine will and intuition thrown in upon his impulses, if . . . well, yes, maybe. There was no doubt anyway that Jim's wife, Nellie, was the stronger of the two if it was only because being feminine and maternal made her narrower so that she wasn't so easy a victim to confusion.

Strolling about he encountered Brander Ogden who was as leisurely as he at the moment. "How glad I am to have a few words with you, Peter," Brander assured him. "I haven't been out of my rooms except to go to the bakery for almost a week. It just seemed as if I'd had enough of all kinds of social contact New York had to offer me, so I went into seclusion, but today I thought I'd venture out and look them over again."

"I'm meeting Jim Boyle in a little while, and would say for you to come along with me, but we're up to a great scheme for rearranging the universe that we want to talk over alone together," Peter responded.

"Such a new wardrobe as I've been looking over, if I ever get enough money that I feel I can put out," Brander said, for the moment preoccupied with his own needs. "My god, there are so many exquisite little sensations in life. The ties. The handkerchiefs. The perfumes. The last word. You must walk down Fifth Avenue with me some day soon while I look over the shop windows. Too delightful, some of them." As he walked he strolled along with deliberate eaglelike dignity, his great cold blue eyes staring about him. Peter felt amused at what someone had called his dowager gestures, and noted his high beaklike nose, and his face with its fierce grandmother's profile.

"Oh Brander, it's certainly damned good to see you again. I've wondered if something I'd said hadn't got back to you and upset you when I didn't see you around for a month or more. I've been pent up and disgusted with everything all winter, or I'd come around to look you up."

"Indeed not, I've heard nothing that upset me. New York in the winter just drives me into my hole to hibernate. Don't you fear, I understand you and your rantings. I've never had any doubt about you from the first. You'll land on your feet all right, and what you say . . . you understand me too. Great lads, you and Jim. Tell him we must see each other soon, now that I'm about again."

"He was asking about you last week."

"Is he the same old goat?" Brander chuckled. "He just never will know to handle the many different qualities and personalities within himself. My, I ceased long back ever asking what he thinks about anything, because that puts him in a panic, so he has to run home immediately to try and think out what he does think, and that means another siege of trying to calm him down for Nellie. There is so much wild imagination, audacity, and timidity mixed up in him indiscriminately that nobody can ever know where he is, least of all himself."

"I don't know about that. I think Nellie's pretty hep about how to handle him. He just gets ideas he's becoming too settled and that terrifies him now and then, but now too he's wanting too many 'final solutions' to things to actually break any tethers."

Brander and Peter separated after a few minutes and Peter turned for a moment to watch Brander proceeding down the street like a whole caravan to himself going in orderly procession, that surely had need of a crown and a train. Turning on his heel to go towards the clinic hospital at which he was to pick up Jim, a feeling of aversion to entering the charity ward came to him. Already the dusk was beginning to come upon the city so that it forced consciousness of the smoke in the air, and brought upon him a feeling of depression. There'd be all those screeching youngsters at the clinic, as though their bones were being pulled from them, and their dull, soggy-eyed mothers, Jewesses at the period in life of fruition and opulence of fecundity—ugh—the new generation. Why should life go on to present such diseased, dull, and poverty-stricken aspects? Why should life go on? Does anyone like it?

Jim met him at the entrance to the hospital, informing him that his work had finished sooner than he'd expected this afternoon. His brown oval face lighted up for the moment of greeting, so Peter judged that tiredness had not made him apathetic towards everything today as often.

"After being up almost every night for three weeks I began to get a rest the beginning of this week," Jim commented. "Maybe I'll get a chance to do some of the things I want to, rather than treating kids for bellyaches, or old ladies for colds, or men for clap. Let's go and have some tea, or something."

"I have some ideas in my head about getting writers and painters together. It's got to be done in this country; nobody else will help them if they don't help each other . . . but I don't know; a few minutes' talk with most of them and there's no agreement anyway, but we'll have to start something somehow."

"I don't get this modern art at all, but I can't find the terms with which to condemn it either. Tradition doesn't satisfy. We haven't any base at all."

"Rats, modern art, bunk. Which is modern and which isn't, and what's derived, and what's real? I don't know anything about such class terms. I know only individuals and what they do, and if it doesn't matter to the devil with it. We haven't a religion any more; we don't accept scholastic or esthetic standards, or the old ideas of morality any longer, so we must recognize individual qualities more."

"That's too little; I want something inclusive."

"Anything individual, and really so, is inclusive and simply one of many possible variations. Any other kind of individualism is a stunt, and that's about as old and cheap a trick as there is in time."

"Somebody said that if a fact is a fact why say anything more about it, since talk doesn't create new facts."

"Maybe it rediscovers them or emphasizes them in a new way though. Besides it isn't the facts that matter; it's what can we do in the midst of them that's worth doing. Dance, sing, paint, copulate, eat, sleep, and finally die, and if that isn't all there is to it—show me—I'm looking."

"That damned woman who's been sending me love letters and obscene photographs of herself has taken to coming out to the house in the country and leaving big packages of notes and photographs on my steps. Nellie says she'll call in the cops someday. She doesn't give a tinkers damn, except that it's a nuisance."

"Ah, don't let that old dame worry you. She likes to think of herself as a rampant adventuring conquering superwoman. Take her as a joke. You're too inclined to let little episodes like that frighten you. Have you answered any of her letters?"

"I wrote her two, letting her know I thought she was an old hag, and now she's threatening to blackmail me by showing them at the clinic hospital if I don't come and sleep with her."

Peter laughed. "Oh hell, she won't do that. It's only a bluff, and if she did show them what could they do? You don't depend on them. You just let your imagination run away with you when you thought you admired her for her reckless vagabondage a few months back. A look at her should have told you she was a complete nut."

"I don't know. It bothers me, and I don't know what I'll do this summer, whether I can get a month's vacation in or not. By Christ, I should never have been a family doctor, but it was some idea about duty I had when I was a kid. I'd like to chuck it and go to Europe for a year."

"Why don't you? You've money enough put aside, haven't you?"

"Yes, but there's the youngsters at school. They're too young to put in a boarding school yet, and then—I don't know—maybe I have freedom now, and always have had it, and don't know how to take it. It's in the mind anyway. I want to feel definitely free."

"God, Jim, am I ten years younger than you, or you ten years younger than I? Anyway I lost the idea of definite freedom at least a year back, in the way you mean it. I don't think one can insure it anyway. You just have to take a leap and if you slip and bang your ass in the mudpuddle, tra la, c'est la vie."

A cat scurried past them with a dog in pursuit. Suddenly the cat whirled, as though to say "to hell with running away," and stood baleful-eyed, hair-erectedly terrifying before the dog. He barked yappingly, but did not go too near the green eyes, alternately yellow with ire-flame. Suddenly a claw reached out and dug into his nose, so that he rushed off yelping with his tail definitely down in retreat. The cat, the cold fighter, sauntered away in dignified contemptuous victory.

"That's the answer," Peter commented. "Run like hell. Fight like hell when you have to. There's the cat with nine lives to protect and madame cat takes the protection of them upon herself and doesn't leave too much to nature. Maybe that's definite freedom."

Jimmy, having promised Nellie to be home for dinner, had to depart, without their having discussed plans that seemed to have become too impractical for Peter to suggest when he was confronted with Jim's temperament and situation. He walked away, wondering, as Jimmy went down into the tubes to ride home. Home, and is it a place for the spirit, or a place of bodily security? Well, a situation that, and what does one do with situations? Use them, or search continually for new situations that are doubtfully more valuable. What did he himself want, finally, knowingly? It was too damnable that every time he and Jimmy got together Jimmy's occupation made him go back home, or on a sick call, before they could have a decent conversation. But that's how things were.

The Dream

Peter was on the street walking leapingly, but beneath his zest, and the taste of flavorless chilly air in his mouth that his lungs drank in gulps, there was an undercurrent of storming rebellion. He flung his body into a more rapid pace, throbbing with unrest inside. "Good Christ," he swore to himself, "what's to be done with energy, with heat, with blood, with flesh?" It struck into his senses, as it had frequently before, that every impulse and thought struck and broke finally against barriers. Perhaps intelligence was the greatest barrier in life, making, when small, the narrow moralities that oppress life, and ravaging the emotions with a philosophical sense of the barrenness of life when comprehensive. Animals have their physical reactions freely, but discretion stops the human species. He was detesting himself and life for a tolerance that was being made to grow within him because his perception saw all people the victims of nature, their own blind subconscious yearnings making cowards, or knaves, or imbeciles of them. All any of them wanted was gratification and if they had no wisdom in their means of getting it, who could be blamed?

Going up the three flights of stairs to his skylight room, he noticed that a larger front room was empty, and the door into it was open. It occurred to him he might ask Mrs. McCarty to let him have that as it had a window and was bigger than his present room. He stepped inside to look it over but by the time he'd taken three steps he'd realized the floor had been freshly painted. A panic came over him, and he turned back quickly and went into his own room, hoping that Mrs. McCarty wouldn't know it'd been him who'd stepped on the floor she'd just painted, but he was the only lodger on that floor so she surely would guess it was him. Perhaps she'd be good-humored about it, but if she had a headache . . .

He was undressed when he heard her steps on the stairway, so he quickly jumped into bed after turning out the light. He was as quiet as possible, listening in a keyed-up half-amused dread to her as she plumped around outside. Waiting, he heard her talking to herself as she frequently did. Then her voice mumbled out in a louder tone, "Ah, the devil, some god damn fool has been walkin' on me new painted floor; the bloody fool, and me workin' so me back aches a paintin' it."

Peter stayed as still as possible, praying that she could not hear him breathe or know he had gotten home yet, and then she might think it was some lodger from the floor below. He hoped she wouldn't knock at his door as he'd have to answer or she might unlock with her key and look in on him. After a minute of muttering, however, she went on downstairs, and he felt a part relief as he might get out of the house before she embarrassed him with questions in the morning.

Within a few minutes after she'd gone downstairs, however, his mind was back tearing away at him with savagely brooding ideas. Why did he have expectancy, or make any kinds of demands on existence; why question all the time, analyzing, dissecting, destroying? But how could he stop his consciousness from running on; that inability in itself was a thing to rage at, that he could never know when it would buoy doubt, unbelief, and bile to its surface. Futility was all his intellectual processes could think, and how could he accept that?

Sleep finally began to pour its thick smoke upon his waking mind. He was going under like a drugged man, drowning apathetically; and apathy, it appeared, was coming to be the chief emotion in his life. But sleep, not a paleness, sleep, not a blackness, not a heaviness, not unconsciousness, not anything of quality, just sleep,—nonknowing existence for his mind, for his emotions; this sleep was upon him. He sunk, sunk, to temporary extinction.

For how long? Nonknowing time, unrelated to events.

Then the nothingness of unaware being was populated. He was in the midst of people moving and talking about him, but he could not see them, or hear what they said. Gradually a feeling of impending danger numbed him with a motionless fear. Someone led him into one room, then away again, through a throng of people hurrying by unceasingly. He should call out, or break away, but his will was paralyzed. A man near him was sharpening a butcher knife. The scenes shifted without sequence but always the menacing people were there. He saw a cow butchered and its glazed-eyed head dropped into a pit. Perhaps they would drop him there and he would go sliding down in the slime. Stale terror was all through him. How absurd. He could remember that he was no longer a child. He could protest, but he did not. They took him into a dark room and he knew they were muttering about him outside. An old man (like his father) was going to put him in the stove. Then he was cold with terror. A bloody horse— it was Nellie, his old saddle pony, who'd strangled herself to death by getting her foot caught in her halter rope—was sliding down upon him, having broken away from the tree in the middle of the sidewalk to which her corpse was tied. She slid on, towards him, and his arms were pinned to his side so that he could not move. She was upon him. With a jerk he rose into the air by the nervous reaction of his horror, and was falling, falling, falling. . . . He awoke. Fear was in him yet, and a druggish utter hopelessness that weighed upon his part dormant mind. He was recalling life of now gradually. He would go to sleep again. There was nothing to think of he wanted to face with thinking. Life or ghastly nightmares perhaps. It would come morning soon, and the routine of getting up, going through the day, to live till bedtime again, for what? Eating; meeting a few people indifferently cared for; talking talk to them; alone amongst them who were also alone, so little is real communication between people possible except at rare moments. Oh, he'd sleep. He could not let himself be possessed of this ravaging sense of futility, if he was to go on. He ran his hand over his heart and let it rest there to feel the pulse of it, and to feel flesh. Then he embraced the pillow to feel matter, and to sense again reality. In the stillness of the skylight room he could hear the alarm clock tick; through the walls of the room he could hear the clock in the next room tick. Foghorns from the bay sounded, through the solitude of space he felt stretching out all ways from him. Life, his energy, with all its virulence and violence of yearning and protest was devastating itself in the silence and darkness. What could he do, battling his own reason, as well as enmassed indifferences? He must find something to express himself on.

The thought of people came to him; his mother—what had she gotten out of life to have made it worth her while? Was she really a Christian in her beliefs expecting a hereafter? And the others, and many others—he must force himself to sleep. Sleep, sleep, sleep, sleep, and sleep did gradually blanket his consciousness, which became meaningless as the word "sleep" became with repeated repetitions, sleep, heavy sleep—is it a taste of death? The mouldering of all will in the impalpable nonknowing of the mind.

Detestingly he arose in the morning, but immediately that he was up, his detached mind began to ridicule his broodings. Damnfool within himself. Were all people so sentimental in their pity of self,—oozy, sloppy, morbid, brooding self-pity, thinking thoughts of simply staying in bed and passing out of the picture, with tears inside themselves about the tragedy of it all. Bah! What to hell could it all matter? Six thousand, or six million years of the same kind of thing ought to have taught the species to care less about their own emotions. He wasn't any more caught than millions of others; not so much caught.

Going downstairs he encountered Mrs. McCarty, and remembered with a pang his having stepped on her painted floor, which she mentioned.

"I see ye were up to tricks last night steppin' on the floor in that empty room upstairs."

"Oh yes," he said uncomfortably. "I'm so sorry. I couldn't see that it was freshly painted in the dark and thought maybe you'd let me have it since my room's so small. I'll paint it over for you if you'll let me."

"Sure and that ain't needed. I'm getting auld, and me back's aching with these damned cramps, and one gets discouraged with the likes of most lodgers. Ye're no bother though; nor was Mr. Ogden when he stayed here three years back. I like having men of parts around. There have been three writers, and a man's who's become a great philosopher, and a painter on that top floor in the eight years I've been here." Mrs. McCarty conversed, holding her woolen kimona to her neck with a hand.

"Great doings amongst the Irish, aren't there; and in New York too."

"And it's a good thing that they are. Them bloody English. There should be no rest on this airth until they're all wiped out and made slaves of, like they'd have the rest of us—who are of more wit than ever they can be."

"Ah well, the Irish need their sparring partners, don't they Mrs. McCarty?"

"Sure, and they can find them aisy enough without them English. Do ye know I was at a lecture the other night, and a good, sound argument it was the man made too. He said the raison the Irish were so restless a race was that they were by nature poets, and had always been forced to be agriculturists, which goes against their temperaments that crave fantasy. Think of the likes of the English . . ."

Peter interrupted her last sentence saying, "You know some of the Irish, like Synge, with his Playboy of the Western World, are a little hard on the Irish themselves."

"He should have been tarred and feathered and run out of Ireland. It's the likes of him that poisons the minds—don't ye ever think an Irish boy would be a murdering his own father and made a hero for it."

"Yes—I'll have to rush on though or be late again this morning," Peter said, escaping with a feeling of having placated Mrs. McCarty, who followed him to the door to call out a few more temperamental ideas to him as he walked away down the street, reflecting that it was fortunate for him that Mrs. McCarty was a goodnatured old Irish woman, except when she was an aroused old Irish woman. Anyway, she'd let him stay for weeks at a time without paying his room rent.

Walking, he liked the feeling of cold air on his legs that were no longer chilled because fast walking had warmed them. He had so much vitality. What for? Too bad he couldn't pass some of it on to weary-looking individuals who passed by, on their way to work probably, and that work most of their existence—poor devils—perhaps though his mind overimaged what they felt.

A dead horse was lying near the curb. Strange coincidence

that, after his dream last night. A pale face went by. Death. Pale faces. Why was he recalling the still white face of his brother Lloyd as he'd looked in the coffin many years ago? Why did he connect it with calla lilies—there'd been none at that funeral— more carnations than anything else. And he thought a myrrhlike odor. He'd never smelled myrrh. Reading. Death, Lloyd, myrrh, a Christmas tree. He'd recalled the Christmas of the year Lloyd had died when he'd sung a song at the Sunday school entertainment about "Myrrh is mine, the bitter perfume, brings a life of lingering gloom," or some such riming thing. There'd been a scrap between him and Lloyd because Lloyd had teased him for forgetting the lines as he was on the platform. Then Lloyd died a few weeks later, and he'd thought they would meet in a hereafter —strange sensation without emotion of grief, or fear, of only dumb wonder, he'd had looking at the pale young face shining out of the coffin. Why does sophistication overtake one? Why does one feel wearied before sentiment, or calloused, or indifferent, disbelieving in the reality of all ecstasy, exaltation, and even affection? Perhaps he ought now to be doing fairy stories as he'd always told himself them in those years back, and in that case he might be able to ignore the crassness and dull tortuousness of existence. But that was an idea only, he knew. His mind was a knowing one so that it rebelled against any idealism or romanticism but that of any moment's mood. For the rest he wanted almost touchable reality to analyze, and what to hell *is* so irrevocable as that? One makes one's own reality to a big extent. Ah well, he'd go on analyzing, diagnosing, himself and everything else about him. To what end he couldn't know, but that was his temperament, and that was the answer.

The Party

The doorbell had rung. Peter waited in the hall, listening over the stair railing to see if it was anyone coming to see him. Mrs. McCarty spoke his name.

"Tell whoever it is to come up," he shouted down the stairs.

"Shure, and he's younger than I am, so I will without bringing up his card to you," she called back, and within a minute Brander Ogden came up.

"I was around the neighborhood, and thought I just must come and have a chat with you. Things have been so deadly, but I've concluded I must get around a bit again."

Brander sat on the bed, his still blue eagle-glaring eyes—extended with a terror or a hatred or a suspicion of life—persistently coldly surveying everything in the room, with an insolent stare, as though they would vivisect any object, or rape any person they were gazing at.

"I feel as though I've had enough—you know—of the sort of quality about. Not bad for its kind, you know. But I've had enough of the New York quality, and must plan to get away somewhere for the summer; must manage the economic side of it somehow." Brander talked on as Peter puttered about the room, hanging up garments, and putting his writing table in order. "It's so deadly. Nothing happens. I go around, but nothing happens. Surely I remember that things were not that way in Paris, or Germany, when I was there before the war, but these New York people just get together and stand around dumb. At parties I try to be ordinarily sociable, but they will just get together and stand around. Nothing happens. The people don't know how to play or carry on a conversation. The same people too. They're all right, but I know them. Feel as though they have nothing more to give me. In Europe they know how to play."

Peter wondered. Perhaps, in Europe. Perhaps anywhere. "Yep, they give me the gut ache too, the arty art worshippers, the moral ones, and most the others. There ought to be laws against talking about poetry, art, or the social revolution, or any other kind of idea I think when most of them talk. Ugh! One gets fed up listening to ideas, particularly old ones."

"I don't suppose you'll want to go with me to Dora's party, then," Brander queried. "She sent me a note saying she was having a number of people at her studio in honor of—think who—that lady poetess Vere St. Vitus—the jumpy cooey little thing. Oh she's just too much when she gets over in the corner with some coquettish male admirer and the two of them start gurgling."

"Yes, I'll go. I've nothing else to do tonight, and I've learned to take parties like that as though I were visiting the zoo or an archeological exhibition. We'll be protection to each other too, and perhaps Jimmy will be there so we can all clear out a little later on. But lordy, if Dora gets up and starts to evangelize any of that verse of hers! Ouch! Isn't she less than could be desired, and more, when she begins swaying and spouting with a super trance look in her eyes about the perspiring moon or the hot belly of that illegitimate child of industrialism, the city? There are advantages in being a ditchdigger so one doesn't feel called upon to appreciate or even comment on the beauty of that utterly urgeful affectation of sonorous agony. I hadn't ought to go to her party though, as she's aloof to me now, but I can stay under cover somewhat."

Peter started washing himself, and after shaving, did a quick manicuring process. He was conscious that Brander's eyes were on him as he stood shirtless, shaving, and thought, "Gets most of his erotic satisfaction through his eyes," as he recalled a phrase Brander had used in a letter to him at one time, "in my adoration of flesh." Poor, inhibited, virulently passioned Brander, with his talk of the "cold intellect." He'd continually talk of life and art as "scientific and conscious affairs," while all his own repellent force resided in his savagely repressed rhapsody of eroticism. His was a repressing circumstance and temper, since he couldn't actually attract physically those he wanted. Who would want to touch skin and flesh that was so big pored and old looking?

Peter was dressed, and the two started downstairs together, Brander with his arm about Peter's shoulder. Peter could not respond and could only permit it because of some pity and a frozen antipathy that was indifference within him. He quickened his pace and slipped away from Brander's touch, and then on the street spoke, sorry for his emotion of aversion.

"Gad, Brander, I am glad you came around. I've been wanting to see and talk to you. Your mind has a stimulus, and one sees so few people about who offer anything."

"Now, now, don't you start that. I get so tired of people who like me for my mind. I've thought you got other qualities in me; you've always seemed to like me, and even to understand a little."

Peter felt a desire to evade this subject, but responded, "Why certainly. What does mind mean anyway? How fundamental an affection I can have for anybody I've never had time to discover, but . . ."

"Yes, one shouldn't go into that too much. I so much wish I could help you solve some of your problems. If I only had money I'd ask little more of life than that I could have nice looking young people around me to take care of, and see that they never had a moment's bother about the grim side of things. There are some people who have that kind of talent, and I seem to be sought for my sympathy at times too. There's Marie Plummer— such an intellect she has. She's one of the artists of the world— and I understand she delights in giving away her stage clothes to anybody she's a bit attracted by. She just would not want anybody to have a moment's unhappiness I'm sure; not if she could help it."

"Yes, I believe she isn't supposed to care much about going in for repression of any kind."

"Completely nonmoral—that's the only thing to be. If I could only get myself around to the state of feeling that as well as thinking it so decidedly as I do, I'd have much solved. But New England training is hard to escape."

"I know I'd do anything that I really desired to do, regardless of anybody's opinion, or any god's commandments," Peter commented recklessly, though in his mind the immediate realization that Brander, at least, wouldn't be allowed to do many of the things he actually desired to do, because his desires generally involved people who had no corresponding desire as regarded him.

"Who could or would care, and why should they?" Brander said decisively. "Unless this fanciful god, and if he's there he doesn't seem to let anything disturb him much. The man must have frequent naps."

"Too vague a concept for my mind . . ."

"I haven't told you of a new acquaintance I've run into, a boy from upstate in Maine, who used to know my family vaguely.

Such a lovely boy. Such gentle soft qualities. There's nothing in his head of course, but I like him so well just for lovely human qualities he possesses, and he seems so ready to be helpful. Last week when I was staying in my room, laid up because of this damned gut of mine, he'd bring me things to eat from the delicatessen shop on the corner, and that's all I wanted to eat then. How beautiful young people can be, just as things to have about one."

They arrived at Dora's address and started up the three flights of stairs. "I get so weak from climbing stairs. My intestines drop down in me—since that accident—I have to be so careful of what I do and eat," Brander complained complacently. He didn't like making too much physical effort ever; quite apt to take to bed actually and metaphorically when life got rough, Peter reflected, mounting the stairs behind him as he ascended with slow dignity, with the calm hauteur of a camel, neck camel-like, eagle eyes appraising a little camel-like in their assumed ferocity.

In Dora's studio Brander entered at once into the conversation, deliberately gay and facetious. Peter felt ill at ease, and withdrew into a corner, there to sit watching, feeling pent up and irritated at his own feelings as well as at the atmosphere. There was no one he saw he wanted to talk to, and nobody much that he knew even by sight. He saw that Dora's glance evaded his and helped her in the evasion. Darned little she and he had to say to each other; poor old thing, pretending to be revolutionary and flaming with passion when a few good meals would change all of that perhaps, except that she'd still be pathetic.

"Lackeyship to England," a phrase sounded near him, and he turned to see a middle-aged woman discoursing intensely. "We fete all these English novelists and poets, who are second rate in their own country, and not equal to our own artists, but never a fete do we fete our own worker," she was saying.

"Rats," Peter exploded in, not bothering about an introduction, "that's the attraction of the foreign thing, and doesn't at all mean we're lackeys to England intellectually. We have the energy at the present moment, and any country is ours to learn from if there's anything to learn. What the public thinks can't matter anyway, here or anywhere else. Let the Englishmen drag some money out of it here if they can; Lord knows we won't get it anyway." Whereupon a discussion waxed hot, and ended for Peter by his settling back into himself, disgusted with argument.

The evening was not actively painful, however, until Reginald Crackye read an extract from his play "The Mummy" and became dramatic about it, much worked up apparently over his inability to keep his long hair out of his eyes and out of his fervid recitation. "Are these my eyes looking at me in the mirror? Am I then that manner of a man? No, no, away, thou phantom. Torture me not thus. I have loved; I have prayed, now this, this . . ."

Everybody applauded the reading, enthusiastic at all costs. Peter suffered from not being able to get up and walk out into the street rapidly, and blamed himself for having presumed to expect that any variation from the usual might occur at Dora's party.

Verses were read by several ladies, and by one young man whose verses were, according to Dora, "very sensitive."

"God," Peter ejaculated to a woman sitting near him, "isn't this modern poetry movement awful? Lemon water, anguish, sand and sweat. Ain't the moon gangreneous though? How do we survive this atmosphere?"

"Oh my, don't you like what has been read? I think it's all too wonderful. How do you clever people manage to write it? I've tried, but of course my efforts . . ."

"Um—um—yes—well," Peter commenced, eyeing her askance. Then suddenly he looked with inspiration at Brander across the room. "Oh I must go and talk to Brander Ogden," he declared, escaping.

"Say, Brander, let's collect Jimmy and get out of here. I see he's caught up by some fervid lady. I'd like to take art and drown it in the river. Reginald Crackye! Dora! Dora! the gate."

Jimmy needed to be rescued from a woman who was sure that he'd be a greater poet if he would put more social content into his work, and make it more representative of the average person's experiences and emotions. "Certain things exist; but why should they be talked about, unless they can serve to uplift us, and give us beauty? I like to be deeply moved, and exalted, by poetry, if not by prose."

"Mr. Boyle and I have promised to be elsewhere at twelve o'clock and it's near that now, so I'll have to interrupt your conversation," Peter broke in, and soon he, Jimmy, and Brander were out on the street together.

"Ghastly!"

"Too much; just too much!"

"For Christ's sake give me a cigarette, one of you. I wish I could be a truck driver."

"Just too killing Dora is, and I used to think she had a sense of what not to do once, but—did you hear her talking to that poor English novelist she'd gotten hold of? Her reserve and irony couldn't save her from Dora. I thought she'd simply pass out when Dora actually quoted some verses she evidently wrote years back and was ashamed of."

"Yes, I don't know," Jimmy parried. "What's one to think about anything? I used to like Dora, and thought I liked some of her things. What's there to say anyway?"

They went into a coffeehouse to talk and smoke and there Peter sensed a reserve between Brander and Jimmy, and recalled that there'd been some break between them about a letter Jimmy had written because he'd been hearing things he didn't like about Brander, after he himself had written many unburdening letters to Brander, every time life seemed to get unbearable to him. To hell, thought Peter, why in the devil did Jimmy run at people so impulsively offering them friendship, and then break away with some disapproving terror of having them ask too much of him? One can hold people far enough away without that. But it was damnable too that Brander couldn't understand that Jimmy's letters had simply been effusions about life, and his own ego; exuberant in a morbid way generally, but never actually at their recipients except as he or she was somebody to shout through the mail to. But Brander would have to clutch at them as signs of romantic friendship.

The conversation would not go; all three of them made starts but a group interest would not pick up, and Brander looked at Jimmy ever attempting to keep the right degree of coldness without being pettily haughty. Jimmy was simply diffidently nervous. Peter tried flippancy, but the others did not respond, so finally he said, "What the devil! Haven't you two patched up that scrap two months back yet? Why don't you tell each other to go kiss ass, and have it over with?"

"Well now, Peter, you know yourself how little one likes personal comments," Brander said austerely.

"I know it, old kid; but I like this atmosphere of refined restraint even less, and why should two old goats like you and Jim, who should be hardboiled by now if you aren't, stand nibbling at conversation like pet rabbits, with me a bored spectator trying to be the life of the party? We'll all admit you're both damn fools, and I'm a little inclined that way. Let's take it easier."

"What's it all about?" Jimmy said, pretending unawareness.

"Well, as I said to Peter some time back, I've always liked you, Jim, but after that letter I just thought, well, I can do without that friendship too."

"Oh, I just had to get something off my chest," Jim defended, grinning and uncomfortable.

"Hell, sez the duchess who up to this time had taken no part whatever in the conversation," Peter broke in, "explanations and apologies are most incriminating and h'embarrassing. You two haven't anything agin each other. I've got to get up early in the morning so I'm going to beat it home, but let's all three have dinner together some night soon and if you're still scrappy then I'll be the referee."

The Talks

"Just a minute, Peter."

"Huh, Gusta, glad you've come along. If you're feeling gay you can infect me, and if you're feeling as rotten as I am there's a drugstore nearby where we can get something and die enjoying our misery mutually."

"Not me today. I'm going to the country, and wanted to see you to say goodbye. My folks in England finally sent me some money so that I feel a wealthy woman again. I'll go away and come back after I'm rested to start renting out houses, or some such thing."

"Tosh, Gusta, you a business woman?"

"I've been so miserable lately. I do hope the country air sets me up again."

"What is unhappiness anyway, or its opposite? You're doomed to confusion and misery. What does it all matter so long as there's movement of some kind?"

"Don't talk nonsense. You're such an infant. When one's unhappy one can't feel to know whether movement's about one or not."

"Oh, it's type of helplessness you mean—a brooding— Oh, I don't know. What are we talking about? Both happiness and unhappiness are types of stupidity, and what I'm saying is another kind. I'd better head for the country too."

"Who've you been seeing lately? Anybody that matters?"

"Bats, there aren't any such people if you ask me today. Well, the usual assortment. You and the others last night. Jimmy, Brander. Considered in relation they're important enough probably. My intolerations insist upon importance I guess. Oh, Martha Wullus too—know her? I'd like to run around and say hello to her. Come along with me won't you."

"I've just met her. She's rather quaint."

"All of that. She thinks anything, disapproves of little, for other people, and is a churchgoing, cerebralizing moralist who observes sabbath day strictly, herself. I can't quite understand why with a mind like hers agnosticism hasn't eaten into her a little, but it seems not to have, or she conceals it well, for her mother's sake possibly."

"It isn't reasonable to be as rigid as that with the kind of intellect she seems to have. There's some suppression or cowardice there."

"Possibly she isn't emotionally developed much, but still there's the force of experience back of her knowledge; there must be for her to realize what she does. She needs to be seen apart from the background of her mother to be actual though."

Going around the corner at one block they encountered Brander Ogden, surveying the street with his usual air of connoisseurship towards humanity and traffic. He greeted them gaily.

"Ha, ha, so I've run into two darlings at once. It's so natural to see you two together though."

He joined them, to go to Martha's apartment, and chatted with deliberate facetiousness. "My word, I must tell you about the white peacocks I saw at the house of a friend in the country Sunday. They were the final thing in beauty, with their gorgeous whiteness, and the circle spots, of a different shade of white in their tails, that looked like staring blind eyes."

Peter's mind withdrew from listening but vaguely to the conversation. White peacocks. White music. White winds; white with every color in the world in it. He'd write something about that. White and purity. What is purity? It certainly couldn't have anything to do actually with physical acts. White winds blowing, cool and fresh through the white sky. Like the days far back in North Dakota when the blizzards hurled white sleet snow across the snow-covered plains. How tired he was of apathy; how prim- itively clear those winds, that snow, had been; and all the while through the whiteness to the eye the winds had shrieked out a cold blue symphony. What could one say of beauty, of white pea- cocks, of golden pheasants? Why weren't people so colorfully beautiful? The devil with visible reality. Here, where mental and physical weariness were pursuing him, something went on storm- ing inside him, regardless of what he said, how he acted, so that he himself or nobody else knew him. From protoplasm to come, suffer the variegated impacts of experience, reaction, thinking, feeling and responding, how?—there was everything to question and nothing to understand.

"I think I'd be bored to death with Martha Wullus if it weren't that I can't get her angle," Peter broke in suddenly on Brander's and Gusta's conversation.

"Now, now, wait. I like the way this boy tells people what's what, and when, but you have to watch out for him," Brander joked, looking at Peter curiously, so that Peter felt irritation come up in him because of his resentment against the look that nullified him. But the resentment passed in a flash, and he spoke up again, saying, "I think I'll put an ad in the paper and try to get a job in a psychological laboratory. The kind of existence I'm leading is eating me up."

"Yes, do anything but be an artist who's interested in art. I feel myself as though I must get away and never hear the word art again."

"Hell, you'd feel as though you had to get away and never hear the word business, or education, again, if you were in circles where those terms are used frequently. Where human beings consort about ideas and trades, there's a place to want to get away from."

"I know; and of course the only possible thing to be is an artist, and enjoy the divine trivialities. Isn't it too wonderful to feel that the only thing one needs think about is a form, or a line, or a bit of color in a design?"

Arriving at Martha's place Peter rang the bell, and while waiting, Brander said: "Isn't Martha the quaint idea rather than a real human though? She's sort of a Dresden doll thing with those great contemplative Chinese eyes of hers, and that wisplike body with its thatch of carrot-colored hair. So picturesque too in her half-boyish clothes."

"Probably it's best for her to be only an idea too, seeing that ideas is about all she'll have of life," Peter responded, and Martha was at the door inviting them in with formal hospitality that had a whimsical directness.

"Oh good day, and how have all of you been; you, Miss Rolph, particularly? I've so wanted to have a conversation with you because of what I've heard about your work."

"What tricks have you been up to yourself?" Brander asked Martha.

"I haven't been doing much that I want to do. My work keeps me away from—my work, the real kind I'm wanting to do."

"Bother your paid work. You observe things too uniquely to let any paid job interfere much with your writing," Gusta said rather curtly. "Though I presume you believe in self-discipline, and duty more than some of us do."

"It is true that I have never expressed so far any of the things that I particularly wish to say. But I shall soon attempt to put down some of my observations; nothing absolute. To put my remarks in verse though, as I have attempted, is like trying to dance the minuet in a bathing suit, though I do have some things to say about acacias and seaweeds and serpents in plane trees that will have to appear in fragments."

"What a person. What a person," Brander declared. "And how calm and collected you manage to remain through it all."

Martha chortled. "You must not be too sure of that. I was quite unable to control myself at the library today, and I fear I spoke curtly to the head librarian for some of her trite insistences. . . . But I find seahorses, lizards, and such things very fascinating. Also a fox's face, the picture of which I saw recently in a magazine, haunts me like a nightmare, and contradictory as it seems, I am quite able to appreciate the 'bright beaming expression' that Xenophon talks about, on the face of the hound which was pursuing it."

Mrs. Wullus was in the sitting room when they entered, and during their stay drawled out her observations, making distinctions of her exact meaning with a too careful honesty that had its limitations, it seemed to Peter, who felt his impetuosity repelled by the older woman, who was much given to moralizing.

"While I am Irish myself I cannot approve of the way the Irish have been acting in this country," Mrs. Wullus stated. "And no more can I sympathize greatly with Mr. McSwiney in his hunger strike in Ireland."

"Why, I wouldn't starve myself to death for any cause in the world," Martha said, and chuckled. Her mother echoed the chuckle, and laughed in a way that she must have considered immoderate.

"My, you mustn't ever make as funny a remark as that again," Mrs. Wullus declared, and went into a lengthier dissertation upon the Irish.

"Can't you get away now, and let's all go down to Solveig's and have a nice long chat over some tea, or coffee? I know you won't smoke cigarettes," Brander suggested, wanting to get Martha away from her mother, who lacked the whimsicality of Martha as a personality. Some minutes later the four of them came into Solveig's dingy little bohemian café, where several nondescript individuals were lounging about, in groups.

"Solveig's the only person about this section of town who has any reality about her," Brander asserted, after they'd seated themselves. "The first time I saw her last week after a month's absence—she must have heard that I was hard up—she told me to come here and eat whenever I needed to, and she would see me

through. Isn't it fine to know that people like her, with no pretensions of any sort, actually like you for what you are? She
charged upon me and shouted: 'Hell, Brander, old dear. Where've
you been keeping yourself? My God, I've wanted to see you or
somebody who wasn't talking about life or art, but I didn't know
your address. My nose is good, and I'm adventurous, having been
a streetwalker in my day, but honestly, kiddo, I can't smell out
where you're staying.' "

"Was that the truth about herself?" Peter asked curiously.

"Yes indeed. She's had experience all right, every kind. Affairs with prize fighters, policemen, sailors. I guess she doesn't
even hold herself aloof from intellectuals. A wonderful girl she is.
So real. Just one of the plain, dirty, outspoken, big souls of the
world she is. She's one of the real women. It's so nice to encounter fine girls such as she."

Solveig came up to Brander to exchange boisterous joviali-
ties; there were additions to their party from tables nearby as here
seemed the noise center of the room, and the situation had soon
resolved itself to one faltering between banal dullness and forced
brilliance, punctuated by casual conversation, picked up, sus-
tained, dropped, and again re-insisted upon. Now, sitting quietly,
Peter felt tired wonder settling all through him, physically and
mentally, as a reaction from his drunkenness of last night. Watching all that went about, it seemed to him that he was incapable of
an emotion or a conviction about anything, or any person, except
an emotion of wearied bewilderment of wonder. Nothing about
was in anyway related to him; he could sit still, feel burnt out, almost washed out to extinction with a day-after reaction; and no
circumstance could make him to himself an actual part of it, so
removed and dumfounded by all of life and by any reality was he.
His eyes, looking introspectively at Martha's face, and seeing her
gulp in her throat, as though seeking to drink back some inex-
pressible desire, or to drink of some denied gratification, found
pathos in the keen sensibility of her facial expressions. "Hungry
too—and for what?" he reflected, and a dully submerged wave of
rebellion against his own sympathy swept over his consciousness,
taking him back to bewilderment.

"Ah—er—yes, not quite desirable you know. He's rather foul,
you know—hardly a decent sort," his ears heard, while his eye

noted an Englishman speaking. The blur of that face attempting to express correctness angered him. What was beneath that proper exterior, with its "not quite proper" or "not quite desirable" insularities?

"Yes, well, just what do you mean?" a girl asked the man, evidently wishing to tease him.

"Kitty is afraid you might mean he's an ascetic or chaste, which would be an atrocity to her," another girl broke in.

"I'll have to use that in my book on men; just another idea for showing up what a sham he is," Gusta stated, appearing animated now that many people were about. "What tricks men do play on us doting women."

"You know, Gusta, you like the darlings too well to do them the harsh justice they need," Brander told her.

"Don't destroy my inspiration. I must do something, even if it's only trying to be clever," Gusta said, giving an impression of the real discouragement, almost despair, behind her trifling.

"For God's sake, but this is a cheerful party," Solveig said, coming to the table, to lean her mop of yolk-colored hair upon her hand, as she leaned over Brander. "I'm getting too old to be on the qui-vee vi-vee about all the things that are talked about in my exclusive little café. I'll go into a nunnery soon, now that the war's over and I can't be a salvation army lassie or a nurse."

"Dear me yes," a pallid man near forty spoke in. "I'm so glad every time I think of life that I'm an artist. That is the only sanctuary after all, isn't it?" and Peter knew that he'd have to be leaving this atmosphere in a moment, or shriek out some profanity, or some rudeness at various people who talked.

"Put that to music, won't you?" a lady answered the man.

"Oh Doris, do be quiet. You're so coldly intellectual and cynical. What would you have us who feel strongly do, and how should we express ourselves?" a Jewish-looking girl declared. Peter's eye caught Martha's and he began an aside conversation with her.

"This sort of atmosphere drives me wild," he said. "And one gets enough abhorring indifference to existence without staying about here."

"It's pretty bad I admit, still it's restraining oneself in the midst of annoyances to which one is subjected that toughens the muscles. Wildness in itself is an attractive quality, but it fails to take into account the question of attrition, and attrition is inevitable," she replied.

Peter, chafing inwardly at that, answered, "Yes, but I haven't your ability to take into account the inevitability of attrition so readily, or to believe it needs be accepted as much as we have to."

"I lack your swiftness, myself, or rather I have no swiftness."

". . . that places a quickly intolerant judgment upon every situation that doesn't suit your mood as my swiftness does."

"No, no, I was thinking of my writing when I said that. I find many situations as intolerable as you do, and do not hesitate, I fear, to express my distaste."

"It's bad you haven't time to write then; can't you escape some of your routine labor?"

"That wouldn't help me, I'm sure. I am telling you the truth when I say that if I had all the time in the world I should not write anything important to myself for some years. In order to work as I should have to, I should like to look into certain things and make up my mind with regard to the relevance, or irrelevance of certain other things. That may be hard for you to realize but it is quite true, and I have, I think, an intuition as to how I am to succeed if I do succeed."

"Yes, that; if you can know what success is; and not feel that waiting becomes in such a scheme of things the one activity," Peter said, wavering between admiration of, and restlessness about, Martha's attitude. He could not comprehend, more than as an idea, Martha's apparent ability to weigh and balance. "Of course I don't know what there is to express except some feeling about, or perception of—should I say, and take a chance of Brander's hearing—reality."

"What's that you're saying, Peter?" Brander interrupted.

"Shucks, you would hear when I use one of the words that's your pet aversion."

"What one is that?"

"Not life, or beauty, or art, or truth—but I did try to evade being too exact in my appellations by saying reality."

"Don't, for god's sake whatever you do, use those words

seriously. It simply can't be done any longer, amongst a world so full of doting ecstatics, mystics, and other chatterers. I'd like them all taken out of the language."

Martha laughed her nervously spontaneous and quickly passing chuckle, which seemed to crumple and dry up in a moment. Brander, observing her with his eagle eyes, said sotto voce, "Doesn't Martha look piquant tonight? She's a rare one. Something so keen, and diamond hard in her direct observations. She's one of the rare ones too; one of the few who come off into some actuality."

"Yes, probably. She was telling me a while ago that she and her mother lived like anchorites, and that she could work as she was situated better than anywhere else. I can't get that. Of course any situation is the best situation if one knows how to utilize it, but she must want to break away often, and refuses to admit that she's caged."

Brander was looking at Peter's face so keenly that his gaze seemed to penetrate beneath even the bony structure. Then his gaze averted and he was listening in on other conversation, so that Peter's mind reverted to its bewildering analysis and dissection of all conversation and of his own emotions. Within a moment he knew he had to leave the café, the whole atmosphere of which was stifling him with the annihilation of purpose, and the breeding of unrest within him, which it brought about. Saying good afternoon, he banged hastily out of the place, and went catapulting down the street.

For a few minutes only an oppression and depression of the spirit that had crept into him because of the conglomeration of beings collected in the café lingered in him, and then, as he walked at a rapid pace across Fifth Avenue from the park, he began feeling vital again, with a clearer chaos in his mind than had been there before. Ideas on various people, on his own past, and more, an idealess brooding, drifted rapidly through his brain, until suddenly he was aware that he was whistling, and swaying along at a tremendous pace. Not brooding; not resentful; not even a little bit unhappy; scarcely able to understand why he or anybody ever should feel anything but free, and glad of strong bodies and a strong life stream of blood. But he knew this too was only an emotion; but that did not matter either. What had bothered him back there? Why try to remember? He'd go and see if Vera was at her room. No, not that either. She might have company, and he didn't want to have to talk to anybody. Was he composing a new piece of music as he whistled to himself; couldn't recall having heard the piece he was blowing out of his lips before. It was too bad he wasn't a composer, or a painter, so as to be able to dabble around with sound and color now and then to amuse himself. Why did he always want to put color he liked to his lips, almost to eat it? He was always wanting some sensual realization, carnally sensual, to possess anything that pleased his senses. Damned tired of being a civilized man, if he was one; wished he were a barbarian so he could wear barbaric costumes and jewels, nose rings, earrings, anklets—wished he could go and dance somewhere with somebody who really could dance, and in a place where there was color and music that caught him up and lived up to his desire to express his vitality of being physically. As the wind went by him, coldly stinging, he could sense that it was dancing with him, but he could not leap up and dance, whirling around, jumping, striking the wind, here in the city streets.

But he'd walk miles, walk off this spurt of energy. To the devil with any kind of care. Life would happen as it would happen, and he would not allow it to batter him into a gray mass of lethargic protoplasm; not so long as energy enough remained within him to offer an exhilarated response to life. There was nothing to know but wonder, generally, and tiny finite facts that banged him in the face, and the rest could stay open, and unsolved.

(See Bibliographical Note, page 361.)

2. Contact

McAlmon's first publishing venture grew out of his friend-ship with Williams. Together they founded and edited the magazine Contact believing, Williams said, "there was some good stuff lying around that should not be lost. . . . Our poems constantly, continuously and stupidly were rejected by all the pay magazines except Poetry and The Dial. The Little Review didn't pay. We had no recourse but to establish publications of our own." [1] There was another element in McAlmon's interest in publishing: he wanted to belong, as it were, and Contact made him a patron of the arts and a colleague of Harriet Monroe (of Poetry), Scofield Thayer (of The Dial), and Margaret Anderson (of The Little Review). It gave him a definite place in the literary world.

Fortunately, as it happened, he did agree with some avant-garde opinion. Good writing, he and Williams thought, provided "the essential contact between words and the locality that breeds them, in this case America," hence the magazine's name. "Art which attains is indigenous of experience and relations," McAlmon wrote in Contact's first "Manifesto" (December 1920), "and the artist works to express perceptions rather than to attain standards of achievement." Williams explains more fully in his Autobiography: "What were we seeking? No one knew consistently enough to formulate a 'movement.' We were restless and constrained, closely allied with the painters. Impressionism, dadaism, surrealism applied to both the painting and the poem. What a battle we made of it merely getting rid of capitals at the beginning of every line! The immediate image, which was impressionistic, sure enough, fascinated us all. We had followed Pound's instructions, his famous 'Don't,' eschewing inversions of the phrase, the putting down of what to our senses was tauto-

140

logical and so, uncalled for, merely to fill out a standard form. Literary allusions, save in very attenuated form, were unknown to us. Few had the necessary reading.

"We were looked at askance by scholars and those who turned to scholarship for their norm. To my mind the thing that gave us most a semblance of a cause was not imagism, as some thought, but the line: the poetic line and our hopes for its recovery from stodginess. I say recovery in the sense that one recovers a salt from solution by chemical action. We were destroyers, vulgarians, obscurantists to most who read; though occasionally a witty line, an unusual reference, or a wrench of the simile to force it into approximation with experience rather than reading—bringing a whole proximate 'material' into view—found some response from the alert." 2

Who were "we"? A list of contributors to Contact *reads like a roll-call of the new generation. Chief among them was Marianne Moore, "like a rafter holding up the superstructure of our uncompleted building, a caryatid, her red hair plaited and wound twice about the fine skull," Williams said. "Marianne, with her sidelong laugh and shake of the head, quite childlike and overt . . . Marianne was our saint—if we had one—in whom we all instinctively felt our purpose come together to form a stream. Everyone loved her."* 3 *Among the other contributors were Wallace Stevens, Kenneth Burke, H.D., Marsden Hartley, Ezra Pound, and of course Williams and McAlmon.*

At about the time they were putting together the first issue of Contact, *McAlmon declared himself on the business of art and the artist in* The Little Review. *The "jh" referred to below is Jane Heap, the associate editor of* The Review. *McAlmon addresses Margaret Anderson, who had commissioned the piece.*

Essentials

Ask "jh," too, whether one must be "strange," "compelling," "original" at all costs, or whether it is well to be these only when

you mark an advance, or at least grant value equal to the "old."
There is a disease "modern traditionalism" that has little to do
with art, or life. A "modern" who counts, is surprisingly like a
"classic" in scope of comprehension, and neither of them deal
with the dry chaff of words, manner, and form, until they have
some content in which they themselves have faith to put into
form, via words and manner.

Art is essential? If life is. You can take your pick of which is
the bigger thing—life, art, religion, science. If art is essential, it is
so because of the live significance of it. A James Branch Cabell,
Anatole France, type of erudition-wrought writing, with re-
juggled philosophies and theories that come from reading rather
than from contact, physical and mentally perceptive, is deadly,
but it does have some degree of "understanding" within it. A
D. H. Lawrence sullen bull intensity without the clarity of intelligence, or the area, is rather bad too. But both these mentioned things are "genuine" to the conviction of their producers.
One of them believes in life through literature; the other believes
in the white incandescence of the luminous spore-like germ, or
some such thing. Tell me, will you, how many of your lesser contributors have that much genuine quality?

An artist's prime occupation is with life. Art is his outlet. One
does not become an artist by going into the arts. One has some
perception, some interpretation, some essential record that one
must leave. What has Djuna Barnes, or Bodenheim, or Malcolm
Cowley, or Witter Bynner, Ben Hecht, Mark Turbyfill, and a few
others to leave? Omit their names from their work,—all that any
of them has ever done, compiled in a book,—and who would
recognize it as theirs? They produce neither conscious, accidental,
nor perverse art. Cowley, and the poor overdone family cat, slur
at respectability, the tenacles of houses;—if these things meant
something to him more than a mannerism, aped from some artist
who has them a part of a whole, their over-usage by "moderns"
would not matter. It is deemed essential to be subtly satirical
over respectability, over repressed sexuality, over many things
called "modern." Sterne, Rabelais—innumerable ancients did it
better than the pseudos.

A piece of writing should be criticised upon its own basis, but few of the mentioned people give their writing any basis of its own. They swim under a sea of influences—Rodker, doing the Rimbaud thing fifty years too late, and he many years too old to put "belief" into it. Men such as Pound, with crisp minds worshipping at the shrine of LaForgue and Rimbaud, who were simply precocious examples of the "malaise de la jeunesse" and interesting or ingratiating for that reason rather than for art. Art deals with life. Form is something to worry about for the artist, but not the other fellow's form. Joyce is not "modern" in form, but "Joyce." Followers on are procreating mechanics. The impact of experience, environment, realized perception—not literary-gained knowledge—and a will to say something about it produces literature, which is valuable if the producer finds his own form,—valuable both for perception, and for form. What the artist needs first is the faith of his own ego, and the conviction of its knowing, and feeling, so that into form he can put some quivering protoplasm that men of comprehension can look at and not card index.

Freud speaks of the "sexual impulse." Is there such a thing? A voluptuous impulse, yes, which desires not contact with another sex, but satisfaction, and which consequently seeks for it at many destinations en route to the marriage bed which all good Christians declare is the ultimate. And the roots of the voluptuous impulse are a desire for a justification—an art, a religion, a love, a science—and there is no justification but an individual's faith in his own ego,—his vision of the universe as himself transcended and multiplied, with his ego a thing he can be quite detached and abstract about,—a shrine before which he can call nations, politicians, gods and undertakers, and say "worship." But if he doesn't worship himself what boots it?

I haven't *form;* neither have I an aped structure. Christ knows I'm no artist—perhaps en route. I don't know, can't care, must write any way, nothing else I want to do and I have energy and conceptions. Every now and then in some little thing I achieve "form." Then somehow I'm satisfied, and don't care about sending it in—both because I know it to be complete, and because I know it is a lesser "form" that doesn't indicate much to me.

Do you know any "modern" critic, you, "jh," Eliot, or anybody else who would be capable of writing in the abstract a philosophy of art of comprehension comparable to Taine's, or of Remy de Gourmont's, with "modern" understanding,—Oh yes indeed, but we must insist, with equal scope,—however different the texture. Or do we know much about even our individual philosophies of art today. Doesn't *The Little Review* "chance it" frequently on,—say on some simple being—such as the man who wrote the bloody spittle in the bowl story, for instance? Pourquoi moi, I am agnostic. I know of only two writers in whom I can believe—of course I make no stringent effort to "keep up"—but Hardy, and Joyce, with Conrad and Hudson, at least know what they want to do. Hardy has a conviction in some kind of unity of futility in existence; Joyce has insight into people. Conrad I have read but slightly, and Hudson—I don't know. I liked his "Purple Land" and "Green Mansions"—well, he's had space enough. I've nothing to say about him.

The million things I say are attempts at location. You declare you have yours. I ask questions to ascertain your conviction. I only know one person who has his "location" and it isn't mine. I don't write to write, but because I hate, or adore, or don't know what to do about life to such an extent that I can't end it, unsolved. The whole damned process is a frame-up—you're caught going and coming, and at both ends, for every realized impulse.

Hasn't the race been "civilized," such as the word has come to mean, for enough generations, for it to be rather absurd to talk about "primal" impulses, and want to go back to the primitive, naive, child-mind form sort of thing? Isn't a complex man, emotionally, spiritually, intellectually, quite a "natural" manifestation? There have been so many of them from bible times on down.

(See Bibliographical Note, page 361.)

Williams, in his Autobiography, *tells how McAlmon worked to support* Contact, *earning money by posing for art students and laboring on a harbor barge. One suspects that some of the money sent him by his long-suffering sisters went into the magazine too. Whatever McAlmon had he spent, and without a thought. But like so many "little magazines," Contact lived only briefly. Between December 1920 and the summer of 1921 McAlmon and Williams managed to bring out four issues.[4] Toward the end of 1921 McAlmon dashed off a letter to his associate with some further reflections on the magazine's name and on writing in general.*

Contact, I thought was a good title for a magazine, but apparently not, Bill. They think in terms of physical contact there [in America] yet—do here [in Paris] too. . . . The idea of contact simply means that when one writes they write about something, and not to write "literature" because it is a day of publications, and publishing houses. [Kenneth] Burke wanting a manifesto,—hasn't he, or anybody else, copulated, desired, thought, detested, been abused, enough by actual experience, to say something about existance [sic] that has a quality that is his own. . . . it isn't lack of contact that condemns most writing, there or here. It's lack of an individual quality that makes the stuff worth reading, and presence of too much desire to be a "literary figure." . . . And when people justify "conscious art" and an eternal talk about "form" and technique, by mentioning the painstaking Flaubert, they overlook that fact that Flaubert's bigness rests a great deal more upon the fact that he created his characters, understood the psychology of people, and got the drama of his drab situations. Some may like the way he uses words; incidentally, I do too, but if it weren't for deeper insights I wouldn't give a hurrah for him, or de Gourmont, or LaForgue, or Rimbaud. It's the skeleton of intellect and human "understanding." Burke would say that was howling about the great throb drama of humanity. You can look on, observe keenly, understand, and be as cold hearted, and calloused as a butcher. Know that all the problems aren't yours to solve. But the situation is made art by the understanding, and ability to note how the characters spoken off [sic] react emotionally. Flaubert was simply able to be both a formalist—which means a good deal pedantic regarding "style"—and an observing psychologist and intelligence.[5]

"Life would happen as it would happen." Early in 1921
McAlmon's life took an unexpected turn. Through Williams he
had met an English girl, Winifred Bryher, author of an autobiographical novel, Development, for which Amy Lowell had
written the introduction. Bryher—she ordinarily went by the
single name—had "come out to the States" in September 1920
with her friend. H.D. (Hilda Doolittle), the Imagist poet. Bryher
was a short, sharp-featured blonde girl, immensely energetic and
self-assured. She looked about the same age as McAlmon although
she was two years older.

Bryher and McAlmon were immediately attracted, but shortly
after they met she went on to the west coast with H.D., and did
not return until the following February. McAlmon meanwhile
had made arrangements to ship to China on a freighter. Greenwich Village had its points, but he was no more committed there
than he had been in the Middle West, or California, or Chicago.
To his friend Williams it seemed that "Because [McAlmon's]
own poverty anchored him in one place, he felt the world was
passing him by." [6]

When a card came from Bryher telling of her imminent return, McAlmon canceled his plans. On her arrival in New York
she proposed and he accepted; or at any rate they quickly came to
an understanding. They were married on February 14 at a civil
ceremony. Afterwards there was a small dinner in a private dining
room at the Hotel Brevoort. Williams remembers that Marianne
Moore and Marsden Hartley were among the guests. Some of
McAlmon's family had rushed east for the wedding, and Williams
took the couple a boxful of orchids.

The most astonishing part of the story was yet to come. It
turned out that McAlmon had married an heiress. Bryher's legal
name was Annie Winifred Ellerman, and she was the only
daughter of Sir John Ellerman, a shipping magnate and the
heaviest taxpayer in England. Bryher had intended to keep the
marriage a secret to forestall parental opposition to her bid for
emancipation, but this Cinderella story in reverse was hardly one
to be overlooked by the newspapers, and the marriage was played
up by the press on both sides of the Atlantic. In Los Angeles
the story was carried in the Sunday supplement illustrated with
faked pictures. Even the dignified New York Times unbent a bit

*(and in the process came up with a somewhat scrambled account.[7]
McAlmon was confused with his football-playing brother Will;
also, he had only one parent living in the West—his father had
died in June, 1917):*

'HEIRESS' WRITER
WEDS VILLAGE POET

Greenwich Circles Stirred by the Romance of Robert Menzies McAlmon.

GIRL PROPOSED, IS REPORT

Bride Exploited as Daughter of Sir John Ellerman, to Whom Burke's Peerage Credits Only a Son.

Greenwich Village had a fresh topic for conversation yesterday: the marriage of one of its best-known characters, Robert Menzies McAlmon, "editor and poet," of 351 West Fifteenth Street, and an English girl writer who indited a book of self-revelation under the nom de plume of Winifred Bryher.

But the Village talk veered sharply away from the official records of the Marriage License Bureau, which told briefly that McAlmon and Miss Winifred Ellerman —that is said to be her real name—on Feb. 14 obtained a license to wed.

Greenwich Village gossip was that the bride was wealthy in her own name and that she was related to Sir John Reeves Ellerman, the British ship owner, and some of this gossip even went so far as to say that the author of the revelations was the daughter of Sir John. According to Who's Who, 1920, and Burke's Peerage, 1921, however, Sir John was married only in 1908 and has only one child, a boy 11 years old. Face to face with romance, Greenwich Village was willing to admit that this took a little of the tang out of the romance, but it was still romance nevertheless, because—

The woman writer is reported to have
proposed to the "poet and editor" because
she became enthralled and entranced with
a poem that appeared in one of the Greenwich Village publications. According to the
villagers, she then met the poet at a party
given by one of her friends. He whispered
a line or two of the poetry and there was
nothing to do but call a minister.

Captive and captor having sailed away
for England two weeks ago on a White
Star liner, the imagination of the village
could take full wing on this new romance
without regard for any of the facts, and it
is reported that many more new poems and
satires are under way on the subject. And
the villagers are only too glad to point out
that all their literary efforts lack is appreciation—"just see how this romance
turned out on a single poem."

McAlmon was a halfback on the University of Minnesota football team several
years ago, and then became an expert on
aviation, serving in the air service during
the war. Then he saw one of the Greenwich Village publications—so the villagers
say—and decided to come to this city to
become a Bohemian. Poetry was a last resort, and the village publications have had
many of his flings. His parents live in the
West.

The girl writer came to this country
from England last August and has been
living in the village. She wrote her book
there, and had decided to remain in this
country. Then she met McAlmon and—still
according to the villagers—she proposed
and won. All of which has enough fact to
suit the village imagination.

BEING GENIUSES
TOGETHER
1921-1927

Comments on the persons mentioned in Part III will be found in the Biographical Repertory, beginning on page 367.

1. The "Right People" and the Left Bank

In London the McAlmons lived for a time in some magnificence with Sir John and Lady Ellerman. Sir John, self-made and single-minded, and Lady Ellerman, deaf and temperamental, were completely won over by the engaging young man from the Middle West; in fact, he got along with them better than their daughter did, just as she had hoped. Sir John was extremely generous with his son-in-law—who did not hesitate to spend what he got—and both then and later the Ellermans went out of their way to show him kindness.[1]

McAlmon, predictably enough, started out at once to investigate London literary and artistic circles. Through New York friends he met T. S. Eliot and Wyndham Lewis; through Bryher and H.D., Miss Harriet Weaver, Joyce's prim patroness, whose Egoist Press very soon published McAlmon's first book of poems, Explorations *(1921). He and Bryher moved into their own apartment, but before long McAlmon "migrated" (his word) to Paris; and for the next five years he was to shuttle between London, Paris, and the Riviera, sometimes with Bryher, sometimes alone.*

McAlmon's most constant association with the literary figures of his time began in that spring of 1921. Paris, as the center of expatriate literary activity, was his main base of operations, and he quickly established himself in the cafés and bistros of the Left Bank. "I shared Bob McAlmon with the Dôme, the Dingo, and other such places," wrote Sylvia Beach, "but his permanent address was c/o Shakespeare and Company [her bookstore] and at

151

*least once a day he wandered in. . . . Except for his eyes, which
were a bright blue, [he was] not exactly good-looking. Yet, as a
rule, he attracted people, and I knew few who did so as much.
Even his nasal drawl seemed a part of his charm. He was certainly
the most popular member of 'the Crowd,' as he called it. Somehow,
he dominated whatever group he was in. Whatever café or bar
McAlmon patronized at the moment was the one where you saw
everybody. Bob was so busy sharing ideas with his friends or listening attentively and with sympathy to their stories of frustration
that he neglected his craft, which was supposed to be writing. . . .
His talents made him one of the most interesting personalities of
the twenties. His ample means, unique in the Bohemian world,
contributed not a little to his popularity. The drinks were always
on him, and alas! often in him."* [2]

Unlike many of McAlmon's short pieces, which were on-the-
spot reports of current happenings, Being Geniuses Together
(*1938*), his memoirs of the lost generation, was written some years
after "the Crowd" had disappeared from the Left Bank. Its judgments benefit from hindsight, but it is marred by errors of fact
which Martin Secker and Warburg, his distinguished London publishers, could not seem to get corrected. The published book, while
a good deal bulkier than anything he had ever had printed, is yet
only a fraction of his sprawling (lost) manuscript. Breezy, slapdash,
and unorganized, the book remains a fascinating, perceptive, and
relentlessly candid account of the expatriate world of letters in the
years between the two great wars. Historians of the twenties have
repeatedly pillaged it without acknowledgment.

Wealth Breeds Complication

In 1920 the atmosphere of New York had been postwar despairing, but various poets were then raising passionate voices in
rebellion against puritanism, shouting America's need for an indigenous culture, so that finally London, never a city bubbling

with gaiety, struck me as sodden with despair. One had to admit that there were intelligences and talented beings about capable of invention and execution; nevertheless, from the first moment of leaving the train at Victoria station I found the smoky heaviness of the city muffling as a dull illness driving one into a despairing delirium.

I had married a girl under her writing name, and when getting the licence and informed of her family name it meant little to me. However, I knew she was connected with great wealth, and was warned that her parents were difficult, as her father was a self-made man. The Audley Street house was, as Bryher warned me, "a stuffy old museum," and conversation at mealtimes was cautious and restrained so that servants would not overhear. The rooms, halls, and staircase walls were lined with French paintings of the photographically sentimental and academic kind at their most banal. I recall no picture by any painter of whom I had ever heard. Sir John, however, did have his own tastes, for which I respected him, because nothing can compete with the vulgarity of snobbist or bought correct taste. In the dining room were cow-pasture and woodland scenes; in the library was a glistening white statue of a high-bosomed young girl lifting eager lips to a cluster of grapes. There was also a painting of geese on the village downs, but of that more later.

Although then I violently disliked and was depressed by London and its morale, it would be unjust to blame on the city the involved and unusually complicated household in which I found myself. Wealth, the war, and the phobias, manias, dementias, prejudices, and terrors that come from both, were the dominant factors. Bryher's life had been unfree throughout her childhood years. She had never been allowed proper pets or friendships. One could not do this or that, know so and so, one was being used, such and such a person was trying to know one simply because of the wealth in the offing. People wished to use me to get at Sir John, or to get "something on" the family possessing this vast wealth. There may have been some reason behind these fears, but the nightmare throng of potential blackmailers, people knowing one only for money's sake, and artists seeking to be patronized and financed never struck me as overpoweringly great. On the other hand it seemed that the family led a frighteningly antisocial and lonely life, with their few "friends" or acquaintances, business associates or, more actually, employees of Sir John. Her ladyship was deaf, and Sir John was jealous of her friendships, so that years before she had renounced most of the friends of a more gregarious and buoyant girlhood. I came to understand, soon, that she cared as little for Sir John's dismal sisters as later I cared. If the nephews and nieces—or the aunts and uncles for that matter —had a liveliness within them, all show of spirit which they might possess they resolutely renounced upon entering Audley Street, into the presence of Sir John and her ladyship, who when in a mood was sure to speak her irritations and mind without restraint.

For a man who had a monomania for planning his family's life to the minutest detail—what plays to attend, who to see and when, what motor run to take on what day and hour—Sir John was surprisingly noninterfering with me. The fact of my being a minister's son impressed him at the first moment, and he feared that I might disapprove of his serving wines and whisky at and after meals. That theory of his was soon discredited, but my being an American caused him to view me as alien, strange, one whose reactions he could not judge. In fact after two weeks of our presence in the household he looked a bit harried. Bryher had theories on education which she thought advanced, and which no one but a person of great wealth could put into practice. She was pert also about telling mamma and dada her ideas, and in front of the servants. I too never did learn to be careful in front of the servants, feeling sure that they would gossip downstairs as much if we restrained ourselves as if we didn't. In fact my first move was to let the butler realize me as a weak mortal, so that I could have an ally in the household when returning home late at night in a condition which the Spanish call "joyous."

The parental attitude towards John, the twelve-year-old son, appalled me. It was impossible to think it improper for the lad to walk across Hyde Park in other than a bowler hat; there was no sane reason why he should not ride in taxis or buses and learn to pay for himself, realizing costs and the value of money in relation to various objects or pastimes. He did not then know the difference in value between a sixpence, a shilling, or a halfcrown; he was taken wherever he went by his parents, a governess, or tutor, in either the Rolls-Royce or the Lanchester. Too much protective guarding certainly then cramped that boy's life, and his sister talked to him of what a disgrace it was that the parents should treat him as helpless, as they had her, a girl, and in so doing ruined her capacity for full self-expression and enjoyment of life.

It was six weeks before we moved into a service flat, and that was a great error for me, who already had a belly-full of London without that contact with the dim and stuffy anglo-respectables. Of nomad stock, my unrest became more of a fever than ever. Bryher, with her fervor for education, had taken on the up-bringing of Hilda Doolittle's infant. It had black hair and eyes, an utterly blithe disregarding disposition, and at the time looked a Japanese Empress in miniature. Hilda, an American, understood my wails, but explained that the war had cleaned out all of the best young people of the generation. She produced red-haired Brigit Patmore, and Brigit in turn endeavored to produce some gayer young women of the town, but London had me against it. Taking a chance that Wyndham Lewis might know of me I wrote him a note, was answered by telegram and 'phoned him to make an appointment for that night, so quick had been the exchange of postal-telegraph service.

At five there was no Lewis at Verrey's, nor at five-fifteen, but at about five-thirty a figure emerged from the shadows of the nearby corner. His hat shaded his eyes and a faded blue scarf was in disarray about his neck. His overcoat looked seedy. There was a pause and I spoke to ascertain that it was Lewis. He peered suspiciously at me out of distrustful brown eyes; his small mouth was tight. After the first appraising glance, however, he relaxed. Later he confessed he had expected to meet an older man, for at the time I could pass as nineteen, and my open American manner lulled his distrusts. His manner soon became patronizing and sympathetic about my wail against the heaviness of London, atmospherically and socially.

It was not long before Lewis was doing what I came to look upon as a London pastime: informing me whom I could, or could not, properly know. Intrigue and distrusts and the talk of groups and cliques made up most of the conversation. Chelsea, Kensington, and Bloomsbury meant almost nothing to me, because my interest in the arts had always been for things Russian, Scandinavian, Italian, French, or Spanish. At the time things were very interesting as regards paint in Mexico, too, with the names of Rivera and Orozco gaining réclame. This talk of London group intrigues was vaguely irritating, because I intended to meet anybody regardless, and trust to healthy instinct and wit for self-protection. There were groups in New York, too, but why be alive if you can't like the battle of measuring your contempt or indifference or interest against that of others? In any case, somewhere, silently and without fuss or desire for réclame there is quite apt to be a man or woman who will turn out the masterpiece that puts to shame all the intriguers or politicians.

Believing that he knew of my relationship with wealth I mentioned Sir John, and when Lewis discovered that I was his son-in-law a peculiar change came over his manner. He became— not less protective and ready to show me about London, to warn me against the people whom I should not meet—but let me say, as Lewis would say, I mean to say, more interested in my personality. It seemed that there was nobody one could safely know in London; all of the painters were cribbing his style, or if not that they would not prove interesting to an alertly informed young American such as myself. I felt dismal about it all, because always I have been gregarious and used to companionship, and mainly undemanding.

Before the evening was over Lewis struck me as very sympathetic. He relaxed with a bottle or so of wine, was what we call boyish and confiding and almost lovable. I recall deciding that he was English and reserved, and that whenever I met him again I must let him remain so and see that we quickly drank enough for him to relax his reticence. By midnight he was talking subtly of how much could be done with a man of wealth like Sir John by one in my situation. There was art, there were artists, and there was a tradition that rich men should patronize contemporary artists.

I agreed entirely with Lewis about the futility of money not expended, but I was sceptical about my influence with Sir John. He was by no means the first rich man with whom I had been in contact, and I had some time ago decided that the money-makers on the grand scale are monomaniacs and fanatics and self-willed. Sir John had his own tastes in art, and when he talked of books, which was rarely, they were of boys' adventure books, mainly *Dead Man's Rock,* by Q. As regards finance he had the thing that need not be looked upon with awe, *genius,* but in many other aspects he was a perfect case of arrested development suffering innumerable childish fears. It was highly improbable that he could be interested in the paintings of Lewis; for already he was trying to woo me from the pitfalls of modern literature to secure for me a position on some proper publication such as *The Tatler, Sketch,* or *Sphere,* all of which he at the time controlled. He presented me to Clement Shorter, a man whose presence gave me the willies. The latter no doubt had his points, but his tobacco-stained moustache, his leering interest, his aversion to modern writers, and his wounded haughtiness when I did not care to attend some old-fogey literary club left me frozen. Having the young man's resentful belief that the war had killed off, in Europe and England, the best of my generation for moralizing hacks and elders, most worm-eaten old men with a patronizing attitude gave me the creeps in those days.

Nevertheless I did plan a campaign to help Lewis, whose drawings I liked. His paintings might have done if he had admitted them as literary or illustrative, but he would be "abstract." I might work through her ladyship to Sir John. She and I were definitely of the same spontaneous strain, and had got together to complain that none of the rest of them were human. Once any one of them got an idea in his head never would he consider what another might feel.

If in those days I had known a few of the sound, hearty, humorous London types whom I came to know later on other visits I might not have had such a hate on the city. But on every side I was warned that one doesn't go here or there, and I assumed that the warners meant the places were plainly dull and boring. Certainly the secretive whispering atmosphere of one restaurant was that, unless it was hysterically dismaying. It was there that Lewis took me the first night, and it was there that at one time he stopped my making some harmless remark. "Sh," he whispered, touching my arm and pointing with his thumb backwards towards an empty table. "They're listening."

One time, calling at his studio by appointment, he came to the door, opened but two inches. "Wait," he cautioned and closed the door. He was gone for two minutes before admitting me. I wondered where the model or naughty rendezvous or corpse was hidden, for there was no back exit to the studio. Recalling my earlier decision I suggested that we go to a pub and have a pale ale. After two ales he was "normal," and we went back to his studio, and it appears that he was doing a sketch of Lady somebody, whose name meant nothing to me. I gathered that he feared I might tell Dobson, or Roberts, or Wadsworth, none of whom I knew at the time. It was about that time too that he asked me had I ever heard that he looked like Shakespeare; at other times he was looking like Shelley or Swift; and again he asked if "they" had been telling me that his teeth were false, he wore a wig, was Jewish, and took five years off his age, and then he immediately explained that as the war had taken five years out of all our lives we had a right to lower our ages. Probably he never believed me when I told him the truth, that I knew absolutely none of the people about whom he talked. At least he sometimes took the attitude that I was a devilishly clever deceiver.

I decided to get in touch with T. S. Eliot, although his cautious articles on criticism did not impress me with his enthusiasm, erudition, scholarship, or sense of either life or literature. His mouldy poetry did strike me as perfect expression of a clerkly and liverish man's apprehension of life, and to me he was Prufrock. I prefer his then main influence, La Forgue. (Eliot never had Ezra Pound's health and vitality.) La Forgue's outlook at least had a fever and an alive wit, without the perverse intent upon being a "hollow man." Much of Eliot's poetry had been written before the war, so that I knew his "spirit" had not been created by war events.

At this time the Egoist Press published a book of my poetry, *Explorations,* but as nobody paid it any attention I need not apologize, and can dare to say that much worse had been done before and is being done yet by others. In it was a poem which was rather harsh on Eliot, and in America I had written an article which caused me to think he might not receive me with pleasure.

Don't Be Common

I telephoned Eliot so that if he wished he could quickly dismiss me. It was for me a method of escaping Audley Street and that awful service flat, and I had promised to stay in London for at least three months to placate the family. When Eliot was at the other end of the line and caught my name there was a pause, and he agreed to an appointment, but not today and not tomorrow, but would I 'phone again? I thought if he wished for an appointment he could drop me a note. He did. I was surprised to find him very likeable indeed, with a quality—to save sparring for words—of charm that few people possess. He looked tired and overworked, which was understandable as he was then employed in a bank. Present that first evening was J. W. N. Sullivan, who at the time was religious and worshipful about Dostoevsky, mainly *The Brothers Karamazov*. We drank a quantity of whisky and the evening was amiable and entertaining. Eliot and I indulged in a bit of "leg-pulling" with Sullivan, trying to convince him that Dostoevsky was too much a soul-searcher to be an artist, but Sullivan brought in higher mathematics and a wealth of earnestness. We none of us proved a thing, but we did have a sociable time. After leaving Eliot, fairly early as his wife was an invalid, Sullivan took me to the Café Royal, but it was a bad night, and I didn't click to the fact that so much as there was a general hangout for "people of the town," this was it.

During the course of the evening at Eliot's I had evidently regretted my comments on him in a New York paper. At any rate he wrote me: "As for your criticism, it was so intelligent that you need not worry about my opinion of it. I like your mind and that is all that matters."

I mention this for this matter of intelligence and Eliot comes up later, in connection with a magazine, which called itself *The Criterion*.

While in Paris I heard from him again and his letter made me feel that distinctly never would he and I agree on what makes literature or life. He said of Paris that the right way to take it is as a place and a tradition, rather than as a congeries of people, who are mostly futile and time-wasting, except when you want to pass an evening agreeably in a café. When he was living there years ago he had only the genuine stimulus of the place, as he knew no one whatever, in the literary or artistic world, as a companion—knew them rather as spectacles, listened to, at rare occasions, but never spoken to. Joyce he admired as a person who seemed to be independent of outside stimulus (had he read Joyce's *Ulysses?*). He was sure Julien Benda was worth knowing, and possibly Paul Valéry.

There was your snob-governess attitude. Possibly the lives of the Elizabethans and Greeks would indicate Eliot's attitude wrong, and it is hard to understand what gives validity to a tradition if it is not the lives and conventions of living people. Is Eliot afraid of the interchange of relationships, with their attractions and antagonisms and experiences? Derain, Brancusi, Proust, Picasso, Satie, and quantities of others of various races were in Paris at this period, and many of them spent much time in cafés and bistros, drinking considerably upon occasion.

Eliot appeals to the adolescent emotions of despair and defeat, it appears, but his cerebral tearfulness, his liverish and stomach-achey wail dominated his poetry during even his college days long before the war, at the time he was writing *The Portrait of a Lady,* and with artifice having people come and go talking of Michelangelo, while the long-haired Pole plays Beethoven. He became then quite a butler to the arts, the "classes," and later to the church. If Ezra Pound wrote of tradition and discipline it could be interesting, because he has interiorly disciplined his craft (when he is not scolding, but is being the poet he can be). He has at least not subjected himself to the sterile cant of a vested interest or religion, and when reading, for example, the compact impressions of Marianne Moore, does appear to understand what is being said, and that Miss Moore is as definitely modelling or sculpturing as, let us say cautiously, Benvenuto Cellini. However, others have detected that Eliot, in his essays, seems unable to realize the clearly stated meaning of certain sentences so that perhaps overcaution and gentility are so inherent in him as to stultify his "intelligence."

In Paris I had a note from Harriet Weaver, publisher of the Egoist Press, to present to James Joyce. His *Dubliners* I much liked. The Stephen Dedalus of his *Portrait of the Artist as a Young Man* struck me as precious, full of noble attitudinizings, and not very admirable in its soulful protestations. He seemed to enjoy his agonies with a self-righteousness which would not let the reader in on his actual ascetic ecstasies. Nevertheless, the short stories made me feel that Joyce would be approachable, as indeed did passages of *Ulysses,* which had already appeared in *The Little Review.*

At his place on the Boulevard Raspail I was greeted by Mrs. Joyce, and although there was a legend that Joyce's eyes were weak, it was evident that he had used eyesight in choosing his wife. She was very pretty, with a great deal of simple dignity and a reassuring manner. Joyce finally appeared, having just got up from bed. Within a few minutes it was obvious that he and I would get on. Neither of us knew anybody much in Paris, and both of us like companionship. As I was leaving he suggested that we have dinner together that night, and we did meet at eight for an apéritif and later went to dine.

At that time Joyce was by no means a worldly man, or the man who could later write to the Irish Academy that living in Paris as he did it was difficult to realize the importance of their academy. He had come but recently from Zurich, and before that Trieste, in both of which cities he had taught languages at the Berlitz school to support his family. He was still a Dublin-Irish provincial, as well as a Jesuit-Catholic provincial, although in revolt. He refused to understand that questions of theology did not disturb or interest me, and never had. When I assured him that instead of the usual "religious crises" in one's adolescent life I had studied logic and metaphysics and remained agnostic, he did not listen. He would talk about the fine points of religion and ethics as he had been taught by the Jesuits. His favorite authors were Cardinal Newman and St. Thomas Aquinas, and I had read neither. He told me some tale of how St. Thomas once cracked a woman—possibly a prostitute—over the head with a chair, and explained that the Jesuits were clever at logic. They would justify anything if it suited their purposes.

He was working on *Ulysses* at the time and often would make appointments to read rather lengthy extracts of what he had most recently written. Probably he read to me about a third of the book. It was impressive to observe how everything was grist to his mill. He was constantly leaping upon phrases and bits of slang which came naturally from my American lips, and one night, when he was slightly excited, he wept a bit while explaining his love or infatuation for words. Long before this explanation I had recognized that malady in him, as probably every writer has had that disease at some time or other, generally in his younger years. Joyce never recovered. He loved particularly words like "ineluctable," "metempsychosis"—grey, clear, abstract, fine-sounding words that are "ineluctable" a bit themselves. Had I been older and less diffident before him in those days I would have given him *Irene Iddesleigh* to read. Her author also loved words, and flung her work "upon the oases of futurity," hoping as did Joyce of *Ulysses* that it would not be consigned to "the false bosom of buried scorn." I don't think I ever did get to telling Joyce that the high-minded struttings and the word prettifications and the Greek beauty part of his writings palled on me, as did Stephen Dedalus when he grew too noble and forebearing. Stephen's agonies about carnal sin seemed melodramatic, but perhaps they were not so. Several years later a son of Augustus John, Henry, who was studying to be a priest, wrote essays and letters equally intent upon carnal desire and the searing sin of weakening. Mercifully I was not brought up by the Jesuits.

Almost every night Joyce and I met for apéritifs, and although he was working steadily on *Ulysses,* at least one night a week he was ready to stay out all night, and those nights he was never ready to go home at any hour. We talked of the way the free mind can understand the possibility of all things: necrophilia and other weird rites. We agreed in disliking mysticism, particularly the fake and sugared mysticism of many poets and writers. We spoke of what a strange man Robert Burton must have been to have compiled his *Anatomy of Melancholy,* and he didn't know in the end a bit more about it than we did. Sir Thomas

Browne, not to speak of Ezra Pound and Eliot and Moore and Shaw, we discussed, but sooner or later Mr. Joyce began reciting Dante in sonorous Italian. When that misty and intent look came upon his face and into his eyes I knew that friend Joyce wasn't going home till early morning.

One night he wept in his cups when telling of the fertility of his forefathers. His father had parented a large family, and his grandfathers before him had been parents of families of from twelve to eighteen children. Joyce would sigh, and then pull himself together and swear that by the grace of God he was still a young man and he would have more children before the end. He didn't detect that I, the youngest of ten children of a poor minister, did not fancy his idea. He would not listen when I suggested that if one is to produce children one had better have the money to educate and care for them in the childhood years.

One night at Michaud's we picked up with two men, supposedly Frenchmen. One of them, slightly bald, with light, curly hair and a round, naughty-schoolboy face, talked to me and scoffed at Joyce, Pound, Wyndham Lewis, etc. He did not apparently know that Joyce was the man present. He refused to speak English, however, although he seemed to know contemporary English writers and their works. When asked his name he said "Clive Bell." Having assured me he was French I answered, "Yes, there's an English phrase-slinger with the same name. Are you a relation of his?" I recalled that Eliot had told me Bell was a most agreeable person if you did not take him seriously, and a waste of time if you did. The Bell lad was too full of mischief for me, the rascal. Joyce was busy talking to the other man, really a Frenchman, a painting critic, but he was as ready to depart as was I when I explained that Bell thought it bright to talk only French, which I understood poorly.

At the time Valéry Larbaud, the French author-critic, was keen about Joyce's work and had written his article, noting *Ulysses* as the first Irish book to belong to world literature. He dined with us at times and we generally went later to the Gypsy Bar off the Boul' Mich'. It was generally empty, a large bar-hall, but students and their mistresses collected there some nights, and a three-piece orchestra played American jazz very badly, and the *poules* pranced about, dancing together and waggling their behinds with much energy to indicate that they were enjoying themselves. They laughed shrilly and were bawdy and reckless and ready for arguments or battles among themselves.

Wyndham Lewis arrived for a stay in Paris and he was a different man from the Lewis of London. He was free and easy and debonair. Indeed, too many Englishmen will do on the continent what it does not do to do in London. Lewis was intent upon going to the Picasso exhibition; he must meet Picasso and Braque and Derain, although these painters of Paris were cagey and suspicious about English painters of talent. Picasso at the time was doing his pneumatic nudes, which always made me want to stick a pin in them to see if they would deflate.

Lewis was most gracious and jovial and instructed me with a constant flow of theories on abstraction and plastic values. It would not have done to let him know that I had heard most of what he was saying before, in New York. Somehow there was no wonder in Lewis' discovery that the engineering demand of structures often give them an æsthetic value. The Egyptians, Greeks, and Mayans seemed to have known that before Lewis.

It was spring, however, and for a time Lewis, Joyce, and myself met nightly, and upon occasions would stay out till nearly dawn. The Gypsy Bar was usually our late night hangout. The patron and the "girls" knew us well, and knew that we would drink freely and surely stay till four or five in the morning. The girls of the place collected at our table, and indulged in their Burgundian and Rabelaisian humors. Jeannette, a big draughthorse of a girl from Dijon, pranced about like a mare in heat and restrained no remark or impulse which came to her. Alys, sweet and pretty blonde, looked fragile and delicate, but led Jeannette to bawdier vulgarities of speech and action. Joyce, watching, would be amused, but surely there came a time when drink so moved his spirit that he began quoting from his own work or reciting long passages of Dante in rolling and sonorous Italian. I believed that Joyce might have been a priest upon hearing him recite Dante as though saying mass. Lewis sometimes came through with recitations of Verlaine, but he did not get the owl-eyes and mesmerized expression upon his face which was Joyce's automatically. Amid the clink of glasses, jazz music badly played by a French orchestra, the chatter and laughter of the girls, Joyce went on reciting Dante. I danced with Alys, and even sometimes with Jeannette, but she was six foot and buxom, and dancing, seemed not to realize that I was there at all.

Frank Dobson, the English sculptor, also turned up and joined our nightly wanderings, and with him was Stephen Tomlin, student-sculptor to Dobson. In those days the English did Paris frequently; they seem not to now; but in all I think that in spite of or possibly because of it being postwar, people were better willed, more reckless perhaps, but gayer than now. They had not suffered peace long enough to have grown cranky and sour; and of course as regards these of whom I am writing, no one had become an acclaimed "great man" or "genius." There might have been slumbering envies and animosities, but Paris lulled them and each knew that not only he but the others had to struggle for recognition of any proper sort.

Ezra Pound was in town also, and I dropped him a note. He had been a boyhood friend of William Carlos Williams and of Hilda Doolittle (H.D.), and I wrote to him as a friend of theirs and not as to an older poet. He had not written any of his cantos at the time (to my knowledge), and while I mildly liked a poem or so of his, I disliked his critical work generally. Emanuel Carnevali had, in *Poetry* of Chicago, written a review of Ezra's work, declaring the main impulse behind it was irritation. I agreed, but Bill Williams and Hilda both assured me he was—he was—Ezra. I could understand that he was a bit of a character and perhaps difficult, but I'm not easy.

We met and had lunch together. Ezra hemmed and hawed and talked of writing, being very instructorial indeed. I was merely wanting to find out about Paris and its pastimes. Over coffee he sat back from the table, hemmed and hawed, threw one leg over the other, then reversed. He had a Van Dykish beard and an 1890-ish artist's get-up. I did detect that Ezra was shy and within limits kindly, but I was and am shy also if anybody will believe it. Having been a reporter and an advertising copy writer and salesman, and between times more or less a hobo of a not too sublime order, I may have been forced to hide shyness more than Ezra, who has been mainly and perhaps too exclusively literary and the poet, a bit troubadourish.

When editing *Contact* with Bill Williams I had written two

big-worded "poems," razzing Ezra and Eliot. At lunch I mentioned Carnevali. Ezra knew both my poem and Carnevali's
criticism, I thought. At any rate there was discomfiture in the
air for us both. That might have passed, but two days later somebody informed me that Ezra made a comment, "Well, well, another young one wanting me to make a poet out of him with
nothing to work on."

My answer when told that is unprintable, but it said clearly
that he had better discover whether these young ones liked his
work and mind before being the martyred schoolmaster. I had
looked him up at the behest of Williams, for comradely and not
for art reasons. Perhaps remarks of mine got back to Ezra; at any
rate it was about a year before we stopped avoiding each other,
although often we would be in the same group with Joyce, Lewis,
Rodker, Dobson, and others. Joyce and Lewis talked to each of
us, persuading us that we shouldn't be antagonistic. The thing
passed off; perhaps I, perhaps Ezra, became less touchy and
precious about sensibility. In any case, while I still do not care
for the irritated portion in his work, I thoroughly admire his
poetry and much of his criticism, and would hand *How to Read*
to every youngster with brightness by the time he is twelve years
old. There is much about the sociologic, psychologic, atmospheric,
and documentary values in literature that he does not mention
in the book, but he makes no pretence of covering the entire
field. Ezra may be a bit too much the poet poetizing, but no one
touches him for craft and the power of evocation when he suc-
ceeds. Where Eliot is mouldery and sogs and is everlastingly the
adolescent who will perversely be an old man blubbering, Ezra
is hard, and his images flash at you and awaken clear and stimu-
lating response. Where Joyce goes Irish-twilighty and uses words
for their isolated beauty, without attaining much more than the
beauty of the word alone as it stands in the dictionary, Ezra gives
entire passages, which evoke historic and legendary memories, and
satirizes coolly. His cantos do not carry on throughout. They are
jumpy, often axe-grinding, pedantic, scolding, but there are other
passages which compensate, and no poem of such length carries
on throughout the whole. Homer's *Iliad* and *Odyssey* are narrative and epic novels; but *The Divine Comedy* of Dante and
Milton's *Paradise Lost* are insufferably boring through long pas-

sages—and to me particularly, because they possess the medieval or Catholic mind.

Ezra once said that advice does nobody any good. We must learn by experience. He won't keep on knowing that. He will be a bit the pedagogue yearning for pupils to instruct, and I, whether I write well or badly, have my idea of how I want to do it. Since we have been friendly, now some ten years, he has given me many a pointer which sometimes I am able to use, but I wonder does he still think that young writers put themselves into the hands of older to be taught how. We have such different approaches and things to say.

The influx of people who came to be called "expatriates" had begun before this, but they hung out in Montparnasse at the Dome and the Rotonde. At the time I was doing Lipps, the Deux Magots, various bistrots, all around St. Germain, or Boulevard Saint Michel. I was hardly aware of Montparnasse. In the day-time I was busy writing the short stories which went into *A Hasty Bunch*, a title which Joyce suggested because he found my American use of the language racy. I was at that six weeks, and as it was finished a flock of "expatriates" descended upon the rue Jacob, Saint-Pere, St. Germain section. They were Kate Buss, critic for some Boston paper, Djuna Barnes, the *Broom* outfit— Alfred Kreymborg, Harold Loeb, Frances Midner, late of the Washington Square Bookshop, and Kreymborg's wife, Dorothy. They all stayed in the same hotel, and Vicki Baum's *Grand Hotel* couldn't touch the drama and intrigue which occurred in that hotel, but as I didn't stay there, that is somebody else's story, and I fear the rest will be silence. At any rate the *Broom* outfit meant to be literary at all costs. How that little group of pilgrim ex-patriates loved each other. As some child once noted to the re-mark "little birds in their nest agree," "They do since when? That's my worm."

I had known Djuna slightly in New York, because Djuna was a very haughty lady, quick on the uptake, and with a wise-cracking tongue that I was far too discreet to try and rival. It seemed, however, that once I had written a letter to *The Little Review*, asking how came it that Miss Barnes was both so Russian and so Synge-Irish. Some comment in the letter Jane Heap ap-parently used frequently to cow Djuna, and Jane kept assuring her that McAlmon was not taken in by her cape-throwing gesture but understood her for the sentimentalist which she was. In the end Djuna had gathered the idea that I disliked her, and that I was a very sarcastic individual. She was wrong about the first idea at least, for Djuna is far too good-looking and witty not to command fondness and admiration from me, even when she is rather overdoing the grande dame manner and talking soul and ideals. In conversation she is often great with her comedy, but in writing she appears to believe she must inject metaphysics, mysticism, and her own strange version of a "literary" quality into her work. In her *Nightwood* she has a well-known character floundering in the torments of soul-probing and fake philosophies, and he just shouldn't. The actual person doubtlessly suffers enough without having added to his character this unbelievable dipping into the deeper meanings. Drawn as a wildly ribald and often broadly funny comic he would emerge more impressively.

With Frances Midner, Djuna and I went one night to the Bal Bullier, where we had a few drinks. I finally asked her to dance with me, drink having freed me of the fear of a rebuff. As we danced she said, "Bob McAlmon, why do you act nice to me? You know you hate my guts." Of course denials and explanations took place, over more drink. For with late spring on Djuna and I were all over Paris, as though it was a college campus for a boy and a girl, as it seemed for the masses of Americans who arrived in Paris that year.

Joyce had to go into retirement after a particularly hard week. And for whatever I say later or have said before about Joyce "nobly the martyr," during these days he suffered, and physical agony is distressing to watch. I realized that his eyes were weak, but I didn't know that he probably was doing heavier drinking than he had for years, worried about money, and too intensely at work on *Ulysses* so that Miss Beach could publish it.

We went one night to the Brasserie Lutetia, and he ordered, as usual, that horrible natural champagne. I did not know wines then and thought he did. We had but one glass when suddenly I saw a rat running down the stairs from the floor above. I exclaimed upon it.

"Where, where?" he said nervously. "That's bad luck."

Earlier in the evening he had been superstitious about the

way the knife and fork were placed on the table, and about the way I poured wine. I thought his superstition more or less *blague*. It wasn't, however. Within a minute after my exclaiming about the rat Joyce was out, blank. I got him into the taxi and drove to the rue Cardinal Lemoine, where he was living in a flat lent him by Valéry Larbaud. There was a huge iron gate to the court-yard, and a key which was about a foot long. I wobbled it back and forth in the lock for ten minutes and finally got the gate open. The taxi driver carried him through the courtyard and up two flights of stairs, where we deposited him and I explained to Norah. She had started to scold him, but turned tender at once, realizing that it was a fright and not drink which had put him in this condition.

The next night we were having coffee and liqueur at the Café d'Harcourt when Norah suddenly called a taxi. Joyce's face showed that he was in terrible pain. I saw them home. For the next several weeks Joyce was in bed, suffering torture with his eyes. For many days the doctor pumped cocaine into the eyes to relieve the agony. After a week when I called to see him his face was a death mask drawn with pain; mere skin over bone. It frightened me and I decided never to drink heavily with Joyce again, but that decision was useless. Like myself, when Joyce wants to drink he will drink. Furthermore, when months later I next saw him he had finished *Ulysses,* it was just about to appear, and he was feeling anxious but lively, and enough had happened to me so that I had forgotten the picture of him suffering eye-torture.

Mina Loy passed through Paris en route to Florence to pick up her children. She lingered, naturally, having known Paris before the war, in the days of Apollinaire, Arthur Craven, Picabia, Marinetti. As summer came, crossing and recrossing between the Dome and the Rotonde of an evening—I had discovered the quarter by then all right—anybody from the writing or art world of any country was apt to appear and quite as apt to be dead drunk or mildly intoxicated. I know that many of them betray their own strong or weak moments, as you wish to call them. They went back to their own countries—the Americans were the worst—and wrote righteous and moralizing articles and editorials on ex-patriate life on the continent. Such articles always disgust me, because knowing London and her pubs, New York and her speak-easies, as well as Paris, I see no use in the lousy pretence that people who drink don't drink elsewhere than in Paris. I never have been able to fix just what it is that make some of us expatriates either; many others who spend as much time on the continent do not get so dubbed.

One night Djuna Barnes and I were at the Gypsy Bar when Sinclair Lewis barged in. He evidently had written a story about Hobohemia in which he feared Djuna would believe he had used her as one of the characters. Or perhaps he merely had an admiring eye for Djuna or a respect for her undoubted talent, however uneven it may be. But Djuna was not going to get chummy. I recall that Lewis looked wistful and went away from the table, without Djuna having introduced him.

A few nights later I was at the Jockey and had ordered pancakes, but upon seeing them decided they would not sit well on the firewater in my stomach. Lewis was there, with Lewis Galantière and George Slocombe, both of whom disclaimed a desire to have the pancakes. Lewis wanted them and went to my table where I introduced him to a girl there. I had been shaking dice at the bar myself, but now sat down. Some woman rushed up exclaiming, "Red, I'm so glad to see you," kissing Lewis.

A tough little flapper who was looking on muttered something not complimentary to Lewis and his personal beauty. The phrase "withered carrot" occurred. Lewis turned redder than usual and said, "Do you know you are speaking to a man of international fame?" The flapper was unimpressed. I saw Lewis grow pale, his hands trembling, and assured him the pancakes were too heavy. He had better let them go. This man who wrote of Main Street and Babbitt was thus upset by a flapper trying to be clever. I told her she was a silly bitch and she understood. Soon Lewis went away, although not before several of us assured him that there wasn't a beauty, male or female, in the joint. He remained upset, however.

Another night a group of us sat on the terrace of the Swedish restaurant, the Stryx. Mina Loy, Harriet Monroe, and others were at the table. Sinclair Lewis came by and said to me, "Bob, I want you to meet Gracie. People say she is difficult, but maybe you won't find her so."

One had heard of Gracie, and there seemed no reason for my meeting her particularly. However, I answered, "Rot, you aren't, are you? Come into the bar and have a drink where your husband can't pick on you."

She went to the bar and we ordered gin fizzes and then suddenly she fired three questions at me, which asked if I thought Lewis the greatest American writer, a fine artist, America's first. Her questions were too fast, and I said so, whereupon she flew out of the door refusing to drink with me. At the time I had read neither *Main Street* nor *Babbitt,* and had read only the short stories of Lewis written in his pulp-magazine days. His Hobohemia had struck me as a concession to the newspapers' ideas of Greenwich Village and Bohemia, and I conjectured that he didn't know a bit more about Main Street, or Minneapolis, or Babbitts, than did I. Our backgrounds were not unlike. I did, however, suspect that he carried Main Street about in his own mind, and that he chose to write the dullest aspects of small town life and types, and I had memories of rather alert and lively people in those middle western towns. They were types who later went away, and they were as ironic about the pretentious village-intellectuals of the sort Lewis depicted as Lewis could be. No, Gracie, I didn't then and don't now, after having read *Babbitt,* think Lewis even a good second-rater. He gives to the travelling salesman, the fake-superior pseudo-intellectual, and to the Europeans a picture of America which they like to believe, to feel their superiority. He fits in with Mencken and his Americana, but before him there had been Stephen Crane, Henry James, and at the time Dos Passos had drawn wholly and in a characterized way, several human beings in his *Three Soldiers.* Edith Wharton's *Ethan Frome* is worth more than all Lewis has written.

Gracie later consented to finish her drink and to talk to me, but she was sure that I was a *Little Review* snob, although at the time *The Little Review* girls and I did not care at all for each other. It occurred to me that perhaps Lewis had secret "art" yearnings. He had apologized to Djuna for his Hobohemia, and here was his wife thinking me *Little Review.*

Another season Lewis was silenced at the Dome. An admirer was assuring him that he drew better characters than Flaubert, but that perhaps Flaubert had the better style. Lewis, a bit intoxicated, insisted that he depicted character and also had a better style than Flaubert. He asserted it while standing, and someone shouted, "Sit down. You're just a best-seller." Again Lewis was crushed, and amazed old quarterites by bothering to boast in the Quarter or the Dome. If he were the world's greatest artist some nobody would shout him down there, very likely.

It appears at one time that he thought Wells great, and Wells smilingly admits himself not of the first rank. He is still more interesting to read, however, than Lewis. Lewis might better have read a bit of Trollope, however, to learn how to depict character and situation and also to placate the *mores* of the larger public. As he writes his penetration is not keen, for he misses all but the hick-uplifters and the boobs of American small towns and cities, and Europe also produces a great variety of sappy and pretentious morons. So far as art or writing is concerned I recall not a paragraph written by Lewis which gives one a joy in its velocity or suggestive quality. He is too intent on types to depict character.

The Nightinghoul's Crying

Miss Harriet Weaver of the Egoist Press had subsidized Joyce so that he was able to complete *Ulysses*. She had at the time given up the publication *The Egoist* and the publishing business. Before and during the war she edited the paper, first as a feminist sheet, and later as sponsor for the new poetry movement. In *The Egoist* appeared the works of Ezra Pound, William Carlos Williams, H.D., Richard Aldington, Wyndham Lewis, Marianne Moore, Storm Jameson, Joyce, and others, many for the first time in any publication.

There had been an episode when I was last in Paris. It seemed that Miss Weaver got word that Joyce drank, even to intoxication. She was frightened of drunken people, and pained to hear the report, and she wrote to Joyce expressing her fear. Since Eliot believes Joyce capable of working without "outward stimulus," it is not surprising, considering Miss Weaver's background, that she should have read *Ulysses* without noting that he knew a bit about bars and brothels. Perhaps she did not even know what particular passages in the book meant, or thought it all "pure" imagination.

Miss Weaver told me a little of her background. She had grown up as a Quaker and her family were most orthodox and severe. When she was nineteen she was caught reading George Eliot's *Mill on the Floss* and was publicly reprimanded from the pulpit by the village minister. Later she had freed herself intellectually, but still she disliked hurting people, namely her family, so that she feared she was a bit of a coward about "facing reality." She published the works of Dora Marsden, who was writing an apparently endless book dealing with metaphysics from the feminine aspect. It was for Miss Marsden's work that Miss Weaver began publishing a paper.

Joyce in Paris worried because of her anxiety about his drinking. I wrote her a letter explaining that he drank, but in moderation, and my letter assured her that so gentle a type as Joyce became merely released with drink, but never did he fail to hold his drink properly and as a gentleman. His courtesy was unfailing. In London I called upon her. She is . . . reticent or shy? Difficult to get at in any case. She would let me talk and answer with a short-gasped "yes" or "no," and looked into space. Whether she heard or was bored stiff I couldn't say. I feared that she believed I led Joyce astray, and his income then was dependent upon her. At last she came through with a confession: she feared she had never faced life with sufficient courage to know reality. She had been afraid from her childhood days of people who drank, but she agreed with my point. Joyce was working and well, and it was by that she was to judge him, but she hoped to be spared seeing him intoxicated, and she did hope some day to meet him. Yes, she would consider visiting Paris if she would not be in the way; she would cross over with Bryher and H.D. and myself when we left in a few days' time.

It is some kind of commentary on the period that Joyce's work and acclaim should have been fostered mainly by high-minded ladies, rather than by men. Ezra first brought him to Miss Weaver's attention, but she then supported him. *The Little Review,* and

Sylvia Beach, and she brought him into print. Somebody else can draw conclusions from the fact that now an amazing number of women are to be considered as artists without asking consideration as feminine authors.

There was a charming old man for dinner at Audley Street one night, asked in by her ladyship because Sir John's associates always talked business over their after-dinner cigars. His name was, I believe, Smedley, and he had a valuable Shakespearian library. It went later to a museum in America. Mr. Smedley was intent upon proving Shakespeare Bacon, and gave me a book telling of Shakespeare's life as a draper's assistant. His proofs sounded perfect and he was far too sweet for me not to agree with him that Shakespeare was whoever he yearned to have him. After dinner, however, Mr. Smedley, nearing eighty, became very sad about my generation and there having been a war, and he was depressed about life. There were tears in his aged eyes, so thinking to buck him up by proving that my generation was not licked yet, and that there had been the spirit of futility in the world before, I mentioned St. Augustine, Job, and quoted Hamlet's soliloquy, suggesting that even Bacon had felt despair. The old man broke into tears. Sir John and I looked helplessly at each other, and each reached for the bottle of brandy to fill first Mr. Smedley's glass, and then the other two. The old man was a staunch soul, and not gone in senility. He had lost a son in the war, and his tears were doubtless for more than a sentimental notion about the young. During the spell of his weeping there was a true bond of sympathy between Sir John and myself, and little as I could ever understand his financial and other obsessions, there were small moments that revealed delicacy and sensibility in his nature.

Her ladyship had a spell of the grippe and we prolonged our visit. Frank Dobson suggested modelling my head and to pass the time I submitted, thinking that perhaps her ladyship might buy it. Dobson at least understood that had I the say-so I'd have had several artists, good, bad, and indifferent, subsidized by Sir John. The other man's art is not my affair and so long as I saw that he was a serious worker my attitude was to give him a chance. I hadn't any say-so, however. Sir John believed that a writer's or painter's work should sell and that an artist should make his own way.

At one sitting for Dobson a man named Lawrence came and watched for well over an hour and talked of excavating near Sumer. He brought a small statuette, which he gave to Mrs. Dobson. It was not until after he had left that I was aware that this was the Colonel Lawrence of Arabia. I would have been more curious, for there were varying reports as to his achievements and as regards his personal magnetism. At the time he was feeling let down and disillusioned because of his treatment by the government; at any rate the impression he left on my memory was not a strong one. It is difficult to conceive of him as a bold leader of desert bedouins.

Dobson finished his head of me and it looked like a gaping fish. Perhaps Dobson has spiritual insight. But her ladyship looked at the head, made little comment, did not buy, and there the matter dropped. Perhaps it would not have fitted so well into the library interior. There the high-bosomed girl eating grapes bespoke herself the star with glistening white.

As her ladyship kept to her room while ill I took my chance to eat out every night, and generally at the Eiffel Tower, which was the rendezvous for what people I knew, ones mainly I had met in Paris. Tommy Earp, Nina Hamnett, Nancy Cunard, Curtiss Moffat, Iris Tree, Dobson, and others. And Augustus John drifted in frequently to hold court. The place was small enough and the habitués well enough known to each other so that usually we got together, often upstairs in the private dining room if strangers arrived in any quantity.

Tommy Earp and I were sitting together when Ronald Firbank came through the door. I knew of him by name only. He was introduced, tittered nervously, covered his face with his long hands, and would not stay to talk. "I'm nervous," he giggled. It was possible for me to believe that this was not affectation, as I looked Ronald over. He was tall and thin, with a high nose and cheekbones and color. He belonged to the Aubrey Beardsley tradition, or more properly to the court entourage of one of the more decadent Cæsars, such as Heliogabalus.

He wouldn't stay and he wouldn't go. Finally I said, "Sit down, Ronald. I'm just a cowboy from the wild west, too dumb to cause you nerves."

He tittered and sat down, delighted to meet an American,

and at once began to show me letters from Carl Van Vechten, who certainly threw adjectives out of joint in expressing his admiration for Ronald's writing. Ronald was so pleased at the praise that I didn't answer when he asked about Van Vechten's writing, which he hadn't then read. Later he talked of the book which he was then doing, *The Flower Beneath the Foot,* and he was brightly malicious about what he would do in the way of caricature of an Oxford man against whom he had a grudge. Lewis came in that night, and Firbank, with some ten cocktails in him, was mildly at ease and consented to sit for Lewis the next day, for a sketch. He did, and the sketch was a fine one, although Lewis claims he couldn't get Ronald to stop fidgeting for ten seconds. However, he gave the sketch to Ronald, who promptly gave it to his publisher, Grant Richards, to use as a frontispiece in *The Flower Beneath the Foot.* Upon hearing of this Lewis was angry and insisted that either Ronald or the publisher pay him. Ronald, however, for all his butterfly flutterings, was strictly a business man. He was difficult to find, and the publisher said that the affair was not his.

The night before we were to leave for Paris, I was with Lewis and he said that we would drink quietly and have a good talk, but the Eiffel Tower, which he wanted to avoid, was just where I wanted to go. Lewis had been telling me that I must read a book by a Frenchman, Sorel, on the necessity of revolution. He was on the verge of bursting forth into an endless book, an endless series of books, and he told of Bogaraz, a Russian anthropologist of a past generation, who wrote that on the Peninsula of Kamchatka there were Shamins given to homosexuality. He mentioned Lewis Morgan (?) a little-credited sociologic-anthropologist of America, some fifty years back, who had said this and that. In all I gathered that Mr. Lewis had been spending a great deal of time at the British Museum, doing research work, and never would he deign to look at anybody contemporary or more or less respected by specialists in whatever particular line. He was researching for out-of-the-way and older and what he hoped were unknown authors and books.

In all, Lewis these days was being very much a man of many ideas, but most of them were other men's.

In London at the time it was being said by painters that

Lewis was a good writer but couldn't paint, and by writers that he was a good painter but couldn't write. I added mentally that he was naive if he thought that spending his days at the British Museum, in what he called research, was going to make him know what it was he wanted to prove. Reading books he has turned out by the volume since I wonder if he ever will know what he wants to tell the world, for the facts and statements in one of his paragraphs are destroyed by those in the following ones; just as he piles up adjectives to be horrifically satirical, only to have one adjective ruin the force of the other. In *The Apes of God* he is supposed to have been cruel to several people, whom I also know, but I could feel no force in the strained narration.

I submitted to a Bass at a quiet pub, but was restless; we had Bass at another pub, but still I felt restless. With every pub we got nearer to the Eiffel Tower. I was going there whether he came or not, but he came. He generally relaxed his intense aversions and became easy with a few drinks.

We were seated over a bottle of Moselle when Tommy Earp entered and stood, rather Pelicanish, looking dumbfounded with shyness as only Tommy can look. His arms dangled woodenly. It was a safe bet he'd had an absinthe or so and felt lonely. He seemed pinned to the floor. I went and asked him to join us.

"Really, Bob," he squeaked in his strange, semi-falsetto, or shattered, voice. "I rather fancy Lewis doesn't fancy me."

"What of it? Some people pet him too much in London and take too much from him. I'm off to Paris to-morrow, where they support artists better and cringe before them less."

It had not taken much over a year for me to get decidedly weary of the way in which certain types of English look on in awe if Augustus John, Epstein, or some well-known English artist heaves into sight, and the same artists go on year after year looking Whistlerian or 1890-ish, or arty-arty. Broad-rimmed hat, flowing tie, longish hair, velvet coat—the gesture. I never have recovered from the way newspaper reporters treated Brancusi in London, where he was showing at the same exhibition as Augustus John, Epstein, and Dobson. He did not speak English, but it would not have changed things if he had. They virtually ignored him. I fear also that the great English artists were none too courteous to him. Luckily I had an apartment then and took him there for drinks, and Brancusi being really unpretentious was happy enough. The English are a sporting race, no doubt, but it is rarely a book by an American gets reviewed in England on its merits. There is generally an undercut comment about it being American, and using the American language, of all things. Cocteau was wise enough never to bother giving any of his little shows in London. He let the Sitwells imitate him and the elderly ladies of the various sexes who are their public were just as pleased, since they were buying British.

Earp came to the table, slowly, his beady brown eyes glistening in a face that gave the effect of rosiness. At the suggestion of Lewis we went to the small dining room upstairs as it looked as though there might be a heavy after-theatre crowd this night. We were all jovial now. The waiter soon informed us that Mary Beerbohm was downstairs and had asked if anyone she knew was here.

"Poor Mary. She is so hating London. She wants company," Tommy Earp quavered.

Mary was hating London; so was I, and the others generally declared that they were too. Some of them were, because depressing as London can be normally, in those soon after the war days it shrieked ennui and despair, and no form of activity seemed worth the effort. Naturally Mary joined us.

Mary was authentically whimsical, by nature. None of the Peter Pan or Milne tosh. Mary's whimsy had a sense of reality and irony within it, but her manner was that of being in a continual state of wonder that she should be alive. She isn't now, and not because of that, but because Mary was what she was, every memory that remains of her to me is sweet.

She never was strong. Her face was a child's on a tall, slender body, and her legs looked breakable. A slight rash on her face gave it the appearance of a child's who has been at the jam jar. "Do give me some champagne," she wailed as she came into the room. "I'm so glad somebody is here. It's been too awful the last two days. Do you think we're going to have a thunderstorm? I woke up last night and thought I was going to faint in bed. I'm sure there's going to be a thunderstorm. They terrify me, and my heart beats so weakly." She looked around, her weak eyes bothered by the light and then smiled a wistful, understanding and sympathy-asking smile.

Mary was always thinking there was going to be a thunderstorm. It was her way of explaining that she had never recovered from air raids over London in the war. Her brother, of whom everybody who knew him expected great things, had been killed in the war. Mary had no defences. Some of the others had recklessness, hardness, rebellion, or hatred, or somebody to fight or to take care of. Mary had an elderly mother, but she was well provided for, and Mary was not made for defiances.

Tommy was sympathetic, as always. "Mary, darling, I understand how you feel, but I assure you it isn't going to thunder. You mustn't really stress the horrible things we can feel. It becomes too much to bear."

The atmosphere in those days was most terrifyingly afterwar, or was it only that I was young and did not know London?

"I'm sure if one were a scientist this would be an interesting age to live in, but one isn't a scientist and it isn't amusing," Mary said.

Lewis was feeling merry, but felt called upon to be sardonic. "War," he said prophetically. "An internal war that blasts the bourgeois aristocratic idea. Must happen every second generation."

He was at it again, spouting his old Frenchman, Sorel.

"I should die, simply die," Mary wailed.

Lewis explained how machines would fight the war, and talked of how ultimately we could have machines live our lives, and I added, have machines be our egos, too. In the end Lewis flowered into tremendous fantasy, and simultaneously Tommy Earp and I accused him of being a frustrated writer of tales for children. It did not daunt him. This was one of the nights when he forgot his idea of himself as a ruthless intellect.

The waiter, bringing more drink, told us that Ronald Firbank was downstairs and Mary Beerbohm at once wanted poor dear Ronald to join us. I went to collect him. Downstairs Ronald hid his face in his hands when I spoke to him. "I couldn't come up. I'd bore you all," he tittered.

Rudolph, the patron, chest pompous and protruding stomach, came up, "Ach, dis man," he said of Ronald. "Vot will ve do vit him? Alvays he drinks de cocktails, and eats de caviarre and pairheps de strawberries, but nefer he eats a meal. Und such good food ve haf. He vill be ill."

It was true. Of all the people who knew Ronald few ever saw him eat really solid food, and he frequently put twenty cocktails down in the course of an evening. He refused still more to come when he understood that Lewis was with us. "He is angry at me."

"Not if you'd give him a cheque for the sketch he did of you."

"I'm afraid," Ronald tittered. "He might tear up the cheque and throw it in my face."

"No chance. Let me hand it to him."

To my surprise Ronald made out a cheque and did come upstairs, and all was peace between him and Lewis, who certainly looked upon Ronald as an exotic. Once there Ronald ordered more champagne but would not sit at the table. Instead he sat on the floor in the corner. As he drank he fumbled his coat buttons with long nervous fingers. Soon he was completely intoxicated and talked constantly, as though to himself. As he had the habit of going off to lonely villages in France and Italy and living entirely alone for months it is probable that he did so talk to himself. One could not judge a Ronald by that rather silly idea "normal." He never was, never had a chance to be, and as Mary Beerbohm commented, no greater cruelty ever happened than his being sent to Eton, and made to indulge in "games."

"I love my hands," Ronald crooned, holding them out before him. "They are too beautiful. Don't you love my hands?" He minced and draped them one way and then another. "When I am alone I am never lonely, because my hands are beautiful."

"They are really," Mary encouraged.

They were; long, beautifully manicured and cared for. They were a dream of Aubrey Beardsley's. Ronald's head was beautifully formed too, but his neck was a stork's.

Ronald was struck by the word *reality*, and recalled that I had spoken in praise of one of his books. "Don't ever say the word 'reality' to me. Where should I be if I admitted reality? You needn't laugh. It is so. But I do love my hands and my lovely books that are beautifully obscene but the censors don't understand and never bother me. But reality is too awful." He turned his head birdlike to the side, tormentedly registering tragedy. He was being Duse or Sarah Bernhardt, or, no, he was being Ronald, and what he was saying was too true if one was serious. "Life is too awful, too tragic. How do I bear it? I have only my beautiful hands. I love to sit before a mirror and watch their gestures. See how beautiful."

Ronald's idea of grim realism in literature was George Meredith, he revealed one night in Paris, when with Curtiss Moffat and myself he swallowed twelve cocktails, having, he said, eaten nothing since the day before. That night he was intent upon taking a taxi to Maxim's, for what reason I don't know. I would not go with him, and neither would Moffat. He was repeating his "Life is too too awful" wail steadily, and we realized that it was, for him, but there was nothing to do. His last remark before getting into a taxi was, "Save me. Save me." It was grimly, hyssterically funny, for Ronald was being a tragic actress while being distressingly real also.

Rudolph, knowing Ronald, came into the room. He realized it was time for Ronald to be put into a taxi and sent to his hotel, but Ronald must believe that the rest of us were being turned out too. "Ladies und chentlemen, ve close," Rudolph said with pompous austerity, but there was a twinkle in his eyes. "Fritz, you ged de taxi vor Meester Firbank. He is a goot man und a goot customer, put he is trunk."

That night I recall as one of the less grim London nights in those years. Too many nights there was no talk except about how bored we all felt. It was doubtless my fault that I didn't discover another London, but that point will come up later.

Before leaving London Harriet Weaver went with several of us to a music hall to hear Nora Bayes sing, and declared herself highly entertained, particularly with Nora's rowdy "No one ever loved like Samson and Delilah." My idea was that as Miss Weaver generously helped artists, she might learn to be not afraid of their less high-minded pastimes. We persuaded her to do a Paris cabaret, namely Bricktop's, where she would hear snappy songs and see, close-to, dancing that clicked. Dorothy Cole, an English illustrator recently turned novelist, accompanied our party and the second night there we had a dinner party at

L'Avenue. Djuna Barnes, H.D., Bryher, Thelma Wood, Harriet
Weaver, Miss Cole, William and Sally Bird, and myself were
at the party but Ezra was to come in after dinner for coffee.
Throughout the meal everything went charmingly. Several were
newly acquainted with each other, and Miss Weaver's obvious
dignity and reserve dominated the affair. However, Hilda Doolittle, who had known Miss Weaver for years, urged with me
that she should have at least one glass of wine. Having decided
to "face reality," she did sip at a glass of wine. The rest drank
more generously. By the time dinner was over Miss Weaver may
have sipped half a glass of wine, and Ezra Pound arrived.

Ezra had left England some years before and not seen Miss
Weaver since, but surely he recalled that she was reticent. Ezra
doesn't drink to an extent that one can mention. He seemed
gay as he entered, however, so that he may have had an extra
cognac or so. In any case he greeted us all jubilantly, and suddenly turned to Miss Weaver, saying, "Why, Harriet, this is the
first time I've ever seen you drunk." His eagle eye had spotted
her half-filled wineglass.

Hilda gasped and her eyes caught mine, and we both let
out a gasp of laughter, and both turned scarlet upon seeing Miss
Weaver. She sat back as though struck. Later Hilda and I agreed
that she thought she did look drunk because of that thimble-full
of wine. The party was dumb with consternation. Ezra realized
that his comedy had not gone over and sat down, self-conscious
and fidgety, looking at Djuna and at H.D., at Bill Bird and at
me, hoping that some one of us could rescue the situation.

Djuna did best. She saw that Miss Weaver wasn't going to
recover through a wittily made remark or even a short and earnest
explanation that it was a joke. She asked her quietly if she wished
to leave. It was well past ten, and Miss Weaver did want to leave.
Hilda saw her to her hotel, across the square, and returned, explaining that Harriet thought her very brave to venture again into
that scene. When H.D. said broadly, "I haven't seen dear old
Ezra for ages. I'll walk home with him," Miss Weaver was overcome with admiration at her dauntless courage. All as Ezra was
sitting cowed and self-conscious, reflecting how once more he'd
been awkward.

The next morning I called on Miss Weaver and we went for

a long walk, across the Seine into the Place de la Concorde, down the Champs Elysées with a stop at Fouquet's, where we had coffee. It was discouraging for me, for not a sign of believing me did Miss Weaver show. I argued that Ezra was to a good extent a thwarted comedian; he hadn't been intoxicated; he was a self-conscious and shy individual and had made an awkward remark to cover his entry into the party which seemed gay. As I was leaving her at the hotel she said, "I am sure you are right. If you will give me Ezra's address I will call on him at teatime. I have always admired his work and must not let my prejudices get the better of me."

I guess Ezra gathered the amount of persuasion Djuna, Hilda, Bryher, and myself put up to bring Miss Weaver round, and I suspect to this day that she nurses a fear that she, once a good Quaker, was intoxicated that night. Fortunately it did not seem necessary for me to be present at the Ezra-Weaver tea because surely one's heart would have had to bleed for Ezra; his self-consciousness is enough to put one ill at ease in normal circumstances.

Miss Weaver never went to Bricktop's; never saw a Paris cabaret. She went back and was soon worrying about Joyce's *Work in Progress,* which she could scarcely believe the work of a rational being. Because of this, Sylvia Beach invited Miss Weaver to Paris a year later, and somehow the Paris atmosphere helped to persuade her that when a man has proved his genius it is not for others to ask explanations about his new and unfinished efforts. As Miss Beach has said of Miss Weaver, "She is an authentic saint," but saints can be difficult. However, if American and English reformers and censors could be brought to "see the light" as easily as she because of a morning's walk, things would be far nicer for artists in general.

(See Bibliographical Note, page 362.)

2. Contact Editions: Paris

A catalog of McAlmon's tastes—"music, mainly jazz, and dancing, mainly my own, and gregarious life and lots of it. Low, or high, but always salted with a little disreputability"—suggests how he put in a good part of his time.[1] But not all of it, by any means. In the late summer of 1921, he showed his first collection of stories to James Joyce. When Joyce asked him, "Are you going to publish it through Shakespeare and Company or on your own?" McAlmon went into action.[2] Much too independent to ask Sylvia Beach to do for him what he could do for himself, he got in touch with Darantière of Dijon, who had printed Joyce's Ulysses, and gave him the book Joyce had titled, a bit ironically, A Hasty Bunch. "Ulysses was published on the 2 February [1922], my birthday," Joyce wrote McAlmon a few days later. "I sent you a telegram that morning to tell you of it . . ." McAlmon's little collection occupied Joyce's printer next.

Although in time McAlmon came to feel that writing was "the more entertaining part of bookmaking, as printing and publishing is a grind and a drag," [3] in 1922 and 1923 he began to think of himself as a publisher. Rather thoughtlessly he slapped "Contact Publishing Co." on his second collection of stories, and in no time his room at the Hotel Foyot was engulfed with manuscripts. They were piled on the chairs, in the wardrobe, under the bed. He couldn't escape his writing friends, and the truth is, he did not try: he enjoyed being sought after. By January 1924 he had brought out eight books, including three of his own and one by Bryher; consequently, his announcement in the transatlantic review (January 1924) that he was a publisher was very much after the fact—and in character. "At intervals of two weeks to six months, or six years, we will bring out books by various writers who seem not likely to be published by other publishers for commercial or legislative reasons," the announcement said in part. "Three hundred only of each book will be printed. These
184

*books are published simply because they are written, and we like
them well enough to get them out. Anybody interested may com-
municate with Contact Publishing Co., 12 rue de l'Odéon, Paris."* [4]
*The address was that of Sylvia Beach's bookshop. "Contact Edi-
tions are not concerned with what the 'public' wants," McAlmon
said in another policy statement. "There are commercial publishers who* know *the public and its tastes. If books seem to us
to have something of individuality, intelligence, talent, a live
sense of literature, and quality which has the odour and timbre
of authenticity, we publish them. We admit that eccentricities
exist."* [5]

    *The auguries were good. Arriving in Paris that January,
William Carlos Williams was pleased to find that "Contact, the
venture [Bob] and I had started in New York . . . had . . .
become an influential one with many leading writers of the day.
Due to Sir John's fortune, he was an extremely important factor
in bringing out many books."* [6] *Sylvia Beach confessed that she
"never quite understood what the 'Contact movement' was about,
but the books McAlmon published in Contact Editions were quite
out of the ordinary. For instance, there was a small blue book
called* Three Stories & Ten Poems *by a new writer named Ernest
Hemingway. It sold out immediately, and made both Hemingway
and Contact Editions famous."* [7] *It also resulted in McAlmon's
alliance with William Bird of the Three Mountains Press. But
not all Contact books were sellouts. Publishing had its problems—
and problem children—and McAlmon recalled them, not without
asperity, when he came to write* Being Geniuses Together. *The
following excerpts from its pages are supplemented by information from William Bird, McAlmon's partner, and editorial commentary as needed to fill in the picture.*

Not What the "Public" Wants

    By this time I was with William Bird, publishing books in
Paris, and, most of them, books that I am yet glad to have pub-

lished, but so far as getting distribution was concerned silence is better. The mere fact that the books were printed in English on the continent made them suspect, both by the English and the American customs officers. One shipment of *A Hurried Man,* a distinguished but certainly clean book by Emanuel Carnevali, was rejected and never returned. Even one shipment, later, of Gertrude Stein's *The Making of Americans* was refused entry at New York. It was a shipment of five copies, and already one hundred copies of the book had been sold to a publisher in America. John Herrmann's boyish and, for the present-day, naively innocent book *What Happens* was steadily refused entry, even after Herrmann protested with a pamphlet signed by several noted people. As we printed only 300 to 500 copies of each book, of works for which America was the logical market, the venture was not a cheering affair. It was not only the customs; reviewers in America were ruthless against them. They would not comment on them as books; they were always mentioned as expatriate and Paris publications even when the authors never saw Paris. Since, some of the books have been republished in England or America and have been greeted with praise; Robert Coates' *Eater of Darkness;* Mary Butts' *Ashe of Rings;* Hemingway's *in our time.*

Wanting to get a copy of Gertrude Beasley's *My First Thirty Years,* while in America, I was asked $40 for a book for which we had charged $2.50. Some three hundred copies of that were lost in America. The author, not having registered her residence in London, got into trouble with the authorities at the time proof was being sent her. The ensuing newspaper publicity made it impossible to attempt distribution of her book in England. In the publishing of some twenty books only two authors got "temperamental" and they were both Gertrudes, Stein and Beasley, and may it be said, both megalomaniacs with an idea that to know them was to serve them without question about their demands.

[William Bird—described by Williams as "a tall, sharp-bearded American businessman who looked as though he'd been mellowed in Chambertin, gentle, kindly, and informal" [8]—became McAlmon's partner almost by accident. Here is his account of how it happened and how he got into publishing in the first place: "I started the Three Mountains Press simply to have a hobby. Most of my friends were golfers, but sports never interested me greatly, whereas ever since my childhood I had had an interest in printing. I discovered on the Isle St. Louis a French journalist, Roger Dévigne, who was printing books on a hand press of about the Benj. Franklin vintage. I arranged with Dévigne to print English books on his press, after acquiring a full series of Caslon type for that purpose. After a short time, however, the adjoining shop fell vacant, and I bought a hand press of my own, also of a model about two centuries old.

["Hemingway, who was then a young journalist and whom I had met when we both covered the Genoa conference * suggested that Ezra Pound, then living at 70 bis r. N.D. des Champs was busy writing a long poem and might be willing to have some of it printed. I went to see Ezra, and after a couple of days reflection he came up with a series of 6 long books which he proposed to publish.† He said the thing to do was to have a series of books that went together, and not just print things as they came along. Thus Ezra became editor of the Three Mts. Press.

["It took an ungodly long time to get these done, as I could only work in spare time. (The second one in the series I had printed outside, because Dévigne needed his press.) Hemingway got very impatient, as his book was last on the list, and gave another MS. (Three stories & Ten Poems) to Bob McAlmon, who thus got it out a few months before 'in our time.'

["McAlmon got quite a handsome present from his father in law Sir John Ellerman (about 14,000 pounds I think) and began publishing books by almost any writer who came along. Soon his hotel room was full of them and he consulted me. I was all clogged up with my own unsold books but at least I had an office and a secretary to handle such orders as we got, so agreed to join forces so far as distribution went. I printed a list of books in print headed 'Contact Editions, including books printed at the Three Mountains Press.' My idea was that the Three Mts. was a

* The Genoa Economic Conference, 1922.

† The six books were *Indiscretions or Une revue de deux mondes* by Ezra Pound; *Men and Women* by Ford Madox Ford; *Elimus: a story* by B. C. Windeler; *The Great American Novel* by William Carlos Williams; *England* by B. M. Gould Adams; and *in our time* by Ernest Hemingway.

printing office, and that Contact Editions was a publishing house. McAlmon, with his usual distaste for fine distinctions, never understood the arrangement and put both imprints on both his subsequent books." [9]

[But he did understand how to make himself useful to authors. He was particularly attentive to James Joyce, who was amused by his American speech and his gossip about "the Crowd," and who was his regular drinking companion. Joyce "regularly asked McAlmon's opinion of his latest pages. But McAlmon had his own books to write and did not give Joyce unqualified adherence; he also took less interest in subleties of Catholic thought and Irish politics than Joyce wished," Joyce's biographer, Richard Ellmann, has written. "He treated McAlmon as a colleague, and was pleased to find some resemblance between their short stories. To another friend [Samuel Beckett] he said indulgently, 'Maybe McAlmon has a *disorderly* sort of talent'. . . ." [10]

[From the first days of their friendship—they had met in Sylvia Beach's bookshop—McAlmon had generously and cavalierly provided Joyce with a hundred and fifty dollars a month of the Ellerman money "to tide him over until *Ulysses* appeared." [11] Sylvia Beach, who published it, needed subscriptions to help defray the great expense, and in her memoirs she has told of McAlmon's "untiring" help. "He combed the night clubs for subscribers, and every morning, early, on his way home, left another 'Hasty Bunch' of the signed forms, the signatures slightly zigzag, some of them. When *Ulysses* came out, I met people who were surprised to find themselves subscribers, but they always took it cheerfully when McAlmon explained it to them." [12] Actually McAlmon's connection with *Ulysses* was not confined to promoting it. He had a portable typewriter which he pounded with more enthusiasm than accuracy, and it was from this machine that there emerged the last fifty pages of the book, Molly Bloom's famous interior monologue.]

The husband of the English typist who was typing his work had destroyed some forty pages of the original script of *Ulysses,* because it was obscene. Joyce was naturally scared about handing work out to typists, and most typists would insist upon putting in punctuation which he did not desire. He knew that I typed not well, but quickly, and spoke suggestively of the point as we were drinking. I thought then, fifty pages, that's nothing, sure I'll type it for you.

The next day he gave me the handwritten script, and his handwriting is minute and hen-scrawly; very difficult to decipher. With the script he gave me some four notebooks, and throughout the script were marks in red, yellow, blue, purple, and green, referring me to phrases which must be inserted from one of the notebooks. For about three pages I was painstaking and actually retyped one page to get the insertions in the right place. After that I thought, "Molly might just as well think this or that a page or two later or not at all," and made the insertions wherever I happened to be typing. Years later upon asking Joyce if he'd noticed that I'd altered the mystic arrangement of Molly's thought he said that he had, but agreed with my viewpoint. Molly's thoughts were irregular in several ways at best.

[Joyce must have altered most of McAlmon's alterations. In a letter to Miss Harriet Weaver (13 June 1925), in the Joycean manner he mocks McAlmon's imprecision, manner of speech, and opinion: "Did Fossett change those words? They was two. Doesn't matter. 'Gromwelling' I said and what? O, ah! Bisexycle. That was the bunch. Hope he does, anyhow. O rats! It's just a fool thing, style. I just shoot it off like: If he aint done it, where's the use? Guess I'm through with that bunch. (With apologies to Mr Robert McAlmon)" [13]]

Wyndham Lewis turned up in Paris, but this time for a very short stay and he had a mission. Somebody, Roger Fry or Augustus John, had told him that an Ingres exhibition was on and that he must by all means see it, and although Lewis purported to think little of English art critics' opinions, he was curious. I went to the Ingres exhibition with him, and certainly if ever a man worked at his craft and technique, if ever a man studied anatomy to be more anatomical than is anatomy, it was Ingres. If genius is the infinite capacity for hard work, Ingres was a great genius. I have doubts though. There wasn't a picture in the exhibition I craved. Before Ingres I agree with Man Ray, Marcel Duchamps, and others, why not the camera? Lewis hardly saw his friend Joyce on this occasion. He was probably preparing his attack on several writers in *The Enemy*.

During all this period I had a room at the Foyot, and for very little, having kept it by the month, whether there or not. Through the months innumerable acquaintances stayed at the Foyot. Tommie Earp, Curtiss Moffat, Mary Butts, Radiguet, Edith Taylor—and I believe Dorothy Parker. Sorry to say I never met her, and one is curious to know whether she does originate all of New York's brightest wisecracks, or if, having the reputation, anything clever is attributed to her.

Curtiss Moffat made an art of boredom, and advocated a tornado of it. His voice drawled and expressed boredom, and though an American his accent was more English than any educated Englishman's I have ever known. Curtiss let me in for one of those typing sessions, too.

I was having coffee at the Dome bar one day when Curtiss approached and informed me that Michael Strange (then Mrs. John Barrymore) was in his taxi. "She has a short play she wants typed, by tomorrow night, and I thought you might do it, Bob. Only half an hour's work."

I wasn't pleased, but had heard that Michael Strange was beautiful and entertaining. I told him to bring her in.

The next day Michael Strange came to my room at the Foyot. She was in a tailored suit with pockets in it, and after a little chit-chat we got down to the typing of the script. It was a play about Anthony and Cleopatra, and Cæsar's son played a part. Oh, glamor, and draperies, and poetry which pours voluptuous colour and rhythms upon our prose-worn minds!

Miss Strange put her hands in her pockets and strode back and forth across the room, brushing back her hair with an inspiration-fevered hand. I sat stolidly at the typewriter and wrote as she dictated, only now and then halting her as her inspiration sprang to flower too quickly for my not so nimble fingers. I was far too busy catching her fervid words to laugh, and much too riled at Curtiss for having suggested that I do this typing. Miss Strange singularly failed to strike me as beautiful, clever, or attractive, and the play was the most awful tosh I have ever allowed myself to sit through hearing. She should properly have paid some

poverty-stricken typist the highest commercial rates rather than
impose on the unknown acquaintance of a friend. Miss Strange
had wealth then, and I didn't forgive the imposition.

(See Bibliographical Note, page 362.)

All Men Are Musicians

It developed that Ezra Pound was writing an opera, namely
the setting to music of several of Villon's poems. People who had
known Ezra for some time did not take Ezra's music-compositional
abilities with great seriousness, as, they claimed, Ezra was virtually
tone deaf. He was not a trained musician, and it was said that he
plunked away at a mandolin or banjo and jotted down notes,
to the end of getting back to musical values which an older world
had known, and which sentimentalized tradition had destroyed.
Ezra at the time had elected himself sponsor for George Antheil,
so Antheil claimed. I never knew. At one time, not being a musician, and as her ladyship found Antheil "boyish," and "needing
to be taken care of," I managed to get him subsidized for a two-
year period. Now I must confess that George always struck me as
a bit too deliberately boyish, naive, and ingenuous, for the lad
never neglected to cultivate, in his naive manner, whoever might
serve his ends. Sometimes he got his dates and acquaintanceships
all confused.

William Carlos Williams was in Paris, and sat one day with
Hemingway, myself, and two other writers. Williams confided
that George Antheil had appointed him to write the libretto
for an American opera, as he, Williams, was the one writer most
sure to get into the spirit of America. Hemingway and I ex-
changed knowing glances, and noticed that the other writers also
looked "so that's the way it is."

George had talked warmly and with much enthusiasm about
how I was the logical writer to do this libretto. His innocent and

childlike ardency about my quality was heart-appealing. The others had thought his fervor about their work most pleasing too. I wonder if he had actually read any of our works.

As elsewhere, secrets in Paris have a way of becoming public, everyone bravely concealing the secret sorrows of others from all but their most intimate friends. At one time Ezra came to me with a sad tale. Living in a tiny studio in the same courtyard as was Ezra's studio was a wrecked American poet, who for the last several nights had been virtually insane. His screams kept Ezra from sleep, but Ezra's romantic nature was touched because this poet was truly in the Villon, Rimbaud, Verlaine tradition. He didn't eat enough, and surely he took drugs; in short a self-destroyer.

At the time life was striking Ezra as far too complicated, for after years of marriage his wife suddenly gave birth to a son who was named Omar Shakespeare Pound. Homer was not needed, that being the name of Ezra's father and an anticlimax in its way. Ezra also got himself a piece of marble and started to sculpture in "taille directe," but perhaps the chisels did not guide. At any rate Ezra made noises on his bassoon, sorrowed for the romantic hop-head poet, and betook himself to Rapallo, thinking others could life-save his friend. In Rapallo Gaudier-Brzeska has a bust of Ezra which stands in the town square of that city today, honoring the sage.

Ezra's idea was that I was the American most about town and most aware of low and night life. The poet was in a bad way, because he no longer could procure himself opium, and it was dangerous for him to cease using it suddenly. Surely I knew where to get him opium.

Ezra overrated my knowledge of the low-life world. I knew dives and cabarets and *poules,* but never had I been interested in the dope-dives. Narcotics do not interest me, or rather have no desirable effect. Drink and reality are the best drugs so far as my feelings go. Nevertheless I did some inquiring, but nothing resulted at first. The afternoon after Ezra had told me of the poet's sad plight I encountered Hemingway at the Closerie des Lilas with Ford and Williams. Discreetly, without mentioning names, I told of the need for locating opium. Hemingway looked at me questioningly. "Hell, Ezra's told you too," I ejaculated, and we wondered how many others Ezra had let in on this secret.

We got wind of an Indian chief who knew about getting opium, it was said. I looked him up, and left him a note as he wasn't at his hotel. Finally a can of "opium jam" was delivered to me and I was about to hand it over to the poet. Another person, however, informed me that it needed preparing, "cooking," and that the poet was far too mad at the moment to bother. It would be highly dangerous to let him have the jam in that condition. Naturally I did not give it to him. Instead, with Mariette Mills and Oleg Skrypitzin, we took him to the American hospital, where he was to go through a disintoxicating treatment. He would not stay. He was back at his room the next day. Three times we got him to the American hospital, where they swore they could not hold him against his will unless there was a medical certificate declaring him insane, and they did not deal with cases of insanity. Finally, through a French doctor, a friend of Mrs. Mills, he was placed into a French sanatorium, where he remained for two months. He came back to the quarter forty pounds heavier and healthy looking. The cure was not permanent, however. Later he died, but more from hunger than from dope, it was said. He was miserly about food.

While we were trying to aid this poet we tracked down several people who had been his or his mother's friends in the years past. One was an English woman with a twelve-year-old daughter, who had more poise than I have ever seen in any human being, of whatever age. We took the poet to the woman's flat, as she might convince him to drink a glass of milk without imagining that people were trying to poison him. The woman was not in, but the twelve-year-old girl was. She took one look at Blank, and said, "Oh, he is out of opium again." Immediately she went to the telephone and rang up a man in a bank who also knew Blank. "This is Mary," she said. "It's about Blank. He's off again and must have some opium if you can't get him into a sanatorium."

Blank at first refused to drink a glass of hot milk which the child handed him, but she curtly said, "Stop being silly, Blank. Why should I want to poison you? Drink that and stop being such a problem for us all."

Blank drank. Suddenly he looked at me, and said, "What have you against me?"

"Nonsense, Blank. I hardly know you and why should I have anything against you?"

"Then why did you linger about the grounds of the American Hospital yesterday until long past midnight?"

"Blank, you're barmy. I was in Montmartre last night from eleven o'clock till four in the morning."

"Oh, no. You came into my room at two o'clock last night. You spat at me, snapped your fingers, and said, 'Foiled again, and we've got you where we want you this time.' "

Oleg, the child, and I spent an hour convincing Blank that he was having hallucinations, for he began to see things in the room which were not there. That day we got him to return to the American Hospital, where the Directress was not at all glad to see him. He did not stay, however, and the next day Mrs. Mills took Oleg and me in her car and we spent some five hours getting the poet settled in the French sanatorium.

His poetry was a horrible backwash of Swinburne and the 1890 decadents, except when he injected a bit of Eastern mysticism. Painted on the walls of his musty and unclean studio were hieroglyphs and phrases. "Not pity but scorn." Poor Blank was as mild and beaten a specimen as could possibly exist. The legend was that he had been dominated by his mother, and that upon her death he never recovered. He had always felt persecuted, and even in boyhood suspected others of trying to put poison in his food. For all that he was not quite another Francis Thompson, or even a Dowson. All who are mad are not necessarily inspired.

With much ado among the Anglo-American populace of the art world the night for the production of Ezra's opera approached. We all in those days delighted in attending such affairs, whether they be American or French. People moved en masse and every English-American person in Paris—excepting the staid "exclusive" set—was sure to know, or to know about, every other one. It did not mean that they dearly loved art. In fact most of them attended Cocteau's shows at the Cigale—*Romeo and Juliet*—because there was a bar at the rear of the main theatre room. Yvonne George was also playing the rôle of nurse in this production and she was one of the livelier steppers of Paris at the time. There was always a question as to which end of the auditorium attracted the most attention. Surrealists and enemies of Cocteau would be shouting down the actors and the play from all parts of the house, and the drinkers at the bar retaliated by shouting at the surrealists to pipe down. Nothing, however, interfered with the serious drinking which went on at the bar. The Anglo-American lot were strangely unimpressed by the obstreperous violences of the French advance guard. Louis Aragon, "the wild duck," as he was known, might become very passionate in his hatred of Cocteau and his productions, but Aragon failed to strike terror into an American breast.

In a similar way people flocked to the Swedish or the Russian Ballet in those days. The turnouts were interesting spectacles, the women elegantly gowned, the men generally in evening clothes, except for a few defiant French or American rebels. During the entr'acte everybody promenaded to display themselves and to give the others the once-over. Often, after the first act many retired to the barroom and did not return to the auditorium. The dramas and comedies of the bar were much more real than the lackadaisical pantomime of the Swedish Ballet dancers, who lacked fire and zip.

Ezra's opera was in a small hall and was not so well attended as these French affairs and ballets, but still a sizeable audience arrived on time and waited patiently for the performance to begin. I was with Jane Heap (*Little Review*), Djuna Barnes, Mina Loy, Kitty Cannell, but near us were very few people that we did not all know well. As the performance was under way I saw T. S. Eliot come in and slip into the back row. Mina Loy and Jane Heap said that they would like to meet him. Thinking that surely he would remain to go behind and greet Ezra, I thought they would meet him. He, however, slipped away as he had come. Perhaps he was living up to his belief that to know people is mainly futile and a waste of time. Or did not approve of Ezra's music or the Paris congeries, certainly unlike those of London.

The performers of the opera, or rather the singers, held our attention more than most of us had anticipated. Perhaps Ezra had caught the right sort of music to suit Villon's poems. The night was hilarious, and Ezra's delight in having held an audience as a composer was, for the time being, flawless.

Ezra, however, was no jealous composer, for he arranged various musical affairs at which George Antheil's music could be heard. The first was at Mrs. Christian Gross's apartment, and was well attended by both French and American people of the art and diplomatic worlds. Later Natalie Barney gave an afternoon at which a new symphony of his was played.

Virgil Thomson tells a tale that when he showed up at Antheil's concert at Mrs. Gross's, Ezra pointed him out and shouted, "There is the enemy." Ezra claims no memory of the incident, and does not take Thomson's music seriously, but now that Florine Stettheimer's stage designs and a chorus of Harlem negroes have given a New York success to Thomson's and Gertrude Stein's opera it is no time to doubt either the force, originality, or genius of the Stein or the Thomson. Thomson ought better, however, to have set Mary Butts and Villefranche to music. There were more than four saints there, with Cocteau the "Master."

By 1922 or 1923 there were quantities of Americans who had settled in France, to stay indefinitely, either in Paris or at houses which they had rented in the small towns nearby. The American bars had not yet come into being and there was a great deal more entertaining in the home than now occurs. Never a week passed without its one or more cocktail parties, and people dined at each others' homes frequently. Man Ray was settled into his studio with Kiki, spoke French fluently and was getting a French public, in a measure due to the help of Marcel Duchamps and Tristan Tzara or other dadaists. George Biddle, John Storrs, John Carrol, Ford Madox Ford, Sisley Huddleston, George Slocombe, Clotilde Vail, and Laurence Vail with his then wife, Peggy Guggenheim, Jane Heap, Mina Loy, Kathleen Cannell, the Arthur Mosses, Mme. Champcommunal (who hadn't then opened her couturière shop), William and Sally Bird, and many others were about and most of them entertained fairly often. There were a quantity of the more seriously commercial artists about, generally intent upon their careers in the world of success and fashion. Frequently they had strong-minded wives who saw to it that they did not over drink or indulge in companionship with people who could not be of definite service to them. A goodly lot of them, nevertheless, did wander frequently from the right bank to slum in the Quarter. Gilbert White, Jo Davidson, Paul Daugherty and Manship (guarded austerely by their wives).

In the year 1924 there were appearing in American magazines and newspapers a number of articles about the life of the deracinated, exiled, and expatriate, who lived mainly in Paris leading, the articles implied, nonworking and dissolute lives. An American journalist, long a resident of Paris, was riled and asked me to collect a list of the foreign artists who had been in the Quarter throughout the last year or so. He suggested that I note also what work they had accomplished, and jot down a note about their dissipations, if any. One night, with several others who had been in Paris for some time, we noted down a list of two hundred and fifty names, English and American, and some were the names of persons responsible for the American articles against so-called exiles in Paris. The report indicated that said righteous article-writers had been known by several to have indulged in Montparnassian dissipations as extensively as any. In that list were the names of none but working writers or painters; one of the writers has since gained the Nobel prize; several others have been Book-of-the-Month Club selections, or best-sellers, or acclaimed great writers. The same is true amongst the painters and sculptors, and I now, looking over the list which we compiled and which was never used, remember that a quantity of these people started and completed books which brought them fame, in Paris and during those days. One wonders what fixed idea American newspapers had, and what obsession persisted in the writers who returned to America, which caused them to find it necessary to throw off on Paris, a city which gave them material and stimulus, and which helped them to grow up mentally, if they did.

It has been said that Paris is the parasite's haven because it is easier to go to hell there comfortably than anywhere else. On the other hand, if somebody stands its racket for a long period and emerges purposeful and a producing person it means talent and strength, and it means that he had dissipated a quantity of soppy ideas and has a sounder chance of being an artist in a respectable sense, intellectually. For the rest, any art quarter is tolerant of weaknesses, and the hangers-on might as well go to hell in Paris as become equally spineless, futile, and distressing specimens in their home villages. A Parisian drunk is not nearly so sad to watch as the small town down-and-outer. He isn't alone or lonely.

(See Bibliographical Note, page 362.)

McAlmon's largest single publishing venture, Gertrude Stein's Making of Americans, *turned out to be one gigantic headache. The book had been written between 1906 and 1908, and in the years since then it had been seen by a goodly number of the more emancipated British and American publishers. Among them was B. W. Huebsch, whose letter (1912) to Miss Stein was typical of many: "I find that the novel is not suited to my list, but I am glad to have had the opportunity of examining it. Will you be good enough to send me remittance of $1.32, the amount of charges which we had to pay upon receipt of the box containing the book?"* [14] *But finally in 1924 things began to look up. As told in* The Autobiography of Alice B. Toklas: *"Hemingway came in then very excited and said that Ford wanted something of Gertrude Stein's for the next number [of the* transatlantic review]*, and he, Hemingway, wanted* The Making of Americans *to be run in it as a serial and he had to have the first fifty pages at once. Gertrude Stein was of course quite overcome with excitement at this idea, but there was no copy of the manuscript except the one that we had bound. That makes no difference, said Hemingway, I will copy it. And he and I did copy it and it was printed in the next number of the Transatlantic."* [15] *But this was still no substitute for book publication, and Miss Stein and her friends (including McAlmon) continued to try to interest commercial houses.*

In the end McAlmon was elected: at the author's request in January 1925 he agreed to undertake the book. From the beginning it caused trouble. First, Miss Stein made a difficulty about the contract. Then McAlmon discovered that the manuscript was a good deal longer than he had bargained for—it was a third again as long as Ulysses— *and received no cooperation from her when he insisted that they must begin getting subscriptions to help out with the unexpectedly large production cost. Next he tried to sell sheets to two enterprising publishers, Cape and Liveright,* *for distribution in England and the U.S.; and at the same time, independent of McAlmon, Miss Stein and Jane Heap, her self-appointed agent, were conducting negotiations elsewhere. (They had a nibble from Albert and Charles Boni, but the Bonis backed away when asked $2500 for a thousand sets of sheets.) Subsequently, Jane Heap offered McAlmon $1000 for the same number of sets—an offer which infuriated him: the cost of printing alone was more than three times that. When Stanley Nott of London offered to distribute four hundred copies in England, and Miss Stein on her own initiative telephoned the printer to send them to Paris for delivery, McAlmon hit the ceiling: the sheets were his property, not Gertrude Stein's. Although Nott apparently got out of his tentative agreement, the break between McAlmon and the author was complete. On a number of occasions thereafter Miss Stein tried to patch things up—she herself admitted that his anger was "not without reason"* [16]*—but McAlmon was through (was through was through).* The Making of Americans *failed to sell despite its author's protestations that she knew at least fifty people who would buy it, and he sent her a cold little note: "If you wish to purchase the rest of the books you may do so. . . . If you wish the books retained, you may bid for them. Otherwise by Sept.—one year after publication—I shall rid myself of them en-masse, via the pulping proposition."* [17] *At the same time Jane Heap, helpful to the end, wrote to Miss Stein: "I had a short talk with Sylvia [Beach]. Bob had told her that you are cheating him or trying to cheat him. . . ."*

Gertrude Stein did not buy the remaining copies of The Making of Americans *and* McAlmon did not have them pulped, but what became of them nobody seems to know.

Genius All Too Simple

The name of Gertrude Stein was one which newspaper columnists used to twit. There were innumerable legends about her since either she or her brother Leo "discovered" Picasso, Braque,

Matisse, and so on. Her *Tender Buttons* was amusing enough, and perhaps at the time of writing it Miss Stein had not been so religious about herself as the one and only. She had written, by this time, one sound book, *Three Lives.* The second life, of a negress, Melanctha, and her romance with an idealistic, intellectual, and dumb negro doctor, is a masterpiece. It reiterates, stammers, and moves slowly but with a pure force to the conclusion: Melanctha's annoyance at the sensual lack of understanding in the doctor, her wandering and her end. In this, Gertrude Stein's sluggish but virile feeling for life emerges.

I had not much curiosity about Miss Stein as a person. She appeared on the streets in her "uniform," wearing sandals with toes like the prow of a gondola. She could be seen driving about Paris mounted on the high seat of her antiquated Ford. There was no doubt that Miss Stein knew how to stage-set herself to become a character and celebrity. With Leo she had purchased a good many of the pictures by painters who came to be called "cubists" or "moderns." She had sufficient money to conduct a salon, and many people who later became famous attended gatherings there. Some of them went because her teas were bountiful and they were hard up and hungry. Others, then as now, were ready as people are in the bohemian world to attend to regard the menagerie. Gertrude, who has a child's vanity and love of praise, believed their soft-soaping flatteries and one gathers still believes them. In a recent book of hers where she becomes Alice Toklas and Alice Toklas becomes Gertrude, and they merge into one, singing the praise of Gertrude, Alice-Gertrude tells frequently of what people think of her, of how they love her. Unfortunately for her belief other people know many of the same individuals and, therefore, are inclined to find Gertrude too credulous.

Miss Stein is a pronounced example of the protected child, never actually allowed to face real hardship. Her brother Leo discovered painting for her. She had inherited an income. She ensconced herself securely on the rue de Fleurus and let herself be known as a patron of the art of painting. The word spread. Painters desire to sell their pictures, and it came to be that shortly it meant réclame to have Miss Stein possess an artist's picture. Not only would hangers-on see the picture; they would believe they must think it fine because Miss Stein owned it. That some of her paintings, certainly of the more recent years, are horrible trash—namely those of Sir Francis Rose, who paints everybody's pictures but has no manner of his own—people did not breathe in those younger days of abstraction.

During the early years of Paris and Florence, Miss Stein was protected from "reality" and vulgar contact by hangers-on who sat, looked, and listened to her as the oracle. Otherwise she knew an occasional person such as herself—wealthy, secure, and protected, and capable of assuming a "great personality" quality because he or she could afford to entertain freely, and be kind to the flatterers and curt to the independent if they intruded and dared assert a contrary opinion. Such a one was Mabel Dodge. It would be interesting to surmise what these women would have been without inherited security.

Before I had come to Europe it entered my mind that Amy Lowell and Gertrude Stein were much of a type. Amy certainly preferred second- or third-raters, who talked of her art and genius, to people of understanding who might occasionally find this or that poem of hers not quite a success.

In consequence of my attitude towards Miss Stein, although my admiration for *Melanctha* was great, I had not in several years of Paris life met her. However, I went to see her one night with Mina Loy. Surprisingly she struck me as almost shy. She did seat herself in a large, higher chair, in the middle of the room, and she did monologue and pontificate and reiterate and stammer. But she was much more human, indeed, a much better specimen than Amy Lowell, although the species were of the same family—doubting and spoiled rich children, hurt to discover that they can't have the moon if they want it. Perhaps she was extra shy with me. I can't say. Perhaps my manner is critical or analytical, and I may have said a doubting "yes?" to some of her pronouncements, but in the main we got on well.

We discovered a mutual passion for Trollope's novels, for documentary, autobiographic, and biographic things. I added travel books, but she wasn't so sure of them, although she would read anything. She would read every book of Edgar Wallace's. I'd read any one of them which one could feel wasn't a rewrite of the others. She recommended Queen Victoria's letters, and I recommended those of Cardinal Manning. I left thinking that one could become fond of Gertrude Stein if she would quit being the oracle, descend from the throne-chair, and not grow panicky every time someone doubted her statements, or even bluntly disagreed. It never resulted in friendship, however. Miss Stein apparently is interested in people who sit and listen before her. That does not mean that she will not take a blow at their solar plexus later, however, for she does detect the craven, hanging-on spirit in those who intend to succeed and believe in praising the great for all their qualities, even their worst ones.

Having used the word megalomaniac on others we will add Gertrude Stein to the list, and also say that on occasions she can be much of a mythomaniac. In her recent autobiography extolling herself, she says that McAlmon wanted to publish her *Making of Americans,* and she graciously allowed this. The fact is that she wrote to that individual asking him to tea and suggested that he publish the book in a series of four to six volumes throughout a two-year period. Thinking it over, he thought, "All or not at all. It's a unity." As Miss Stein assured him that she was sure of about fifty people who would buy the book, he took it on.

Months later when the book was in the process of being bound he had tea with Miss Stein and assured her that he would not allow the lot of books to be shipped to a New York publisher for distribution without a definite contract, or the payment outright by those publishers of the printing bill. That interview was in Paris. That night he went to London. The next day he received a wire from the printer at Dijon, M. Darantière, asking if it was his wish that the lot of books be shipped at once to a Paris shipping agency for shipment to America.

After wires and letters it devolved that Miss Stein had telephoned M. Darantière that it was McAlmon's instructions that this shipment should be made. As it was in direct contradiction with his last interview he was very angry and not without reason. Miss Stein explained in a letter that she understood McAlmon would allow the shipment. Jane Heap told her so. Miss Heap had never been McAlmon's agent, or in any way involved with him in business, and he had not seen her during his trip to Paris. McAlmon's anger did not cool when Miss Stein tried to involve Miss Heap. Since she so believed in her own genius, she might sell a painting which had cost her little for fifty times that amount and pay her own printing bill. It appears she has now rewritten *The Making of Americans* and brought it down from one thousand pages to four hundred. With its dodderings and hesitations and repetitions, it doubtless could be made shorter. She contrived to sell not more than ten at the most of her purported fifty, and she did send as review or gift copies books to friends who were her then only public.

The book got few and mainly unfair reviews. I wrote a review myself. "The Legend of Gertrude Stein," quoted here in part. It appeared in *The Outlook.*

Gertrude Stein is a writer of quality in that she uses words in a new way. She handles them repetitiously, darkly, sluggishly-understood, slowly-utilized, in vast quantities like mud and plenty of mud, and mud can with difficulty be made to take on a suggested sculpturesque effect. Unfortunately, Miss Stein, a naive, fairly childish person, has had thrust upon her a legend as a leader of modern literature. Those who elected her are generally too insistently "modern" and "stylish-minded." She is sounder than they if only in her lethargic vitality and heaviness. Her manner of writing may upset people; what little she has to say cannot. She has a deep, aged-child kindness and resignation to certain inevitabilities. In her later years she has perhaps lost her stride trying to live up to the "innovator" legend which has been imposed upon her.

There is a monotonous, slow, unidentified, pulsation of sluggish life, and too great though a sound insistence on middle class virtues. Her property sense is sternly Hebraic . . . she does not allow the existence of imagination based on sensibility and she suggests a human order of organisms, which vibrate without nuance of personality, and which move with the thickness of protozoic slime. The book is thick with a heavy sense of life . . . monotony, soil, and yet more soil, and yet more more soil, mediocre, not too fertile soil . . . gives the sensation of being written by a low-tensioned being.

One feels that Miss Stein triumphs within herself to think that she can put words together, and having done so feels charmed enough to repeat them again and again, as a three-year-old child who is playing with clay might say to a nurse, "Shall I make a man? Shall I make a man?" Her characters have not the distinguished qualities of the baby's clay man. They go on being. She is obsessed with being.

She might object to what is high praise. In Hebraic, Sumerian, and primitive literatures, in the realm of incantations, and in the way children think and write when they are allowed to do so on their own, a sensitive reader might find the "secret" of such style as Miss Stein possesses.

Now it seems that Miss Stein believes that she has put down the history of all mankind. Well, hardly. She never has so much as indicated an awareness that high-strung, witty, and highly imaginative people exist and to whom her characters have interest only as the dullards whom they must learn to find, in their way, somehow dependable people, or at least some part of the foundation which makes up our faltering society.

The year 1925 I wrote a portrait of Miss Stein with no intention of publishing it. Knowing that it would please Ezra Pound, however, I sent him a copy. A year later Pound wrote telling me he had sent the portrait to Eliot, of *The Criterion*, anonymously. He enclosed a letter from the journal saying that the enclosure was the best criticism of Gertrude Stein that the editor had seen. He did not decide whether it was possible to use it. Until decision "did not inquire name of author, but wished to know whether it would have to be published anonymously."

Naturally I wrote Ezra it must not be published anonymously. Months after, Ezra informed me that Eliot had accepted with gratitude the article on Gertie, while making several comments, mainly to the effect that it was too intelligent for his public. This is the portrait which appeared finally, in 1928, in Ezra Pound's *Exile*.

PORTRAIT

Gertrude Stein being a Sumerian monument at five o'clock tea on Fleurus Street among Picassos, Braques, and some Cézannes; slowly the slow blush monumentally mounting as in dismay pontificating Miss Stein, loses herself in the labyrinthine undergrowths of her jungle-muddy forestial mind naively intellectualizing.

Early 1925, speaking of herself, Miss Stein said, "No, nobody has done anything to develop the English language since Shakespeare, except myself, and Henry James perhaps a little.

"Yes, the Jews have produced only three originative geniuses: Christ, Spinoza and myself."

Miss Stein has been disconcerted by her thick intuitions having slowly suspected that her oracular proclamations are being adjudged rather than accepted as mediumistic deliverances of nature's slow-aged, giving-taking, un-interruptable continuance.

Slowly the slow blush mounts and her tone is of naive plaint; embarrassment struggling suspiciously to exasperation. "But my manner could not remind you of anything Sumerian. I have never gone in for Babylonian writings."

Being, biblical, being obsessed with being, biblical, repetitively being, biblical, massively being, the slow slime breathes to being, slowly the biblical slime evolves to being. The aged elephant mastadonically heaves to being, breathing in the slow slime slowly with aged hope, breathing to be slowly. Slowly burdened with a slowly massive clinging slime, agedly the slow elephant ponderously moves in the ancient slime, slowly breathing to move heaving the idea, being; disconcertedly the slow blush mounts and the infant elephant idea panics at being adjudged rather than consulted as an oracle; the ancient mastadonic slow idea with slow suspicion moves agedly suspectful, resting to pause in the ancient slime, effortfully feeling slow being, going on being, to be evolving towards the slowly massive idea elephant, while slowly the elephantine idea evolves to the idea slow aged elephant, suspiciously being, heaving from the slime.

"She is shy, very unsure of herself," the mind warns a listener. "Don't frighten her or she won't talk and when she talks one can, if keen, select an idea which may be heavy but which may also be unique. The elephant's sensibility is not that of the humming bird's."

Shyly pleased by "Of course, you are not touched by time, so you need not think of your generation. Even the youngsters have not the sense of modernity which you had before the war," Miss Stein is monumentally deaf to the tones of flattery or irony. She confesses confidingly, naively being naive.

"I sometimes wonder how anybody can read my work when I look it over after a time. It seems quite meaningless to me at times. Of course, when I write it it seems luminous and fine and living, and as you say it has a tremendous pulsation."

The slow earth slowly moves agedly, massively the mastadon stirs in the mud, and slimed with mud is mud, pulsating with and in mud, but ponderously this mud slowly evolves to the identity, slowly to ponderously identify itself as an idea, slowly evolved, slowly dredged through the slow clinging mud, slowly to capture the slow slimed identity of the aged slow idea, elephant.

Leo Stein has said, from 1917 on: "Gertrude does not know what words mean. She hasn't much intuition but thickly she has sensations, and of course her mania, herself. Her idea of herself as a genius."

Leo Stein has said often: "Gertrude write a thesis against pragmatism which would win William James' admiration? She couldn't. Gertrude can't think consecutively for ten seconds. It was only after I discovered Picassos and had them in the studio for two years that Gertrude began to think she senses a quality."

Gertrude, in speaking of her work. "No, oh no, no, no, no, that isn't possible. You would not find a painter destroying any of his sketches. A writer's writing is too much of the writer's being; his flesh child. No, no, I never destroy a sentence or a word of what I write. You may, but of course, writing is not your métier, Doctor."

The Doctor-writer: "But Doctor Stein, are you sure that writing is your métier? I solve the economies of life through the profession of doctoring, but from the first my will was towards writing. I hope it pleases you, but things that children write have seemed to me so Gertrude Steinish in their repetitions. Your quality is that of being slowly and innocently first recognizing sensations and experience."

"I could not see him after that," Miss Stein said later. "I told the maid I was not in if he came again. There is too much bombast in him."

Slowly moving towards a slow idea the slow child repeating the idea being, slowly the child entangles itself in slow bewilderment of the forest of slow ideas; slowly the shy slow blush slowly mounts in suspicion slowly tormented by the slow harassing distrust, an idea, slowly but finally lost, slowly re-discovered, slowly emerging, slowly escaping, slowly confusion gathers, the dark blush mounts, while slow panic reveals that surely Miss Stein has slowly entangled herself and has slowly allowed the slow idea she was slowly expounding to slowly escape and slowly lost in slow confusion of slow panic shyly slowly Miss Stein wishes these people who listen adjudgingly rather than as to an oracle were away, slowly she is ill at ease, and slowly she realizes suddenly that she wishes these people quickly away, and quickly they go, slowly controlling themselves to quickly realize laughter upon relentlessly realizing being, surely, being outside, away from Miss Stein.

Incidentally, *The Making of Americans* is a beautiful bit of printing and make-up and binding, and Miss Stein compliments

M. Darantière for the job. M. Darantière did do a very fine job, but the publisher chose the paper, the print, the binding, and designed the jacket and make-up of the book.

Nevertheless, Miss Stein has qualities which command admiration; she has vitality and a belief in the healthiness of life, too great a belief for these rocky days.

(See Bibliographical Note, page 362.)

In 1926 McAlmon and Bryher separated and in 1927 they were divorced. Bryher promptly remarried. In Being Geniuses Together *McAlmon made only one comment on this development: "Incidentally it was my suggestion that I felt my marriage was not a go. It represented to me more things that I did NOT want in life than I could cope with."* [18] *His friends were not displeased at the divorce, for they felt that while he was married to Bryher he had failed to do any significant work. It seemed to some that he had become increasingly a dilettante and all were agreed that he was touchier and drank much more heavily than before. "McAlmon was much liked by his friends," Sylvia Beach wrote, "but he was too intolerant of restraint, personal or literary. As he himself said to me, 'I'm only a drinker'."* [19]

The divorce seemed to have little effect on McAlmon's way of life; he had received such a handsome settlement from the Ellermans that he was known in some quarters as "Robert Mc-Alimony." He continued to hang around the Left Bank, though "the Crowd" was beginning to thin out and the "wrong people" were taking over. Kay Boyle has a vivid memory of him at this time: "One summer night we sat at the bar of a Montmartre night-club, the two of us saddened and embittered and outraged by the ugliness and the opulence of the middle-aged people, French and American alike, who danced, and ate, and drank, and threw their money away in handfuls instead of giving it to the poets and beggars of the world. God knows what we were doing there at all. And then, in the piece of night that showed between the silken draperies hanging before a window that stood open on the lonely street, there was a man's miserable hand reaching in from the dark, a black-nailed, dirty, defeated hand, with a

*foul bit of coat sleeve showing at the wrist. Without hesitation,
and without a word, [McAlmon] placed his fine, full glass of
whiskey and soda into the empty fingers of the stranger's hand,
and the fingers closed on it and drew it into the dark outside."* [20]

In-Between Ladies

Sven felt oppressed. As he came into the restaurant he felt
gaily nonchalant, but encountering Grovere altered that. It wasn't
that he was confused. He understood Grovere too well. People
aren't complicated—enough. Grovere had for himself a difficult
nature, but he did endeavor not to throw off on others: still
there he sat, having life; life, something he had in common with
the fishes and insects. It was about everywhere, so damn com-
monly, and contemplation is easier to talk about than practice
constantly. Yes, things can be simple. Sven felt himself simple.
Walking down the Boulevard Montparnasse he had felt good
about being, and hadn't thought more about it.

Having come out of the hospital but a month before, to be
alive meant—that he was alive, and it's a being condition. He had
liked the feeling. Driving over the Grand Cornish from Monte
Carlo to Cannes with a damn fool who will have tormented
moods has its chances, but Miles had been another person, not
Sven. He was one more of people and their moods and problems,
generally fanciful. In the hospital Sven had been delirious, but
things get that way for impressionable people when they aren't
sick. He had sense enough now not to remember past deliriums.

The orchestra played a waltz, deep-swingingly luscious; the
Montrachet was refreshing. Sven felt France a most gracious country. The woman across the way isn't bad. She had trim ankles and
a manner. Nevertheless Sven couldn't feel free in Grovere's
presence. Grovere's eyes had a painful way of dissecting the person
he looked at: a glare of too many passions died from fright within
their depths. The thing they call the New England or some kind

of "conscience" has a vicious way of retaining its carrion long after a decent burial had been indicated as a necessity. Mercifully though Grovere didn't talk with that scolding high-mindedness that many frustrated people believe conceals their real selves.

"Marvelous, simply marvelous, the way the French utilize stallions," Grovere said. He said things so emphatically he must mean them although he did strive for the right tone of a worldly man who knows that life is best for the pursuit of pleasure. "There seems an idea elsewhere that they are dangerous, but the French manage them."

Talk again! "Yes, aren't horses marvelous?" Sven answered, thinking he might get the vaunted quality, balance, sooner if serious people like Grovere did not bore and oppress him so. "We must have brandy with our coffee. Horses are beautiful, but what can one do about them? We can't be riding horseback all the time, though the Italian officers think highly of their steeds."

Grovere smiled with his grimmest intention to be jovially gay. Sophistication is a silly word: aristocracy too; a servant's idea of a grand world. There was this amount of freedom to be had, Sven reflected, one need not envy the lots of other people, understanding them all too well. "I have to meet somebody across the river," Sven said, feeling fidgety, and thinking of Lydia. She wrote awful tosh in her notes about spending dreary hours waiting for word from him. He knew. She kept her days full, in cities, as did he. She was as happy an animal in the country or by the sea as was he. She was at the phone at once, in cities, if it looked like two unengaged hours ahead, and now she was going in for black boys since that Persian gentleman had departed for his homeland. It was all right though if they pleased her. He'd meet her. She rattled on well if her machinery did need lubrication, but she needn't fancy he fell for her letter. They understood each other, and would be loyal, in their ways, to a short period several years back. They didn't have to make efforts with each other. "Sven darling, one can always depend on you. You're the only one who really understands me. I do want to see you. I'm longing to, but you understand. I feel I must see what Rome has become since 1921. I can tolerate Paris only till Saturday."

Yes, Lydia darling. Why did Eustace write her such silly ass letters? He might know she showed his letters to other lovers when she felt confiding over champagne, and her sense of the gaga-ness of existence was uppermost. Eustace's letter was literature and rot. He was sentimental, and aware of himself, too. Right now he was writing another end-of-things novel, and what would his heroine be up to this time? "Waiting for you to make another moment precious, Lydia, darling. Longing to have you sitting across the table just as delight and comfort."

Sven felt the aged impatience: Life must have more design and purpose than any of them let it have. Anyway, he and Lydia didn't wail together. That was a good thing about her. Hell, he was always having these flash moments of purposefulness. He felt cranky. "That was a depressing woman you introduced me to at the Deux Magots yesterday," he told Grovere.

"You silly boy," Grovere was gay. "If you come to the table and seem spontaneously accessible what can you expect? She wasn't one to see how cool you are beneath your boyish, wistful quality. You were spreading charm. Blame yourself. It's to find experience that women of her kind come to Paris. You looked so debonair and interested, what could the poor frump think?"

"She drove me balmy: talked about the negation of life. She was dismal saying that we're too clever in this generation, and intelligence too common, and we disperse our energies. I had to leave when she became sympathetic about my having to earn a living. What would one do with leisure among people such as she? I felt too rottenly nervous to help her if I had been a kind young man, but I did present a young Italian to her. She can have him and reasons for emotional scenes. He won't give a damn."

"You look healthy," Grovere advised severely. "How could she know you feel nervously wrecked? You ought to go to bed for a few nights. You're a wild man, tearing about before you're two weeks out of the hospital."

"I'm not a nervous wreck with some people. I can't stand my room. Cities drive me crazy, and I can't be alone. Maybe I'll go to the seaside, or to Italy," Sven answered. Yes, Italy. How would it be in some small hill town? But he hated the fascisti regime. Probably Mussolini was who Italy needed but that didn't help an individual's life. And he didn't want to be hounded by the past, tourists, or English Colonials. Their voices killed him. And little towns turned lonely, dismal, and dirty on one as night fell.

But Benozzo Gozzoli; a hound pursuing a stag; negroid faces; lithe muscular tightness of modeled kneecaps and legs. Italian hills conventionalized into glistening terraced mounts. Mist and silver and olive trees; blue sparkling Mediterranean sea and sky. He wished the orchestra would quit playing oozy waltzes, or Puccini, about the same rate of loose voluptuousness. "Blue as the blue in your eye." And faces that cut into one's visual memory of primitive paintings. No, he was feeling too impressionable for Italy to soothe him now.

"It's strange how Italy depresses me. I don't find the Italians less sympathetic than most people, as individuals," Sven mused.

"You should rest," Grovere was maddeningly complacent.

He doesn't understand how any other person can feel, Sven thought, and said, "I have to go." He was away from Grovere. Depression dropped from him. The thought of Italy pleased rather than depressed him. It was Grovere who depressed him, physically and psychically, but no matter. Paris was in the spring-time and his heart beat high as he walked across the Louvre Bridge. Paris was casual; she made few demands. He felt light and ethereal, thinking of the nurse at the American hospital. She was a reposeful sort; the kind he should cultivate. "I'm seeing too many people," he told himself, and decided he'd make himself paint some pictures even if they did turn out unsatisfactorily.

Lydia was on time when Sven arrived at the Boeuf sur le Toit. "Sven darling, I'm so glad to have found you. Why didn't you write me? I do want to talk." At once the springs began to unwind. "I've been so busy this morning, but strangely too, re-membering so many things. You and I talk to each other as we do to no one else, I'm sure. Sven darling, it is good to see you again. Kiss me."

Sven kissed her, feeling a bubble of droll mirth at her timed utterances. "Who have you been seeing?"

"Ernest Homer, last, just an hour ago. It was amusing. Poor Homer. He was charming. He came to the studio door looking sleepy. His studio is three times removed from the street. He says he has no consciousness of time. It would be perfect for a person who likes drugs and can't stand people. He believes himself Chinese-souled."

"Ernest doesn't care for drugs, and he can't stand people."

"Dear Ernest. He became tender as he sat beside me, and quoted poetry, while I was thinking, 'With Ernest? Well yes, and why not, if it comes to that?' But it meant nothing to me."

"He must emulate Casanova, and the troubadours. How would poetry continue without the great-lover legend?"

"Sven, angel," Lydia's dry voice was stifled lushly. "I don't know how I would have gotten through the last year without you to write to. We do understand how awful things can be, don't we?"

Sven was uncomfortable and couldn't play up to Lydia. "I thought we'd learned enough to refuse to understand awfulness."

"I'm glad that Ernest is, just is," Lydia wailed. "There aren't many one can say that for, I can tell you." Her voice had rue and driven desperation, but behind the wail was something more. She was a brittle, wound-up statuette of jade and silver and ebony. She was a crashing bore. She hadn't more than twenty sentences out of which to make conversation. She was only human in weak moments, when asked to judge something which synthetic information hadn't let her know how to appraise. "I hate mirrors before me when I'm eating," she said. "It's too awful to feel that one's most attractive years are over. I remember that devastating season in Monte Carlo when I was so sure of myself; that utterly weird but brilliant time. Every time I entered the gaming room I felt myself a magnet that would give off sparks if anyone touched me. It was a fabulously successful demi-mondaine feeling. I wonder if I shall ever feel that way again."

"With drink," Sven was quickly sure. "I'm still ready to get off with anybody, in theory, when I'm lit up. It's not for them; for me. Narcissism."

"You blessed darling. Don't talk as though you were old yet."

"But older, and not readily pleased."

"I love the line of your head, Sven. Sometimes you are beautiful. You understand how one can look, and suddenly that feeling of seeing someone absolutely beautiful comes over one, and one wants him. I'm furious if I can't get him, and helpless. It's strange with one I've known so long as you. It's discovering a new miracle in the world. Sven darling, how did we ever, not quarrel, but feel furious at each other?"

"Because both of our eyes wander and neither of us are faithful," Sven joked.

Nan Adams and Luella Parsons came into the place. Nan peered near-sightedly out of her strawberry mottled and child-whimsical face. Her tall, slight figure appeared breakable on her slender legs. "It's been dreadful the last few days," she said, helplessly bewildered. "Do you think we are going to have a thunderstorm? I woke up last night and thought I was going to faint in bed. I was sure there was going to be a thunderstorm. They terrify me. My heart beats so weakly too." She blinked as her head wobbled on a slight neck. She groped in naive wonder at being alive.

"We must go somewhere to dance later," Lydia said.

"Oh yes, I feel like anything but going home early these nights, if one ever does any more," Nan agreed. "I get so terrified in my room, and the hotel people aren't nice. There is no one to call if I feel ill. It was too dreadful last night at the Noctambule. The most repulsive fat man came to sit at the table next ours. I thought, well that really is too much, and left. I so much didn't want a dull last night too."

"Nan darling, why don't you come to my hotel?" Lydia said, but she, Sven, and Nan knew that Lydia was never in, and that Nan could hardly summon energy to pack and move. Two young men came in from the taxi to join Luella and Nan, and Sven saw at once that Lydia would feel "that way" about Luella's companion. He was young, had pretty ears, a fine skin, boyishness, a smile, a lost wistful air which always meant "charm" to Lydia. Lydia danced with him as Doucet played.

"What should Lydia do?" Nan asked. "She's so restless and her affairs are meaningless to her. She could kill herself, but she doesn't want to do that. Do you suppose this age is worse than other ages, or do people always think their own age awful?"

The waiter told Nan there were no oranges. She stamped her foot and wept helpless tears as she caught her breath. "I did so want an orange."

"Nan dear, you're being hysterical," Luella said, so British with calm sense. Sven did not like her. Nan and Lydia weren't heavy human flesh as she was. They were ideas, and rather comic.

"We're all children," Nan told Sven. "What will become of Lydia?"

"She'll manage to be wherever she emotionally wants to be; and later she'll be a patron of the arts to keep people around her. Like her mother," Sven said.

"I love you for that," Nan said childishly. "It's nice to hear somebody speak who can crystallize thought."

"Rather than paralyze it," Luella spoke, grimly watching Lydia with her young man.

"We must go elsewhere to dance," Lydia said, back at the table.

"But Howard is taking me to the hotel," Luella explained, sweetly patient. "I go to London tomorrow and can't be out late." Her eyes met Lydia's in combat. Lydia was angry within herself, and suggested by a look to Sven how really vulgarly Luella handled situations.

"But darling," Lydia urged, sweetly too, "we'll drop you at your hotel if you won't come dancing. Can't London wait? We could have a quiet cigarette in your room before we went on. Do come. You understand how one feels."

"I do understand," Luella said, making Lydia angrier. Lydia wanted her way and intended to have it. Soon Luella said she must go and Howard had taken too many cocktails to suggest accompanying her. He laughed a silly giggle. Luella left, frigidly. Lydia's metallic quality was mesmerizing Howard, if she kept him sober.

"That young man is droll," Nan said when Lydia was dancing again. "He goes completely under when drunk. Luella adores him, but he doesn't care. Poor Lydia. She's off again. She can be attracted by the most awful men, and he's just a weak pretty boy. I am glad I have had what I wanted and have given up hunting."

The waiter told Nan there was no chartreuse. Nan made a helpless gesture and was tearful. "I did want chartreuse. This is going to be another dreadful night."

They went to the Palermo where Howard wandered to the bar. Sven went to collect him for Lydia, chuckling at the way these girls liked taking each other's men. That gave more kick to their romances. At the bar Howard stood drinking with two *poules,* but he wasn't talking to them. He was muttering, "These damn frogs. Take every cent a guy's got." One *poule,* who Sven knew, indicated that Howard was *fou.*

"Come to the table and drink with us. These girls will slip bills over on you if you don't watch them. You're new to Paris, aren't you?"

"I've been here two weeks and spent five hundred dollars. I sold my ticket to the states too," Howard brooded. "That English woman I was with was paying for my drinks, but she's gone. I don't savee her. Who is she?"

"All of the girls were snappy youngsters before and during the war, but they don't get petted as they once did. I'll buy you drinks. Are you just here for the summer?"

"Hell, I thought I was going to be a writer, but I don't know what to write about. I thought I was a genius in college, but the old man wants me to go to work in his business," Howard said, going to the table.

"You gave him too much to drink," Sven told Lydia. "He's broke. He'll go with you, if you take him. I'm going back to the bar."

"No, stay with me, Sven darling. He's going to sleep on the table. I will go home. This place is too awful. I have had enough of taking care of people when they are drunk. One gets so angry, but that kind doesn't suffer, or even know what one is feeling. You understand. His type does appeal to me. I'm sorry he came along."

Nan soon left with her companion, wailing, "I do hope there won't be a thunderstorm. And that champagne is awful. I shall be sick. But Lydia darling, do call me up tomorrow. What about lunch? You too, Sven. Do call me up. Paris is being too awful."

"Let's go elsewhere, Sven," Lydia said. "Maybe we shouldn't leave that boy but he has picked up some French girl. If you find out where he lives you might ask him to my place for cocktails tomorrow."

"Nan knows where he stays. You can send him a blue tomorrow. He'll be about surely. He's on the town until money arrives for him from America."

"You are an angel, Sven. So sympathetic. It's too ridiculous, my feeling about that kind of boy. I remember my first lech, when I wasn't twelve, mind you. There was a young man I fairly worshiped. I used to be furious at mother for not understanding how he needed drink. It seemed she didn't appreciate how sensitive he was."

"Yes, there is always sensibility."

"How well I remember when he asked me why I always ran away from him. He couldn't know how cruel that remark was. In the country I went to his room mornings. It upset me the first time when I saw he wasn't so beautiful as I had thought. I think he used make-up. I leaned over and kissed him, and he mumbled, 'You Lydia, so good of you to come and say good morning.' I saved pin money for a month to buy him a gold cigarette case when mother wasn't watching. I did adore him.'·

"Love has its drawbacks," Sven chuckled.

"My governess knew what I was feeling. When I was fourteen there was a boy who wrote me letters and she found one and raised the devil. 'Remember, Lydia, young ladies do not receive letters like this from young men. It is vulgar.' I hated that woman. As if I did then or was born to care what is done."

"No, you don't."

"But things get better every year. I stand less of any one person. There can be so many. But Sven, I will go on. Don't come. I feel ghastly. How about tomorrow? And don't go away soon. I need you. Should we have dinner or perhaps lunch, or maybe we might meet after dinner?" Lydia was putting her wrap on. Her voice was level, leaving the question of an appointment between them unforced. "You will see if that boy can come to my place tomorrow. I must see him again. Darling, you do understand. Do call me up, or I may give you a ring towards noon." She walked briskly across the floor, tall, lithe, with a self-assertive swinging poise. Sven danced with a French girl and went to the bar. Howard stood there looking dazed.

"Do you feel ill?" Sven asked.

"Yes, I'll make myself sick, I feel hellish. Dad might have let me study in France for a year but he'll raise a racket when he knows how much money I've spent. Mother might send me money if I wrote her I was doing Italy and Greece."

"Do that then. You'd be confused in Paris, I take it. I'm going home. Do you want me to drop you at your hotel?"

"That's it. I haven't taxi fare. Do you mind waiting?"

BEING GENIUSES
TOGETHER

GREENWICH VILLAGE

Edna St. Vincent Millay with Arthur Ficke

Maxwell Bodenheim (1933)
auctioning his poems

Alfred Kreymborg with two
members of the cast of his play
Manikin and Miniken

Sherwood Anderson

William Carlos Williams

Marianne Moore

Mabel Dodge Luhan

Amy Lowell

Bryher

Photos courtesy of Norman Holmes Pearson

Bryher and McAlmon

McAlmon and his young brother-in-law,
John Ellerman

LONDON LITERATI

Wyndham Lewis.

Richard Aldington

Augustus John

Mary Butts

H.D. (Hilda Doolittle Aldington)

Photos courtesy of Norman Holmes Pearson

McAlmon, two unidentified women, Tristan Tzara, Sylvia Gough, and Kiki, the famous model-songstress

McAlmon with Eileen Lane at La Rotonde

Alice B. Toklas and Gertrude Stein

"GENIUS ALL TOO SIMPLE"

Nina Hamnett, Suzy (described as "one of the old-time *poules* of the Quarter"), and McAlmon

THE "RIGHT PEOPLE"

McAlmon with the Philippe Soupaults

Sylvia Beach in her bookshop

AND THE LEFT BANK

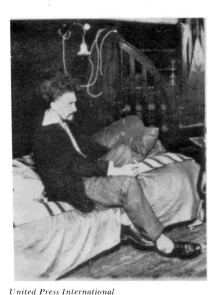

Ezra Pound in his Paris studio

Ethel Moorhead at Monte Carlo

Eugene Jolas and James Joyce

Berenice Abbott

Jane Heap

Berenice Abbott

Peggy Guggenheim

Berenice Abbott

Margaret Anderson

Wide World

Frank Dobson

United Press International

Constantin Brancusi

Wide World

Jo Davidson

Wide World

George Antheil

United Press International

Iris Tree

Berenice Abbott

Kay Boyle and daughter

Daisy Fellowes

Djuna Barnes

Nancy Cunard

Samuel Putnam

VISITING FIREMEN

Sinclair and Grace Lewis and their
son Wells Lewis

Florence and William Carlos Williams

United Press International

Courtesy of Norman Holmes Pearson

United Press International

United Press International

John Barrymore and Michael Strange

F. Scott Fitzgerald and Cornelius Vanderbilt, Jr.

Hemingway and McAlmon in Spain, 1924

Photos courtesy of Norman Holmes Pearson

"Either Ronda or Aranjuez," according to **McAlmon**

MIGRATIONS

Mallorca: McAlmon wearing a matador's uniform

Photos courtesy of Norman Holmes Pearson

Boarding the bus at Pampeluna   William Bird (waving), Sally Bird, and McAlmon

SECOND TRIP TO SPAIN, 1926

Pampeluna: Hemingway (white trousers) playing the bull

Le Canadel: McAlmon, Kiki, Louis Aragon, Peggy
Guggenheim, and Clotilde Vail

THE RIVIERA AND MALLORCA

Theoule: Edwin Lanham, Joan Boyle, McAlmon,
and Felicia Meyer

Mallorca: McAlmon

THE SUN ALSO RISETH,
AND THE SUN COMETH DOWN

Courtesy of Victoria McAlmon

Malcolm Cowley (left) came back to the U.S.A. and took the measure of a day that was ended in the autobiographical *Exile's Return* (1934). In 1934 McAlmon (above) still an expatriate, was at work on his memoirs. "Paris had changed," he concluded, "but Paris was the same . . . I had not changed either."

"No, go ahead and be sick."

"Sure, tell her I'll be at her place tomorrow," Howard said later to Sven. "I might as well get free drinks. She's the heroine of that book, is she? I might as well belong to her past. I'm getting one of my own quick these days. If the old man doesn't send me money I'm apt to be one of those gigolo boys, if I can stand the racket. Hell, I don't know what I want any more. I used to think I was a serious man with ambitions."

"Do you mind?" Sven asked.

"They want me to marry, and suggest girls. I don't want to marry, certainly not the girls they pick. They want me to go into dad's business. I don't want that. I say, let's go somewhere else. I can't go to bed. I don't want to be alone."

"All right, let's go to the negro place around the corner. I don't want to be alone or go to bed either."

"Come to my hotel when we go home then."

"No. Your laugh is funny. It gives me the willies," Sven said. "I think I'll stay up all night."

"You have to sleep sometime."

"To hell with the negro place. Come to my hotel. I'll have drinks sent up. There's a jazz band crew staying near my room. They'll drink with us. My hotel's loose as hell, full of American rounders. It doesn't matter much what rooms we wander into. Everybody there is liberal and believes in a full life."

"Hell, this town is as crazy as New York, even if the liquor isn't rotgut."

"Americans, you know. We go crazy in America and come here to stay crazier where it's less trying on the pocketbook. I'm going south tomorrow night myself. If you're wise you'll miss the summer season here. Once you get started on night life it's hellish hard to stop."

(See Bibliographical Note, page 362.)

PART IV

MIGRATIONS
1924-1934

Comments on the persons mentioned in Part IV will be found in the Biographical Repertory, beginning on page 367.

1. Europe at Large

McAlmon was no more able to stay put in Europe than in America. He moved restlessly about from country to country, from city to resort, with Paris as his point of departure and return. Life was a succession of "migrations" whose "essential record" can be found in his short fiction. In the early twenties he made several trips to Berlin. Postwar inflation had encouraged an astonishing wantonness, and the night life in the German capital was more dissolute than anywhere on the continent. McAlmon described it as a world of total abandon where nothing remained stable, not even gender. His Berlin stories were collected in Distinguished Air (Grim Fairy Tales) *(1925) which William Bird brought out in a limited editon—115 copies—set on his hand press and printed on fine paper. A good many critics would agree with William Carlos Williams that this volume "heads the list of [McAlmon's] writing. It is a brilliant piece of work." Unfortunately—as Williams adds—*Distinguished Air *is "all but unpublishable because of the nature of the material."* [1]

A Note on the Berlin Stories

All three stories deal with Berlin night life. In the first story, "Distinguished Air," which was McAlmon's favorite, the narrator is a deracinated American who takes an old friend, Rudge Kepler, on a tour of the *nochtlokalen*. Early in the evening they encounter Carrol Timmons, a painter with an "elderly, aunt-like visage," and inquire about an acquaintance, Foster Graham. Timmons reply explains the story's title: "Oh yes, Foster. Tiresome boy. I'm so glad it's you I ran into. When you first spoke I was afraid it might be some of the awful rats who have come to Berlin because of the low exchange. Just too tiresome most of them are. I just feel as if I would have to give up seeing people altogether. And with this after-war atmosphere, and poverty amongst the few really likable Germans one knows. It's all too tragic, I suppose, but I just can't feel any further about that sort of thing. People will starve to death; people will die; or kill themselves, or drink themselves to death. Now Foster has, or had, an air—real distinction—but life has become just too much one thing for him. It's more than enough having one's friends, let alone acquaintances whom one accepts only because of worldliness, forever thrusting their awful and limited realities in one's face. Foster can be a nice thing, when he isn't drunk or in love, or both, but such times are too rare. And when there are such lovely window displays in the shops I can't be bothered by people who bore me. But I suppose the natives can't buy. How they must hate us foreigners. Of course, they know me—from before the war.'

One of the "queer cafés" is the first stop on the tour. "While we were there an elderly fairy, well known to the various psychoanalysts in Germany, came into the place. This night he was dressed as a blond-haired doll, and his fat old body looked in its doll's dress much like that of a barn-storming burlesque soubrette grown a generation or so too old for the part she played. All about the room at various tables were scattered the queer types of Berlin, many of them painted up, two or three in women's clothes, and a great number of types who were not obvious; who might have been mere sightseers, except that Foster generally knew them by sight and swore they were male whores."

They are joined by Ruth, a casual acquaintance, at the moment operating in haze of alcohol and cocaine. "[She] was holding her third whiskey and soda in her hand, and tried with wobbling dignity to sit straight. She held a jewelled walking stick in the other hand and attempted to get some support from it. Pausing for several moments while her fuzzy mind performed a few slow volutions and seemed to stop at the idea that she had better assert her purely detached and scientific interest in all of this, she collected herself to say:

" 'Never in all the times I have come here have I ever been treated as anything but a lady. I'm a Gale-Cawkins, and I do know how to assert my dignity if it is necessary, but a lady does not need to advertise the fact,' she assured me, and twitched her head 'to look the lady' before she lapsed into blinking at space. She came out of this semi-coma only now and then to murmur sentimentally: 'You dear thing. You will come and see me, won't you? There are so few Americans about, and you do look so much like my husband.'

" 'Hell, let's get out of here,' I jerked out suddenly to Kepler as a sudden coagulation of aversions occurred within me, and bad temper robbed me of any ability to laugh. I'd noticed Foster getting increasingly maudlin with a soldier, and Carrol Timmons, down the room was being sloppily affectionate with the boy at his side. . . .

"Feeling somewhat tired, and potentially sleepy, I was, however, ready to make a night of it, but suggested that if we were to go on we'd better take a sniff of the cocaine we had to liven us up. Getting under an archway entrance, away from the wind, and under the light of a near street lamp, we unfolded the paper containing the cocaine, and cautiously sniffed a little. Feeling no immediate sensation, to be aware whether we'd actually taken any into our nostrils or not, or had blown it away, we sniffed a second time. My nose soon began to feel numbed, and in the back of my throat there was a dryness that was mildly disagreeable, while a feeling of nausea was within my stomach. However I felt exhilarated, strong, leapingly light-bodied, and capable of going on without thought of tiredness. Kepler was affected in a similar manner, so we started off at a great pace towards a big dance hall, where I knew there would be plenty of girls to dance with.

" 'They won't insist upon your buying them unless you want to,' I told Kepler, 'and if you slip them fifty cents' worth of marks that will seem a fortune to them.' "

After two o'clock they move on to an after-hours club frequented by dope addicts and down-at-the-heels aristocrats; they meet "a rather dowdy, dark-skinned girl," a Russian refugee, who "took a silver box out of her bag and offered me cocaine on a

tiny silver spoon which was an accessory to the box." They continue the rounds of the all-night places and, having picked up a
couple of girls, head for the O-la-la, "an after-night place into
which all night-lifers in Berlin drifted, as a round-up ôf their
pastimes." It is mid-morning when they leave the O-la-la, and now
in addition to the two girls their group includes a cocaine dealer,
a Polish boy, and two other men. The narrator takes them all to
his hotel room where the girls sprawl "in uncomfortable postures
across the huge bed, . . . the men slumped into chairs, on the
lounge, or on the divan," and at last they sleep.

The second story, "Miss Knight," was highly regarded by
both Ezra Pound and James Joyce and was translated into French
at the latter's suggestion. It too concerns male homosexuality and
manages to be simultaneously funny, pathetic, and repulsive.
Modeled on a well-known expatriate figure, the main character is
Miss Knight, "apparently he to the outside world of not acute
observation," a man who seems to possess only female instincts.
"With her it was 'now I'm tellin' you, Mary' or 'now when these
bitches get elegant I lay 'em out stinkin'',' many times a day, if
her mood was a vital one. . . . She would hastily apologize had
she used the Mary phrase on a man who did not know her well, or
who might resent queerness and undue familiarity. 'Just a way
I talk, yuh know,' she would explain in a conciliatory tone. But in
a group of sister bitches she had few thoughts but to see that none
of them rose above the proper clan manner in elegance without
being 'raised proper.' 'I'm so glad I'm a real man,' she shrieked
across the room or café every now and then to relieve the tension
of ennui that might, and does, settle upon all atmospheres at
times. Properly she believed herself appointed as a camping
comedian, ready to earn a right to her presence by keeping undue
seriousness from making dullness exist through an overlong period." More a character sketch than a story, much of it in Miss
Knight's own words, it is a real tour de force. The third story,
"The Lodging House," deals with the joyless vagaries of hetero-
sexual relationships, blurred and complicated by cocaine and
whiskey.

Life has become just too much for the people McAlmon describes: the male whores close to starvation; the silly fairies who
desperately pretend passions they do not feel; the degenerate

aristocrats who beg marks to buy "snow"; the snickering college boys after a cheap thrill; the neurotic Americans who live impoverished lives, confined by their aberrations to their dreadful cafés; the artists who cannot paint, the writers who cannot write, all the deluded, feebly talented, lost and abandoned men and women of a decaying world.

Shortly after its appearance *Distinguished Air* was reviewed at some length by Ernest Walsh in *This Quarter*. The people in the stories, Walsh said, "ought to be disgusting to the average reader but they remain comic. Just as in life they are comic. McAlmon never writes disgusting books. He isn't disgusting himself. He doesn't exclude anything from his world and is like Walt Whitman in his completeness but different from Whitman in that he doesn't argue with his readers. He doesn't explain either. He doesn't apologize. He is a great white father watching the brood and because some of the brood are a queer lot according to the world McAlmon doesn't shut the door and refuse them what he didn't give them, their life. . . . McAlmon has seen the humanity that is in the lives of these twisted characters and gives us the humanity and leaves the rest out." [2]

McAlmon summarized *Distinguished Air*'s achievement a good deal less portentously: "At any rate the stories did deal with variant types with complete objectivity, not intent on their 'souls' and not distressed by their 'morals'." [3]

(See Bibliographical Note, page 363.)

One of the most famous "migrations" in modern fiction is the trip to Spain in Ernest Hemingway's lost-generation novel The Sun Also Rises. *The incidents on which the fictional account was based have been related at length in Harold Loeb's reminiscences,* The Way It Was. *(Loeb, the original of "Robert Cohn" in the Hemingway book, remembered McAlmon as "a handsome young Westerner with clear blue eyes and the straightest of noses . . . [who] dressed like a Midwestern expediter of freight cars"* [4]*). Previously, Hemingway had gone to Spain in the company of his two publishers, McAlmon and William Bird. The tour, according to William Bird, "extended from Madrid to Seville to Ronda to*

Barcelona (I think) and none of us knew before going that it was not the bullfight season. Hem had heard about bullfights from Gertrude Stein. He talked Bob into a trip at Bob's expense, then suggested to me that I should join them. I caught up with them in Madrid about their third day there and we went on to Seville, then to Ronda which Gertrude had described as a great place for bulls, and then Granada where we had heard there was going to be a novillada *but it rained, so we had to be content with going to see the gypsies dancing in their caves, as all tourists always do. McAlmon was in the chips at that time, but he did think Hem was unreasonable in requiring that he should always be supplied with bottles of Johnny Walker—scarce in Spain, and hellishly expensive."* 5

McAlmon tells of the trip, and of other experiences with Hemingway, in Being Geniuses Together. *His account is inaccurate in some details—but then, as all McAlmon's friends well knew, he was always impatient with detail.*

Let's Be Shadow-Boxers

Intending to return to Paris, I stopped en route at Rapallo, having proofs of books I was publishing to read [1923] (Carnevali's *A Hurried Man* and Mina Loy's *Lunar Baedecker*). It was the town Ezra Pound had chosen for permanent residence, but he was not there at the time. Ernest Hemingway, whom I had not met, but had heard was a Canadian newspaper man, and Mike (Henry) Strater were there with their wives and I met them naturally, there being few restaurants in the town. Henry Strater, a painter, later did illustrations for the Three Mountains Press edition of Ezra's first sixteen *Cantos*.

Hemingway was a type not easy to size up. At times he was deliberately hard-boiled and case-hardened; again he appeared deliberately innocent, sentimental, the hurt, soft, but fairly sensitive boy trying to conceal hurt, wanting to be brave, not bitter or cynical but being somewhat both, and somehow on the defensive, suspicions lurking in his peering analytic glances at a person with whom he was talking. He approached a café with a small-boy, tough-guy swagger, and before strangers of whom he was doubtful a potential snarl of scorn played on his large-lipped, rather loose mouth. Mike Strater was a far more simple and direct, clear-cut young American, unpretending and actually modest.

We all worked those days. There was a French painter about with an American wife who was a stage designer and interior decorator, and one of the other wives was inclined to think she was designing in other ways. Nevertheless we worked, Strater painted portraits of his wife and infant son, the Frenchman painted, Hemingway and I wrote, and at nights we all drank, moderately. Rapallo is situated in a bay which I find emprisoning, although along the coast are hotels beautifully situated. They, however, are generally occupied by elderly English people, and although the Sitwell trio seemed happy in the environment, Rapallo after the sun goes down struck me as dismal and depressing.

Hemingway was suffering a minor tragedy. His wife had lost a briefcase of his containing the script of writing which he had done for nearly a year's period. However, he had three short stories and a few poems on hand; he knew Sherwood Anderson and Ezra Pound and perhaps Ford then, and talked of Ring Lardner's work. I was publishing books in Paris and decided to do his three stories and ten poems. One story, *My Old Man,* was distinctly in the tone of Sherwood Anderson's *I'm a Fool,* and some other race-track story of Anderson, but the other two stories, or rather sketches, were fresh and without derivation so far as I detected.

It is difficult to say who started the attitude in writing which occurs in *My Old Man* and much present American work. It is not so much a style or an approach as an emotional attitude; that of an older person who insists upon trying to think and write as a child, and children in my experience are much colder and more ruthless in their observations than the child characters, be they of child age or old men, in this type of writing.

Ring Lardner wrote about boob baseball players for boobs to read, but he knew it, and therefore his work took on a satirical value amusing to adults. Anita Loos, a sophisticated woman, did the same thing in *Gentlemen Prefer Blondes*. Whether these two took the manner from Sherwood Anderson and added adult wit, or whether Sherwood Anderson took their ironic attitude seriously and became childishly soulful about this naive outlook, one cannot judge. Since, however, Hemingway and a number of others have written in that, to me, falsely naive manner. They may write of gangsters, prize-fighters, bullfighters, or children, but the hurt-child-being-brave tone is there, and all conversation is reduced to lone words or staccato phrases. Possibly I forget my childhood. Some day I'll write to the new air director of the United States, Eugene Vidal, and ask him to check back in his memory. I have a theory that quite a gang of us in South Dakota—a wild and dreary plains state—talked whole sentences and paragraphs, and calculated and often outwitted our elders as very astute intriguers. During those days I was growing up with football and baseball players and track stars, and roughnecks from the roundhouse gang. Several of us used to hop freight cars and bum about doing the harvest seasons and mingle with the hoboes in the jungle. My sceptical nature tells me that in war books, and in this false-naive type of writing, there is altogether too much attitudinized insistence upon the starry-eyed innocence and idealism and sentimentality of not only the child but of the "sensitive roughneck." Possibly South Dakota's hot summers and freezing winters and its pioneer qualities of that not-so-far-back period made us different, however. As it is I read with an incredulous eye when reviewers comment much about this or that writer's ability to capture the "inflection" and "intonation" of American types and the American language.

This incredulity never arises when reading the work of Dos Passos, from *Three Soldiers* on through his trilogy. He has put down types I know and have been intimate with. Some are college educated or good-family types; others are wanderers, restless and grousing and young. They, however, talk in paragraphs and sentences, and they have opinions rather than grunts expressing bewilderment and the thwarted emotion of arrested development. For a time Whit Burnett and Martha Foley, editing *Story*, appeared to think no story "sensitive" or good unless it was about children or somebody child-minded. Collecting statistics at Camp

Zachary Taylor after the armistice, I found that out of 250 men from Kentucky and Tennessee, ninety were complete illiterates, several were actual imbeciles, two had syphilitic rheumatism; and any number had married at childhood ages from twelve—the youngest—to seventeen. They had married girls from nine—the youngest—to fourteen. Because of this I am ready to believe that the Faulkner and Caldwell depictions of ingrown sections of the country are based on existing conditions, but don't they concentrate on the extreme cases too much?

Dos Passos manages to suggest horror enough without picking complete mental deficients, prize-fighters, gangsters, or hurt children of whatever age. Possibly the old Spanish writers of the picaresque novels got their tough lads better. Certainly now in Barcelona, in Berlin and Paris, it is possible to talk to virtual children of the streets, and find no hurt-baby wail in their conversation. They're tough and they're knowing. I may be wrong, but it appears that there is a new-preciousness in one stream of contemporary American writing, and that is the fake child-mentality quality. It was not there in Hawthorne, or Henry James, or O. Henry, or Dreiser; it is not there in a quantity of present writers, but reviewers seem to adjudge it as the true American, and surely America produces many adults and types who are as alertly aware and sophisticated as any in the world.

One night in Rapallo the lot of us were talking of birth control, and spoke of the cruelty of the law which did not allow young unmarried women to avoid having an unwanted child. Recalling an incident of college days I told a story of a girl who had managed to have herself taken care of. Her attitude was very casual. "Oh, it was nothing. The doctor just let the air in and a few hours later it was over."

Two years later there appeared in some magazine a story by Hemingway called "Hills Like White Elephants." A young couple are arguing about whether the girl should or should not do something. It isn't immediately clear. After several beers she retires and when she returns she says sadly, "Well, it's done." I didn't see the point of the story and reread it and encountered the phrase "Let the air in." Later Hemingway informed me that my remark suggested the story.

Yes, Hemingway was a new type for me. He must be actually

young and naive, for he, in telling me, still seemed to believe that young ladies could help themselves out of difficulties while at the same time many undesired children are being born. Later, a protesting flapper who had read his story and was made hopeful, one gathers, commented bitterly that the tale was all lies, like white elephants.

Later the lot of us were in Paris at the same time and after a trip to London I talked of going to Spain. Hemingway, who knew Gertrude Stein—I didn't then—wanted much to see a bullfight. I had missed seeing one in Mexico, at Juarez, mercifully, as they are generally bad shows: small bulls and poor matadors. After a week or so of talking about it we headed towards Spain. Hemingway and his then wife had a fondness for pet names, which they called each other, their baby, and their puppy. Beery-poppa (Hemingway) said a loving good-bye to Feather-kitty (Mrs. [Hadley Richardson] Hemingway), Bumby (baby), and waxen-puppy, and he and I well lubricated with whisky got into the train.

The next day, on the way to Madrid, our train stopped at a wayside station for a time. On the track beside us was a flat car, upon which lay the maggot-eaten corpse of a dog. I, feeling none too hale and hearty, looked away, but Hemingway gave a dissertation on facing reality. It seems that he had seen the stacked corpses of men maggot-eaten in the war in a similar way. He advised a detached and scientific attitude towards the corpse of the dog. He tenderly explained that we of our generation must inure ourselves to the sight of pain and grim reality. I recalled that Ezra Pound had talked once of Hemingway's "self-hardening process." At last he said, "Hell, Mac, you write like a realist. Are you going to be a romantic on us?"

I spurted forth some oath and went to the dining car to order whisky. Not only was the sight of the dog before my eyes, its stench was in my nostrils, and I have seen many dead dogs, cats, and corpses borne in on the tide of New York harbor when working on a lumber barge. That dog had no distinction or novelty as a corpse. Several years later Paul Rosenfeld informed me that Hemingway had told this story to prove his assertion that I was a romanticist. He was realist enough himself to join me in the dining car and have a whisky, however, but he surely had duly analyzed all of his sensations "on seeing the maggot-eaten corpse of a dog on a flat car in Spain while wondering what it is that makes a guy who has seen so much of life as McAlmon shudder."

[According to Sylvia Beach: "Joyce remarked to me one day that he thought it was a mistake, Hemingway's thinking himself such a tough fellow and McAlmon trying to pass himself off as the sensitive type. It was the other way round, he thought." [6]]

The day that we were to see our first bullfight we agreed that the horse part of it might repel us, so we had a few drinks before taking our seats. We would doubtless have had them anyway. We had a bottle of whisky with us, with the understanding that if shocked we would gulp down a quantity to calm ourselves. My reactions to the bullfight were not at all what one had anticipated. At first it seemed unreal, like something happening on the screen.

The first bull charged into the ring with tremendous violence, and did not refuse a charge. When the horses were brought in the bull charged head-on and lifted the horse over its head. The horns did not penetrate.

Instead of a shock of disgust I rose in my seat and let out a yell. Things were happening too quickly for my mind to think of the horse's suffering. Later, however, when one of the horses was galloping in hysteria about the ring, treading on its own entrails, I decidedly didn't like it and looked away. Since, I discover that many a hardened Spanish "aficionado," even the brother of a bullfighter, does likewise.

Hemingway at once became an "aficionado," that is, a passionate bullfight fan or enthusiast intent upon learning all about the art. If I suspect that his need to love the art of the bullfight came from Gertrude Stein's praise of them, as well as from his belief in the value of self-hardening, it is only because his bullfight book takes a belligerent attitude defending his right to love bullfighting. There are quantities of English and American people who have been bullfight enthusiasts for years before that summer of 1924, when Hemingway and I each saw our first.

By the end of that day my temper about all connected with the bullfight was much what it is now. I resented the crowd's brutality, and the way they would throw mats and articles into the ring at moments dangerous to the matadors. The crowd was taking no chances. The bull was—when he was—a magnificent animal, a snorting engine of black velocity and force. The matadors moved beautifully and did their dance well, and played seriously with death. The horses I decided to overlook as a Spanish brutality no worse than many a French and Anglo-Saxon cruelty. It has always been the Portuguese bullfight which I prefer, for the bull is properly killed from on horseback, and the horse is a magnificent Arabian mare or stallion, and beautifully trained and never injured by the bull without disgrace to the "rejoneador" or rider. In this there is breathless speed and terrifying beauty of power and velocity. It is not so intricate or so daring an art as Spanish bullfighting, but it has more throbbing and breathtaking excitement, for me, generally. The wonderful matadors and their fights are rare and I recall too many degrading exhibitions.

William Bird, who was then associated with me in the publishing of books, joined Hemingway and myself in Madrid and we did a tour, seeing Granada, Seville, Ronda, and more bullfights. Bird also liked bullfights, and neither he nor I were putting ourselves through a "hardening process." After the first bullfight we each took them as matter-of-factly as if we'd been seeing them all our lives, and our criticism of the matador without art was as ruthless as any Spaniard's.

Before leaving Paris Hemingway had been much of a shadowboxer. As he approached a café he would prance about, sparring at shadows, his lips moving to call his imaginary opponent's bluff. Upon returning from Spain he substituted shadow-bullfighting for shadow-boxing. The amount of imaginary cape-work and sword thrusts which he made in those days was formidable. Later he went to Key West and went in for barracuda fishing and I wonder if he took then to shadow-barracuda-fighting, or if in Africa he will shadow-lion-hunt. He has a boy's need to be a tough guy, a swell boxer, a strong man.

All of this shadow-boxing was to keep himself fit, naturally, and a couple of years later when Morley Callaghan, also a bit of a boxer, arrived in Paris, he and Hemingway staged bouts. Before, Hemingway had a bout with a young French writer, Jean

Prévost, but it seems that it was a draw, a sparring match with no referee.

The Callaghan-Hemingway bout, however, was apparently not a draw, and it was reported to me several ways, by Hemingway, Callaghan, and from Scott Fitzgerald. Callaghan's report was that Scott was to referee and they were to have three or four two-minute rounds. Scott got very interested in the boxing match. Hemingway was the taller and heavier man. Callaghan was short, inclined to a look of flabbiness and rotundity. Scott was sure that Hemingway would need to play with Callaghan and let him down easily without showing him up in a mortifying way. The first round did not come out that way and Scott forgot to tell time, Callaghan had Hemingway backing away, and getting winded; but the fight went on and on. Neither of the boxers would suggest that the round-time was up, but after some minutes Scott called time. Callaghan was sure that Hemingway thought Scott forgot to call time purposely.

Hemingway's story was that he had been drinking the night before and was boxing on three pick-me-up whiskies so that his wind gave out. The decision results were, however, that neither Hemingway nor Callaghan could decide what the bout proved. Was one a better boxer but not so good a writer as the other, or was the other a better writer and boxer, or had Scott framed one or the other of them?

At this time Hemingway felt that Callaghan was imitating his style, and it is true that Callaghan was writing about prize-fighters, gangsters, and inarticulate roughnecks, but there was Ring Lardner who had done a bit of this before either of them. Gertrude Stein was the repeating child, and Sherwood Anderson had injected highfalutin' sensibility into the hearts of childish boobs. Possibly then their writing bout was a draw. The final bell has not rung. Callaghan, admittedly a pedestrian writer and perhaps dull—but it is the fashion in some quarters to court the dull —seems interested in wider and more normal phases of life. At least much less of his writing is a defence and explanation of himself and of the reactions and emotions which he feels he ought to have. Hemingway is always protesting and explaining his emotions so much that one is able to wonder if he has not invented some convention for himself as to how one should feel in each particular circumstance. To be brave, professionally here, tough there, gentle and inarticulate with tenderness there, the rough man, reticent but full of sensibility.

[According to William Bird, McAlmon was one of those who served as Hemingway's sparring partners: "I met Bob in a Montparnasse bar—his upper lip was covered with surgeon's plaster. He could speak only very indistinctly, but made me understand that Hem had socked him. It was during that same period when Hem was assaulting Dreiser, Max Eastman, and I forget who else. Bob was quite cheerful about his wounded lip, it even seemed to me that he felt flattered to be in such good company." [7]]

In Paris there were a constant stream of old-timers and new-comers pouring into the Quarter, from America, England, and Scandinavia, and I have always had a number of Swedish friends. If told to pick the people most civilized and sympathetic to me I believe that people would be the Swedish. They have the advantage of time behind them without the ennui and decay it so often dumps like garbage upon a race's apprehension.

John Herrmann was about with his wife, Josephine Herbst (now a very "Proletarian" novelist), and he had the manuscript of his first novel, which I decided to publish. *What Happens* was not startlingly great, but it was a direct and authentic picture of American youth and not marred by idealized "love" scenes. Today it would appear milk-pure, but it wasn't permitted into either London or America then. It probably would not have sold well in any case. What recommended it to me was its obvious young-ness and undecorated directness, and its unawareness of the "glamor" and "romance" and "great love interest" needed in a book which is to sell. As a later publisher in America said to Herrmann, "Your book reads, but we can't publish it. It's about the sort of people we know in an ordinary way. It's too much what happens." It would have been improved by a touch of wit, no doubt, but it would have lost the gangly, awkward, fumbling-bewilderment of its youthful quality. Perhaps too few people read other than romantically, however, for it to have been a commercial venture. Later, some publisher took on Bob Coates' *Eater of Darkness,* which Contact Editions published. It was by way of being a surrealistic novel, or satire and burlesque of surrealism, of Stein's and Joyce's style, and of itself. Properly it should have been a brilliant and intellectually racy story, highly amusing to an intellectual or an author. It was a book for authors. In some way, however, it failed to come off. Mr. Coates has not, in person, a sparkling presence of wit. His manner of speech is rather slow and fumbling. Perhaps he pondered too long a book which should have been written with gay and malicious joy. The script he handed me was a beautiful affair; a work of art in itself with the cover and inside pages designed by himself; a modern illumined manuscript. He had to retype that wonderful affair, however. The French typesetters could never have unravelled its mystery, and we couldn't afford to photograph the binding and pages and have them reproduced in color, even had we thought the book worth that expense.

2

Hemingway had become much of a bullfight enthusiast since his 1924 trip to Spain. In one of his earlier short stories one character says, "It's no fun if you can't skee any more," and the other character responds, "No, it's no fun if you can't skee any more." He now carried this manner of perfect dialogue and the intonation of the American language over to bullfighting and bullfight stories. It was all muscular and athletic prose, but for this period in the spirit of "it's no fun if you can't see bullfights any more."

He talked a great deal about bullfights as the great art, the beautiful dance involving death, and withal one summer, quite a number of people decided to do the July fiesta week in Pampeluna, Spain. Having done a quick trip to Egypt, and back via Athens and Constantinople, I also hied myself to Pampeluna, and there before me were Donald Ogden Stewart, Dos Passos, William and Sally Bird, young George O'Neill, Hadley and Ernest Hemingway, and an English captain [Donman Huyler Smith] from Sandhurst, who had known Hemingway in Milan after the war.

The days and the nights were hot with a heat that sweated through one's flesh and bones. However, the fiesta spirit was rampant, and everybody was willing to drink plenty of pernod and forget the heat. The town, the first two days before the bull-fights came on, was quiet till noon, when the café terraces were crowded. After lunch the streets were empty again, but at six o'clock the fiesta gaieties began. Innumerable throngs of peasants from the mountains filled the town, their necks encircled with necklaces of garlic, and various shaped goatskin bags of wine thrown over their shoulders. Some were made in the form of ships, or of dolls or animals. To drink one held the goatskin high, squeezed, and a small stream of goaty-tasting wine poured into one's open lips. This took learning, but the natives were adept. Continually little crowds of natives came and went, blowing whistles or playing more or less primitive musical instruments. Groups formed and danced solos in circles. Donald Ogden Stewart proved himself a born comedian with an inherent clowning instinct, for after his first solo dance he was the friend of the peasants from all the surrounding countryside. He knew how to utilize his yankee professor's appearance. With the Americans he had the advantage of having his "crazy-fool" cracks and witticisms understood, but he managed to troupe his comedy across to the Spaniards without a common language.

All of the American-English gathering proceeded to lose each other generally the first two nights. Each one tagged on to or got picked up by some wandering group of musicians and boys from the mountains, and the dancing and drinking continued till early morning. The town slept till well past noon.

We all went to inspect the bulls which were to be used in the corridas. The third morning, the day of the first bullfight, everyone was up by six o'clock, and in the boarded street down which the bulls for the day were to be driven. Hundreds of boys and young men, natives, stood along the sides of the street and ran ahead as the bulls dashed towards the bull ring. A few got butted or knocked against the walls by an excited and bewildered bull, but no one was badly injured or killed, as does happen sometimes. Later, when the fierce bulls had been driven into their corrals to wait for the afternoon corridas, the amateur fun began. A heifer, light-bodied steer, or yearling bull—but seldom —would be released into the ring. Hundreds of aspiring bull-fighters were in the ring, and the bewildered heifer, steer, or young bull would dash here and there, sometimes charging, but as often merely looking for means of escape.

Hemingway had been talking a great deal about courage, and how a man needs to test himself to prove to himself that he can take it. I am doubtful. If one takes it too much one may begin to get nervy, or shellshocked, or plainly fed up. Hemingway, however, had persuaded himself that he must prove himself. With his coat he tried to attract the charge and the repeated charge of a steer, but the two hundred odd others in the ring were all trying to capture that mystified animal's attention also. Finally, Hemingway took a charge straight on face, and then catching the steer's horns, attempted to throw it. He did break its strength and got cheered by the crowd. When the steer was released it ran away bellowing a bewildered moo, its tail wagging pathetically, and an expression on its face indicating that it was having no fun at all.

Bill Bird and Dos Passos were either the bravest or just plain quitters. Anyway, they didn't get into the ring to play with them calves. George O'Neill, then about seventeen, Don Stewart, Hemingway, and myself, however, were all there. The first day only Hemingway proved himself. My idea was to evade getting butted, and the others ran out of the path of a charge also. Later, however, Hemingway talked about bravery to Donald Ogden Stewart. Stewart confessed to me that maybe one might as well save one's courage to use when an actual crisis occurs, if it is there to use. You cannot judge one's reaction to one type of danger by his bravado.

I was drinking altogether too much pernod and goat-skin tasting red wine, and eating heavy Spanish food. The idea of having a calf, steer, or young bull, charge into my breadbasket did not appeal to me. I never did anything but dodge out of the way of those cattle, and if they appeared to pursue I jumped the fence.

All members of the party liked aspects of the bullfights by the skilled matadors, but no one ever became the fervid enthusiast which Hemingway elected to become. Bullfights that are truly great are too rare, and one must see many to see fine ones. For the rest, nothing is more vulgar and disgusting than a bad bullfight, and clumsy killings of the bull are more horrible than the horse part of the fight. The lost, baby-calf look of wondering stupidity on a bull's face is heartbreaking, particularly when it is a brave bull, but does not want to fight or to charge horses. It is complete nonsense that all bulls are naturally attacking and fighting animals. Even goaded by torture some of them remain brave but fight only to be let alone.

The fiesta week over at Pampeluna, Bill and Sally Bird and I boarded a bus and went to Burguette, a Spanish town near the French border. It was tiny and quiet, with one bare peasant inn, and but a few cottages. Herds of sheep and goats flocked in the surrounding hills, and muleteers drove their donkeys down the road, bearing cordwood or wine bags. Some miles up in the mountains was an old mine shaft and a stream where trout-fishing was good. After a few days Hemingway and his wife joined us, and we took walks to the fishing falls, and it was here that Hemingway fished one day while thinking out his story *Great Two-Hearted River*. He was so intent thinking about what it was that a man who was fishing would be thinking about, and what Bird and I would be thinking about, that he didn't catch many trout, but he jotted down notes for the story. Some declare it great. I find it a stunt and artificial, and do not believe his mind works that way at all. I think he is a very good business man, a publicist, who looks ahead and calculates, and uses rather than wonders about people.

For a few days things were restful and pastoral at Burguette, and the country about was beautiful with innumerable walks to be taken. Later Chink Smith, Dos Passos, and George O'Neill arrived, and the next day these three and I started to take a walk in the Pyrenees, intending to spend about a fortnight with the little republic of Andorra as our goal. Hemingway accompanied us for about five kilometres and then dutifully returned to his wife. We made some thirty-five kilometres that first day and were well into the mountains. In the beginning we agreed to take it leisurely rather than to make a race or a show-up competition of the jaunt.

However, young George O'Neill was full of vim and vigor and youth, and he carried a cane. Apart from striding along at a great pace he took swings at passing stones with his cane. Chink Smith, the army man, had the maps, and while swearing that he wouldn't try to show up the rest of us he noted that Dos Passos and George both set a pace hard to follow. The next day we did forty kilometres, and another day, when we had been lost twice in the mountains, we did well over sixty kilometres. Eleven o'clock at night found us faltering footsore and leg-worn over a rocky road which was endless into a rather sizeable mountain town. That night we had to sleep in a haystack, but we slept all right.

At one little village, hardly more than a shack and a pig-pen, George O'Neill noticed a letter on a fence post. It was for him. He had seen the name of the village on the map and gave it as an address, but in these little so-called towns the mailman came seldom and then on foot from miles away. For days George had been expecting money from his father, and this letter contained that money. It was pure luck to have found it.

Life in these villages was going on much as it had hundreds of years ago. The costumes were skirted trousers and leggings, of bright colors. The mountaineers had an air of nobility which simple and primitive people have. At one time, crossing a field, we inquired our way and one old patriarch offered us a drink of wine from his goat-sack and told us that we need not have fear. They knew our kind here, and many of their own were like us. Dos Passos translated and we were naturally delighted that he had taken us for smugglers.

What food there was to eat had no variety whatever. There was goat cheese, black bread and continual "tortillas" (heavy egg concoctions filled with potatoes and sometimes onions). There was coffee with goat's milk also. In one village at noon we seated ourselves in the peasant woman's kitchen. In the corner was an old hag certainly past a hundred years. At short intervals she coughed and gurgled as though it were her death cry. Chink Smith and I didn't feel like eating then, and I never got to like the goat-skin tasting wine. Dos Passos, however, loved it all, the food, the wine, the bread, the walking. There are not many men in the world with more gusto and enthusiasm and zeal than Dos Passos. It is just possible perhaps that he was overenthusiastic at moments when Chink or I would have as soon had him say

"We've started so let's go on. We're in for it." That wasn't his way though. He and George O'Neill had exuberance and vivacity for all events.

I had started the walking trip unprepared, not having planned it ahead as had the others. My "alpargatas" (canvas slippers) were not suitable for mountain paths; my achilles tendon began to ache.

Rheumatism, gout, and blisters on my soles began assailing me the second day. They did not cease either, and climbing up mountainsides was hard work, and going down steep mountains I went slipping and sailing and flying too fast. It had become a race and I discovered that if I kept ahead there were more chances of longer rests. On the sixth day, however, we struck a fairly large town which had a bus that ran towards the French border, and here I decided that Andorra could wait for a later visit. These long walking trips are very fine, if the companions will let them be leisurely, but in this case the distances between towns and the lack of places to sleep in many of the villages did not permit leisure. And en route we drank a good deal of "agua gigante," a powerful and effervescent drink of the absinthe family. It tastes like ethereal nectar, and however tired we arrived in a village, after a drink or so of this we felt wings on our feet.

The others continued on to Andorra, but it is to be regretted that no one kept notes of the trip. At the time no one of the party but Dos Passos spoke any Spanish whatever. That was dampening to my enthusiasm and curiosity, but finally a five- to six-day walking trip is long enough for one who isn't fanatic about the pastime.

(See Bibliographical Note, page 363.)

William Carlos Williams, according to Kay Boyle, was "a soil, a core, a homeland, to which McAlmon returned and to which he gave total loyalty." [8] *When Williams and his wife Flossie came to Europe in 1924, McAlmon did the honors in Paris and accompanied them on some of their travels.*

Williams

William Carlos Williams and his wife Florence intended to spend a sabbatical year on the Continent, his first lengthy vacation from doctoring for fifteen years. He had not been in Paris long, however, before he was worrying about his "practice." He was a child specialist, but as he practiced medicine in the same town in which he was born, he was easy prey for numerous old ladies, poor people, negroes and Italian working people, who wanted no other doctor. He was not severe about his charges and not much good at collecting accounts, and in consequence he had always done a great deal of general practitioner work.

Possibly it was his generation, or his earlier association with Ezra Pound and Hilda Doolittle, but Williams was inclined to go literary and nostalgic about things Greek. It is not unreasonable to ask if the Greek and classic tradition is not needlessly restrictive, because much fine literature has been entirely outside that tradition, as we are now discovering. Arthur Waley having translated *Lady Murasaki*, Pearl Buck having done likewise for *All Men Are Brothers,* we are permitted to see a literature which indicated an ongoing panorama and which does not inflict an arbitrary pattern upon life. That pattern does for small nations and races whose conventions have hardened into a mould, England, Denmark, provincial France, etc. It is not suitable to a polyglot America, any more than it is or ever was to Russia. It is quite possible that Russia with her *Dead Souls* and various lengthy novels of family life in the process of decay because of a social order has more to indicate to Americans than the so-called classic tradition, derived from Greece through English literature. In contemporary times Proust, Joyce, Dorothy Richardson, Dos Passos, Jules Romain, and others have broken with that "classic" formula, as indeed had Cervantes long ago. Joyce did retain a precious and literary nostalgia for the Greek poetizing, word-prettifying qualities dear to Pound's heart, *melopœia, logopœia, phanopœia*. That is, an interest in words as words for their evocative and suggestive qualities to the extent of being indifferent to the larger qualities of material, content-concept, and the whole compositional realization of relationships rooted in a social order.

That "I am a poet, a bard, a singer" attitude has disposed many people to view poets as flighty creatures incapable of observing reality or of coping with experience, and it certainly has bred a spirit in the universities which makes very precious lads and lassies indeed out of young people, who, if they must be poets, would be much better poets using the idioms and symbols of their own time. We simply do not live on an island in the Mediterranean, where the sun flashes on the sea's wine-dark waves, like the reflection of light on shining helmets. Greek gods and mythological figures mean nothing more than Hans Christian Andersen or Grimm characters to most. Today one gathers that there are many children as interested in primitive Mayan or Toltec civilizations as they are in the Greek. Certainly these civilizations produced an architecture as worthy as any, and we know little of what literature they may have produced.

Williams would tell amazing experiences which occurred to him through his years of doctoring. On the outskirts of his town was a colony of settlers intact throughout a two-hundred-year period, ingrowing and interrelated, with the customs of long ago. Because Williams is kindly and understanding he had quantities of patients amongst Italian settlers and negroes, and some of his stories were weirdly amusing or tragic, but deeply based in life. Now and then he wrote poems about these characters, or short stories, but these stories he seemed not to rate so highly himself as some precious poem inoculated with nostalgia for something Greek or poetic in a way that the pedants conceive poetic: that is, poetic in a way that they have been taught was metrical and had "beauty," in a convention.

Williams as an organism was and is one of the most interesting "sensibilities" which America has produced. He was over-impressionable, in that the quiverings of his sensibility were so constant that he never had time to clarify his observation, but instead was lost in a species of life-wonder, bewilderment, and torment. He has written many fine poems and short stories, but

he is apt to think his best not worth publishing because it has
come straight from a direct and stark impulse, it does not perplex
and torment and irritate him and make him restless. In New York
I kept him from destroying one such poem, one of the most
beautiful in any language. It was the *Portrait of the Author*,
which appeared first with Contact, and later in his book, *Sour
Grapes*. Marianne Moore later commented on it, saying, "It pre-
serves the atmosphere of a moment, into which the impertinence
of life cannot intrude."

But Williams thought it too intimate, or not art, or whatever. Miss Moore, I believe, forced him to save various others of
his better poems which he was inclined to reject. I cannot go
deeply into the reasons for this blind spot in him. Joyce and Ezra
Pound and H.D. and many others strike me as being "bards,"
Greek-spirited and worded and traditioned when to be so is un-
called-for and precious. It may be literary, but it does not make
literature in a sound sense. Pretty words and their lovely rhythms
and colors are not enough, and an obsession about these qualities
in words is, I suspect, a preoccupation for the younger and de-
veloping years. The first and autobiographic novel of almost
every writer who has later emerged as first rate in the last few
years has devoted passages to ecstasy and rhapsody on words and
their lovely flavors.

There was a good deal of party-giving in Paris for Williams
and Florence, his wife. Sylvia Beach and Adrienne Monnier had
him to dinner with Valéry Larbaud, and both the American and
the Frenchman came away feeling powerfully stimulated, for
both had quick and responsive minds and broad sympathies, and
a tremendous expectancy which made me feel a jaded cynic, not
less than ten million years old, and on his last incarnational sentence before joining the infinite.

Williams was intent upon meeting young French writers, the
dadaists, Tristan Tzara, the surrealists, to get to the root of what
it was that they were driving at. I suppose he felt I let him down.
I never was romantic about French groups, and knew many of
the dadaists who seemed to like being dadaists because dada is
nothing, so they could do nothing and feel fine about it. It was
impossible to know them and to glance at their work and to be
impressed; they were often likeable, bright, good conversational-

ists; but Williams would not at first be convinced but that they were profound and moved by a significant impetus. He would not have it that this one was a calculating opportunist and publicist, that one a likeable young man intent upon becoming a man of affairs with a sound status in the bourgeois world, and a few others aspiring lovers with definite ideas about establishing themselves to enjoy leisure.

Before Williams and Florence headed towards the south of France there was a party at the Trianon, then the restaurant at which Joyce always dined. Mina Loy, Sylvia Beach, Adrienne Monnier, Kathleen Cannell, Laurence and Clotilde Vail, in all some twenty people were there. Williams had expected Joyce to be perhaps more staidly the great man of letters, but Joyce had been having apéritifs and dearly loves a party. He wanted there to be singing, preferably of Irish songs and in an Irish tenor voice. He wanted general hilarity. Williams wanted these too, but he also wanted there to be profound discussion, one gathered. Someone at the table asked Norah Joyce if she read her husband's work.

Norah said, "Sure, why would I bother? It's enough he talks about that book and he's at it all the time. I'd like a bit of life of my own." Later, she admitted that she had read the last pages of *Ulysses*, portraying Molly Bloom's thoughts. Her comment was short, but to the point, "I guess the man's a genius, but what a dirty mind he has, hasn't he?"

I assured Norah that had it not been for her keeping him down to earth Joyce would have remained the word-prettifying bard, the martyred sensibility, Stephen Dedalus. Norah would not have it that he had learned about women from her. "People say that I have helped him be a genius! Go along with you," Norah scoffed. "They'll say if it hadn't been for that ignoramus of a woman what a man he would have been, but never you mind, I could tell them a thing or two about him after twenty years of putting up with him, and the devil take him when he's off on one of his rampages."

The party became joyous as Joyce wished. He sang Irish come-all-you's, and everybody got together on a few like "Love's Old Sweet Song," or "Carry me back to Old Virginny." Clotilde Vail knew a few "blues" songs, and I knew some spirituals and

cowboy songs. The Trianon stayed open late that night, but it
ended when Norah decided that Jim was going too far and there
would be no handling him if she did not get him home now.
"It's you who see him in a jolly state, but it's me who has to bear
the brunt of it if his eyes get ailing, and what a martyr the man
can be you've no idea," she apologized.

Williams revealed one day that he was annoyed by a comment of Mencken's, which mentioned one of Williams' books
and stated that Williams was a village horse doctor or some such.
There the difference in generations was a barrier between Williams and myself. It hadn't occurred to me that he would look
upon Mencken as other than a Babbitt-iconoclast for Babbitts.
In college several years back there had been two girls with the
intention of making their living as writers, since they felt it
would permit them more freedom than set positions. One of them
discovered that Mr. Mencken delighted in exchanging flirtatious
letters with lady writers, and the two of them had a wonderful
time carrying on mail flirtations with that romantic editor. It
simply was not in the minds of our, the younger, generation to
think of Mencken as a person with a feeling for literature.

Mencken is a "case." There is hardly a travelling salesman
or a store clerk, insurance or real-estate salesman, who is a
"great hand for reading something that makes you think" who
does not view Mencken with awe. Gertrude Stein believes she
belongs to a great and common public; and perhaps Williams
has the germ of that same feeling within him. Permit me to suspect that any of Mencken's public who read books of literary
value do so because of blurbs, misunderstanding, and for all the
wrong qualities. That does not mean that many simple people do
not have tremendous and authentic appreciation for the fine
qualities in art. It merely means that Mencken's public are not
simple and honest, and when the yokels and hicks and medioc-
rities take on what they think intellectual and ironic pretensions,
it is time to worry about their getting control of the book market.

Williams has said that I have a "genius for life," while be-
moaning his New England soul and his not having ventured far
or long from the town of his birth. He may be right about me; if
despair, a capacity for indifference, long and heavy spells of ennui
which takes bottles of strong drink to cure, and a gregarious but

not altogether loving nature is a "genius for life," I have it. However, with Williams I always feel more or less gay and he is one of the few who can tell his soul problems and probe life's deeper darkness without irritating or boring me. He, Florence, and I headed to the south of France for a period and there I remained when they went later to Italy.

(See Bibliographical Note, page 363.)

"All of us who were interested in Robert McAlmon," Sylvia Beach wrote, *"were looking forward to his contribution to the writing of the twenties. Unfortunately, the more he thought of it, the more he was convinced of the uselessness of effort. 'To hell with grammar,' he once wrote to me, 'have thrown mine out of the window.' He would tell me he was leaving for the south of France, to look up some place where he could get away from people and do some work. I'd get a telegram: 'Found right place and quiet room.' Soon somebody would mention seeing Bob down there. 'His room is above the bistrot and they all meet at the bistrot.' "* 9

On the Riviera McAlmon observed the directionless life of the rich and indolent. This was Scott Fitzgerald's country, the world of his expatriate novel *Tender Is the Night.* If Fitzgerald treats his characters with deadly seriousness, McAlmon treats his dispassionately. Fitzgerald's account, for all its diamond-hard, many-faceted brilliance, is ultimately adolescent; McAlmon's account may be rough, but it is adult.

Evening on the Riviera, The Playground of the World

It being six o'clock evening, two hours before dinner, Toodles had already began to talk about how she would not serve any cocktails, to herself, or to the other people about her, that night.

"I'm through; not another cocktail does anyone get from me for three weeks, so unless you all love me for myself—and you do love your Toodles, don't you—you needn't come around. The General tells me I've run way into my next quarter's allowance. Think of it, my bill for drinks last month was over three thousand francs, and that doesn't include things I sneaked through on the General by paying for them on the spot," Toodles, otherwise Mrs. Dawson, chortled.

To see Toodles one had best think back forty or even forty-five years, when she was a girl of between fifteen and twenty. She must then have been a plump, cuddling, elfish-like creature, full of giggles, high spirits, and confiding, never-ending prattle. She still at present saw herself as a joybird, claimed to be but forty-five years old, and explained that the photograph of her three sons, the youngest of whom could not be less than twenty-three, must make her seem very aged, but she'd married so young, at seventeen. About the question of age, however, her own or anybody's, she was shy, and inclined to halt for a moment in her prattle, distrustfully.

"I'm sure she's still a beautiful woman, and that men are as wild about her as ever," she was inclined to comment if some friend of her earlier days was mentioned. Toodles bore no one ill will, except at moments when they stood in the way of her desires to bubble on, irresistibly seeking to be the center of attention.

"I must dress for dinner now," she told Allen Cowles, who was thrumming out ragtime on her piano after others had left the room. "And of course you'll stay, and play music for me. And listen," she whispered, "I'll make you just one wee little cocktail, but don't you tell the General. You know, there's nobody can make cocktails like your little Toodles, is there?"

Tonight Toodles, always high-spirited in action, was feeling more than usually high-spirited as she'd rested much in the last few days. Her right eye, that became decidedly crooked at moments of fatigue, looked almost direct, and a flush was on her cheeks so that her face flesh looked firmer and younger too. Really it could not actually matter how old Toodles became; she'd remain somewhat elfish, exuberant, and primitively child-like to the end.

Because she could not abide living with her sons and their wives, not to mention the places they'd chosen to live in—South Africa, and two other out-of-the-way places—Toodles had for the last two years been a paying guest on the Riviera in the home of an ex-Russian general and his wife. Whatever other paying guests stayed too were generally friends of Toodles who liked visiting or staying about her because of the constant stream of people coming and going around her. Toodles did not want to be alone much; more than five minutes at a time, during daytime, and not at all during the evening until she retired. For this reason, the General and his wife, Madame Cavallera, found her at moments wearing because she'd be at them during busy hours to come to her part of the house and chat with her.

Remaining at the piano, Allen Cowles began playing some Puccini, which he and Toodles both adored; as soon as he started an aria section from *Tosca* a great exclamation of delight came from Toodles' room, and she appeared at the doorway just loosening her day dress at the shoulder. Standing, posed dramatically, she raised her hand then and began to sing with mighty fervor. That section finished she said, "Did I tell you the joke on the General? He heard me singing while he was working in the garden and asked his wife who the woman with the wonderful voice was I had calling on me. I tell you, I could have made a go of it when I was younger, but Fred wouldn't have it. No sir, he wanted his little Toodles in his own home, and I must say never a moment's worry did he ever give me because of his attentions to another woman. That's why I've remained single these ten years he's been gone, though many a chance I've had; and the Princess Gura tells me I'm foolish not to take a lover."

Allen went on playing, as Toodles slipped back to her room to continue dressing. He was a young American she'd picked up weeks back when he was playing jazz music at a casino dance, and Toodles said she could see at once he was more of a gentleman than jazz players are usually. At any rate it was quite the thing at the moment to be enthusiastic about jazz, and to entertain jazz players.

"You're my boy, aren't you, Allen?" Toodles commented, coming out of her room, dressed now in a black dinner dress that fell in loose folds about her short, rotund figure. "See, I'm wearing this string of pearls for you tonight. They're not my best. The General makes me keep them in the vault in Paris for fear I'll be tempted to pawn them sometime, and he's right too. I always need a man to look after my money affairs for me. Smell me too. Isn't that wonderful perfume? Now I tell you, there'd be less unhappiness in marriages if all women knew how to handle and please men the way I did Fred. I always dressed so he'd be proud of me; kept the house cheerful, full of flowers and fresh odors, and he never ceased being my lover."

There was a shout to Toodles from outside, so she slipped to the balcony which overlooked a mountain and seascape outside her room.

"Ha, ha, there's another one of my boys. And your Juliet speaks to you from the balcony. Come on up, Eddie; you'll stay for dinner. And just one cocktail, no more, remember, but don't say anything to the General. He's been frowning at me for the last three days because of my drink bills, and declares he doesn't know how he can manage to make my allowance meet everything if I go on."

Eddie Campbell, Toodles declared, looked on the dark side of things too much, but not when he was around her. "I give you a cocktail, dance with you while Allen plays, and you feel better, don't you? What you're needing is a woman with the right disposition to keep you cheered up," she informed him some minutes after he'd come up. They were standing together out on the balcony looking at twilight come over the mountains and upon the ocean, as Allen was playing the love music from *Tristan and Isolde*. As he played Toodles chanted forth a phrase, and gestured with her hand over her heart to Allen, and then to Eddie. When the music ceased, however, she stopped her fervent gesturings and came back to the balcony, waving in her right hand a long ivory cigarette holder.

"Now I'm a woman of the world, and you mustn't think that I don't have profound thoughts. As Fred's wife, when he was Ambassador to Munich, and in circles that I've always been drawn into, I had to know how to parry a point and how to conduct myself. It's matter of philosophy for me to be cheerful. I say, keep the bluebird in your house, and in your heart. Now look at nature, that sea beneath the colorings in the sky, and the mountains. You, Eddie, you should certainly be able to write poems of ecstasy on that. Ah, ah, ah—well, but let's stop mooning, and I'll slip into my little kitchen and make my boys one of Toodles' cocktails, you know them. But just one."

"Not tonight for me, Toodles, I think," Edward said. "I don't want to get buffy tonight; have to work tomorrow."

"Now, now, you want cheering up, and Allen there's looking thirsty."

Edward chuckled. "Neither of us would insist on one, Toodles; I'm afraid you have the taste for alcohol."

"I, tush, go on with you. As if I ever took too much. I know how to conduct myself," Toodles asserted, prone to be offended upon this point, which was a delicate one to her. She retired, and soon returned with three cocktails of double strength in double cocktail-sized glasses.

"One of Toodles' own cocktails; she knows how to make them, doesn't she, my boys?" she bubbled forth, setting one cocktail upon the piano before Allen, and handing the other to Eddie.

The cocktails downed, Toodles wanted Allen to play some dance music so that she and Eddie could dance. "There's no debutante that can dance better than your Toodles, is there, Eddie? I am light as a feather to dance with, aren't I; get the rhythm of jazz steps? That's all there is to it, but I have such a feeling for music. My soul just sings and dances," Toodles prattled and danced closely to Eddie. "If only you could play so dear Allen would have a chance to dance too."

Ceasing to dance with the finish of the piece, Toodles went over to the piano to stand back of Allen. "You do love your Toodles, don't you, Allen? We two understand each other; both just children in our hearts, and music is such a bond. We aren't serious and gloomy like Eddie, are we?"

At a quarter to eight Madame Cavellera came into the room, and after her a slender young woman who was introduced as Mrs. York, and who looked Javanese. Her slight figure was dressed in a long clinging apricot white dress that fell in Grecian lines from her shoulders to her ankles.

"Well, Toodles," Madame Cavellera said suggestively.

"I know, I know—well, maybe—the General won't be up,

will he? Look and see. All right then, we'll all just slip out into the kitchen and have one tiny cocktail before dinner. But don't you tell on me."

"Yes," Madame Cavellera argued, "I've been working hard all day, and a little drink lets one talk so much more freely at dinner. Now that the boys are staying, and that we'll have some dancing after dinner we might as well do what we can to be gay."

Mrs. Green, a blonde woman with intelligent blue eyes and a sensual mouth, came into Toodles' room, and slumped her well made body into a chair in a way that emphasized the animal quality of her being. "Hoh," she exclaimed resentfully, "this beastly climate. I *am* so bored," accenting her words with middle-class English intonations. "I *do* so want some excitement. It's *extraordinary* how dull days can be."

Soon Toodles had six cocktails prepared, and saw to it that the two young men got double-sized ones; whereupon, after the cocktails were drunk, it was time to descend to the dining room to eat, which was done in a gay procession, with Toodles confiding to Madame Cavellera what a noble woman she thought her. She diverted her remarks then to Edward, saying, "Such a brave woman as Madame Cavellera is—and if you only knew who she is the daughter of—but she manages all this house, and has to keep the General in spirits besides, as he becomes depressed so easily. There's no littleness in her, I can tell you, and," she lowered her voice to a whisper, "let me tell you, she's very attractive to men, even if she is a plain woman, and I'm sure she has her affairs on the side. She's no prude."

The General sat at the head of the table, a tall, slender man, with a well made head, and fine features that betrayed, however, a tendency to neuroticism. He apparently was worried this evening, because he talked little, except to parry Toodles' patter. Mrs. York sat along the side of the table with precise dignity, like a Javanese statuette; Mrs. Green ate silently, a bit morosely, evidently annoyed by Toodles' constant prattle. Madame Cavellera, at the foot of the table, helped carry on the general conversation, or talked aside to either Allen Cowles or Eddie Campbell, who sat on either side of her, the former next to Toodles. It was difficult for there to be any conversation except that of, or directed by, Toodles, who was persistently playful, and who indubitably possessed the greatest facile energy and vivacity, to pun, prattle, coquette, and essay childish paradoxes.

"Of course she's never touched much of life," Madame Cavellera said in a low aside to Eddie at one moment, "and one must hide one's impatience at her eternal need to be amused however inopportune the moment may be to oneself. Certainly she doesn't possess enough imagination to understand that, dear and kind as she can be, she's obtuse about other people's suffering."

"That's not a bad thing either at times, is it, because it might make the other person less intent upon his or her emotion. But she can wear a being down. How you must want rest from Toodles at moments," he responded.

Mrs. York spoke in a low-toned voice of strange timbre and vibrance, coming from so slight a being. The quality of her voice carried with it a significance, a sense of power, that her words had nothing to do with. "I ran onto Mrs. Rice this afternoon, Toodles, and she said she and her husband would drop in on you after dinner, so it is nice that Mr. Cowles is here to play music for us all."

"Isn't that lovely. You boys will just adore Mrs. Rice. She's a famous beauty—and Thomas Rice too—how I love both of them, and they think the world of their Toodles too. But everybody likes Toodles. She's never done harm to anyone, and she so likes making people happy, doesn't she?" Toodles chattered.

"You say how we all love you so often for us, Toodles, that we have no need to tell you," Mrs. York commented.

"How nasty of you," Toodles exclaimed, woundedly pouting.

"No, no, Toodles, you really know I did not mean it that way," Mrs. York responded quaintly, giving a sense of naiveness direct.

Dinner over, Toodles went to her drawing room with the two young men, inviting all of the others who wished to come with her. There she gaily rolled up the rugs so there could be easier dancing, while Allen played. Her maid brought in two liqueur bottles, one of cognac, one of benedictine, and Toodles sympathetically saw that Allen, at least, had a liqueur. "If he's to play we must reward him, mustn't we? I see that my boys aren't neglected."

Mrs. Green came into the room, and seated herself on a double seat with Edward Campbell. Observing Toodles, she commented acidly, "She's too obvious, really, you know. Did you notice how she looked at me? She likes me in the daytime when she wants companionship, but not at night when any men are about. She must have all the attention."

"Yes, but there's no far-reaching design in any of her dislikes. She's made only by each moment's emotion."

"So I am too, for that matter. I'm so pent up in this atmosphere of old women, and with worry about getting hold of money to keep up appearances. Of course if it weren't for Toodles and her money, and the people she brings here, the General and Madame Cavellera would be completely on the rocks, and it all bears down upon Madame because the General is a fussy old maid, pinpicking at everything. I help run things, you know, to pay for part of my keep as my income's so small. I *do* wish my husband would get his leave—he's in the army—and we would get off to Egypt where we intend to settle."

Mr. and Mrs. Rice arrived, and soon Mr. Rice was leading several arguments into the conversation. Irritatedly Madame Cavellera moved away from him and came to sit near Mrs. Green and Edward.

"How cross Mr. Rice can make me. He always deliberately chooses his subjects to antagonize one. I will not listen to him when he scoffs at patriotism, decries England, and praises the spectacle which the German Kaiser made of Imperialism. Mrs. Rice too, whom I so like for herself, and who is lovely to look at, is a nuisance with her assents to his pretentious triteness. I had thought she was an intelligent woman, but she's lived with him for eight years and still thinks 'Thomas is so original.' Utter rot, that," Madame Cavellera asserted.

Mrs. Rice sat languidly in an easy chair. Her long body was clad in a blue Chinese-fashioned robe. Upon her ears she wore large-sized blue earrings; these and her blue gown emphasized the blueness of her eyes, and possibly accented the perfection of her profile. Viewed full face she was not so perfect, as her lips were overheavy, and there was not sufficient firmness to the oval of her face.

"Aristocracy seems to be a past concept in this age," she was drawling at one moment. "It puts me out when I remember a State parade I saw in Berlin under the Kaiser's regime—when Thomas and I had just been married. It was magnificently stage-set. The common people should certainly have been happy to have someone ruling them who had such a sense of statecraft and stagecraft."

"This *modern generation*," Mr. Rice exploded vehemently. "As if all the vulgarity, the modern improvements, and the cheapness of democracy were anything new to the world. What is most disgusting, too, is talk about science—the degradation of a civilization— What we need are a few emotional geniuses who illuminate the subconscious, and know what the throes of inspiration mean. I'm a snob. We're all snobs. Good healthy snobbisms are good for the world. Some men are made to serve, and some are made aristocratic. I don't want my servants becoming chummy with me."

"All one asks, though," Eddie Campbell broke in, feeling that he, being of the generation Mr. Rice deemed modern, "is that aristocrats be aristocratic. Too many imbeciles, degenerates, and obtuse-minded individuals come in the wake of old families and wealth to think that either of them form a good basis by which to judge aristocracy. I can't quite think of a way in which the lines between classes can be so strictly marked as you wish to make them. After all it's only a matter of what's interesting, and neither class nor wealth are that in themselves, while intelligence and ability to produce are. And perhaps beings who possess intelligence don't emerge solely, or even often, from what you call the aristocratic classes."

"Huh, huh, but it takes the aristocrats to subsidize and patronize them; to recognize them."

"That's it; they don't want to be patronized perhaps, and resent needing to depend upon patronizing subsidies. And also the willingness to subsidize doesn't too often occur. Sometimes the aristocrats are preferring to devote their attentions to themselves, and to getting acclaim for themselves that they haven't earned."

"The proofs are earlier civilizations, where class lines were distinctly drawn, and which produced great works of art—"

"That's an involved discussion, isn't it, and doesn't take into account modern and scientific improvements, which whether we like them or not have occurred, and which we don't eradicate by disapproving of."

"You say then you like this present social order; this revolting, money-grabbing, psychoanalyzing, disrespecting of our wives and mothers, system. I tell you this is the vilest age that has ever existed on the face of the earth."

"I wouldn't be surprised; still there was Sodom and Gomorrah, Rome under Nero, and others we don't know too much about. The Aztec race lived through a civilization about as flagrant and barbaric. I can't judge social orders, but can only think, or rather feel, that one has to do what's possible in the time one happens to be born in. Anyway emotion doesn't turn the clock back to the hour we want it; it's more apt to turn it only to fanaticism."

Mr. Rice was getting redder in the face where it could be seen around his sideburns and above his whiskers. His smoky blue eyes were concentrating into intense gleams; he moved his chair nearer, and then away, nearer and then away, from the man he was speaking to, in a nervous anxiety of antagonized vanity. The discussion went on for a few minutes, and Mr. Rice condemned names which he obviously had never heard before; painters, musicians, writers, brought into the discussion by Edward in trying to indicate that even this age could let one hope a little.

"I tell you, all the times do to me is drive me into my country home, and make me wish to see nobody but my lovely wife—and my children—my son, who, I tell you, I'm bringing up to be the president of the United States so that then this damnable vile filthy democratic idea will be done away with."

"You are driven? Perhaps if you're driven enough you'll be driven finally to meditation, even the kind that produced the sort of cryptic wisdom you say you find in the old Chinese art; or the enigmatic quality of removal from temporal experience that the Egyptians possessed. Perhaps that's the answer; if one is driven enough one quits storming about today and the things in it that change overnight, and becomes either a producer or a philosopher."

Toodles had listened to this argument all she could. She feared that her younger guest, one of her boys, was being rude to Mr. Rice, but she was quite incompetent for several minutes to break in, so ferociously had the two talked in each other's faces. Toodles did not understand what was being said, but she did understand that it was not about her, and that it was not the sort of thing that was socially gracious and easy. Finally, at loss to know what to do, she whispered to Allen to start playing.

"Now, now, we've had enough of that very profound talk, and little Toodles is going to sing you a song, or start to, and then we'll dance."

The evening had begun to tire Toodles. Her bad eye took on a more crooked expression than it had had earlier in the evening. It could even have been thought that Toodles had drunk too many cocktails, and perhaps a liqueur or so, unnoticed during the discussion. Standing by the piano, she waited till Allen began to play *La Bohème,* whereupon she assumed an operatic pose, hand over heart, other hand uplifted, feet sprawled a little apart, and started to sing, rolling her eyes, she believed, seductively, and swaying her plump torso for the same effect. The first moment or so Mr. Rice was fidgety in his seat, and moved it about two or three times. However, his emotions within themselves began to quell; his courtesy reasserted itself, and he listened politely as Mrs. Dawson—he never called her Toodles—sang. When she had finished there was applause and exclamations of approval.

"Bravo, Toodles. There's nothing Toodles can't do, is there?" the General commented facetiously.

"You're in such wonderful spirits tonight, Toodles," Madame Cavellera stated. "It's a joy seeing one who can be so eternally young and irrepressible as you. Such energy, you dear thing."

"Dance music, Allen, your little Toodles wants to dance," Mrs. Dawson requested. "And Mr. Rice is going to dance with me. Give us something soulful. You do like so to dance with me, don't you, Thomas?" with an amorous gesture.

Mr. Rice arose gravely as the music began, and circled with slow steps about Toodles, who was cavorting around the room tossing her arms about her head, and swaying her plump little body in a way meant to be willowy. No one could accuse Toodles of self-consciousness. Mainly she danced alone, but at times she would face Mr. Rice, and lean towards him sirenly, lifting her plump birdlike face with its crooked eye towards his as she thrust out her arms in invitation that turned, upon his response, immediately coy, as Toodles again turned to dance the dance of the pursued nymph. Long before she, Mr. Rice was exhausted as well as ill at ease, commenting in a whisper to his wife that "Mrs. Dawson is making a display of herself, and she's a grandmother, but she puts all the sensual desire of her nature into her wriggles."

Ten o'clock came and Mr. and Mrs. Rice made their departure. The General retired; Madame Cavellera took herself off, having first had a whiskey and soda; Mrs. York too bid a quiet good night to the others. No sooner had she left the room than Toodles said, "Did you notice that somebody looks—don't say I said so—as though she had nigger blood?"

"Do you mean Mrs. York?" Allen asked.

"Don't repeat it; but nothing much is known about her. She came from New Orleans, and doesn't seem to want to talk about her family. The poor little thing married a man much older than herself—she mentions her mother, but never her father. When that old man, her husband, died and left her hardly anything, she came over here. My son almost married her, but he stopped that when I suggested to him that she might have—of course it may not be true—she's a dear little thing too. And she seems to love being about me, but everybody loves Toodles."

Edward, sitting with Mrs. Green, having heard this, asked her about it, and she answered, "It may be the case but she's obviously of good breeding."

"Certainly that, and lovely in a porcelain statuette way. She must sense that people think that negro blood story about her, or probably she thinks it is true herself. There's a restrained tragic quality about her. As I talked to her a few minutes this evening her attitudes struck me like those of a quaintly romantic boarding-school girl. Toodles hadn't ought to start that story. She might let people discern it and think it for themselves."

"Not Toodles. Mrs. York is too attractive for that. Several men have been quite taken with her, and she needs marriage as she has almost no money, and there's nothing she can do."

"Many men who'd marry her wouldn't want children either, but the snobs in this part of the world wouldn't pass a thought like that up. It's too bad."

Toodles was leaning on the piano whispering to Allen in an affectionate manner. "We'd better go out on the balcony and let Toodles and Allen have the room to themselves," Mrs. Green suggested. "She almost ought to be told not to show so clearly what she feels and wants."

Out on the balcony Mrs. Green stood looking into the night for a time beside Edward, whom she finally leaned against. He put his arm about her, asking her if she was cold.

"Oh no, not that, not that. But—oh, I'm going to make a bloody fool of myself—but—I want you—oh, I must control myself." In speaking she bit her lip, and turned her head desirously around to be kissed. He kissed her.

"Have me, then," he answered. "Should we go for a walk, or can you take me to your room?"

"I wouldn't dare; everybody in the house would know about it. Oh, I am a bloody fool. I hate my husband. I hate my life. Why am I here, wanting money, and that woman in there has so much she can tear it up. Oh my god, I want you. I'll go tomorrow and throw myself over rock end if I can't have you."

"Nonsense; you can have me, for tonight, if that is enough. Walk back to my room with me. You can be back here and in through your window by five, or six, if that's before anybody else gets up."

"I can't. I can't. I'm a bloody fool. I can't make you understand why I can't. I hate my husband. Why did I ever marry him?" As she spoke she twisted herself about writhingly in his arms, and brushed her hand nervously across her forehead and through her hair, loosening it.

"Yes, you are being foolish. You're perhaps right not to have me because I have no particular interest in you, and wouldn't want to make things more difficult for you if you'd try to make more of me than an affair in passing."

"Oh, I wouldn't; I wouldn't. I could make you care, I know I could make you happy for a few minutes anyway; for several times. But—I can't—I can't—"

"If you can't then—"

"But you had not ought to listen to me. You should go right ahead, you know."

"Come on; we'll go out for a walk."

As they went through the room to go downstairs Edward noticed that Toodles and Allen were not there. He concluded that they'd gone to the kitchenette to have a drink. Standing just for a moment before the fireplace he heard Toodles whispering huskily.

"Don't go, Allen. Don't go home tonight. My boy. My boy. Stay with Toodles."

"No, no, I can't," Allen answered in a pettish voice. "You don't mean that to me."

"Don't go, Allen. Don't go."

Allen's answer was in a weakening voice, pettish yet.

Mrs. Green came to the door, and she and Edward went downstairs together. "The age is never by, I take it," Edward said to her. "I suppose you heard what I did."

"I wonder—do I strike men like that?"

"Um—oh, no—well, what if you do, you get what you want."

Going to her room, Mrs. Green got a shawl to throw over her shoulder, and reappeared, tiptoeing. She put her fingers to her lips, and indicated that Edward should come through her room.

"We can step out of the window there, and go out. I daren't let you stay there because the General's and Madame's room is next . . ."

"Would they mind—"

"No, not she anyway, but he—one can't judge. He'd disapprove, and I can't stand his pecking and prying about into my affairs."

(See Bibliographical Note, page 363.)

In a story written about 1928, Kay Boyle has sketched the Robert McAlmon of the late Twenties. *"He had no one to put back his buttons on his clothes when time had seized them by the forelock. To see him with his lean mouth closed like a wallet, his eye like iron and as cold as, would it ever have come into your head that the mouth of his heart was open, was gaping wide like a frog's in dry weather, requesting that into it be drained not glasses with frost on their faces but something else again. It was easy enough to see that his bottom was at ease nowhere except upon a stool at a bar but other things, if you had a mind to, you might see as well.*

"If you could forget yourself for two minutes you might see his eye peeled for the sight of a new face coming in, his ear harking for a word that would set him to thinking at last. Whatever you said to him it was drawn with labor word by word from the bog of his interest in something else. Up and down and around he was looking for something that might catch his curiosity. If I stay up all night was he thinking perhaps something will happen after all. By staying awake all night I might get a whiff of it. But what if it came to pass in the morning then, in the morning early when I was recovering from what my thirst had left me. . . .

"Denka [McAlmon] came back from where he had been and he said There's something going on across the street. The record of it could be read in the faces of the people walking arm in arm back and forth among the tables. A night as hot as a warming-pan of coals between your sheets. There's something going on said Denka. He looked for it in every eye that passed him by. A couple of words that slapped his ear he took and used them as his own. There's something going on he said. Where he couldn't remember. There's something happening around the corner. His ears were starting from his head to capture the direction of it. There's something happening somewhere else he said. Into these places and out of them we went. There's something happening on the other side of town said Denka. We stepped into a taxi to track it down. Before the café mirror we sat still and surveyed the landslide of our faces down the glass." The narrator remembers his tales of working on a ranch in the West—how he would lie, his ear to the ground, listening, *"harking all night for the sound of horses' riding or a grasshopper turning over in his grave."* But now he seems only to be waiting for events that never occur.[10]

But if McAlmon waited in vain for *"a word that would set him thinking at last"* and if the same old faces confronted him daily at the Dôme and Rotonde, nonetheless he could still write of the café habitués with humor and curiosity. And write well enough, it might be added, so that the following story appeared in

company with work by Ezra Pound, Apollinaire, Par Lagerkvist,
Boris Pasternak, and Samuel Beckett.

The Highly Prized Pajamas

Girls such as Yoland used to be called of the half-world,
though it can not be explained why their world is more half than
the world of aristocrats, workers, or the bourgeois, few of whom
take so much into the range of their experience as Yoland did.

She was about the Latin and Montparnasse quarters for two
years before people commented upon her archaic Greek beauty.
I associated her with a type of low-class *poule*, who without mind
and abandoned, soon grows bloated and ugly and disappears. One
may hear of them as dying of consumption back in little villages,
on farms; or one may forget to remember if they are mentioned.
Integral a part as they are of the French social organism, no one,
or one year's crop of them, is essential. Each season brings its new
recruits.

Yoland went about with Andra, of young pig-faced charms,
and Arlette, who, darkly striking, soon disintegrated into bovine
aspects and was soddenly drunk nightly until she became con-
sumptive and disappeared. Any of the three was apt to be in
some bar at any time of day, from noon till five in the morning.
There was little outward evidence that they were plying their
trade. However, they had money to drink on, dressed well, and
rather than gold-dig off foreigners they were inclined to gather
in flocks with others of their kind. Their laughter taunted like
that of so many hyenas as they sat before their drinks, jeering and
laughing at the strange habits of foreigners.

Seated in the Parnasse bar, which was empty but for Jimmie,
the barman, I was having a sandwich and a beer when I noticed
a copy of Proust's *Sodome et Gomorrhe* on the table next to mine.
I picked it up to scan and Yoland came from the ladies' room to
stand waiting for me to hand her the book. I was surprised that a

girl of her sort should be reading that, so I asked her to have a drink. She would, and sat down. When I asked if she liked to read she crackled a dry, inhuman laugh, unlubricatedly metallic. Mechanically the laugh had cuteness.

"I don't like sentimental things. Sometimes I read. This," she indicated the book, "is of things we all know if we aren't stupid. The author I wouldn't like," her rusty crackle of laughter sounded, "but he wouldn't like me. He liked only men. His heroine is a man he has made a woman in the book, but I like his manner."

It occurred to me that I'd underrated Yoland's perceptions considerably. We chatted, but she had no intention of telling much about herself to a stranger. Thoughts of her past apparently irritated her. She did say that until she was thirty or no longer good-looking she would live a life of freedom, abandoned, if people wanted to call it that. She didn't want marriage, or family life, and why should she give up freedom to become settled or a woman of the home? She knew when young more than she wanted to know of these things.

As we sat, a photographer who liked doing studies of unusual looking people came into the place. I asked him to sit with us, and said, as Yoland did not understand English, "Have you ever noticed how beautiful Yoland is? A more perfect and delicate profile doesn't exist, and her eyelashes are really long and black. It isn't *maquillage*."

Her teeth too were straight, not too small, and glistening white, and her eyes large, and softly grey if one didn't detect that their softness was no evidence of a tender nature. The photographer, as we sat analyzing her perfections, agreed, and asked her if she would pose for him.

"My body is not good," she said finally, assuming at once that he meant for her to pose in the nude. "I have more than enough breast, and my waist is not subtle."

When assured that he wanted to photograph her face, three-quarters or profile, she agreed, and said she often made money posing for romance photographs one can buy in postcard shops. The idea amused her; she mimicked sweet young love poses she had taken for these pictures. Incidentally she appraised the photographer with her soft gaze, not assuming that he wished too to make love with her, but, she informed me later, to judge whether she was willing if it came to that, and whether he was another man who pretended he wanted her as a model when he had other intentions. With such, she declared, she was ruthless.

The photographer left and Yoland's cute, unhuman laugh creaked after him. It struck her as droll that he should want to photograph her when she had posed for so many sentimental postcards which sell as a joke or to simple-minded people. "You know his friend, that dirty old man with white hair who would be droll if he was a negro?" she asked, chortling, menacingly this time. "He asked me to pose for him, and they say he is famous. I believed he wanted a model. He showed me screens and pictures," she shrugged her shoulders. "I didn't care for them. He was to pay me two hundred francs for the afternoon. But the foolish old man thought he could make love to me too. I was cold and said 'no' and meant no, but he battled with me. Then I showed him my nails, on this hand." The nails on her hands were long and sharply pointed. "I can handle them when they get difficult. I would have torn the skin off his face, and then I said, 'You give me two thousand francs, and I will go. I won't pose for you. Without the two thousand francs, now I will tear your face, and call the police.' Never before have I done that. I don't like that sort of thing, but if he thought he could be brutal to me I would show him."

Yoland didn't need to inform me that she was hard. She wasn't apache class, but she had many of the tricks. I'd seen her break a glass and threaten to thrust its broken rim into the face of a man who annoyed her; and had heard her quarrelling with some girl she did not like. Then she had been aflame with cold menace.

Yoland evidently decided that she liked me, as a comrade, though she didn't like Americans generally. She wasn't flattered by my remarking on her beauty; she rather wondered why I commented on it now, when we had seen each other about for over a year. Just now she had the idea that she was making me think her cruel, and said, "I am *sensible* with those having emotions and sensibility, but usually I find little use for sentiment in this life."

"Independence of spirit is a quality I like too," I told her.

Her unlubricated rusty laugh chortled and she looked at me mockingly. "Ah, yes, you are independent, but as a passion."

Her remark struck home, and I hoped that one more clear realization of needless lack of detachment had functioned into my emotions.

After this she and I were comrades whenever we met and hadn't more intimate friends with us; we sat together and chatted pleasantly, without inquiring into each other intimately. Yoland drank copiously, and stayed up most nights till five o'clock. Her laughter mingled with that of other girls to make hyena noises. She threw glasses, cursed out the *patrons* and *patronnes* of bars and restaurants, and she was not unique in doing these things. However, she began to dress better, and people were soon commenting on her beauty. It was when she came forth in a pepper-red coat and dress, wearing a hat made of shiny black cock feathers that curled above her forehead and about her ears, that her profile stood out luminously white and perfect. Her teeth, when she smiled, were the perfection of dentifrice and glistening beauty; and her deep grey eyes glowed, but were aware people knew that their glow came from the dilation of drugs rather than from emotion stirring within her. In the emotion of anger they flashed hatred as she glared through her narrowed lids.

Yoland had, as had many others, fought with so many of the *gerantes* in the various cafés and bars in Montparnasse that she was a well known figure to the police. When a small and stuffily cozy bar opened near the Jardin du Luxembourg she changed her rendezvous spot; so did many old-time Quarterites, to follow Jimmie, the barman, who went to work there. Jimmie, a Liverpool Irishman, and an ex-prizefighter, was genial, tittered readily at the careless habits of his clients, was openhearted, and informed of the open-secret lives, amorous and financial, of about everyone in the Quarter. Eight years before this time he had arrived, naïf to Paris and full of alive curiosity. His first night he got drunk too, and seeing a fire-signalling box, banged it, and stood. Not then understanding French he didn't know what he had done. But the firemen arrived and wanted to know where the fire was. Jimmie didn't understand, but the police understood Jimmy, and he spent three weeks in the Prison de la Santé. When liquored up he was apt to remember his fighting days, and insist upon "protecting" friends he drank with. Sometimes his protection resulted in a night in jail for both Jimmie and his friend, but as the police took him with an ironic sense of comedy his sojourn with them was seldom overnight. When his blood pressure was too high from overeating and drinking, Jimmie had a habit of going to his room, banging his own nose so that it would bleed, and thereby reducing his blood pressure. Sometimes he would slit the lobes of his ears to lose more blood. In all, Jimmie suffered the pangs of loving and losing, and was a barman prone to understand the habits and attitudes of his clients in all their various types of drunk-ons.

In the New Bar Yoland collected an Argentinian lover. She wasn't attracted to him, but he persisted; he was wealthy; he gave her expensive clothes and jewelry; he gave her money, paid her apartment rent, and submitted to her tempers, so she accepted him for a time. He, José, was a thin, fidgety man, given to drinking vast quantities of pernod, but he seldom ate. When intoxicated he wanted to dance, and humped epileptically about the room, singing. The song was always the same. "Toreador, Toreador." His rendition was one apt to irritate anybody, let alone a nervous person. It surely irritated Yoland and one night José found himself sitting on the floor with a sore jaw. He'd sung one "Toreador" too many and Yoland slammed him. From then on she was apt to beat him up nightly, until it was a bar joke and comic even to Yoland. As fist-hits from her seemed only to please José, she took to scratching his face with her lengthy fingernails. The Madame of the bar would take him upstairs, put plasters on his face, and José came down ready for more punishment from his ladylove.

It became too much for Yoland, however. He bored her; he drove her wild; she crashed a broken glass into his face one night, tore from her neck an expensive pearl necklace he had given her, threw it at him, and departed. José was disconsolate, but as Yoland was not to be located for several weeks he moved elsewhere, and was out of her life. She, hearing of this, began again to make the bar her nightly rendezvous. She stayed in the hotel above. Madame Camille, thinking that Yoland would find José when she needed money badly, permitted her bill to mount, but when she argued that some amount of the bill should be paid, there was a violent quarrel. Madame Camille indiscreetly suggested that it was like stealing not to pay one's bill.

"You dirty cow," Yoland spit at her. "I am not a thief. That remark you will pay for," and a series of glasses flew in Madame

Camille's direction. She hid behind the counter, too afraid to say she would call the police. Yoland, highly insulted, stopped her when she tried to make a placatory remark, for Madame Camille knew she'd never get money if she stayed enraged.

"Madame Camille," Yoland said, frozen with hauteur, "I will not dispute further with you. You are a woman without education or breeding." At this she went out and took a taxi to haunts in another part of town. She was not seen about the Quarter for several months, and when she returned it appeared that she was amply provided for from the elegant clothes she sported.

Seated at the Dome bar one afternoon Yoland chatted amiably, when Madame Camille appeared with a look of insecure triumph on her face. At last she had found Yoland and might collect what was owing her. Yoland was frigidly courteous, but Madame Camille got nowhere with her. She did finally get an address, however, and went away, saying that she would call on Yoland to collect.

Yoland's eyes were stony black with rage. "She calls me a thief. Ha, ha, ha, ha," her menacing laugh rattled deathbones. "I did not give her my address. I gave her the address of my friend, and he will break her face in if she comes."

Yoland passed through a period of being *"une femme sérieuse"* while she lived with a wealthy Egyptian for several months, and she confided that at last she had found the race which knows how to make love. Before, love-making had been more or less of a bore to her. However, the Egyptian left, and she then lived with a forty-year-old Polish man, who, to my amazement, Yoland permitted to strike her in the face without her using either fingernails or broken glasses on him. Later she said that he was irrational. He was very gentle, but when he drank much he went crazy because of shell shock. "It is not me he hits at. It is a crazy something he sees," she said, and shrugged her shoulder, thinking me foolish to suppose she'd mind being beaten up under such circumstances. Could one fight back at a crazy man? He gave her a squirrel coat and various pieces of jewelry; and their romance was either successful or not, in that Yoland never got to the point of doing him physical damage. He, however, departed after some months, and Yoland was again about the Quarter daily. She now did only the better-class bars, and came into them generally alone. Andra, her pig-faced ex-friend, was about, and a very successful bourgeoise *poule,* but to none of her two-year-ago girl friends did Yoland pay any attention. She wasn't curt. She had decided that what amused them in life didn't amuse her, and she, instead of having lost her looks, was more elegantly and glisteningly beautiful than ever. Her pallor glowed; her teeth had a diamond sparkle, and she had learned what a hat and a color could do to give her beauty a setting. Nevertheless before long she was hard up. Probably she would not make love to men she once considered. She'd grown more definite and positive in her tastes. I wondered if she was calming down and yearning for a settled and secure circumstance.

2

I found one day waiting for me a letter from Arthur Stout, who had been given my address by a friend. He had no reason to look me up except that he did not know Paris and I might tell him what to see and what to avoid. Also he understood that I was the friend of a psychoanalyst and interested in the subject myself, and as he had a deep affection (platonic, of course) for a woman who did not care for men he would like to talk to somebody more worldly than himself. A book-lover and scientist, he hadn't sampled any variety of life.

One gets used, in Paris, to having acquaintances and friends of friends think of residents as convenient guides and hosts, and I felt no inclination to conduct this unknown Mr. Stout to sights and other places I'd seen or didn't care to bother about. However, liking the man who'd given him my address, I dropped a note saying that he would be apt to locate me at the Coupole bar at aperitif hour almost any night. My morning letter reached him that day, for when I went into the Coupole the barman told me that the gentleman in the corner had inquired for me.

Stout presented himself and offered me a drink. He was quiet-looking, and I understood at once that it is hard for a man not speaking French to get around in Paris at first, and Stout confessed that he had only one week before sailing back to America. "And I have three thousand dollars with me and don't care if I spend it all. There's more where it came from. I rather gathered from Morris (our friend) that you'd be the chap to locate an attractive sort of girl to keep me company when I'm at loose ends. In any case, whenever you or any of your friends are with me, all the bills for eating or drinking are mine."

I didn't jump off the barstool and run outside to blow the fire whistle, but certainly during the course of the evening I let various regulars of the always-broke quota know what had come upon us. It seemed cruel on Mr. Stout, but Morris should too have informed him that Montparnasse, where deadbeating is an art, is no place where he need make an offer such as the foregoing.

Mr. Stout said that he'd just come from the Riviera where he had read Frank Harris' *Life and Loves*. As I'd never more than glanced at the book, and then not to be interested, excited, or amused, we couldn't go far into that subject. Next Stout spoke of a cellar where Verlaine, Baudelaire, and others had once sat in discussion while drinking absinthe. He spoke of Dr. Hirschfield of Berlin, of sexual variants, and asked, reticently, what curious places there were to visit in Paris. Not too decisively I concluded that he was in search of subtle, aromatic vice, as imagined through literary gleanings. He obviously was a small-town product, and showing me his notebook of addresses such as college boys, Legionnaires, and business men collect, he wanted me to tell him about the various places. As most of them were of *bourdelles* where people go to see poses, or for mass promiscuity—mainly for tourists—his interest lapsed, so I told him of more exotic places. He looked only mildly physical and sensuous, and his manner was slowly kind. It was probable, I thought, that he was merely sentimental and afraid that he was missing experience in life. Again he spoke of wanting a girl, and an aware, worldy girl, with intelligence.

Yoland came into the Coupole and spoke to me as she seated herself at the end of the bar. She smiled enigmatically. I concluded she had been taking heroin or opium, because though her smile seemed directed at me I knew she wasn't even looking at me. But her gleaming teeth glistened blue-white between her lips incarnadine, and as she turned to arrange her jet locks beneath her hat her clear profile gleamed white against the shiny shadow on the mirror.

"Who is that girl?" Stout asked, and there was tensity in his curiosity now, where before he had been merely casual.

I concluded that Yoland was a good answer for him.

At my suggestion Yoland came over to drink with us, and

Stout admired the crystal clarity of her skin, and the modelled perfection of her facial contours. He couldn't speak much French, and I had to translate between them. Yoland noted Stout's admiration and looked at me to chortle a low metallic crackle. I told her that he found her grey eyes lovely, faunlike, and tender, that he was sure she had a sweet and tender nature. She chortled cutely again, and her long eyelashes swept down over her drug-dilated eyes which had such liquid beauty. I suggested to Stout that he'd better not be too moved by Yoland, to listen to her laugh as much as he believed the mysterious glow in her eyes. He was appearing altogether too much the small-town man in middling years wanting to break loose, and if Yoland had been taking drugs, she might get him into some row that he couldn't handle. I had no intention of spending the evening with them. Every warning I might give Stout, however, but further interested him in Yoland.

"I know by her face that she has an old soul," Stout said. "I don't go in for reincarnation, but I knew when you came into the bar that you have an old soul too. I knew it was you before you spoke though nobody had ever described you."

His talk would sometimes have made me uncomfortable, but I felt easy, knowing that soon the night aperitif crowds would be filling the place. I told Yoland that Stout wanted me to tell her that she was beautiful, and she merely rattled her machine laugh, knowing that she was so, and that I knew the matter didn't much interest her since so many people who liked her beauty irritated her.

"He likes you very much," I translated.

She asked, "He is rich?"

"Enough. He's ready to spend quite a sum of money while he's in Paris. He wants you to have dinner with him."

"Very well. I need a new coat, and dresses. I'm disgusted with the clothes that dirty pig José bought me. If he would see me in them he might still think he could come and speak to me." She observed Stout with a sidewise glance. He was charmed. "He is nice. He is sentimental, but that does no harm for a few days, since he goes in a week," she concluded.

Stout took her hand to kiss, and wanted me to tell her that it was an aristocrat's hand, that he knew she had lived before. She leaned towards him and straightened his coat collar with a caressing pat, and looked at me again to chortle dry rattling laughter.

"I love her laugh," Stout said. "You say she is Basque? They are a race thousands of years old. She has lived many times before. Her laugh is cleared of emotions."

"Go careful on her temper though. See her fingernails. She keeps those on the right hand long and pointed to tear strips off a person's face when she's in a fight. Well-kept hands and nails are fairly general with French girls."

"Ask her why she has never married, if she intends to marry. Say she is too beautiful to live this kind of life."

"She might resent it. She is not given to thinking of herself as a lost soul. But I'll ask her about the marriage part."

"I want liberty," Yoland said curtly, and relaxed a little. "I don't love love if it binds me. What would there be for me to do if I was married?" She left us for a few minutes and when she returned the pupils of her eyes were huge black; she had put on more *maquillage* too, and looked smarter because her black hair was sleekly peeping from under the rim of black cock feathers on her hat. Quickly she saw that I noticed this, and crackled a laugh that came out in sharp hard spurts of metallic sound. Her glance agreed that it was funny that she should be acting coquettish because she saw that the simple, sentimental Stout expected that of her. She wondered at me too, that I asked her questions about her life, her family, and her first experience in love. Although she knew I was merely translating for Stout she didn't connect that type of question with me. She, however, answered, since she knew me well enough for two years past.

"He thinks that he will be serious with me," she jeered, cutely taunting. "When I was fourteen, I was seduced by a woman. Women didn't and don't interest me, but no matter. Soon after I seduced my seventeen-year-old boy cousin. And before either—" she hesitated before she decided to say the last, "I had known my father that way since I was twelve. In every case I was willing."

"And your mother?" I asked, having translated her remarks to Stout.

"My mother? I don't know. A country woman. She was not a wife. My father's family took me. He said I was mature and beautiful at twelve. At fifteen I was disgusted with my town and my father's home. He was old; he handled me. I didn't hate him, but I didn't want him, so I went away with an older woman and she wanted me to become a coiffeuse." Yoland laughed, harshly disdainful. "Me, a coiffeuse! I did not like small villages and I do not like people enough to fuss over old women's hair. Always I intended to come to Paris, to be free, and abandoned if I liked. You may tell him I am sufficiently well educated. My father has money and would send it to me but I want nothing more to do with that old man. I know life is nothing. Never have I expected anything of life. For me it is amusing only to be in bars and cabarets and with people who pretend no class."

"Let me read your hand?" I said, lightly curious.

"No, no," she answered, with a quick hardness, drawing her hand away. It was the first evidence of anything noncynical or superstitious I had detected in her. "Why should I be curious about the future? I take what comes and will always do so." Again she said that at thirty, or if she lost her looks or health, she might consider marriage, but that was eight years to wait yet.

"She is damned quick," Stout admired her. "The old race knowledge. She has lived before. It's my luck to fall for girls who like their own sex, I guess." His mild Teutonish face had a pleased expression. "She likes me, though. I don't know why." Yoland responded easily as he stroked her arms, and she smiled her glistening, mechanically glamorous smile, into his eyes, he thought, but she was looking at Andra too, with whom she had taken up anew in the last few days while she had been in financial difficulties. If she drank she might get rid of Stout and go away with Andra who had some attraction for her. Possibly the young pig-faced Andra took drugs with her.

Stout was evidently hoping that he was the man to awaken a soul in this girl, and as that is a hope aged with tradition I was glad that Yoland and Stout were holding hands and no longer asked me to translate back and forth. Other people came into the bar, among them four men I knew well, and with them I was wandering off to dine when Stout reminded me that I and all my friends were to be his guests if we wished. We waited, and had more drinks. Sporty, the hearty, hardy, and more generally used girl of the Quarter, came in, and she too joined us, and we all went to L'Avenue for dinner.

As Stout and Yoland kept gazing at each other Sporty engrossed the interest of the other five men. She told Groenlun that she would pose for him for nothing, but her face, he could see, was battered. She had been drunk three nights before and had fallen downstairs onto her face. But her body was not cut. No, no lover had beaten her this time. Later she confided to the party's youngest man that she knew a very rich man who liked boys, and who liked her too. "We will sleep three, non?" she asked the boy with generous hope.

The boy looked shy and indicated that he was not interested. "You no like?" Sporty accepted his rebuff with three of her ten words of English. "No go. Hello, goodbye then." She had as usual done her best to arrange things so that as many people as possible could enjoy themselves in this human world of ours, but with her sweet peasant sympathy for all desires, she understood not wanting everybody too. She decided to leave us, and as she was Sporty, with catholic tastes, she was sure to find company for the evening.

With her departure we others left Yoland and Stout together, as Yoland wanted to go to La Cloche. By eleven o'clock they came back to La Coupole, however, and came up to me. Yoland was laughing her unlubricated laugh, steadily now as she was intoxicated. The jeer and taunt in her weird laugh wasn't at anybody in particular so much as it was at everybody, at fate, at the world.

"My little girl nearly got me into a jam," Stout told me proudly. "As we were leaving La Cloche in a taxi a girl tried to take her. I was afraid she would go, but the three of us went to a small bar. An Argentinean was there. I didn't understand the quarrel, but Yoland smashed a glass in his face. The Madame fought with her too, but she started to scratch the Madame's face. She just came away at the sight of the police. We slipped out a side door."

"It's good you slipped away. That Madame is after her. Probably the police have a silent sympathy for her though, and weren't as bright-eyed as they might be," I said, and asked Yoland her version of the story.

"That dirty cow, Madame Camille, calls me a thief. I decided to show her I wasn't afraid of visiting her place. She was sweet to me, saying that José would pay my bill. I told her José could do it, he meant nothing to me. And he tried to talk to me. When he sang

'Toreador' I told him to shut up, but he didn't. *Toreador,"* she made her voice nasal and mimicked José's jerky way of singing. "He gave me disgust. He tried to kiss my hand when I was not in the mood, so I struck him with a glass. He bled. He will have scars for weeks."

"She'll kill that Argentinean some day," I said. "He is awful. He gave her syphilis, I think, but he did pay for her treatments afterwards. But she damned near killed him the night she discovered she was sick."

Stout was more sentimental about Yoland than ever now. She confided that he had given her five thousand francs and promised to give her more in the morning when he'd been at the bank. She laughed a warmer rusty chortle now and her clear face was carved above the blue-grey fur on her coat collar. She smiled sphinxly. "He is foolish. He nearly weeps that I don't talk love to him seriously."

When Stout disappeared into the washroom for a few minutes Yoland told another girl of his generosity, and they shrilly shrieked laughter. He was unbelievable to them. Yoland, however, was gentle to Stout when he returned, and they soon left for his hotel.

For six days they were about together. Each day Yoland arrived with a new outfit, a jewelled cigarette case, jewelled vanity box, bracelets, shoes, etc. And Stout continued not only willing but anxious to pay bills for people. Several times when I asked the barman what I owed he told me that Mr. Stout had paid.

At the end of the week Stout departed for America, and I didn't see Yoland for several days. Coming one night into the Dome bar I saw her at the end, seated with Andra, Sporty, and two other *poules.* They were having a hilarious time, and Yoland's voice was higher and more abandoned than usual. It shrieked, but rustily mechanical rather than human. Their jokes could not be heard because of the laughter, in spite of their being loudly spoken.

"Hello Yoland," I greeted her.

Her long lashes went over her grey eyes lizard fashion, and her head swayed towards me, brightly staring, and then it registered in her brain who I was. Whether only drunk, or both doped and drunk, I couldn't judge. She gave an inebriated rasp of laughter, and gasped out, "He wanted my photograph, but see," and showed me a cabinet-sized picture of herself. "He paid two thousand francs for a face that sells on postcards for five sous. He said he would send me money from Canada, whenever I need it. He wants me to write him and he'll have my letters translated. Ha, ha, ha, ha." There was no unkindness in her voice. It was simply ruthlessly unhuman, ironic, unbelieving.

"And he cried at the station, that man. He wished me to marry him but said he understood I wanted freedom. He would wait and if I ever wished I should write him and he would come for me. He is droll. A really sentimental man."

"I guess he finds small town life doesn't furnish enough exotic excitement," I said.

Andra made a remark that caused the other girls to shriek their shrill hyena laughter again. Yoland's cute crackling ripple sounded more subdued now, because she had laughed too much before at Andra's joke, or because she felt that I might resent their laughing so at a man I'd introduced.

"His pajamas," Andra sputtered, "his beautiful blue paja-mas!" She was overcome with mirth and held her hand over her heart.

"They were magnificent, they were blue, but he would not give them to me," Yoland explained, crackling. "I had worn them when I stayed with him. Instead he would give me a necklace, a bracelet, whatever I wished. But the pajamas he would keep, always, without washing, because I had worn them. He liked it that I cared for women. He was droll. What a *type!*"

(See Bibliographical Note, page 363.)

2. Between Two Worlds

Although McAlmon liked his nomadic life of casual associa-tion, he recognized that it did not satisfy his deepest needs: through all his "migrations" his discontent remained uncured. He hated what he called "soulprobing," but in such stories as "Deracinated Encounters"—which pictures a rootless man who, having rejected his heritage, finds nothing else to which he can be loyal—he is diagnosing his own situation even if he can not prescribe a remedy. McAlmon was not romantic about "Old Europe"—he had come there, he said, "because of events"—and his attitude toward his homeland was equally ambiguous. He could not live happily in America, but he defended it.

In "Deracinated Encounters," the protagonist tries to explain his feelings to a Turkish friend who asks if he is not soon return-ing to America. "I feel no wish to be there. There are stretches of sea-coast that are marvelously lovely there; mountain regions, forest and lake districts; the desert, and many scenically wonderful things in America. But—I can't explain easily to you. Our back-grounds are so different—there is a weariness in me about the country. I can see a foreigner loving it, as a spectacle, for its vibra-tion, and for the beauty of the people too. They are beautiful en masse, and individually, just as bodies, as healthy animals. Can I make you understand? They pry, and permit little privacy to any-body. Mainly they are neither simple or cultured but they are ag-gressive and pretentiously ambitious. Advertising there goes in for impertinences about peoples' personal habits as though the whole population were still unwashed, badly bred school children to be taught how to take care of themselves. They are too eager to be cultured, but it isn't generally so much a wish for culture as a sensitive thing, as it is a commercial impulse to increase one's so-

275

cial market-value. Can you understand that, having been born to class and caste, and the traditions and responsibilities of that system? You might be most unhappy in America, except that there is a kindness, in a manner, apart from the custom there of judging so much by money standards." [1]

Late in 1929 one of McAlmon's "migrations" took him to the United States. A story written at that time reflects his state of mind. Despite his dislike of "soulprobing," he seems to be asking himself if life is so pointless that no values exist at all, not even the values of personal satisfaction. Can his search only show that there is nothing to search for? Would his life have been as free if he had stayed at home, cultivating his own garden?

A Romance at Sea

With thirty days ahead of me on the sea I not only had time to relax; I knew it was necessary, and calm unrelenting glide through the foaming variegated granite water made the necessity a luxury. There were eleven other passengers on the ship, mainly elderly, with a majority of women one guessed to be spinsters. The ship's younger officers weren't to be much help as regards hilarity or even easily casual conversations. They were too eminently British and proper, and the word had come to me that the Captain regarded drinking on board ship with an alarmed eye. I was prone to resent that, but as a passenger could give orders for my own drinks. The younger officers didn't tarry about the salon so the question of my being a bad influence did not come up. It might readily, because while I will drink alone it doesn't strike me as sociable.

Naturally it was a relief to find the Captain of an argumentative sort, perplexed and mild about political questions, and ready to learn about literature. It wasn't novel to me that he should have a manuscript volume of his own poems, about unrest, the sea, strange places, memory, the loves he had lost, and far places. His stories surely could have been taken by many writers and turned into corking adventure stories. There was one about an aristocrat English outcast trying to steal the gold find of a gaucho American real man in the wilds of Argentine. It had a brave note and a moral, and he wasn't too keen about *The Nigger of the Narcissus* at that. The Captain and I got on capitally, because we were tolerant towards each other. He didn't quite forgive me that I thought little of "the white man's burden" idea, but I didn't know China, hadn't guessed what the Chinks did during the Boxer revolution. Because I wanted books and more books I pleased him. He had De Quincey's *Confessions of an English Opium Eater,* Doughty's *Arabia Deserta,* Herodotus, Browning's poems, and they were all books to read when one had leisure to get into them thoroughly. The ship library had books of memoirs by English and Irish aristocrats, hunters, explorers, politicians, and near-court society people. In the sailors' library were books on mathematics and mining, the construction of the Panama Canal, forestry, and travel. These are all subjects one has intended to delve into. I quickly responded to the Captain's melancholy confession that the sea wasn't much of a profession; he hadn't chosen it himself. It's rather the thing, I seem to gather, for sailors to bemoan the lack of home life and the pursuit of intellectual interests. It didn't help the brilliance of conversation when sixty-ish-year-old Mr. and Mrs. Brisbane brought reincarnation into our evening conversations. The youngest other passenger, an ex-army officer on his way to Canada, wanted to talk of the war but he hadn't unusual experiences to relate, and he did want to argue or discuss whether Germany or who started it all, and what England, or France, or America, should have done. I had concluded I was in for a dull voyage into which I would drug myself with that fatalism of resignation that being cooped up on a ship can bring to a rebellious nature. I didn't know that my romance awaited me. For three days seasickness had kept her to her room, but her seasickness was, let me say at once, timidity with meeting strangers and venturing forth into the new, large, and strange world of many new people who frightened her.

I stood at the bow of the ship watching the lights on the horizon from that sun which will sink every day. Flying fish shot frequently into the air and flew along. Uninformed, I had at first wondered how bluebirds were so far out at sea. It was my bad luck that the ship was too high for any of them to land on board as all flying fish should in a sea story. I had to content myself with remembering that the night before a sailor had crawled up the mast to bring down a seahawk under a rug, but no one dared try to touch it once it was in view. Porpoises plunged, dived, and raced the ship, to find it a silly game.

"It's lawvely, ain't it?" I heard a voice, and turned. Beside me was a tiny, weazened woman who looked actually, and not as exaggerated description, like a bewildered monkey. I agreed, remembering having seen her just for a glimpse the first day out. Her cheeks were even now ruddier, and her dwarfish figure sagged less. She must have taken on courage to address a remark to a stranger.

"You're a great lover of music, aren't you?" she queried eagerly. "I hear ye playing the machine, but I dinna come in because maybe you wouldna play the pieces you like best then. You have an ear for the things I like."

"Oh, I play what there is. There aren't many pieces," I told her. "We'll go to the salon and play some of them now if you like."

She—Miss Forbes—hesitated. "But we're looking at them lights on the water now."

Of course we were. I knew at once that for the rest of the voyage it was "we" between us. Not married and having no intention of being a father of a family I could have protective feelings about such a lost, withered little being as Miss Forbes.

"You've never been out of England before?" I asked, sure that she could not have been from her timid manner. She had just told me she had never heard a phonograph before coming on board the ship.

Her eyes brightened. "Oh yes. I was in Australia and New Zealand. I'm going to Vancouver. I have a friend there who told me to come and stay as long as I want to. Do you suppose I could go to Australia for a short time after I've been there a while? I'd want to come back to Vancouver. My sister in New Zealand might not want me to stay long with her."

"Yes," I hesitated, wondering where she thought Australia was, but still she must know if she had been there. "You could go to Australia and New Zealand again. I don't know how much it costs, from Canada, but probably not much more than from England."

"Would it take as long to get there from Vancouver as we take from London to Vancouver? I couldn't go then. If it took only eight days I could go. I like to travel on the sea, but I haven't since we went to New Zealand. Mother always said we would go again, but she was ailing the last few years." Miss Forbes was eager and palpitating. I was sure she was conversing more than was usual.

"Was it long since you were there?"

"About fifty years, but I remember it all clearly."

"Don't you want to go and hear some phonograph records now?" I volunteered, feeling that my blunt questions had made her shy.

"The sky is so pretty. I never knew whether there were really flying fish or not. Are those things we see all the time sharks or whales? I wanted to ask somebody."

"They are porpoises, sea pigs, and quite harmless. Are you finding it restful on the sea? I wish they had more books aboard one might read."

"I have a book I will give you. It is sweet and nice. It is about a poor old lady who is left without money. She begins to wander the streets and forgets everything," Miss Forbes' voice trembled with tender excitement. "She is so hungry, and the city is big and nobody knows her. But some nice people find her and the book is happy at the end. I liked the book. Would you like me to lend it to you?"

"Yes, do," I answered quickly, wondering how much of her own possible future she had read into the book. She obviously was not rich. Just in time I stopped myself from saying how brave she was to travel alone to Vancouver. She was too childishly innocent of chance to have that idea presented her.

"Let's go in now, and if you will, have a port wine with me," I invited. "We'll pick the records you like and play them. I've gone through them all."

"Yes, do," she quavered. "Play anything you pick. I don't know what any of the pieces are. I love them all. I like sweet things."

"Waltzes, and swaying music?"

"Sweet things, that make me feel soft inside. I will have the port wine if you are so kind."

Inside, I was sure from the way she looked as she sipped the port that she had never tasted it before. She told me that she had been twenty-five when she went to Australia and New Zealand. She and her mother had stayed there for one year, and then come back to live in a small London suburb for fifty years. "My mother was ailing the last few years so I couldn't travel. She just left me six months ago."

"She lived to quite an age," I said without condolence as Miss Forbes spoke without sadness in her voice. I looked keenly at her as I could without having her observe me. Was she a dwarf or humpbacked? No, she wasn't, simply tiny and withered, and very naive.

"She was one hundred and three, and I hadn't been further than the grocery store away from her for fifteen years," Miss Forbes confided as something utterly as it should be.

I played a Galli-Curci record and delighted in the coloratura gymnastics of that metallic brilliance of soprano. Miss Forbes sat, her face beaming. I wished she'd move to express her joy, but she sat tight, afraid that her joy was too expressive. She loved a Viennese waltz; and her eyes glittered as a jazz orchestra played a lilting one-step as it might have been done in any fashionable cabaret where there was a good band. It was no use trying Beethoven on her, and she said, "Yes, it's nice, but I like sweet music," when I tried McCormack singing "The End of a Perfect Day."

Mr. and Mrs. Brisbane came in and soon the Captain was there. They talked of Mexico and how some day one of the more upright races would have to direct the destiny of Mexico. I felt cranky and said, "They haven't done such good jobs elsewhere as they might."

Captain Roberts made a discouraged gesture, and said, "Not that I believe in anything, really. One gets cynical after one has been about and seen all sorts and conditions of life." He was apologetic towards Mrs. Brisbane for being so skeptical, because she talked to him frequently of how a new religion would start us all off right again. They worried me, and I saw that Miss Forbes was afraid she wasn't being quite nice in drinking the port wine as Mrs. Brisbane didn't drink.

"I have a feeling that Mr. Ross is one of the people we were talking of," Mrs. Brisbane said, smiling towards me. I didn't mind her, but she tried to impress one as being very well read, travelled, and experienced. She'd have been nicer as a sweet old lady, perhaps a little austere rather than placatory as she was. If I was a soul who had lived before, I had no awareness of it within myself, whatever she might say. I suffered ennui of a very temporal worldly sort. I drank, and went to cabarets and bars, and led a night life generally when in cities. No, I had no feeling of reincarnated wisdom. Reflection and contemplation and resignation and fatalism were ideas to me, and I had moments of trying them as attitudes, but I was searching, still wanting something out of life as action. Her messages gave me no solutions.

The days after that had themselves arranged. Mornings there were deck walks and swimming in the pool erected on the deck. After lunch there was an attempt at reading if any possible book could be located, but the result generally was a nap. But at five Miss Forbes joined me and we walked around the deck until we went to the bow of the boat to watch the flying fish, porpoises, sunset, and the churning colors the boat made in rushing through the water. It was all simple and quiet, and Miss Forbes told me of scones she had served her mother at tea, and of what good times they had had talking of their trip to Australia and New Zealand.

I was to get off the boat at Los Angeles harbor, and for days before our arrival there Miss Forbes told me that she didn't know what she would do without me to play the phonograph for her. In her eyes I was apparently a great musician. I tried to show her how to play the records, but she resignedly declared that she couldn't. She believed, evidently, that the machine would respond only to my bidding. The Captain was nice about saying that he'd play the machine for her, but I knew he wouldn't. He rather wondered why I bothered about the old lady, not realizing that she was my ship romance and far more to me humanly, and every way, than anyone else aboard ship had been.

As the boat docked at Los Angeles harbor I was impatient to get off and be headed towards my destiny, a visit to my mother. It would have been cruel, I think, if Miss Forbes hadn't been standing on the deck watching with eager eyes. I would have forgotten to say goodbye that morning, though we had all said farewells at the last dinner. She was there, however.

"It was good of you to play the sweet music to me," she quavered, without pathos, as I stood waiting to be allowed to go down the gangplank. "I will remember you. It seems as though I have known you always. We didn't see people the last years mother was here."

I wavered. It might frighten her if I kissed her goodbye, but it was such an easy gesture and it would be out of my mind as soon as I was away. It was a delicate moment. Would that gesture be nice, or would it be merely without imagination?

I didn't directly. When I got on the dock I turned and waved my hand to her and threw her a kiss. She didn't respond, but she waved her hand, and when I disappeared in the taxi I turned to see her still waving her hand, The taxi was well on its way towards Los Angeles before I remembered. She had told me that her friend in Vancouver had written her a year ago to come and visit her, but she had waited till after her mother died. Suppose something had happened to that friend of hers in Vancouver in that year.

The idea disturbed me, but what was there to do? Still, after many sea voyages I find Miss Forbes has left more impression on my mind than most people I have encountered aboard ship. And why? She was only naive and simple and old, and her life had been without events. Was it that which disturbed me: that with all the chasing and turmoil and struggle for excitement and adventure one's capacity for enjoyment grows no larger?

(See Bibliographical Note, page 364.)

From Katherine Anne Porter and others, McAlmon had heard "rumors about a vital art movement and group in Mexico City," [2] *and at the beginning of the thirties he migrated south of the border to see for himself. But Mexico City was a disappointment —it seemed to him secondhand and* vin ordinaire. *He left after only a week, and went to an out-of-the-way village where he remained for some months. A passage in* Being Geniuses Together *suggests what held him:*

"*There is an ultra-violet ray quality of light in the air in*

Mexico, a clarity and purity of landscape, which can be surpassed nowhere in the world. Drifting down the Nile on a clear, sweet day, in Greece or in the Greek Islands, one senses a not unsimilar quality, but I feel the Mexican quality more. At night when bands of youth wander about, following an orchestra, and when the thin, nostalgic tones of some Mexican song sounds through the still, moonlit space, it can be almost unbearably beautiful, and suggestive of a wonder and loveliness that the jaded mind refuses any longer to believe a possibility. That mind knows also that down in Cucka's shack there are a crew of men and boys, some not ten years old, drinking mescal, and that quite as apt as not one of them will split open the head of another with a rock or bottle. On carcel hill within the year there have been two executions; the mailman within the last month has been stabbed to death; a peon has been killed in a mountain pass because he was taking two gallons of Mexican jumping beans to market. His murderer will surely be caught when trying to dispose of that quantity of the beans, but the Apache Indians (they are in this part of Mexico) hold life cheap, their own and that of others." [3]

Yet actually what did all this amount to? Nothing but a change of scene. McAlmon remained McAlmon. "Suddenly I realize that my stay here has been a vacation of variation only; it has not been release, and I don't want to escape from the world I knew before." [4] *What was this world he had known? The year before he had answered Margaret Anderson's questionnaire for the dying* Little Review (*May 1929*)—What things do you really like? "Music, mainly jazz, and dancing, mainly my own, and gregarious life and lots of it. Low, or high, but always salted with a little disreputability. . . . The world is reasonable enough, and so am I, frequently, but something's wrong. Whether it's the capitalists, or the reformers, or the nice good middle class, or religions or economics, or what-have-you, many people will explain to you, but you don't have to take their words for a fact. Really. . . . Why do I go on living? Because living interests me, and I prefer something to nothing." [5]

Away from "the Crowd," McAlmon felt himself cut off from the life of his time; back in his world, he felt fenced in. And wherever he was, something was missing.

Mexican Interval

I awoke feeling panic swell through the room, and could not at once remember what city or country I was in. There was a beat and throb throughout, a thud against the wall, and the flutter of wings. The pigeon, flying at a velocity into the sunlit clarity of my high-ceilinged room, had struck the wall and now fell to the floor. It tottered dazedly; too stunned and stupid for panic. It would not guide easily, but finally I drove it towards the window and on the balcony it stood dazedly for a second before taking flight towards a group of pigeons wooing on the palazzo roof nearby. The event, with sleepless hours during the night because of innumerable bats entering the room, and circling endlessly with flutterings of blind imprisonment, increased a sense of ever-impending catastrophe that comes often upon abrupt awakening.

From the balcony I glanced towards the mountains. The light was ultra-violet upon the richly subdued coloring of arid country vegetation and silty soil. It was early, but already too hot for further sleeping. In the land of mañana, amid many tomorrows, there is always other time for slumber. The pigeons knew and were unfeverish in their love-making. There are always other days for mating. The foolish dove had dispersed my dreams; and that was as well too. Mañana is time enough for dreams begot from childhood and other lands far removed, and times past for which there is no urge to recall.

The sun burned hotter across the room's bare spaces. Coming through the wide door-window to fall upon my nudity it distressed me to modesty. From the next room came the ever-crying baby's wail. When, I wondered, perplexed by life-birth-death irritation, would the señora depart and take her brood of giggling schoolgirls? Not speaking their language, one could have no mood for coquetry with the half-grown girls who were wont to scramble, tittering, past my private balcony, adjoining that of their room. If they would indulge in such play they could take their chances of seeing me asleep, stripped, on the cot. Thompson, Johnson, I, and Salvador, the impoverished hidalgo who dealt in bootleg tequila, were accustomed to having the hotel to ourselves, as a man's hotel, and these summer graduation girls were an intrusion on our privacy. Pretty some of them were, but well guarded by elderly and forbidding dueñas. And to the girl children one could not respond with coyly impudent gestures, similar to their own. Indeed though, it was only I who was conscious of shyness. The mother left her room door open and flagrantly arranged that crowning glory, her hair, upon her flat back-head. She did not mind the bareness of our male chests as we sauntered indolently, pajama pants flapping, to wash away dawn sleepiness in the cooling shower bath. She hadn't alertness, awareness, and had she curiosity? Could she wonder at the ill-fated loves of the gentlemanly but loco British inventor, Thompson? Could she know why and for how many years Johnson had wandered, seeking continually that mine of gold or silver which was to enrich him fabulously? He trusted his beloved Mexico.

"The postman wasn't three days late. He'll never get here," Johnson said, coming into my room, rosy from a shower bath. "He was killed in the mountain pass. They found him with two knives between his ribs. Some bad hombres got word that he was carrying a thousand pesos. But here are some letters for both of us."

"Ecstasy and adventure have their place in youth, but they prove deceptive. Will you never achieve balance?" Olivia's letter teased me. And no, my conscious answered, but it is not so much ecstasy or adventure I want as that I don't want you. But you know; you are preparing yourself again against disillusion, so banal, but always to you, sudden and precocious. I won't return to your not-so-solacing common sense. What need have I for your quickly forgotten decisions and wiles? Mañana I may write you that neither time nor your ponderings affect my hardly gained tranquility. You are lonely and ask why I don't return? I am lonely too, but cleanly alone, uncorrupted by the loneliness your presence brings tormentedly into being.

"*No le hace in Mexico.* No laughing in Mexico. No matter

in Mexico." Thompson's morning formula of forced gaiety re-
sounded through the patio as he came down the balcony. Which
of his obsessions would be dominating him this morning? "They
needn't tell me I'm crazy. I know it. I tell them first," he came
booming into my room, wanting somebody to breakfast with.
"You men don't mind my craziness. Twenty-five dollars for the
man who isn't crazy, in Canada, England, or America. Twenty-
five dollars. We're all crazy."

"Right, Tommy," Johnson said, grinning.

Thompson strives for gaiety but Johnson's glance admits
that he too knows this will be one of Thompson's intricately
loco days. Thompson helps himself to mescal, sighing, "I know
you don't mind." He gulped the drink, and breathed heavily.
"Yep, we're all crazy. I used to belong to the Scots Greys. Their
beautiful uniforms and swagger blinded what natural sense I had,
if I had any. I believed in war and armies. My namesake's bones
lie in France. Gladiators, they're gladiators, like the Romans and
Greeks. England, Japan, and America, gladiators! All crazy. Hey,
parity, where is your purity, parity? With all the fleets we could
gather in a hundred years a college boy can fly overhead, drop
poisoned powders, and kill the fleet in an hour. It took me sixty
years not to be a damn fool. I belong to fighting stock. My ancestors' bones lie in the Crimea, India, Afghanistan, France. One
was chucked overboard at Trafalgar. Ye-unh! *No le hace in
Mexico.*"

Thompson, sedate, plumply dignified, drew designs on the
floor with his cane. Helping himself to more mescal, he brooded,
breathing heavily, more from reflection than from age. Why, since
he had known Johnson but a few days, he made confidences which
he had not made to me in six weeks, I don't know. Possibly he
sensed that he irritated Johnson, while to me he was somewhat
of a comic figure as I had no intention of brooding upon his
pathos.

"Yes, I am crazy. My wife broke me. I was making good money,
had inventions ready to go on the market to make us millionaires.
She wouldn't wait. She said she had one god, money, and she
would go to the streets for it if I didn't supply her. It cut me
to the heart when she said that. Her voice was harder than flint.
I gave her all I had and cleared out. I don't see even my daughters,

and Clarie, the one I love most, the only one I love, may not be mine, I know now. *Si, no le hace in Mexico.* That little girl loved sleeping with me until she was ten years old. No bed was as comfortable. Nobody understands the human heart, what love is or where it strikes and why. Ten men are rich on my inventions. They needn't tell me I'm crazy. I say so first. They haven't even paid me the $40,000 I was to get for my new water filtering system."

Standing by the balcony window I saw a string of cargador burros bearing brushwood down the mountain sides. They were followed by two lean, barefoot, unwashed arrieros, one of them Juan, who was crazy as well as constantly loco from mescal. Careless rags hung about their sinewy limbs, and apathy did not hide the grace or the animal-lithe strength of their bodies.

"Breakfast, Tommy, breakfast. We can't solve women on an empty stomach this time of the morning," Johnson said, knowing well Thompson couldn't be jollied out of any obsession when he was really intense. He or I were in for having Thompson drop into our rooms continually during the course of this day. We sauntered from the hotel, across the plaza, down to the Alamos where Cucka's kitchen stood beneath the cotton trees. Cucka, years before a schoolteacher, pure Indian, and for years after the main woman of the town, had served many American and English men variously. She knew, at least, their tastes in food. She spoke to me, smilingly, when I was seated. I could not understand.

"That's it, is it?" Johnson joked. "You have been casting eyes on Merceditas, have you?"

"Mercedes," I said, glancing at the child who waited on the table. "She isn't over twelve."

Johnson was serious for a time. "No, she's fifteen or sixteen, not just an overmature child. She came two months ago, from a rancho sixty miles back in the mountain. Some love affair made her run away, and parents don't bother hunting these girls out. Cucka is suggesting that if you have no little friend, here is Mercedes."

Merceditas was laughing at us. She didn't understand what was being said. I noticed that the healthy red, apple clear, was applied to her brown skin. She was pretty, childish, Indian, but light-moving and alert. Cucka was not joking, I gathered. She felt sure that after three weeks in the town a young American would be lonely for a girl friend. I felt ill at ease, for Merceditas and Cucka had arranged things, and the child's eyes were direct and willing; not bold. What was suggested was natural to her. I squirmed to feel what Christian civilization and *morality* create in the way of immodest pudency. I didn't want Mercedes either; she might be sixteen but she struck me as a little girl.

We sauntered back to the hotel, Thompson stopping in the market place to buy figs, I, limes for a mescal-julep. Lemons, melons, papayas, beans, potatoes, and tomatoes rested in piles on the poorly arranged tables, behind which stood draggled, grimy natives. Strings of sinewy black meat, jerked to preserve somewhat, hung along the market rafters. Innumerable flies hovered about, but if one is to travel, in the East, or in Mexico, one must forget undue fastidiousness about sights and about what one eats.

As we loitered back to the hotel we noticed a flock of scraggly sheep scrambling about the mountain side, seeking meagre forage. It was dazzlingly hot now. The two orange cats, lean and wild, and the fat drooping dog moved agedly in the patio, to get out of the way of the cargador burros bringing firewood to Señora. An indolent sense of the town and market lived in me. The muchacha called to Señora that los Americanos had used all the water in the shower bath, and Anatolio was not to be found. He *never was* about when the shower bath tank needed filling.

There came the sound of music, thin, wailing, Indian music, and the beat of drums. A group of Indians straggled by, going to some ceremonial dance. Johnson felt lazily talkative. "You should have seen this town before 1917, before the last revolution, when they played native music rather than this banal jazz the boys think they must try now. You will hardly believe it. There were bars, clubs, rich stores, and the nightly promenade around the plaza had aristocratic class. Peons never dared walk on the inside circle in those days. The train nearly made this town a mainline stop. Old General Orozco stopped all that in the 1917 revolution. He took two million pesos and 30,000 head of cattle from Alamos alone. The next year he was served arsenic in his soup. No one knows who got the money he stored away. And now there isn't even a drugstore here. The people don't value education. The teachers don't go above the fifth grade themselves. Their last governor absconded to the States, owing the teachers of this state five months' salary. They should have been paid monthly, but they didn't raise a row. No use having hope in these parts."

Johnson's guile did not keep Thompson's mind off his lonely complications. *"No le hace en Mexico,"* Thompson boomed out the most maddening of his repeated phrases. "I expected a letter from my sweetheart today. Maybe she's angry at me. No matter. She's only one. I have others and more to be had by answering notices in the matrimonial journal. This one has me worried for her though. I feel her grandfather. She writes that she's eighteen and in love with a married man. She's ill, and can't see him often. I told her to look before she leaps. If his wife won't divorce him for three years he will have done with her by then. No laughing in Mexico."

"If my man, Felix, gets back with the car I'm going to rancho San Bernardino," Johnson says. "Do you want to come along, Kit?" I saw that Thompson was getting on his nerves.

"Yes, Felix is probably downstairs chewing a straw and talking to Anatolio. I'll look him up. We need variety."

"That's all right, boys," Thompson said, really kind. "I know I'm a dull old bore. I can't help it when my mind gets filled with problems. You go along. I'll look in on Señora Marcur. She may have some American magazines to give me."

Within half an hour we were in Johnson's Ford truck jogging across the desert. Innumerable long-eared jack rabbits loped frantically across the sagebrush stretches on the approach of the car. In the luminous light, from a distance, they appeared magnified to deer size and looked amazingly deerlike. Felix and Johnson were silent for a spell, and I was wondering.

Yes, silver, copper, and gold were in the region; and fertile soil, and foraging land for millions of cattle. There was too the story of the hidalgo who paved the street from his casa to the church with silver slabs, for his daughter's wedding. Next year he was put against the carcel wall and riddled with bullets.

Now silver bullion prices were low. These people don't know when they are well off. When everything was going well, with people richly prospering, they had to have a revolution.

A neat native, surely an Indian peon, passed by and spoke

greetings. His donkey was extra precious, deer-lithe, neat, and sweet, with dainty feet prancing as though the mountain paths were intricate lace. Some Indians rode right pretty steeds these days, prancing, rearing, champing, but gentle too. Jacinto's Andalusian stallion was *brioso* but docile, and needed no mouth-breaking bit. He danced a pretty dance, coy with his dashing long-tailed beauty. I wished we were headed towards Jacinto's ranch rather than San Bernardino. Bad hombres loitered about that ranch.

"Gold in them hills," Johnson said breezily, to break the silence.

"Guarded by rattlesnakes, cactus, and the Mexican government," I said.

Johnson turned regretful. "They don't mine themselves, and won't do business with anyone who will."

"They have had experience with those who want to and do."

Johnson's mind deviated from desires which he had not fulfilled. "Once the Señoritas all wore black, and veils, and went every morning to say their prayers. They've left off their veils, but they're still cagey. Their short dresses are a sign though. Do you notice how you can always spot a girl with German blood? Thick ankles."

"The Spanish or the meztizo have the quality. At a ball for the Governor last week, you could have seen twenty girls dressed as though they were from a recent fashion show in Paris. How do they know?"

"They make their own dresses," Johnson mused. "They sew, stay indoors all day, do the plaza at night, and wait for mañana. Would our girls consent to that routine? Oh boy! You wouldn't sense, if you didn't know, how hard these people can be. Three days before my arrival, last year, they shot five bandits. They were still hanging on jail hill, as warning, when I got to town. They picked the prettiest spot in the country for their jail too. If they catch the Indian who killed the postman we'll have another killing."

From far away, from some ranch off any main or even minor trail, came the beat of drums. "Hey, Felix," Johnson is boisterous, "are those Yaqui drums? What messages are they sending? Are they coming after us? Felix loves the Yaquis."

Felix looked perturbed, his Indian face less a mask than most because of seven years' labor contracting with Johnson in Los Angeles. "Yaquis, me no like," he said with stolid automatic insistence.

"Why, Felix?" Johnson joked. "They're fine fellows once you get to know them. You didn't make friends with them that time they captured you. Tell Kit about it."

Felix, subnormal anyway, pondered with deep fear an experience of his childhood. Johnson has teased him too much. He feels he must tell the story and does so haltingly. "One time father had fine hacienda, San Bernardino, where we go. Me just kid, with mother, brother, sister. Yaquis come, two, t'ree hundred. Burn house, kill twenty people, sister, mother, father. Me and brother they take. One man they hamstring. We walk three days in mountain. No shoes. One man's leg, he break, leave me guard him. I see. He dying. I only twelve. I see him die and pretty much quick I run away. See brother dead, hanging to tree. I run quick, hide. Yaquis no find. Yaquis pretty much tough guys. Me no like."

"Felix nearly shook out of his pants as we rode across Yaqui country coming down," Johnson said, bothersomely teasing and jovial. "Why don't you get chummy with them, Felix? They're fine fellows once you know them."

"Yaquis, me no like," Felix insists, dumbly, apparently unaware that he's being teased.

We arrived at San Bernardino to find a wedding fiesta going on, for the third day. The groom was drunk on mescal, and surely had been taking marijuana. Porfiria, the middle-aged woman who called herself Felix's wife on this ranch, said that one man had been killed the night of the wedding, in a drunken fight.

"You drink with us. In America we drink with you, we do as you. Here you drink mescal, Mexican drink." Alvaro, the bridegroom, talked challengingly to Johnson. He had come from San Diego, with his father, to marry a true Mexican girl. Johnson hated mescal, but Alvaro was far gone and combative. We drank.

Our drinking pleased Alvaro and the other ranch Mexicans. We tried to join in their songs, as they repeated the melodies and words to us. They called us best friends, but Alvaro disappeared. Later he was on a rampage. Loco with mescal and mad with marijuana, he wanted to fight everybody. His friends could not get his gun or knife and he brandished both, threatening murder. He ran down to the stream nearby and fell in, but when friends tried to rescue him he threw rocks at them. When the water had cooled him a bit he swaggered into the hall and up to his bride. There, in the center of the floor, he threw her down and raped her. Two Mexican children rushed up to Porfiria, who was in the kitchen. Alvaro had, they told her, plunged a knife into his bride. They had seen the blood spurting. Porfiria, already knowing the incident, nodded drily and glanced at a pair of ducks waddling about the kitchen. "Yes, Señor Drake murders Señora Duck so every day, many times."

"He'll kill his wife before the month's up," Johnson predicted. "That boy's a bad hombre. No good. His father is ashamed of him. His sisters have left the party ashamed of what he has done. They're American trained. The natives don't mind."

The wedding celebration goes on. The peon orchestra keeps twanging sad music, patient, but insistently wailing nostalgia and love desire. An owl hoots from the primitive church top. Dawn isn't far away. Bats are returning to the palm tree they chose to nest in. In the hills nearby the dogs are at their barking which demands, perhaps, that something will happen that doesn't, never does, happen. Roosters, tricked by the brightness of the night, crow early dawn's oncoming. The descending moon sheds deep lavender on the hills. The cool atmosphere is an effervescent current. Still there is no feeling of peace or rest about this night.

"Let's clear out and drive back to town," Johnson talks sotto voce to me. "Porfiria and the Chink and a few of the drunk Indians are planning to snitch a lift in my car back to town. They're too drunk and hopped up. I'll get Felix."

San Bernardino ranch is too removed, Porfiria too embedded in dirt which has collected upon her through the years. Her food is impossible. The memory of the murder and the rape make the place sinister. There are no decent houses, or rooms, to retire into. The ranch is only a group of uncared-for buildings. We would not feel safe sleeping on the ground or in the midst of this crew of drunk, doped Indians. No telling how they might resent us. Johnson found Felix, who drove away from the ranch. There we joined him, to depart, undetected by any of the wedding party proper.

"A sweet honeymoon for the bride," Johnson grunted. "But believe it or not, away from these parts I always feel its romance dragging me back. It's in my blood."

A letter from Olivia has arrived, and therein she reveals herself in one of her phases of staunch simplicity. Rather wistfully she compliments me and envies my tranquility amongst really simple people, and she would be, is, simple, but I refuse to accept her thus.

Well, well, Olivia, tranquility isn't so placid or simple as to make one unaware of confusion. These people are just more people and it won't be from me that you will hear of the deep enigmas in their eyes. What simplicity there is might be in ourselves alone, but I don't think these people are simple. They know revolution, sudden death, dancing, color, music, resignation —but boredom, or ennui—no, they are not endangered by the philosophy of defeat and too great a sense of futility. They don't soulprobe; aren't spiritual. Olivia, I believe simple is a word to apply to people obsessed with ideas, and should I write that to you will you find me deteriorating not to value either ideas of your precious simplicity, much?

Roberto comes into my room bringing figs, grapefruit, and three quails, which Cucka will cook for me. He is happy that I am pleased, and by the way he looks at me and laughs I know that he doesn't think that such animals as me really exist. It tickles him that I want to make wine out of pomegranates, but why, he wonders, when I seem so ready to be happy on mescal or tequila? Like Señor Thompson and the idiot cripple and José, the half-wit, I am loco, and Roberto has an Indian-gallant sense of protectiveness towards me. My silly lemon yellow hair and blankishly blue-blue eyes somehow fascinate him. His serene belief that a two mile walk is more than I can do makes me realize that he looks upon me as fragile, if not as an invalid.

Having a quantity of American papers to bring to Señora Marcur, I take them to leave for her on my way to the post office. In her way she is my contact with a world I understand, and don't like, but familiarity holds one in its way. She scandal-mongs in a way one has known in village and group life, always.

Señora Marcur is puzzled. My entrance into her patio caught her unaware, reading, so that she had not time to stage-set an entry. She cannot place Roberto, she, a Marcur, who has known all of her Alamos townspeople for years. He is courteous, with a manner; he is clean, alert, and not shy before her. Still she sees that he is not of pure Spanish stock; not of a best family, or she would know him. She does not know that his mother, who was a woman, evidently, of character enough, has taught Roberto to be proud of his Indian blood and rather disdainful of his Spanish. She doesn't and wouldn't know, as a Catholic, a pure and moral woman, that Roberto has never known the idea that it is shameful to be the child of a man and woman out of wedlock.

As Roberto speaks no English, Señora Marcur talks of him to me, in front of him. She is bothered that he does not show peon awe before her. She is resentful that he does not realize that she is an Aramaza, the original owners of most of Alamos, an aristocrat to whom his ancestors bowed, before her ancestors had brought Christian knowledge to save them. She is curt when I say that Roberto has grace, with a Chaldean youth beauty which recalls the best quality in archaic sculpturing. Some sign of respect which she desires is lacking from both Roberto and myself.

"You Americans," Señora Marcur reprimands me, "think no Mexican has a cultural background. You make me speak your language. That means I'm your inferior." There is a flash of malice in her eyes.

"No, no," I quickly explain, "that means merely that you have superior linguistic talents. You speak French, German, Spanish, Italian, and English, and I speak even English not too well."

Señora is placated, but, not quite directly, she implies that only because I am a foreigner who does not understand would I accept Roberto as a personal friend. She has placed him, and knows that his mother was unmarried. At cross purposes with her high ideals she starts talking of "the best families," and I gather that there has been much intermarriage, with the usual result of degeneration. Heredity tells. Blood will out. The Dossiers and the Almadas are upstarts, and it does not do to exaggerate their weaknesses by intermarrying. Señora Marcur has a grimly joyful period of discussing the decay which happens in old families. She talks of Russian, German, French, and Dutch novels which have depicted such decay. Particularly she remembers the "Small Souls" novels of Couperus.

Roberto, not understanding the language and too lower class to cope with Señora's intellect had he understood, recalls that he has promised to get pomegranates for me. He departs, leaving Señora Marcur to puzzle that he, a bastard, of native stock, should have poise and well-bred boy courtesy, but no inferior's shyness before her.

"No, no," Señora is soon setting me right. "The Almadas have never been one of our best families. Four generations ago one of the boys, Spanish, yes, and of good family, lived with an Indian girl. He married her when they had four children, and it is from him and his children that the Almadas are descended. Naturally we have never quite accepted them. Señor Almada went to live in Los Angeles, but he had no wealth according to American standards. One of his girls eloped with what she thought was a Frenchman. He thought she had more money than the family has. She went abroad with him for a year. When she returned she had so little education or taste that she talked. Her husband, we found, had been Egyptian. He took her into the depths of Egypt. Had she been intelligent she would have known she had lived virtually in a harem. She has been back for three years now. I believe there has been a divorce, but of course the Almadas have no culture. We do not associate with them, except to be kind when necessary."

Since the revolution, one reflects, Señora Marcur's impaired fortune has caused townspeople to be less impressed by her great culture. Her family name does not create the atmosphere of awe she claims it once did. She has retained ideas about the divine right of kings, one gathers, and feels possibly sad for her that she is not viewed with fearsome respect for being a Marcur. In this town they respect neither age nor culture, she sighs, somehow accusing me of failing to understand the superiority of old age. She has, she claims, no desire to go abroad, though she could afford the trip now. In Alamos they do not understand culture, but abroad they would not understand that she is an Aramaza-Marcur.

Señorita Marcur comes into the room. Somehow she is meek and self-effacing, not seeming to realize that she is of her mother's blood. She has, however, some of her mother's, or is it of woman's, or of mere human's, tendencies. Or had Señor Seron attracted her? He was, at first glance, a romantic type. His brooding violet eyes, his matinee-idol good looks, his sad, lost air, his manner of chivalry had attracted Elena and other town girls. Señorita Marcur, over thirty, balanced, sensible, not as the other town girls, she claims, is driven to telling me of the scandal of his life.

"It was for Luz Torreon he nearly made tragedy," she talked. "Luz is over thirty. For a time he saw her every day, several times. Every day she made herself a new dress. She was deeply in love, planning marriage. She was furious when I told her Señor Seron was married. When she found out the truth she sent him away, but the silly Elena would not believe her or me. Now neither of the girls nor their parents dare show indignation. As Señor Seron is the tax collector they are all afraid. It disgusts me the way people fuss over that nasty little boy of his. He is defective I am sure. His wife is a rich woman, too. For that reason they fuss over her."

Visions of Señora Seron floated through my mind. Poor Señor Seron. It was said that his wife, when he married her, had been slender and beautiful. Now she was tremendous; short, dwarfish, and certainly weighed 250 pounds. Señorita Marcur continues discussing him.

"Señor Seron must be mad. At Pancho's, the Chinaman's, restaurant, he got a fourteen-year-old girl drunk. As she became sick he did not have his way with her, but nobody would have reprimanded him if he had. It is disgusting how men in politics are immune, when in power. Now that Señora Seron is here she guards her husband well. He is afraid of her. She is a sensible woman, but I think there is little doubt that her husband is mad. Mad about love. She knows and understands. He has a look in his eyes I do not like. It is not difficult to be a Don Juan in a little town where the girls believe the tax assessor a great man."

The day is quiet, so calm that a burro's bray, birds' notes, the cooing of doves, a dog bark are cameos of sound against the blue, dry silence. At the church the ceremony for Grandfather Goyceola is being held. He had died some days before, well beyond eighty, and upon the plaza for the last few nights none of his numerous descendants were seen. From the States and from other parts of Mexico, surely, descendants come, faithful to their father's or grandfather's or uncle's memory. Old Goyceola had too much wealth, as had his many relatives, for this funeral not to be a ponderous family affair. In the afternoon the fat fifteen-year-old, Pepe, loiters past the hotel and speaks to Andrés and myself. He is brooding, but he is acting sadness somewhat too. He sheds a few tears, saying, "I loved my grandpapa" in infantile tones.

A dirty, minute boy is playing in the plaza, a desolate baby. Pepe, as he goes on, speaks to the child, and comes back to Andrés, leading the child. "He has no papa, no mamma," Pepe explains to me. "He rode in on a cargador burro because he has no home and at Rancho Francisco the woman told him his papa and mamma would never come again."

Pepe, whose father is school superintendent for the district, led the child away, saying that his father would find a home for him, and his mother would feed the child. "We always got the place for the little boy with no papa, no mamma," Pepe lisped, giving the impression of being proudly patriarchal and also communal. Surely there were several children in town who had no papa, no mamma, and no set home, but they were taken care of in some manner, as were the beggars, idiots, and helpless cripples of the town. Being a strayling did not necessarily mean cruel times here. Pepe's orphan was not frightened, was full of play and spirits, in fact.

Late in the afternoon Johnson comes into my room to advise that we go to the cantina. "Big doings there," he said. "All of old man Goyceola's men relatives are there drinking beer, wishing they could be back at their own homes, since they've dutifully attended his funeral. Let's get in on the wake."

The evening was sweetly soothing; the landscape so soaked with beauty that mañana-drifting should be the attitude towards living here. Through the clean cobblestone streets two cargadors with five burros were hawking their last loads of firewood. Barefoot, lithe, indifferent now, beneath their apparent apathy dwelt the will to have mescal and be loco this night. The town lamplighters are out, and we observe that they do not lay down their guns even when they mount posts to light the lamps. They have been ordered not to, as some Indian might grab the gun and run away. The days have been going on with such peaceful tranquility that one forgets tales of brutality and violence; that the natives, when fighting drunk, often have to be killed or knocked unconscious, to be made to give up fighting. There is desperate, uncaring violence beneath their apparent whipped resignation.

At the cantina there are seven of grandfather Goyceola's male descendants, and how like a gathering of Rotarians, drummers, or Deacons-on-a-tear they are! One, a grandson-in-law, has a luxurious undertaking parlor in Hermosilla, and he is gaily buying whiskey. Accustomed to funerals, declaring himself modern-minded and American of ideas, he has dared suggest that perhaps old Goyceola had lived his proper day. He and a dapper-looking grandson of the old man mildly suggest that this funeral has taken them away from their businesses at inopportune times. Johnson and I know, however, that they are saying this to us only because their other relatives with them can not understand English. The dapper, El Paso-broker grandson assures me that in America we are viewing family and relationships in a proper light. I wonder if, in the States, he does not belittle his Mexican blood. He is too proud of having attended an American private school, as the only Mexican boy at the school.

It is so that these Goyceola males, who have not seen each other for years, and who have varying degrees of wealth, do not know what to say to each other. They are glad to play poker and to drink with Johnson, myself, Arturo, and other Mexicans who are not relations. The brewer grandson invites us to visit his brewery in Juarez; the undertaker is proud too of his establishment, but invites us rather to stop off at Hermosilla someday, and he will show us what a promising town it is. The lawyer grandson finally admits that old man Goyceola has left much less money than had been expected, and with so many heirs—it was hardly worth while for any of them to have taken time away from their business to come to this out of the way town for the funeral. He catches himself being indiscreet, however, and decides to drink no more beer or mescal.

This gathering is not Mexican; it is timeless, raceless. It is a group of descendants little interested in each other going in for the convention of mourning, while wondering what money each is to inherit. Unrest, ever ready to breed, gains force in my heart. I have imagined much that is primitive, archaic, communal, into this town and its inhabitants. The peons and Indians are nearer to a state of nature than are most people I know. They have both the kindliness and the ruthlessness and the lack of conscience of nature, but these only as uneducated beings have, elsewhere. Romantic history and literature has been causing me to see this town and its people in the light of ancient Sumerian, Italian, Greek, or Egyptian towns, but coldly the business men descendants of old Goyceola reveal themselves as Babbitts, but harder Babbitts than the American type. They are distinctly suspicious of and on their guard towards each other. Suddenly I realize that my stay here has been a vacation of variation only; it has not been release, and I don't want to escape from the world I knew before.

I am not antisocial; I do want my own kind and familiar qualities. I want cities and traffic and turmoil, which is not turmoil when one is habituated. Too often have these Mexicans questioned and wondered why I am staying in their town, since I am not, as is Johnson, a prospective miner, nor as Thompson, a loco, antiquated engineer, striving to find intermittent employment on irrigation and electric light projects. Mine is not a mañana nature; there is for me no Mayan-masked enigma about tomorrows for one has aggressiveness and makes plans and decisions. This has been a nerve-soothing rest, but to Arturo I now confess, after the Goyceola males depart, that I am keen to get to the States.

"Me too," Arturo says. "This month I have made good money selling the jumping beans. Now I go to the States and see if I can get a job, with a canning company, to travel between here and the States. For you, you laugh at Señoras Khrem and Marcur, the buzzards, you call them. For me, I can't hear more their telling what once this town was. To hell with what was, with them or in the town. They are old cocks trying to crow who never crowed well. Tonight I drive us into Navajoa, if you like. You get you the morning train for Nogales, if you like. We get us a bottle of mescal, and go to your room while you pack."

Arturo too is restless and depressed. The funeral group depressed him, for he is married into a Mexican family similar to the Goyceola, and Arturo confides that marriage and family does not solve life for him. Forty is a bad age when one remembers how little one has accomplished and how little satisfaction the past has given one, or so it seems. Mexicans do not give a damn, do not hope or plan much; it is no use giving a damn, but Arturo is thinking romantically of two successful years in Philadelphia. Then he felt himself very American. Here, ambition is rather futile, and it mars tranquility. Arturo is not resigned to letting fate manipulate his situations. Mañana may not have all imagination for him, for Arturo has an idea of making himself good money by operating perhaps illegally between the States and Mexico. I do not ask indiscreet questions about mescal, opium, or marijuana.

Roberto joins us in my room. He too has become restless during the weeks. Señora Marcur has been irritated because he forgot to bring her fruit she hoped to have from him for little money. She has become too cosmopolitan, no doubt, to understand that Roberto is another boy become restless. To him she is an old woman who talks unimportantly of her class and family background, and such talk solves none of his desires. His imagination is opening to receive new ideas. He too has doubts about waiting for tomorrows, and wonders could he not get into the States, rather than go to Mexico City. A mixture of race bloods is torrenting in him, and soon he will be another young man who has gone away. Is there not good money to be made in the States? He doubts my warning that he might be deported, and if not, be forced to work as a mere day laborer. Two days ago I could have advised him more strongly to stay here, where life moves easily among the charcoal stoves; in the market where women pat tortillas; where nights he can eat menudas with Duba. There have been warming nights in Duba's hut, where steam from her pots add greasy shine to already glowing faces. There, menudas-eaters have seen each other darkly, comfortable in their bellies, feeling night develop into another casual day when worry will not be more needful than on this night.

Roberto, for the first time in his seventeen years, will go to the cabaret in Navajoa with Arturo, Andrés, Jesús, and me. The younger boys do not know; they will dance with the girls, but they admit frankly that they are shy. With boys their own age they would abandon themselves to young bravado, but neither Arturo nor I are anxious to drive them into Navajoa. We will forget, but we have no wish to sponsor their first crop of wild oats.

As Arturo's rheumatic car drove up to the hotel two barefoot Indians were being led by the policia to the carcel. They were drunk, as ancestors for centuries had been drunk. One's eye was cut deeply by, the policia informed Arturo, a sharp stone. The other's face is battered beyond having features. It is seldom worth while asking what caused these fights. They are dirty by ancestral tradition too; and have, sadly I admit it, more trust in mescal than in mañana.

As we drive into the desert buzzards are circling against the primitive blue above a mountain. Where scavengers float there has been death, and has death a mañana? The little Mexican town has already retreated from my active conscious as I strain forward to an American tomorrow. Because of this, the experiences of the last five months have become a keenly sketched painting of warm colors. Reluctance has me; reluctance to turn back, and reluctance to go on. I am leaving something peacefully sociable, and protective, beneath the sinister brooding quality of nature grown strange upon a temperament too little primitive. I feel Alamos and its people as an entity; for it I have a fondness, as it has fondness for me. Like all entities it has its limitations as well as its beautiful qualities. Still, it is not my tempo. I am of the machine and scientific age, and time does not go backward.

It was dark before we came into Navajoa. On the way in we thought we saw a car approaching. The lights were, however, merely the luminous glare in the eyes of a wildcat, mountain lion, or puma, who gazed fascinated at our approaching carlights. As it leaped from the roadway into the brush, the darkness and magnifying quality of our lights made it appear tremendous. Further on a deer sprang across the roadway.

The slow moon was coming up, and the mountains were more clear of outline. Nostalgia possessed me, but I rejected it. Beyond the mountains and mist mañanas persisted, mystic-masked, concealing the future with their original enigmatic smiles. I wondered if a little of mañana-feeling might not stay with me in more active countries to make existence less flurried and nerve-driven.

(See Bibliographical Note, page 364.)

PART V

FULL CIRCLE
1934-1956

Comments on the persons mentioned in Part V will be found in the Biographical Repertory, beginning on page 367.

1. Return to Paris

After the Mexican interval began a migration eastward. Mc-Almon stopped off for a short time in New York where he saw a good deal of Berenice Abbott, who had photographed so many of "the Crowd," and met Louis Zukofsky, an admirer of William Carlos Williams and publisher of his collected poems. David Moss and Martin Kamin, who had a bookstore in the Barbizon-Plaza, tried to persuade McAlmon to edit a magazine, but he thought that the purely literary periodical was passé, and they were not interested in the kind of inclusive review that he proposed—one that would take notice of the increasing general awareness of political and economic problems induced by the depression. Moss and Kamin also "suggested that they should take on the publishing of books under the name of Contact Editions. It did not much matter to me, although I was supposed to retain the editorship of such books as they issued." [1] Though momentarily tempted, McAlmon finally refused the job. "Contact Editions, now completely out of my hands in fact though not in theory, published an adolescently smart and naughty novel, The Dream Life of Balso Snell [1931], *by Nathanael West. It was, as Ezra Pound told me in a letter condemning me for lack of discrimination, the sort of thing we should get off our chests by the beginning of sophomore year in college. Fortunately I could disclaim having ever seen the book before it appeared. Mr. West obviously had read too much of Anatole France at his most senile-mischievous, and tried to convince himself and his readers that he was still concerned about soul and Christ and the insularities of religion. Later, however, he redeemed himself by writing* Miss Lonelyhearts, *which was a brilliant production."* [2]

From New York—and his friend Williams—McAlmon went back to "Old Europe." ("I fail to discover fewer morons and bigotries in other countries than the United States," he once observed. "The other countries do not publicize their defectives so constantly.") [3] *Through the first four years of the thirties he bobbed about here and there, still without an anchorage; it was a period during which he published some of his best fiction, but he was living intemperately, going the pace at a sharper clip than ever before. "And what iz gone wrong with McAlmon," Ezra Pound wrote to a mutual friend. "The kid just playin' the fool, or whatever? . . . I hope he ain't gone plumb to hell."* [4]

By January 1934 McAlmon had nearly completed Being Geniuses Together. "Joyce asked him to read the manuscript to him, and McAlmon did so during several afternoons," according to Richard Ellmann. In the parts about Joyce "the tone was quite different from that of Frank Budgen's book [James Joyce and the Making of "Ulysses"], which was to appear later in 1934. While Budgen never lost sight of Joyce as a writer, McAlmon was more concerned with him as a member of the heavy-drinking Bohemian set. The result was a less amiable portrait than McAlmon intended. Joyce confided to Miss Weaver that the book made him feel 'actionable,' but to McAlmon he only laughed and said, 'You should call it Advocatus Diaboli.' McAlmon answered forthrightly, 'What in hell do you think the title means, that I take genius without salt?' But when it was reported to McAlmon later that Joyce had referred to the book as 'the office boy's revenge,' he was in turn displeased. Joyce speculated to Miss Weaver on the source of McAlmon's 'malice,' which he thought he detected in passages referring to her as well; but McAlmon had not intended malice, only candor. Joyce did not break with him, but their friendship, which had lost in warmth over the last few years, became perfunctory." [5] At least Joyce remained friendly enough to warn him off literary agents. *"They are very unsatisfactory except for the handling of commercial 'copy,' " he wrote to him in May 1934.* [6] *McAlmon was then in London trying to find a publisher for Geniuses, which he had completed in March. The closing pages of the book telling of his return to Paris had been written while he was on yet another "migration," this time to Strasbourg.*

When I got back to Paris in the beginning of 1934 after two years' absence in Germany and Spain, Paris had changed, but Paris was the same. The Stavisky scandal was in full swing. After dinner one night with Ford Madox Ford I left his studio to look in upon a communist meeting in the Salle Bullier across the street. In the stretch from there to the Dome bar there were numerous groups of police, at least five hundred, to stop rioting. A few nights later some twenty French citizens were shot down on the Place de la Concorde, and new evidences of corruption were being unearthed daily. The French police were ironic, brutal, bullying, or jovial, as the mood took them, as always in history. In bars when a quarrel started between a Frenchman and a foreigner the Frenchman would say, "Moi, je suis français," and the foreigner, if wise, knew that the French were not loving or being polite or fair or decent to foreigners these days. Potential war or revolution was in the air, and hate and distrust.

And Ford Madox Ford was as usual. He told an imaginary story about the meeting between Proust and Joyce and he had a woman introducing the two who had never seen Paris until long after Proust's death. Joyce actually met Proust through Sydney Schiff, who is a novelist under the name of Stephen Hudson. It was at a party where were Diaghilev and Daisy Fellowes, among others. Mrs. Fellowes only this year did a reading on Joyce and rather riled Mrs. Joyce by contriving to have herself photographed with Mr. Joyce and others, but the photograph appeared with the others cut out and Mrs. Fellowes appears alone beside Mr. Joyce. Norah wonders what kind of a publicity-seeking woman that is and does the woman think she wants her husband photographed with another married woman.

Joyce and Proust had neither read any of the other's work upon their meeting and Joyce suspects Proust had heard but little of him, and Joyce did not know what an imaginary and also actual invalid Proust was. Each mentioned some character in his own work to the other and in each case the other disclaimed any knowledge of that character. In fact the meeting was not a marked success, as often happens in the meetings of artists in the same medium. Mr. Ford's account, however, as he tells it and writes of it, is highly fictionized as are many of his "memories."

Soon they were raising hell in Vienna and Austria also. Katherine Anne Porter was living quietly in Paris, seldom appearing in public, as she was writing the biography of Cotton Mather, short stories, and planning a novel. Kay Boyle and Laurence Vail were in the Tirol collecting newspapers from all corners of the world to write comparative fiction paralleling the newspaper stories. Joyce was continuing his *Work in Progress;* Ezra his cantos and his letters to newspapers and his pamphlets explaining economics, reading, literature, and how to think about whatever.

I had not changed either. Quite a few people who once struck me as important have faded out in that way but others have taken their places. Life begins, they say, at forty, as they used to say in school days it begins at graduation. There is a little breathing space to let it begin, so let us go on till it does begin. It ought to be interesting when it really gets under way.

It is that it shall keep going on and with some degree of interest and justification that counts.

(See Bibliographical Note, page 364.)

2. Return to the Plains

*In the early years of the dismal thirties the expatriate population in France dipped almost as sharply as the stock market, but McAlmon, who was not dependent on an income from home, did not take part in the exodus. And yet this is not quite the truth. For although his physical environment was Europe and he continued to make the rounds of the bars and the night clubs, his spiritual environment, the environment of McAlmon the writer, was the American midwest. Except for a few poems and his memoirs, all McAlmon's writing of this period—*The Indefinite Huntress and Other Stories *(1932) and the one uncollected story,* "Wisdom Garnered by Day" *(1934)—harks back to the Dakota villages and the Great Plains country of his earliest memories.*

Green Grow the Grasses

They used to sit on the lawn weaving flower chains or looking for four-leaf clovers. He often put his head on her lap and she would weave grass into his wavy black hair, bright with healthy oil. My *stupid* sister and I were quite as apt as other children to titter and mock at mushiness on the part of lovers, but we did not at them. Probably we sensed bravado. Sister Liz was given to moods and sulking, because my older sister was inclined to tell all of us we were ill-bred or silly. Liz sulked and wept quietly to herself when alone sometimes, because she wasn't school-bright.

However, she could blurt out savagely, and generally struck Rhoda's weaker spots when her amiable nature turned momentarily savage. She was nevertheless aloof, and permitted no one to become fresh with her. Knowing that, it didn't surprise me when Liz didn't register indignant dignity one day when he greeted her. "Hello, sister, has your schoolmarm sister been razzing you again? Give us a smile."

Liz instead gave him a smile, and explained to me sheepishly that he was just an easy-going fellow who'd always be getting himself in messes. Liz and I understood then that each of us liked him very much. When Rhoda scoffed at his tiresome mush with "that girl," Liz retorted, "You needn't talk. Watch yourself in a mirror when you're acting skittish with some of the fool men you have at parties. You just can't stand seeing that they like each other."

I wasn't without haughtiness either, and didn't know him, but one day after a quarrel with Rhoda I sulked down the street. He was in his oil truck and gaily jumped out, and flipped me a dime. "Here, son, sneak off to the movies. That sister of yours likes to ride you kids. She's too healthy and has to take her heat out on somebody."

I understood what he meant very well, and though I scrapped with Rhoda she represented to me elegance, and the outside city world. Whenever she returned for a vacation I adored her with awestruck wonder. Nobody else, certainly none of the usual sort of town male, could have made such an insinuation without my flaring up. His manner and gesture, however, were spontaneous; and he took me by surprise, understanding so well what I was brooding about. He made me shy, but he made me adore him and feel that he felt as I did, that there was some understanding between him and me.

At first I thought him merely nice and clean-looking, for a workingman, but soon I was thinking him the most beautiful person I had ever seen, and beauty wasn't a word I thought could be used in mentioning a man. He was supple, with a nonchalant swagger of amiability. While his manner didn't take away my shyness it let me act similarly towards him. His smile flashed brilliantly out of his dark face. I knew nothing of sculpturing, but one day as he passed and spoke absent-mindedly I noted the contours about his dark eyes, and their beauty struck me. I know now that my first awareness of how the loveliness of a sculpturesque line can cut into one sharply occurred at that moment. My sympathy went out to him with a pained leap, because he looked sad and worried. It tormented me that I couldn't ask why, or help. I noticed that she was not waiting at the door for him, and generally she ran out to embrace and kiss him. I missed that for him as much as he missed it; possibly more, because he knew why she wasn't there this evening. For two or three days I missed and brooded over not seeing them on the lawn. Yet the picture of them playing on the lawn's green grasses persists in my mind. Paintings by Watteau, Renoir, Cézanne have recalled their scene, but none of the paintings have the essential naive sweetness their picture left in my conscious. I am not saying innocence or purity, because I was always an aware child, and anything that innocence can mean, meant then that various interests were not awakened in me, or were not inherent, and so I failed to question various things I observed. Things between them were sweetly all right. I knew, as young animals know, and I knew as children know what one does not say or do around certain people, older, or with attitudes which bring out the actor in children.

I was reserved, but I was not by nature timid, however shy I might be before older people whom I knew had reproving or patronizing manners. Now it strikes me as strange that I did not know they were unmarried. My mother didn't indicate disapproval of them, however, but remarked that "she is a flighty girl, though there's no harm in her." As mother was given to austerity, and was for me a model of correctness, I knew they must be all right. In any case mother could not know that Liz and I adored them, him particularly. He was only the driver of an oil wagon, and mother could have no way of knowing how vividly aware we were of them, wishing that we could join them evenings as they sat on the lawn. Poor Liz was sixteen, and impulsive, and had a shamed fear that she must never let anyone see how she adored him. Intuitively she knew I wouldn't tease her about him, particularly, and Liz and I seldom teased each other about our "crushes." We were both given to them. Before we had always picked much older people to look at worshipfully, and people of "our" class.

Walking in from the country one day I saw his truck and he offered to give me a lift back to my house. Had it been anyone but him I would have said no, because I was looking for birds' eggs and had no desire to be at home as it was early afternoon. There was an oil can on the seat and I crowded in. Not wanting to be in the way of his steering I shrunk against the can. He saw and put his arm about my shoulder, patting me. "Sit close, bucko. You're not in the way. You're a nice-looking kid. How old are you?"

"Fourteen," I said.

"You have the prettiest eyes I ever saw, except for my girl. I noticed you the first day we moved in. That younger sister of yours is a cute one, and I'll tell the world she isn't dumb if your old sister does ride her. She tickles me when she imitates the old hens in the neighborhood. I saw how you felt the other day when your sister caught you talking baby-talk to your kitten. She ought to be married. She's a fine woman, too, but if she was married she wouldn't tease a kid like you for being affectionate with his pets. She doesn't think much of us though. Your mother's not bothering to treat us chilly. She gave my girl a little talk, but Enid didn't mind. She knows your mother's a fine woman."

I didn't know what to say. Something was not as people thought it should be in their lives. That Rhoda was scornful about their mushiness meant nothing, as she was given to grand disdain. However, I felt happy to be with him, and he was carefree and spontaneous. As the auto swerved around the corner I was thrown closer to him. He put his hand on my leg and patted it. "You're a well set up kid. Have you got the lead in your pencil yet?" he said lightly. "I tell you I'm nuts about that girl of mine."

I didn't feel uncomfortable or teased in an unclean way. I remarked that I knew from seeing them on the lawn that they thought much of each other. It seemed to me strange that I didn't feel uneasy. He actually was the first older person who had spoken to me without seeming objectionable about a subject which I was accustomed to think must be spoken of secretly. He went further to suggest that the lawn scenes were but preliminaries to joys later, and told me I'd understand soon. There was no innuendo, no indication in his manner that had a thought of saying anything I should not hear freely. I listened with animal curious alertness.

While he didn't tease me, he was older about my being yet a child. I was drawn to him when he said I was a well set up kid, and talked about the innocence of a boy my age. I thought him naive to think I didn't understand. There was nothing strained in either his feeling or mine. It was mere human sympathy, and a deep satisfaction in regarding somebody likeable, capable of feeling or of later to feel the benefits of being a healthy, unafraid, physical being.

"I'll be a pop before long," he boasted as he helped me down from the truck seat. He patted my back, gently. His tone was youngly vain and he regarded me young-paternally. "Your mother can know things will be all right between the girl and me, as she sees things. To a kid like you what kind of a pop do you think I'll make?"

His dark eyes glistened in his olive skin, and the flash of his teeth charmed me so that I wished to embrace him. I did stand to let his hand rest on my shoulder, when with most people I would have moved away. I felt older than he. His black hair gleamed about his shapely head which sat beautifully upon a clear neck. I say I adored him. I couldn't say how marvellous a pop I thought he would be, because I thought of fathers in terms of my own, and he was an elderly man, fussily officious, much as small-town professional men often are. I did not then so analyze it, but I knew my father would never have tousled me to comment with satisfaction upon my being well set up.

Rhoda had a friend from Columbia University, and towards her, Hortense, Rhoda was almost humble. At first the glory of Hortense did not strike me. She had carrot-colored hair, a clear pale skin, a large mouth, and an awkwardly-graceful, free-moving body. It took me several days to think her beautiful, and by then I was awestruck by her "intellect." One Sunday, as Rhoda did not care for long hikes, I went with Hortense. We struck across the fields and walked five miles. Her stride was long for me, but I felt her vitality and the rhythm of her easy swing. Sometimes our bodies touched. I was in a daze of sensual happiness. She told me of New York, the theatre, and talked of books, and as if I was completely an equal. It tormented me later when she talked with

Rhoda, and they laughed, agreeing I was a bright child, with promise. Their implication that I was acting old and pretending to understand books we had talked of put resentment into my awed infatuation for Hortense. I hadn't pretended; I had admitted what I didn't understand or know, and had asked questions, trustingly letting Hortense know the extent of my ignorance. Now she was betraying me, and to Rhoda, who delighted in tantalizing all of us younger children.

Rhoda, given to social research work, gave me the Chicago Vice Commission Report and it fascinated me, with horror, but more with incredulous curiosity. She had me read *Damaged Goods*. I heard her talk to Hortense of putting a "wholesome fear" into me. I heard often when they didn't know. My adoration for Hortense was sullied because she pretended, and was different when talking to me alone than when speaking to me before Rhoda. With me alone she had admitted confusion and wonder, and had told me of her own childhood.

My feeling about "them" was clear, however, and now the girl spoke to me whenever I passed. One evening he, Antoine, called me. I went to sit on the grass with them. "Take a look at this boy, Enid," Antoine said. "He has eyes, hasn't he? And eyelashes. His skin is as nice as yours, honey."

Enid laughed a chortling contralto. I blushed. Antoine caught me to him and patted my head, running his fingers through my hair. Then he leaned and held his face against mine. "This boy and I savez each other. Maybe someday we'll have a bright kid like this, and I'll sure like being his daddy."

I didn't ordinarily like being handled, but I did not draw away from Antoine. He kept his arm about my shoulder, and felt of my arm muscles. Looking at Enid with a smile he said, "Do you think the kid feels anything yet? How about it, son?" and patted me intimately.

"Antoine, you embarrass him. You are a tease," Enid said.

Enid was wrong. Antoine didn't embarrass me, and neither did her presence. No sense of modesty in me was upset, and I knew clearly his impulse towards me was nice. I merely felt sheepish and little boy, and happy. They were accepting me as one of them, who understood, and life had much free affectionateness.

Soon they were gone from the neighborhood, and I heard at

last that they were married, because a neighbor woman commented that at last they'd gone decently through with Marriage. Liz told me, defiantly defending them, when I questioned. Enid had been married at sixteen to a much older man, and later had simply gone to live with Antoine. Only one faint rumor that Antoine was in trouble over money came back to me. I adored him, but adoration is a passing emotion. His presence delighted me. When he was no longer there I forgot him.

A few months later my father died, leaving no money. My family moved to the city, and there was little enough so that I got work afternoons to help support myself. Such work as a boy my age could get was that of being an errand boy, a collector, and later a news-office cub. I came to know the Salvation Army, the Civic Flops for unemployed floaters, the Three Sisters, tenements where were housed the inmates of the red-light district, and sometimes copy of mine was used by the yellow journal for which I worked. It was horrible or excellent sob stuff, wrung from my boy-agonies. There was now in me, powerfully, with the force of a high-strung organism, my adolescence. I knew Bowery dance halls, the lake resorts where if I were older I could pick up girls, but I was still small and looked a complete child. It need not be said that the "wholesome fear" lessons taught me by Hortense and Rhoda did not lessen the torments of those years, for I could not see a scarred face without recoiling.

Interwoven with wanderings about town was the experience of reading much, for I was lonely. Unused to a big city, I didn't know how to become chums with young people in the huge high school which I attended. I discovered Chekhov, and Dostoevsky. It was the nostalgia, revolt, and ennui in Turgenev's *Fathers and Sons* which started me, but soon I was reading till all hours of the night, and generally about tormented, epileptic, frustrated characters and emotions. This increased my shyness, and my tendency to feel different than other boys my age. It would have been easy to remain a more or less unawakened boy, healthily consorting with other boys, but not after I had discovered Dostoevsky. He was to me then a passion, what I now think a disease, for the characters' emotions are overimaged.

The year the war broke out I was past fifteen and had visions of getting overseas to enlist, but I was too small, and knew no way to get over. It blasted something in me. Both my feeling of helplessness and the instinct that the war would last made my adventurous impulses despair. I was seared with despondent cynicism and morbidity, and I was carnal. No despair broods more than the romantic cynicism of pubescent boyhood. I imagined wracked and tortured bodies of young men in battle, but this did not have the effect of making me hate or want to avoid war. Rather I thought I might as well be in it, taking chances with the others. If I was killed, I didn't then treasure life as a precious fluid to be preserved; and I was sure that, crippled, I would kill myself. In the midst of the war was where the excitement was, and I felt imprisoned by dullness and poverty. That hatred of the bourgeois insistencies in life is no rare emotion, much as biographers make of it in writing of "artists." One forgets or ceases to brood in older years, but then, much of the time, my conscious was an inflamed plate registering horror-impressions quiveringly.

The next summer mother wisely let me go back to Lansing to do farm work. Soon after arriving there I found an easy job with Mr. Grayson, whose wife was a friend of Rhoda's. He was almost a bright man, rosy, hardy, with a manner of jovial cheer. I trusted him with youth, but not implicitly. It pleased me when he let me hear him tell his wife that I was bright steel. I was willing to get up at five mornings and work till eight nights, since he made a great point of calling me himself when the older men had to be Johnnies-on-the-spot by their own efforts. He liked it that I always sang or whistled at my work. I was such a happy boy, and he understood well how flattery made me work.

He was not bright, however, in giving me a cot in the corncrib with two other farm hands. Soon I found that they were underpaid. They advised me to go at my work less zealously, because he complained that I did more work than they. That made me observe. I did, and they got $35 a month to my $20, and they assured me that other farmers paid their hands $40 or $45 a month, with day wages during harvest season.

I heard the other men speak of Dandalo, the jailbird, and knew that a man and his wife occupied the room above the cow stable. Never having heard Antoine's last name I did not realize it was him. Having seen him across the farmyard I had not recognized him. Two years had passed, and the man looked thin and worn, and his wife was dragged out with apathy from overwork. They cared entirely for twenty cows, doing the milking, barn cleaning, feeding, and the wife also took care of the chicken coops. Dandalo and his wife, the men told me, got $40 a month and the room they had to live in for their work.

The story aroused my curiosity. I learned that Dandalo had served a year in prison for stealing money from the company he worked for. At the time his wife had been with child and he needed money, so the sentence had been light. When released he had trouble getting work, even day labor. Why, I wondered, since a man would have little chance to steal while digging ditches? Mr. Grayson had liberally employed the man and his wife, and now they did the work of several people for $40 a month. The other hired men thought I was crazy to resent the imposition on the couple who, Mrs. Grayson told me, had been most honest with them and were making an effort to reclaim themselves.

"How much did he steal?" I asked.

"Something over a hundred dollars which he had collected. Antoine says he intended to pay it back at the end of the month when he got his salary, but it was more than his salary, and the company wanted to make an example of him. Poor Antoine, he works very hard, and Enid was such a pretty girl. They are very young. He is not twenty-five."

"Antoine?" I said, but I knew. That night I went to the cow shed where they were milking. He didn't recall me at once. He looked tired, and I had grown. His dark eyes were dull. I had no adoration for him then. I was simply thwarted with a wonder at life, overwhelmingly. My memory would visualize them as they looked sitting on the soft grasses of their lawn, playing with carefree spontaneity. How could such a change take place in less than three years? They now had two children and it was obvious that Enid was to have another. Why had they not been careful? Didn't they realize that life can't be let to drift? People would say they were paying for their sin, but they merely had not been careful.

Antoine's face regained some of its luminance when he recalled me. The debonair swagger and spontaneity of manner weren't much there though, and I was no longer just a pretty kid. I wasn't a gangly adolescent; I was still small for my sixteen years, but his attitude was more man to man now. He agreed that he and Enid worked pretty hard for little pay, but he shrugged his shoulders.

"Why don't you go away, Antoine? Why don't you go to the city or to another town, far away from here?" I asked. I knew I was being uselessly full of advice.

He looked apathetic and shrugged his shoulders. None of the adoring feeling I had for him would have flamed within me, but he smiled rakishly and his eyes glistened. His teeth shone evenly, brilliant, white. The dark beauty about his eyes was there, and I felt a clutch within me for the brooding tenderness of grace which his expression evoked.

"You're a game kid, with fight in you. You get that from your mother. She didn't disapprove of Enid, and you don't think a fellow not fit to talk to because he's been in trouble. Well, the wife and I can't get away with the bambinos. Where's the money? We're waiting. I'm not finished, but the girl. . . ." He shrugged his shoulders, tired now. I thought he meant more than that she was finished. Her prettiness was gone. She looked miserable. With a flood of panicky pain I thought Antoine meant they didn't have joy in each other any more. They had only duty. Yes, John Barrymore was playing in "Justice" in New York, and I remembered drab stories: Gogol's "The Mantle," of fugitives, and outcasts. No, no, they should remain indifferent or become reckless. They shouldn't let themselves be made examples for people more sordid. I almost said "Why don't you steal on a large scale, Antoine? To hell with the sacredness of money." Crook plays, particularly "Within the Law," had given me romantic ideas about intelligent crooksters.

"Don't ever do anything you hadn't ought," Antoine said. "Not unless you're well covered. I'm not a crooked bozo, but I didn't think quick what money means to those who have it. The girl had to be in a hospital and doctors charge money."

I wanted powerfully to put my arms about him, to make him understand that he need not explain to me, ever. He got up from the stool with a full pail of foaming milk. It was white-steamingly lovely. He poured it into the container of the separator, and I offered to turn the crank. "Today's been light work for me."

"It won't be next week when the threshing crew gets here,"

Antoine said drily, and patted my side. "You're the one I hear singing around here nights. You keep some of those songs in you for later, when you'll need them. You're going to be as good-looking a man as you were a kid. I hadn't forgotten you, but you've grown."

I thrilled with a warm emotion at the fondling caress of his hand, but the thrill was pained with a devastating pity. "There won't be any hard work for me on this farm next week," I boasted. "I'm quitting and going to work by the day with thresh-ing crews. Old Grayson can't kid me. Ike Nelson, down the road, says he'll pay me $4 a day if only to be water boy, and he's sure he can let me drive teams to the elevator. Then I'll get $5. That Swede is not so goddamned afraid he'll overpay a kid, or give a living wage."

"That's it," Antoine was cheerier now. "Keep your pecker up." Later, as he was milking another cow I asked how much money he needed to go to the city with his family, and would he go if he knew there was a job waiting for him.

"You think you could get me a job?" he said with a flash of happy grateful emotion. "You'd lend me the money out of what you earned?" He shrugged his shoulders, ironically resigned now. "What about the girl? We are caught here till the new one comes."

I left Mr. Grayson the next day and he blustered at me, scoldingly, saying I had a vacillating nature. I'd never get any-where if I did not learn to stick by what I started. I was too shy to say what I felt, but later wished I had been able to curse at him violently for trying to bully me into retracting my resignation. I'd earn more in a week with Nelson than I got from him in a month, and he knew I was only doing farm work for the summer. Going to town, I was full of plans to make as much money as possible, quickly. I might be able to lend Antoine as much as $50 in a month, and I could get work in the city about as soon as I returned. He'd pay me back, I knew. I might tell some employer of a good man who wanted to move to the city if he knew a job awaited him. Surely I would remember Antoine's plight and write him a letter containing good news.

I worked six weeks in the harvest fields and saved up one hundred dollars. About were many Germans who were going back to the old country to get into the war as soon as harvest season was over. Some of them had been sent for. There were a variety of types among the floating workers, and I, trained to be sociologic minded, was alertly interested. The world was full of interesting problems when one felt lively, and in the country I had little memory of the drugged despondency of being lonely in the city. Had I seen Antoine I'd have loaned him the money, but I didn't see him. Going back on the train I had a copy of Barbusse's *Under Fire*. It fascinated me. It hypnotized my rebellious emotions and my morbidity to read what the *poilus* were up against, and to realize what they had been up against in peace times.

I didn't mean to forget Antoine, but I never wrote him about a job waiting for him. There is much chaos, and every man has his problems. Mrs. Grayson wrote Rhoda that I'd be sorry to hear Enid had died in childbirth; the two babies had been adopted by a farmer's wife, and Antoine had disappeared. Possibly he had gone to Italy to be in the war, although he had come to America as a baby.

Anyway there was the war, my future, and no money in the family, so I had to work. Of course I was ambitious. I thought sometimes I'd be a journalist, an advertising man, a dramatist, an author, but also I was most restless and had the usual adolescent despair of life as a process worth enduring.

Years later in Eleusis the remnant torso of a boy sculpted by an archaic Greek struck a pang into me, but what it evoked was elusive. One knows that the quality of beauty in sculpturing is even more undefinable than that in music, or in human beings; still I persisted in recalling that forgotten flowing-image which was dormant in the subconscious.

I thought of a dance scene in which the ballet swept forward stooping to sweep their white draped garments in a movement suggesting the sea waves' rise and fall; of a possible scene when an actress has intoned an intellectual thought at the heat of passion, while poised to catch form at a moment of abstract beauty which is held static for a pained interval. It perplexed me that I thought too of pretty, weak, but lovable young people making a mess of life because of spontaneous joy. The gracious qualities of tenderness and beauty were confused with those of disillusion and beaten disintegration. Suddenly Antoine was clear in my memory, as I had first adored him, as I last saw him, and then as he probably became. I had not thought of him for ten years, but the young-boy torso evoked some quality he had aroused in my emotions. Having located the sought-for image I forgot him, knowing he had been to my awakening adolescence a symbol of faun-spontaneity with the clean sweetnesses of human relationships. The thought of him as another of the used joy-beings which society breaks and throws into the discard was distressing.

I knew resignation would never be complete in my nature. A wish to encourage him and what he stood for leaped hotly within, and I wanted to know what had become of him. My rebellion asked why are not such as he given just enough calculation to be careful? Society has little trust. Why should he have been naively-generous-willed? One can't let one's arrested-development emotions dominate, however, so I forgot Antoine.

(See Bibliographical Note, page 364.)

*Although his imagination found nourishment in recollections of home, McAlmon did not pretend to himself that the land of his childhood was more satisfying than other places. In "Green Grow the Grasses" he asked as he had asked in Post-*Adolescence: *"Why does sophistication overtake one? Why does one feel wearied before sentiment, or calloused, or indifferent, disbelieving in the reality of all ecstasy, exaltation, and even affection? . . . One makes one's own reality to a big extent . . ." And in "The Indefinite Huntress" he asked yet again: "Home, and is it a place for the spirit, or is it a place of bodily security?"* [1]

But in these last stories McAlmon's attitude toward the Great Plains differs fundamentally from what it was in his earlier fiction. Here he is not primarily interested in the country; here the fictional personages are more important to him than the world they live in. Our attention is directed to the single person, not the shaping society. As time has passed, McAlmon's rebellion against the country of his birth has become a thing more of the head than of the spleen. He has turned from an indictment of society to an examination of character. As McAlmon's indignation has cooled, so has his writing. "The Indefinite Huntress" may

*have grown out of personal experience, but the story is objectified
and does not read like a page from his diary.² In theme it is not
different from much of his other fiction. As usual he insists on the
primacy of the tender affections; as always he suggests that the
conventional world represses more than it liberates, and that
provincial America represses most obviously.*

The Indefinite Huntress

Lily strode firmly into the kitchen and threw down her string
of ducks. She knew her mother thought her unladylike qualities
a bad example for her younger sisters, so did not boast now of
having brought down more game than any of the men who had
gone to shoot ducks at early dawn. "There's no use reminding
you," Mrs. Root sighed, "but you look like a tramp woman. I
must lay it at my own door, of course. I tried to bring you up
properly, but blood will tell, and you have your father's blood
in you."

"Your family were the real aristocrats, weren't they, mother?"
Lily said drily, "but what about your aunt Helga, and you did run
away and marry dad? He may not be much of a gent, but he lets
a person be." Lily took off her rubber boots, and went to her
room. Since the birth of the new baby the year before, Mrs. Root
had relapsed again into complaining, but now she complained
at Lily more than at Ole.

When Ole came in he started to speak of what a good shot
Lily was but Ebba's manner stopped him. Instinctively he knew
that antagonism and jealousy existed between Lily and Ebba,
mainly on Ebba's side. Ebba didn't like the new easy comradeship
between Ole and Lily, and she suspected that Ole was drinking
heavily again and that Lily drank with him. Lily openly declared
that clinging-vine women got on her nerves, and her mother
countered by accusing her of imitating her aunt Helga.

"Who's better in your family, mother?" Lily asked. "I hope

I have her stuff, and you know you admire her, if you are afraid of what she can say."

Ole avoided becoming involved in the generally silent antagonism between the women. Since Ebba's having belatedly become tenderly desirous towards him Ole had found that her devotion didn't matter so much that he didn't need his drink. He was settled into later middle age and accepted Ebba as a home commodity now. Her fragility didn't make him feel so awkward, and he had come to know that she hadn't thought so much of her once-vaunted Swedish home background. Lily was a comrade to hunt and talk farm management with. He hoped she might become a strong business woman like her aunt Helga.

Lily understood too that Ole was a simple, tenderhearted man, with the gentleness which hereditary heavy drinkers often have. Having his own weakness he was easily shamed and little critical of others. He and Lily now joked about Ebba's stories of her father's grand estate. "Dat goes vor de old country," Ole said, over snuff, "but from your aunt Helga I get it. Ve are more progressive on our little farm than your mother admits." Another weakness of Ole's, newly acquired, was his snuff-chewing, and he knew with fear that Ebba would object violently if she discovered that he had this habit. He didn't like snuff much, but a naughty desire to do things Ebba thought low class was in him, even when he did them in secret.

Upstairs, Lily found her cousin Helga packing her trunks for departure that afternoon. During the summer the girls had grown fond of each other, and Helga was the first person with whom Lily had any relationship approaching intimacy. Helga was slight, fawn-haired, and dainty. Lily, who cared not at all about fine clothes for herself, delighted in Helga's wardrobe. When the Chatauqua season was on she had been happily aware that Helga commanded admiration from Lansing townspeople. The highest compliment they could pay her was to think her one of the entertainers. Lily had never had an opportunity to know a woman of elegance, but she thought Helga elegant. She talked of Paris, of manner and style. Lily felt perturbedly restless, wondering about the outside world.

Changing from her hunting clothes, Lily offered to help Helga pack. "I'll miss you," she said. "You're the one person who has ever told me of great places, except mother, and her ideas are old-fashioned."

"Aunt Ebba gets sentimental about her old home because Uncle Ole is stolid. At first I thought he was brutal," Helga said.

"Dad brutal? No, no," Lily defended quickly, ashamedly fearing that Helga knew how much her father drank. "I guess I'm the only one that understands him, and he's quiet because mother scolds." Naive with triumph, she added, "Mother gets jealous of how well he and I get on. She needn't. If she stopped scolding we'd tell her things. He's shy with you."

"I would give a thousand to have hair like yours," Helga said, distraitly. "That color is worth a fortune. Let it down and I'll dress it for you. I'll give you any one of my gowns you like. It's too bad you aren't an opera singer. You'd get all the attention just by being on the stage, with your looks and vitality."

Lily chuckled and tore her hair loose with a free gesture. "What would a thing my size do with your finery? There's no use trying to make me elegant." She seated herself, however, and let Helga brush her long yellow hair. A ten o'clock morning sun sent a bright beam of light across the room. From the barnyard came the smell of fresh hay. The quacking of ducks and geese, the grunts and squeals of pigs, and the twittering of birds sounded outside.

"I love the crackle of your hair," Helga mused, running it through her palms. Lily saw the whiteness of Helga's fine hands against her own hair, in the mirror. "It's as lively as you are, Lily. Oh, I envy you. Being in the country makes me restless, but I won't be happy in New York either. Don't go to cities to stay long, ever. They aren't for you. You don't get bored and nervously nauseated here."

"I'm always restless," Lily said, petting Helga's arm. "I don't know what I'll do, but something has to happen for me. I won't marry a farmer, and mother and I will quarrel if I stay here. Dad tells me she disliked her own mother. I have nothing against her, but I'm the sort who ought to clear out. It would be great to think I had a voice like you say, because I might have ambitions. But I just want without knowing what I want."

"I wish you could come with me," Helga said. "But I don't know what we'd do. Father lets me have money, but he wants to stay at his club. I can't stand being with Aunt Signe. You'd be miserable, trying to keep me from complaining."

"Don't worry about me," Lily boasted. "I'm no weak plant. Some days I know I'll be a great woman, but others I don't care."

"You're so strong. I feel like nothing beside you, but you make me feel vitality too. I don't cry defeat easily myself," Helga said.

"If you ever feel that way, let me know and I'll come and take care of you," Lily bragged. "I could do something even if dad wouldn't give me money. I can stand anything."

"Helga, the car's ready to take you to town," Ole Root called. Helga hastily shoved a few last things into her trunk and closed it. "Kiss me goodbye now, Lily. Everything will be rushed downstairs."

"Let me have a bit of your hair," Helga said. "It's the color I'll try if I ever have mine changed." She snipped off a length of Lily's hair and quickly put it into an envelope. "It's wonderful, having a cousin like you, who goes ahead. You always will. I'm afraid for myself."

Lily saw the look on Helga's face. She was trying not to weep. Lily felt cut with loneliness for her, and sad because she was sad. Then Lily broke away and bolted to her room. She wouldn't go downstairs to bid goodbye to Helga and have others see tears in her eyes. She stood at her window watching the car going towards town until it was out of sight.

2

Lily was in the yard beneath the umbrella tree. Her hair was loose and she stroked it musingly, liking the electric crackle, and thinking of how Helga had praised its color and gloss. Across the road from the farmyard thousands of yellow butterflies hovered over a late growth of uncut alfalfa. As she regarded them she saw them as a flood of flame rippling over the fields. If a lake of kerosene were set on fire it would appear that way, she reflected. Tranquility was deep within her. To look at the cattle standing in the marshes, lying in the pasture chewing their cuds, or moving lazily gave her full satisfaction. She wasn't artistic, she told herself, because she had no desire to paint pictures even had she known how. She was drily curt when her mother suggested that she go inside and get the churns ready for butter-making. That could wait. She'd get the butter made easily once she felt like beginning.

"May I have a drink of water, or buttermilk if you have it?" a voice said. Somewhat resentfully Lily tossed her hair back and looked distantly out of chilled blue eyes at the speaker. He was Red Neill, who owned the restaurant in Lansing. Lily knew him only by sight, but remembered that he was one of the men who had been spoken of as a friend of Mrs. Watkins, when she had stayed with Mrs. Watkins two years back. He thought he was a real lady-killer, Lily surmised. Her pale eyes challenged his appraising glance with a glance more coldly appraising.

"There's the pump with a cup beside it and your hands aren't tied," Lily spoke curtly.

"You're not sociable this morning, Miss Root," Red said over his dipper of water. "I interrupted your toilette, I see, and I look pretty dirty with these ducks slung to me."

"That's not a bad string of ducks," Lily relaxed some. "I brought in more myself the other morning though. You're maybe a better hunter of other things than ducks."

"It's not all game that's worth the hunting," Red answered, "and what is, is scary sometimes. You never respond to my greetings in town. Perhaps you think I'm a bad one?"

"What would it mean to me if you were a bad one? I don't know you, and you only tried to speak to me because you thought I was one of Mrs. Watkins' kind. She's all right too, but I paid my board when I was with her, and stayed on because I wasn't going to let gossip bother me. I can be myself and as I want with whoever I am with."

Red shifted the ducks to his other shoulder. "I'll try and speak more respectfully next time, Miss Root," he said. "You deserve it. They don't make many like you in this part of the world."

"And what a favor you would do me! I may answer," Lily said, melting somewhat, and not wanting to believe stories about Red any more than she believed them about Mrs. Watkins. "I know it is girls you think are fine and elegant you really bother to be polite to. You have a fancy idea of yourself, I take it."

"You aren't meek yourself, Miss Root. But those others,"

Red's voice softened, "they have no blood in them. They don't feel anything."

Lily got red in the face and felt temper arise within her. "Pack your ducks on," she said sharply. "What blood or feeling you have doesn't interest me, and I'm busy."

After Red had gone Lily tried to believe she was in a temper at him, but she didn't believe so actually. She had seen rather surprised admiration in his eyes, and realized that he had wished to tease her too. She was resentful towards his patronizing attitude of male gallantry, which while appraising her didn't recognize that she was sizing him up too. She rather liked his ruddy, open face, but she resented his male coquettish attitude, and more, she believed he looked on her as a simple country girl who might be easy pickings, and susceptible to flattery.

Doing up her hair she still sat beneath the umbrella tree, tranquil, but restless too. An antagonistic feeling towards Red did not go out of her, but she imagined a romantic gallant who came upon a legendary herself while she was combing her tresses. The gallant was a mixture of Helga, Red, Dionisio Granger, and her father, but he had Red's curly, mahogany hair and athletic body. He was taciturn and mild like her father, but he had some look of painfully wistful beauty across his face which excited her. Lily, who wasn't given much to imagination or daydreams, found herself fancying a world peopled quite other than any world she knew, and as she had never read much, all her dream world's types were sublime examples of types she had known in life. She was complicated, adjusting herself in this world of delicate and fragilely beautiful beings, because she felt herself large, awkward, overgrown, and horsy. She didn't, however, lose herself in her imagination. A pent-up rage persisted in her. People would think, Mr. Neill had thought, that she was a buxom country girl to be flirted with vulgarly. She concluded, though, her resentment was not against Mr. Neill, or men's or women's attitudes. It was against sex, and the importance it assumes in people's lives. Except for a lazy tranquility now in her, Lily would have been at this moment swept with a sense of futility about life. The day was too lazy for her to feel anything strongly though, but a despair about action lived in her. She felt emptiness about her, and realized that Helga too felt emptiness, while in cities or travelling. Slumbering in Lily was an intense revolt of rage at time, which is too generally dull. Life seemed made of waiting for moments that were worth little when they arrived. She resented Red Neill for being likeable while a brutish quality in him antagonized her. She despised thinking of her mother's wail. About Ole she felt gentle, but he answered nothing for her. Lily told herself savagely if it ever came to a showdown she'd prove to Red that she was stronger than he in every way. Again she told herself she was silly to think she or Red were to have anything to do with each other.

Dionisio Granger came into the yard carrying three ducks, and Lily's heart plunged as she recognized him. He was adolescent now, but quickly she saw he retained the beauty which had cut into her. "You've been duck-shooting, have you?" she asked, hoping he didn't sense the panicky thrill in her.

"No, Red Neill gave me these," Dion said. "I went hunting with him, but it made me feel rotten to see the ducks plop on the ground or in the water. I couldn't shoot straight anyway. Red pretended I hit some. He was going to give me more but I couldn't carry them."

"Why didn't he carry them all, the big husky?" Lily asked.

"I wanted to stop off and see Pete Simpkins at the next farm, and Red had to get back to town."

"He's a good-looking man, or dresses well," Lily conceded. "I like people who look trim. He won't get fresh with me as he thinks he can with most girls in town though. I guess he thinks I'm another foolish country girl while he's a high class gentleman."

Dion sat on the grass beside Lily. "Red came into town a hobo not many years ago. He was one of those wandering newspaper fellows, a drunk, I think. Sister says he's intelligent. He went with her for a while, but she didn't want to go with him after she found out what other girls he hung around."

"He means nothing to me," Lily said. "Your sister's a real lady, the most beautiful I ever saw. I met her this summer with my cousin, but she didn't notice me. She never asked me to call like she did Helga. I'm too big a cow."

"No, she likes you," Dion said. "She thinks you're handsome, but thought you hated tea parties. I'm drowsy. I'm going to nap on the grass before I walk on to Simpkins'. You wake me if I really sleep." Dion rolled over to bury his head in his arm. The sunlight through the leaves got into his eyes. Lily saw how his brown hair grew around his ears and the back of his neck. It made her yearn towards him, and hurt her by seeming so beautiful.

"Put your head on my lap and nap," she said, in terror that Dion might be shy, and not do as she suggested. She placed his head on her lap, however, and stroked his hair once, to let her hand rest caressingly around the back of his dome. "I wanted to kidnap you two years back, did you know that?" she said, huskily tender with fear. "I nearly died you looked so marvellous one day."

Dion blushed and laughed into her face. He felt a tingle in him because of her caress. She was vibrantly alive. He didn't nap, but stirred uneasily. "I'll get you some apple cider. It's hard and will make you gay," Lily said. She went to get the cider, and Dion did not feel like napping any more. Soon he said he would have to go. "I'll walk to the end of the orchard with you," Lily said.

As they walked through the orchard Dion put his arm about Lily's waist until she laughed with contralto irony. "You little devil, Dion, do you want the countryside to be saying I rob the cradle? You'll be a real swell when you grow up, but you won't fall for a lump of meat like me. You'd snicker to think I was your first love."

"You're not fat," Dion said gravely. "Nobody looks at you once without looking again. Sis says that if you bothered about dress people would discover you as a beauty."

"It's hell, Dion. I don't know what to do with myself. I can't stay on the farm. I like fine people around me. But I need the country to turn around in." Lily was gaily melancholy.

Dion's arm pressed her waist. Quickly she stopped, put her arms about him to draw him close and kiss. "If you were older, I'd do things that weren't careful, but I'd scare you. You don't know how strong inside I feel about you. It's that you're beautiful, and maybe you won't always be. I have to have beautiful things or I won't live." Quickly she ran down the path. She would not turn to wave goodbye. She was afraid she had frightened Dion, or that he would think her a common, vulgar country girl. It hurt to think he wouldn't understand how sweetly she felt about him, with agony in the feeling. She was ashamed too to have teased him when he put his arm about her. His gesture had been small-boy companionable, as though he sensed and wished to comfort the desolate restlessness in her.

3

"Sure, Dion, you shot at least five ducks, but I'll send some of mine to your mother when we get back to town," Red Neill said. "This is the last hunting I'll have this season, and I'm taking a week in the city. This town has me run ragged. You've become a swell shot in three weeks." Red was garrulous, and perplexed at his own desire to please this Granger boy.

"Maybe I brought some down when we shot into that flock," Dion said earnestly. "Anyway, I don't feel sick seeing the ducks fall like I did. It got me seeing them fly as though nothing could stop them, and then they fall and are clean dead."

Dion felt sleepy. It was not nine o'clock but Red and the three other men had shot all the ducks they wanted. Dion felt uncomfortable because Ike Sorenson joshed him. When the men began to get drunk he felt scary. Red cursed Jake Isaacs for offer-ing the kid a drink, and Dion felt protected, but scared of Red's savagery towards Jake, Red saw. It made him shy with Dion. Red knew the Grangers had high ideas, and regretted having told Dion to lie to his mother about the number of ducks he had shot. He didn't want the boy to think him crooked, and he couldn't be scornful of Dion's goodie ideas as he was about most people's. Like his sister, Dion had a naive gravity and a confidingly reticent manner. He seemed entirely trustful, but Red saw him look in wondering analysis at the others now and then. There was a qual-ity of hurt wonder in him. Like his sister again, Dion was more apt to venture than most boys in town. The Grangers had real class, Red knew. He didn't know how to get at them.

Going across the fields the hunters scared up several coveys of prairie chicken at which they shot carelessly. By noon they stopped at farmer Matson's for lunch, after which they sat drink-ing with the old man. Red was morose, and swore at his com-panions. He was contemptuous of these hicks. Drink affected him that way, but he seldom got drunk. He was too aware of Dion's shy discomfort. He wanted to feel contemptuous of a too-delicate boy brought up by a protected mother, but instead he found himself gently understanding that the boy would be scared among lowbrows getting stinking drunk. He moved to sit nearer Dion, and started to put his arm comfortingly about the boy's shoulder, but he was afraid of frightening the boy. Dion didn't look scared so much as he looked wistful and lonely, not happy to be with these roughnecks. To hell with duck-shooting, Red thought. Why should Dion think it fun when he hated the sight of blood and couldn't help that feeling in himself?

Taking another drink Red obeyed his impulse to put his arm about Dion's shoulder. The boy was unrelaxed in his arm. "You're a great hunter," Red said, gruffly, ill at ease. "Forty ducks in three hours, you can tell your mother." Red was angry at himself for persisting upon telling Dion to lie about the number of ducks he had shot. He only wanted to help the youngster to prove he was a sort who could do things, but why didn't he get it into his noodle that Dion didn't care how many ducks he had shot, and that Dion always gravely assured him he wouldn't lie to his mother?

Dion fidgeted, conscious of Red's whiskey breath. "I couldn't fool her if I tried. I'll say you gave me the ducks."

"You're right," Red was elaborately placatory. "It doesn't pay to lie." Cursing himself as soon as he spoke he added, "Until you're old enough to know when you have to lie to dumb people."

Red's breath, and a sense of brutality in Red, made Dion move away, and he was afraid, Red noticed. He couldn't lose the idea that Red had been a hobo, and he had further distrust he didn't analyze. However, he felt a furtive triumph in feeling that he was being much a man's man, with men who didn't treat him like a small boy.

Red pondered the Grangers. Why should they represent class to him? They weren't very rich and wouldn't have cut any great impression in a city. Yes, he had been a tough kid himself, but except that his mother was widowed she was as good class as Mrs. Granger. Unconsciously he put his arm about Dion again, and feeling the curve of Dion's shoulder in the palm of his hand he suddenly drew the boy to him. Dion looked up into his eyes, but his expression told nothing. Red didn't analyze, but he had a sharp terror. The boy's clear eyes told him nothing, but Dion's face swam before Red's vision with a beauty that made him dizzy.

A moment later he realized that his sudden clutching at the boy may have frightened him. Dion, however, turned his head and smiled now. His eyes were limpidly clear, but Red knew Dion wanted to draw away. Red hated to have this boy think him brutish and drunken, and he hated his own coarseness. Right now Red knew that if the boy wanted anything, there was nothing he would not do to give it to him, but he suffered, knowing that Dion didn't care what he felt.

Red took a deep swig of whiskey. He felt a horrible desolation of life. Dion had him awed with terror by the unrevealing glisten in his clear eyes. There was no definite quality in their depths; not innocence, knowing, like, distaste; only wonder and questioning, but the questioning did not include him, Red knew. He wanted to think Dion liked him, but instead he feared Dion despised him more, if the boy had known his own feelings. The Grangers had a way of being sweetly well-bred with a tender consideration which annulled a person. If they hadn't that ethereal prettiness, Red told himself, he'd think them pampered snobs, but the look on Dion's face remained in his mind. He recalled that people suspected that old man Granger had suicided, and everybody but Mrs. Granger knew that her oldest son's death had not been an accident.

The look on Dion's face now showed that he was abstractedly unaware of anybody's presence, to care. Red wanted the boy to understand that he was a friend who would stick by him. As never before in his life Red wanted the sympathy he felt understood. It hurt him to think that the boy cringed from him, and from life, probably.

Thwartedly unable to express to Dion his wish to save him any misery, Red took another swig of whiskey. He hated it but finished off the bottle and threw it from him with a curse. He'd mucked around so much he couldn't even express a nice emotion any more, and what had he ever gotten out of his lousy adventures that satisfied him, even momentarily?

"Do you know Lily Root?" Dion said, to break the silence. "She has come to town to live. She visited a cousin of hers in New York this summer, and won't live on the farm. She surprised me, she's taken to dressing so well."

"Yes, nice girl," Red said distraitly, still wanting to remember Lily clearly since Dion mentioned her. She was that big Swede girl who always antagonized him. She had hair and eyes, he remembered from having come upon her while she was drying her hair last autumn. She gave herself airs because her father was a rich old penny-snatcher. "She might make the grade better than some skirts in town," he conceded.

"She's a real looker now," Dion said, "but she doesn't know what she'll do. She didn't like New York, and she doesn't like Lansing, or the farm."

"Hell, I ought to marry her," Red joked. "I'm getting on and ought to settle down and have kids. She'd make a good cow-mother and keep house for me. She's about the rate for a roughneck like me, since I gave up my fancy idea of falling for your sister. It was damnfoolishness. I'm loose as hell. She was right, not to see me for dust."

"Were you really a hobo, the way people say?" Dion asked. His intimate tone made Red desire to talk of his life, to make the boy understand that he wasn't a real lowbrow.

"I'll tell you, Dion," Red said. "My old man croaked when I was a kid, and mother had no money. I don't know what happened to my older brother, and I started to drift when I was sixteen. I worked in a newspaper office and was a reporter, but after I got back from France I didn't feel like taking any work I could get. I bummed around for a couple of years, sort of de luxe. When I hit town and saw your sister, I decided to stay. Later I had a chance to get my restaurant. I decided life was as much here as anywhere, and I sold real estate, and now you see the Honorable Mr. Neill, one of Lansing's foremost citizens. I haven't been crooked, Dion. I had luck and made money. There's lots I could tell you, but I'm not a cheap tough like some people in town think. I don't toady to most the church-going people, so I hang around with whoever there is to be with. It isn't my fault they're cheap. I can stand cheap skirts, but with men who are lowbrows I want to fight when I drink, and you know I drink."

"Did you really want to marry Neva?" Dion asked.

"I didn't think," Red mused. "She got me, that was all. I sort of felt she'd break if I touched her. She scared me, that was it.

Now I figure I was as good as that husband she has. Knowing you don't like him is the only reason I'd let on what I think of him."

"He's just dumb," Dion said. "If Neva had known what a tightwad he was she wouldn't have married him. In college he seemed lively, she says, but he claims he has to be a church pillar if he's going in for politics in this town."

"I'd make a hell of a husband for a delicate woman. It's best she wouldn't have me, I guess," Red said.

It was late afternoon before the men were back in town. "Stick around," Red said to Dion. "Ma Jensen will cook us some ducks. I'll have my nigger carry yours back to your mother."

Ma Jensen waddled out of the City Restaurant kitchen. "Ay tink ve giff de poys a goot feed, all vor de same moneys," she commented with sturdy satisfaction, her face shiny from kitchen heat as she felt the breasts of the ducks.

"Sure, and ma, give any hoboes who come around a handout. No use having the game spoil on us," Red said carelessly. He didn't feel morose now; he felt elation, planning to take the midnight train to Minneapolis. Feeling the bristles on his face he went upstairs to shave. When he came down he looked well-groomed. Ma Jensen saw that he was in a mood again, which meant he'd take the train to the city. "Dot is pad vor pizness," Ma mumbled to the second cook. She didn't trust the cashier. "Sooch a svell guy you is," she complimented Red. "Choost like a traffeling man."

Red grinned and patted Ma's fat shoulder, amused at her busy waddlings, her Norwegian mixture of thrift and generosity, and her garrulousness. Ma loved talk, and being talked to. Red wondered where Dion was until he saw him across the street with some swell dame. It might be one of his older sisters home on a vacation. The Granger girls all had class, and the two older ones who lived in Chicago were not stuck-up, or afraid of townspeople's opinions. They were sure of themselves, knowing that girls in town were apt to copy their style. Red was impressed by them, but he resented the older one who had sold Neva on that freedom-of-women business. Red granted that she had a mind, and he didn't blame her for giving most men the laugh, but all the same, he argued, it's men who supply the world's brains. Red had tried to give her an argument once, but she snowed him under, mentioning books, and quoting people he had never heard of. She claimed they were big noises, and he couldn't prove different.

Red went across the street to get Dion and talk to his sister, if it was a sister. Red was shy. She might wonder why he was horning in, or if he was being an evil influence on her kid brother. Red was restless. He needed a trip to Minneapolis, to cut loose for a couple of weeks.

Red saw that the girl with Dion was large, firm-bodied, and stalwart in a way unlike any of the Granger girls. She was handsome though. "You don't recognize me, Mr. Neill," Lily Root said. "We're both better dressed than the last time we met, that's the truth."

Red didn't show his surprise. He had always thought Lily a big, healthy, strong-bodied farm girl, with keen eyes and startling hair, but now she looked somebody, and had a poised manner. A faint scent came to Red's nostrils, and it was not cheap perfume. That swell cousin of hers had probably taught her a few things. Still Red appraised Lily as a big girl who would go well in a leg show where they want big women who can show much white flesh and yellow hair. He heard her laugh, and its timbre left a voluptuous taunt in his ear. There was a quick flashing light, of gold gleaming tawnily, in the blue of her eyes when she glanced at him. A forbidding antagonism he had sensed in her once was not now present. It pleased Red to think that Dion had perhaps put her less on her guard, which meant that the boy liked him well enough to praise him. "Dion told me you were in town," he said.

"Yes, I can't stand the farm after a few months in the East. If dad can't give me money to stay in town I'll have to go to work. Maybe I can start a dressmaking business, if there are enough women in town to buy fashionable clothes."

"With your style you won't have any trouble getting on." Red was complimentary. Lily was striking him as femininely alluring and poised, rather than as a mere husky country dame. Maybe he had never taken a good look at her before. As she talked the situation became social, and Red found himself wanting to impress her with conversation rather than just kidding her along. He had a feeling that he spent so much time joshing waitresses and tough Janes in town that he had forgotten how to talk straight to a woman with class.

"I'll manage. It's probably that I'm changing, but my father seems to be a tightwad and I have two sisters and a small brother who have to be brought up. I'll have to manage on my own. If I'd known earlier I'd have educated myself more, but I don't want to be a stenographer or a schoolteacher either," Lily talked, somehow consulting Red, or assuming that he would understand her situation and offer advice. Red surmised that she had heard he'd made money off real estate, and had decided she might make a go at him. The idea of marrying a large woman like Lily struck Red as funny. He had always liked them slender and graceful, and Lily was six foot tall, broad-shouldered, and while handsomely proportioned, her size made one think she could walk through stone buildings, and she had a way of progressing as though she meant to get where she was going.

Boys were playing baseball in the street, and one of the throws caught Dion full in the face so that he toppled over. Red saw, and thought the boy was unconscious. Dion was dazed when Red helped him to his feet. "Are you hurt much?" Red asked. "Don't rub your eye. We'll have the doctor see to that right away. He's going to be sick." Red held Dion anxiously, patting his shoulder and feeling enraged at the boys who were playing fly-catch.

"It will be all right in a few minutes," Dionisio said, pushing away from Red, preoccupied with the pain in his eye. "It got me straight over the eye, but it wasn't coming fast. I've been socked in the eye harder than that, but it drove the ball in. I feel woozy and sick in my stomach. I'm going home. No duck dinner for me."

Lily watched with concern. Red's gentleness towards Dion struck her, and affected her strangely. She had decided not to act antagonistic towards him, but still she believed him without gentleness in his nature. There was some luminously tender quality in his treatment of Dion. Lily felt resentful. "I'll walk home with you, Dion," she said, "because you might feel sick and want somebody to hold you up."

"That's all right," Red said gruffly. "I'll take him home in the car. We don't want anything wrong with his eye though. Come on, Dion. We'll have the druggist take a look at it and if it's inflamed, we'll see the doctor." Red had his arm about Dion's shoulder, and pulled the boy around, to lead him towards the pharmacist's. Lily was in his path. She hesitated, and took Dion's other arm.

"Yes, you're right," she told Red. "We'd better see that his eye isn't in danger."

Red sensed that Lily was challenging him. He felt a desire to be rude and tell her that Dion was his friend to look after. She needn't think he meant harm to the boy. Lily's calm, however, cowed him. Let her take Dion home. At the drugstore Mr. Schwarz made light of the blow on Dion's eye.

"It'll be all right in a half hour. The ball wasn't coming fast enough to blacken your eye, sonny."

"I know, but I'm going home. Don't bother," Dion said, petulantly. He didn't like being fussed over, and his eye felt as though it had sand in it. He broke away from Red and Lily now and went down the street. As the druggist had washed his eye and he looked healthy colored they let him go on alone. When he had left Lily looked strangely at Red. "You aren't as tough as I thought you were. I never thought you'd feel hurt for anybody else's hurt. Maybe I act harder than I am too." There was a wistful warmth of appeal in Lily's voice at her last admission. She laughed, nervous because of having been personal. Red felt a fondly human impulse towards her.

"Too," he said, and laughed uneasily. "Yes, you and me both. I'm not hard. I'm not so gentle, but I don't like seeing a nice kid's eye put out, I don't care who the kid is."

"Oh, I know," Lily said quickly. "I saw. You wouldn't be so bothered by every kid who got hit in the eye. I have nearly kidnapped Dion myself, twice. There he is, and suddenly he looks so beautiful it kills a person. I never thought you would be able to appreciate that kind of look on a person's face."

Red looked confused, as well as surprised. "What do you mean?" he said gruffly.

"Let it go," Lily's voice chortled a tender mocking lilt. "Anyway, I like you a little now; not the way you are acting, but how I see you really are. Maybe I placed too much importance on what people said about you."

"What do they say?" Red asked sullenly.

"Things about your attitude towards women, and Dion says his mother thinks you may give him bad ideas. I told Dion if his mother thought he wouldn't learn things from farm boys and other people in town, she had another think coming. What town people think they can get by with in the country riles me."

"You don't like this burg any better than I do," Red said.

"No, but I get lonely in the city and don't know what to do with myself. I don't want to stay on the farm because I've come to feel restless, and get cross with the others. I guess this town is where I'll stay."

"I'm going to Minneapolis on the midnight train. Why not come along?" Red said, with a drummer-like gallantry of implication. He saw Lily flush resentfully. "I didn't insinuate anything," he defended.

"No, you were honest enough. You said it outright."

"I didn't suggest anything."

"Don't be foolish. What right would I have to go with you if I didn't understand it the way you know you meant it?"

"Well, you told me Dion's family thought I wasn't fit to know," Red hedged, uneasy now. He didn't understand Lily. She kept changing before him. There she stood, seeming a healthy, knowing farm girl, very physical, and at moments he got the feeling he had to be more careful what he said to her than he had with the Granger girls. She wouldn't kid or joke about herself. Just now there was a stark, raw quality of blunt and very young honesty in her attitude towards his suggestion.

In her remark upon his tenderness towards Dion there had been a teasingly sympathetic woman of the world's understanding. Then Red felt that she outthought him, and understood more than did he. He knew he was not of a subtle or delicate sort.

"I said they might be mistaken. Maybe I was wrong, but let that drop. I don't accept your invitation, thank you, however you meant it. I have a man's way of looking at things, and if I went I'd want my own money, and I can't afford a trip to the city just now, if I wanted to go with you. We would probably want to do different things there, so we wouldn't be company for each other anyway."

Red laughed. "You're some girl, Miss Root. You have a different line than any other skirt I ever talked to. I say, you eat Dion's duck dinner with me, and we'll go for an auto ride afterwards. I won't act fresh."

Lily became somewhat defiant. "I'm no weak woman. Certainly I'll eat with you, and we might talk sense. If you talk to me and treat me as though I don't think as much of myself as you do of yourself, I can leave, I suppose."

At dinner Lily was on her guard for a time, but mischief came into her. She found she wasn't at all distrustful of Red. Instead she felt surer of herself than he did of himself. "Why would you want me to go to the city with you?" she asked. "That was an idea which would have worried you if I'd accepted, isn't it? You have girls there, I know. You grew up in the city, didn't you? We don't know a thing about each other, so we don't get at each other when we talk, do we?"

Red mumbled and wanted to draw within himself because Lily manipulated the situation rather than he. "There's not much to know about me. I was a bum newspaperman, and a hobo after I got back from the war. Another fellow put me wise to the fact that I could buy this restaurant cheap, and when I saw Neva Granger I had ideas about settling down, and this town looked as good as anywhere else. She's not so good-looking now, with two kids, but I fell hard then. I guess she was meant to be just refined. Anyway, when she heard about my being drunk a few times she was through with me, and I pulled what she thought was a crooked deal getting hold of a couple of farms. One man had consumption and had to get away quick; and the other fellow was bankrupt. I hadn't much money, but managed to borrow and buy the farms, at different times, but she decided I was no good. It wasn't any good my telling her that I sent that T.B. guy money every month, and have for five years. She wouldn't believe it, and I guess she was right to marry that rosy-cheeked nice boy she has."

Lily mused. "Both the younger Granger girls and Dion have something that upsets a person. The one you liked isn't so pretty now, but three years back I used to feel sick about myself, seeing both her and the other girl. I felt like a load of meat. My mother was beautiful in that dainty, delicate way, but you couldn't tell it by looking at me. I don't know why, I never wanted to be that way, still I like looking at girls who are beautiful their way. It's funny too, because Dion's that way, and he isn't girlish. It's just that they are beautiful, and it hasn't anything to do with their being girls. Oh, I haven't enough education to express what I feel, but it's poetical, I suppose." Lily said the last very youngly and for a flash was a crude, romantic farm girl. Before the last romantic admission Red had been bothered by her wondering about his devotion to the Grangers. She calmly assumed that he felt about them all, Dion included, as did she, and it disturbed him to think that she was right. He hated to have her know how keenly he felt about Dion.

Driving out into the country after dinner Lily was not talkative. Her quietness put Red off his guard, and he finally, in a wooded section of the road, tried to put his arm about her. She did not resist until he tried to caress her firm breast. She merely pushed his hand away and sat back. Red was nervous. His legs were jerky, and he felt restless, wishing he was on the train towards Minneapolis. He tried to tell himself that he had this girl going, and that he would tantalize her. A look in the depths of her cool eyes upset his calculations, however. She was warm and full-blooded. He was not going to believe that she was an iceberg, and Swedes are all hot. She bothered him. Her knowing Dion and the Grangers bothered him too. He didn't want her telling that he was a lousy roughneck. Moments of tiredness with the game he believed he was playing came to Red. Why bother with her? She was right. There were girls in the city, and maybe this girl did run straight. He might get into a jam playing with her. Her Swede father might have more money and influence than people in town knew. You could never tell about those Swede farmers. Still Red later tussled with Lily, to kiss her. She resisted only mildly.

"If you treated me the way you did Dion this afternoon you could do anything," Lily suddenly blurted out. "It struck me you were more hurt than he was when that baseball hit him. I knew then you weren't a tough man. I never saw anybody act so tender.

Your treating me this way won't get you anywhere. I never did like being handled."

Red gulped and got red in the face. "Whatcha driving at?" he said gruffly.

"You make me want to be kind to you, because of how I see you can feel, but you don't let me be as much as I can be. I'd talk honestly to you, if you would, but if girls you know want being played with like this, I'm not like them, that's all. If I wanted to do anything, I would, but you act as though you thought you could play a trick on me and have things happen. I'm able to think too, remember." Lily's tones were not antagonistic though. They were confiding, cajoling, and, Red felt, somehow aggressive. He sensed that with a hunting and hard curiosity this girl was tantalizing and analyzing him.

He in no way understood how few contacts with people Lily had had in her life. Whatever she knew she had observed from a distance. Her alone childhood, her early look of maturity because of size, and her mother's mansion-lady attitudes towards farm neighbors had kept her from intimate friendships on the farm, and away at school her self-consciousness had stopped her.

Country quiet and new-cut grain odors were giving Lily tranquility, but a feeling of indifference, or abandon, also. She felt perplexed, for at dinner she saw that she had attracted Red, and now he treated her with a familiarity she thought cheap. Possibly that is how sex is, but she didn't like having him start things. She felt drawn to him whenever he looked helpless or confused, as she had managed to make him feel several times. She liked the feel of him beside her now, but at this moment he seemed coldly detached. She hadn't observed it acutely before, but seeing his hands on the steering wheel she saw that they were finely made with very well-kept fingernails. A sensation of desire went through her. She loved beautiful hands. Seeing that Red's were fine made her appraise him more. His straight shoulders and his strong, elastic body made her feel the pulse of life keenly. Suddenly she patted his arm, and then held it comfortingly in her hand.

"I get crazy blue and lonely sometimes too. Don't look cut off from everything, and fighting about it. I'd be a good friend to you, and just let it go at that if you'd take things simply."

Red was uneasy. Lily attracted him more than he wanted to admit, and he was incapable of taking her comradeship suggestion. Without distrusting her, he was on his guard. She was aggressive in a strange way. He squeezed her hand, trying to believe he thought he had her excited, but also he told himself she was one of those foreign freaks who don't have any passion or feeling. When he pressed her hand Lily responded. He kissed her, and she responded, but not passionately. Lily let him kiss her again, and patted his backhead with a comforting gesture. Red felt somehow timid, but forced to go on, to tussle when Lily's hand against his bosom kept him from crushing her to him. He saw that her strength was greater than his.

Lily drew away finally, saying, "You're afraid of me. Why? I know you don't feel anything much about me. You don't feel tender, anyway, and I guess you know I won't let myself be treated like you're used to treating some girls. Let me tell you, if anything happened between us it would be because I wanted it, but I don't want anything with you thinking I'm just another girl who's gone out for a ride in the country with you. When I do that it will be with someone I pick up and take out riding. I want to be liked." When Lily started speaking she had been antagonistic, but a dismal quality of desolation came into her voice. It clutched into Red. He saw Lily in a flash as a great lonely child, overgrown, and groping. And passion came into him too. "I want you," he said. "You want me. That's it. We want each other." He caught her in his arms and held her close. She did not fight, but let him kiss her deeply, with long kisses. Then slowly she forced him away.

"I'm stronger than you," she said drily. "That kind of kiss means nothing. I was ready to offer you something but you wouldn't understand."

"Some fellows would make you walk home," Red said roughly. Lily was quiet for a moment, looking at him with a stunned air. Then she laughed, tauntingly until real mirth of dismay was in her voice.

"They would have to be stronger than you are. I might put them out of the car and let them walk home. You're funny with your idea that because I'm a woman you can make me do anything I don't want."

Red looked at Lily. Her face was impassive. He thought her icy with fury. "Come now," he was placatory. "I didn't mean that. Don't get all het up."

"I don't understand why you make things bad that needn't be so," Lily said, with childish bitterness. "Drive to town. I'm sick of things, sick of the way people treat each other. I want things nice. You were nice to Dion, why don't you act so with me? When I stayed with Mrs. Watkins people talked about me when I didn't know what they meant at first. Whatever she does she does for money, I suppose. I can't see that she's worse than women married to men they don't like, but I don't understand women like her or most other women anyway. You think I'm a stupid farm girl, but you're only the Irish owner of a cheap restaurant. I have more to be proud of than you, because I don't try to make anyone cheaper than they are."

"Do you want me to offer marriage because I kissed you?" Red said gruffly, it dawning on him that Lily was young, and not as knowing as he had thought.

"Why would I want that when I wouldn't marry you? That would be no compliment to me," Lily said, but she had detected bewilderment in Red's manner. Possibly, she thought, he had known only the wrong sort of women, and men. "We might do as well as most married people at that," she said after a silence. "I wouldn't be a home woman, and I wouldn't stop doing what I wanted to do and thought right because I was married."

"I didn't want to marry till I could leave a little money if I passed out," Red said, blood panicking through him. He told himself this big girl was not his type; that she was being clever and leading him on; but he was afraid too she was as indifferent as she claimed to be.

"I have money," Lily said shortly. Suddenly she felt decisive. "Yes, I will marry you. I have a business head, father will help me stock a ranch, and I can raise horses or cattle. It will be better if I am married, because people won't think they can trick a simple, unmarried young girl then. I want to do something to keep from being bored and restless." There was in Lily's tone no doubt but that now she'd decided the marriage was arranged.

Red fidgeted and felt caught. Lily sensed his trapped emotion and felt sympathetic. It gave her a physical urge towards him and she felt his magnetism. Her wish to have him gentle had passed. She felt the bewildered, awkward maleness of him, and knew she wouldn't mind if he became rough towards her again. She knew she was handling the situation, and she felt protective towards him, even to the extent of wanting to let him feel the master enough not to feel beaten. His arm rested now about her waist simply. She put her arm about his shoulder to look at his face. She felt the sinuous flux of his muscle beneath her palm, and it made her desire to hold him closer. However, watching his face she saw mingled emotions expressed there; panic at being trapped, withdrawal, abashment, and still Red was feeling her presence keenly. She aroused his desires.

Lily wanted him to look her in the face. His profile struck her as beautiful against the moonlight, and she had her old marvel at the wonder of faces. She had too a keen, deep-thrusting emotion that Red had been up against a hard life, and she wanted to pet and comfort him. When she started to draw him towards her he was taut in her grasp, and curiously hunted in his expression. Red wondered if she intended to have him, to force him to marriage. Her aggressiveness made him wary. If she had him caught, she had him licked too, he knew.

Lily's arm slipped away. Red looked at her. She was apathetic, with a beaten, uncaring look on her face. "No, you're not my answer," Lily said. Red felt a pang of pity and sympathy for the cold distance in her voice. She was different. She was something real. He wanted her, by God, and she was slipping away if he didn't act quickly.

"Hell, Lily, let's get married. I don't know why you would want me. I'm not much, and the idea of marrying and being responsible for kids that might turn out bad, or not like the racket, has always put me off." Red was humble with reality now, feeling defeat about life. "I get sick of that damn restaurant, but I haven't much hope. You don't know what you want either. Let's give marriage a shot. We can quit if it doesn't go."

"I was ready to go ahead with you and didn't think about marrying. That doesn't solve anything," Lily said, gloomily. "You think I'm trying to force you into a marriage, and all I want is to know what's nice in you. I don't know people, I guess, and I don't like them much. I want things nice. You don't want to marry me, even if you don't manage to get the kind of a woman you really like."

"You ask Dion," Red became persuasive now that Lily held back. "I said today I ought to marry a girl like you and begin to have sense."

Lily was distant with a distraitness which was that of a wild but unafraid animal. She didn't want Red now, but wished rather to fight him off apathetically. "You're a wise Jane," Red insisted. "Say the word and we'll head towards the preacher's. You don't start things you don't finish. You aren't that sort."

"Don't call me a Jane," Lily said curtly. "Go to a minister's then. Maybe there's a little something between us, and we will stop antagonizing each other. I'm ready to try marrying, and if it doesn't go, I have my living to make, and we can each go on our own."

4

Red and Lily felt evasive towards each other the next day, but each regarded the other curiously when the other was not looking. Neither of them quite figured out how they happened into this impulsive marriage, and Lily felt that she had tricked herself. Red had been gentle, and she didn't feel any virginal resentment towards him. All antagonism had gone out of her towards him, but she didn't want marriage or him, she told herself. He was awkward or things were grotesque, and she felt in no way romantic about marriage or love or sex. She felt a sense of pity for him when Red introduced her to various men at lunch. His manner of pride was pompous and wished to conceal sheepishness as he said, "Meet Mrs. Neill." She wanted to laugh at the droll pathos of his manner, which was perplexed. At dinner that night she made an attempt to get things straight.

"Red, do you want to go on? We are not what each other wants. We could call it quits now; go to the city and I'd stay there, and when I came back after a few months, just let the whole matter drop."

"What's the trouble, girl?" Red said, believing it needful to be a conventional and possessive husband with patronizing protectiveness. "Am I too rough for you? I thought you knew more than you do."

"It's not that," Lily said. "We didn't want marriage. We bluffed ourselves into it. We ought to love each other a little if we stay married. I suppose I'm funny. I've been in love with Dion Granger for two years, somehow. I don't want him like what you did last night, but I get arm hunger and want him to pet whenever I think of him. I want to feel something that way towards anybody who's making love to me. That other doesn't mean anything to me."

"Well, I won't bother you. You wait a while and maybe in a few days you will feel differently," Red told her. "I know some women have to take things easily."

"I don't hate it, but I only felt sorry for you, and I won't go on feeling sorry all the time. I would just want you away. I tell you now, you don't ever need to be faithful to me that way, because if that's what you want, I'm no good for you. Maybe if you treated me or felt for me as you did yesterday for Dion things would be different, but you don't think my being hurt matters much, really."

"Ya, I get you," Red said gruffly, looking strangely at Lily. "You think I feel about Dion as you do, that's it?"

"I thought you and I had something between us maybe, in understanding how he can get a person."

"We might as well stick to the marriage for a while though, I say. I was going to Minneapolis. I'll go today, and you take care of the restaurant. You say you can manage and want to do things. When I get back you will have had time to think things over."

"All right," Lily said, a new idea making her eager. "That's so. We could stay married, and if things don't go I can go into some business of my own, or raise stock. I guess I'm the kind of a woman who ought to be in business anyway. I'm no homebody."

Within a month Lily completely managed the restaurant. When Red came back from the city he paid more attention to farms and bare land which he owned. He opened a real estate office, and was soon asking Lily's advice about all his affairs. Ole, a rich man actually, was pleased that Lily should want to become a stock raiser and business woman as his staunch and independent aunt in Sweden was. He gave Lily blooded beef cattle, and horses, and daily she drove to the farm of Red's where she reared her stock.

Red, having married, believed he wanted children, but none arrived, and Lily's attitude towards him did not alter to make her desirous of him. She confused him entirely, for he had a deeply rooted conventional and male attitude towards women and marriage. Strangely he felt faithful towards her, even when she submitted so indifferently to his few efforts at love-making. He drank more heavily, and, always inclined to laziness, sullenly admired Lily's energy and business capacity, while letting her take his affairs more and more into her charge. He watched with strange emotions one day as she was regarding her blooded horses on the farm. There was more between her and the horses than there was between her and him, or her and humans. Later, one of his increasingly brutish and sullen streaks came over him, and he cursed her horses, which she gave more attention than she gave her husband.

Lily looked at him coolly. "Why, Red, you aren't jealous of my horses. We agreed to make the best of a makeshift marriage that neither of us wanted, but I have played square."

Red didn't answer. Lily, for physical strength and for surety of attitude, was the stronger. There was no use in his trying to bully her. She won; and the amiable, lazy streak in him led him to acquiesce finally with grace. Still, one time when Lily was at the farm for three days, nursing her pet Arabian stallion, Red was disturbed. What kind of a woman was she? She treated that horse more lovingly than most mothers treat their children. He was sure that should the horse die it would be a tragedy to Lily.

Abab, the stallion, was well soon, however. Red drove out to get Lily, and came into the farmyard to find her putting Abab through his paces. He pranced daintily, coyly exhibiting his sweeping tail and arched neck. After circling about Lily, who directed him by his halter lead, he pranced gracefully to her, and elegantly took a lump of sugar from her lips. Lily stood patting his glossy neck, before the stable man led him away to groom.

"Lily, you're a girl all choked up with protective emotions, and not a womanly or mother impulse," Red said suddenly, bitter, but with a flash of insight rare to his mediocre nature. Lily looked abstracted.

Several years after their marriage Dion Granger returned to

town for the summer vacation from college. Meeting Lily, he complimented her on her happy marriage. Lily was preoccupied, remembering the emotion she had once felt about Dion. When she was sixteen, feeling herself an awkward hulk of a girl, she had been hopelessly in love with the twelve-year-old boy, and terrified both that he should know or that he might not understand. Dion still had a quality that got into her, but her heart did not thump at his approach. She was wondering what quality it was she wanted and now felt that she was missing in life. Her farms, her stock, her business enterprises were not enough. Absent-mindedly she answered Dion. "Yes, Red and I are like lambs together. We don't row at each other. He likes being lazy, and I like doing things. Sure, it's a good marriage."

Seeing Lily talking at various times with Dion, Red recalled her confession of regard for the boy. He pondered, at first thickly suspicious and inclined to be jealous, but after reflection he spoke to Lily. "If you feel the way you do about that boy," Red did not call him Dion now; Lily's attitude made him feel estranged, as did Dion's added age, "I guess it's up to me to be a sport. Seeing how, you say anyway, we bluffed each other into this marriage, and don't mean much to each other . . . well, he's too young to marry you, but he likes you, and you're a strong, healthy woman. I just want you to get what I'm driving at." Red was embarrassed and ill at ease, as he mumbled.

Lily regarded him analytically. "It's not Dion. It's a quality he has. I once wanted what you're talking about, but not now, and I only wanted to hold him and comfort him. It was arm hunger. He seemed so fragile, needing to be taken care of. I know you'd mind, Red. You'd be jealous, several ways, if you thought I made a go at him, and it would have to be me. He doesn't understand. You have ideas that all women want the same thing, Red, but I tell you, I don't, and I don't understand myself any better than you do."

The next autumn Red went duck-shooting but once. With each year he grew lazier and less inclined even to hunt, his favorite pastime. Having drunk much whiskey, Red got a chill coming home in a heavy rain. He thought he would be well in a few days, but pneumonia set in and within five days he was dead. Lily felt dumfounded and empty. With Red about, she felt pride in proving to him how competent and fair a person she was. Their relationship had been an easy, sporting comradeship, she felt. To keep from being lonely she went further into stock raising. Constantly she drove about the country, looking for bargain lands or blooded stock to buy. She had become a woman of importance in the town and county now, because of her business ability and wealth. There was little of the lumpish girl about her now. For a time she was too busy to feel restless or to question whether she was happy. Only she felt a drive within her that insisted that she must not stop to wonder about herself. One day, in a fit of memory and curiosity, she wrote to her cousin Helga, from whom she had not heard for several years.

That day a mood of depression had her. In her restaurant she confided to her attorney, who lunched there daily, that there never would be another man like Red. Going into her room that night she looked at his photographs, and felt a pain of yearning. He had had moments of striking her as beautiful, or wistful. A sinking sensation came into Lily. The photographs swam before her eyes, and sometimes they suggested Red, but they became again Helga, and Dionisio, and even Abab, her pet stallion. In all of the heads was a nervously intense quality, a line of beauty which struck into Lily's heart and made her bleed for their torment and emotions of despair.

She was overcome with misery, feeling empty and nauseated in a vast unawakened realm of herself. What was she missing in life? Was she strong? As strong as Helga, and was Helga happy, or perhaps needing her? That night she dreamed of Dion, but in the dream he changed to Red, to Helga, to a horse, which became again Red, and she and Red were running up the sky. With a snap she felt herself falling into eternity, and awoke, startled, with a stale terror and sense of misery.

Upon awakening in the morning Lily felt so nauseated in the pit of her stomach that she went to see a doctor. He told her she needed a change, and a rest. She had overworked and was due for a nervous breakdown if she did not relax. She overrated the physical resistance of her apparently healthy frame.

"Perhaps I do need change. There are qualities in the world

I don't know. I might travel, and find out about them. Fortunately Johnson, my farm manager, can look after my affairs if I stay away even a year."

Lily didn't act at once, however. Nobody in Lansing attracted her, and she hadn't many friends, merely business acquaintances. Still she knew Lansing, and a fear of new places was in her. Helga was married, and had children, so that Lily felt that she would be intruding should she write that she was coming to New York for a visit.

She tried to feel what she hungered for, to reconstruct some picture of Red in her mind to which she might remain loyal. That might calm her. She was too emotionally upset and honest now to trick herself, however. It wasn't Red's kind of quality that ever had or could move her. Dion, as a boy, had meant strange, thrilled, frightened emotions. Helga's fragility she had worshipped. Somewhere there must be people or qualities which meant similar ecstatic emotions.

Helga responded at once to Lily's letter, and Lily, knowing the handwriting, opened the letter with hands trembling with expectancy. This letter was going to solve things for her. She knew before she had finished the first sentence, and was triumphant, with a new purposefulness. Always she had wanted to have Helga with her, to take care of and protect. She had been a child not to have known before.

"Darling Lily: You said that I should come to you if I felt utterly without will to go on. I feel so now. My husband is living with another woman, and accuses me of being silly, and hysterical. He has never meant anything to me, nor have the children, much. I must get away. I want so much to come to you for rest, and to adjust myself. You are so confident and strong. Do you remember the hair I clipped from your head, years ago, it seems? I still have it, and it always reminds me that there is brightness, and you. I'm too sick-hearted to write more."

Lily went with quick decision to wire Helga. "Coming to you at once. Lansing not for us, now. Plan a year abroad. We are saving each other."

As Lily left the post office after sending her wire she felt exuberantly young as she had not felt since childhood. Helga needed her. Helga, a person, felt she had strength beyond mere managing capacity. Helga meant a release into a human relationship, and Helga meant some mystery that was going to be solved for her now.

Encountering the doctor who asked when she planned going abroad Lily said gaily, "I'm on my way to packing, and will be on the train towards New York tonight. Doctor, it's good I have money, because I have a strong feeling I'm breaking loose to learn what living is about. If there's anything in life that matters, I'm going to find it. I've been compromising too long."

(See Bibliographical Note, page 364.)

McAlmon was thirty-eight when he finished his memoirs. He had written then that "Life begins, they say, at forty . . . It ought to be interesting when it really gets under way." If this was intended ironically, the final, cruel joke was on him. After 1935 nothing much happened to him. He made desultory plans, revised an occasional manuscript, and drank. In 1937 New Directions brought out a collection of his poems written during the previous fifteen years. This little book—he called it Not Alone Lost—*was his only work to be published in America. It was received with no enthusiasm. Similarly, when* Being Geniuses Together *was published in England in 1938, it created no stir—perhaps because the British were too intent on steeling themselves for the ordeal to come to pay much attention to a volume of literary gossip.*

When the war came, McAlmon was trapped in occupied France. By this time he had contracted tuberculosis, and the wartime shortage of food aggravated his condition. In 1940 he made his way to Lisbon with some other Americans. His family, who had never deserted him, managed to get him money and he came home to the United States, this time permanently. From New York he went to El Paso where he worked for his brothers in a surgical supply house, although he still had some outside income. When he was no longer employable, he went to Mexico and then, urged by a sister, to Desert Hot Springs, California. This little town was McAlmon's home for the rest of his life.

His tuberculosis grew worse and his letters show a general decay of mind and spirit. He became bitter. Always impatient and consequently irritable, he even managed to quarrel at last with William Carlos Williams. Few of his other friends knew where he was. There in the desert he tinkered with his manuscripts, talked to the local librarian, recalled memories of early days with his sisters. He died in February, 1956. He was not quite sixty.

Epilogue

His death in the desert, as one of McAlmon's friends said, "gave a kind of Rimbaud atmosphere to what was also, in essence, a Rimbaud career." Although no revolutionary, he had separated himself from the ties of place and society and had set out to find his own way, rejecting conventional procedures and rebelling against conventional restraints. He had been born with qualities that made him potentially a fine writer; his personal charm had brought him the cooperation of gifted people in all his undertakings; and through a series of accidents he had attained economic independence while he was young enough to exploit it. He had achieved greater freedom than most men, and seemingly it lay in his hands to accomplish more than most men.

"It was McAlmon," Kay Boyle has written, "who, in liberating himself from genteel language and genteel thought, spoke for his generation in a voice that echoes, unacknowledged, in the prose of Hemingway and that of other writers of his time." [1] Ezra Pound has expressed much the same judgment: "What Hemingway did, nobody could improve on. Mac was different. Others could go on from where he started. He opened up a whole new vein of writing. Tough realism. Not like Glenway Wescott. He's soft. People like Caldwell. Maybe even Faulkner. Nobody's ever given him credit."

In a letter Pound repeated what he had said in conversation:

I did NOT say a better book than Hem's. What I have repeated is that Bob was the one good american writer NEVER published in vol/ in the U.S.
        cause Sinc Lewis et al / publish the vices the yank is proud to possess , but Bob always got under their skin.

also the rising prose writers of the 20/s and 30/s owed more to
Bob than to H because Hem did his job/ finished his work and
they couldn't beat him at it.
                              But Bob wd/ start a sketch , full of
verve. but refused absolutely to revise/
                                         etc. so a lot of 'em went
on and built over his ground etc.[2]

Why was McAlmon incapable of making full use of his gifts
in his own work? "I saw him literally destroy himself with his
total indifference to his fate as a writer," William Carlos Williams
wrote after his death. "And yet he cared for nothing so much as
excellence in his craft as a writer, but he could not be a liar to
obtain it. And he had an eye and a fierce tongue when he saw
others among the writers about him, liars in one form or another,
who were lying to make their reputations. Many of them were
doing just that. Not he. But he suffered for it in the world's
estimation. He would not work to guard his reputation. Not that
he was lazy, he was not, but he was too impatient to apply himself
tirelessly to the job until he had finished it."

It may be that his distinguished friends, glimpsing their
youthful selves in McAlmon, retrospectively endow him with
greater potentialities than he possessed and make greater claims
for his work than his achievement can sustain.[3] Yet it is certain
that in McAlmon's autobiographical fiction one recognizes a
living, breathing, feeling human being—and a remarkable one.
Who touches his books touches a man. It is certain too that his
failure as an artist derives at least in part from lack of discipline—
from his refusal to revise his material, to commit himself to making the most of it. Perhaps even more his failure came from an
almost wilful misunderstanding of the nature and function of
art itself. McAlmon was so determined to appear what he was, no
more and no less, that he falsified the relation of truth to convention; and in rebelling against what he thought of as arbitrary
standards of literary excellence, he rejected the very methods by
which any kind of artistic excellence is attained. Striving to be
free of cultural restraints, he attempted to be free of all emotional and imaginative bias except that which his own experience
forced on him. He aspired to be Adam, and was too proud to be
taught by his betters. A life shaped by another's imagination was

to him a life of illusion; and he wanted no illusions, certainly none born of books. He made insufficient distinction between the creative intuitions of an artist and the conventional assumptions of the unthinking. Life, any life, he thought better than art, any art. The passions were more important than descriptions of them, and the life lived counted for more than the life invented. A genuine work of art, he thought, reflected a full-blooded, living man. He did not see that art is more than a reflection of reality, it is an ordering and an intensification of it; hence, a work of art, far from being a capricious manifestation, is achieved through patient experiment and disciplined toil.

In McAlmon one sees the prototype of the lost generation of whatever century. Impatient with inherited values, he was yet unable to arrive at new values he could accept. Having uprooted himself, he never grew to full stature. At fifty, when he should have been reaching full maturity, his talents and his body were already desiccated. By the time he was sixty he was broken, and he died.

At the end his integrity was all that remained of his high aspiration. This at least was inviolable. Until his last breath he went his own way. But long before he lay dying, McAlmon—with no more illusions about himself than he had about others—must have realized that his future was far behind him. Unable to function as a writer except within the ambiance of the twenties, as early as 1935 he had become an anachronism. But he stuck to his guns, and he backed his judgment with everything that he had. Men of fierce integrity being rare, he does not deserve oblivion.

NOTES, BIOGRAPHICAL
REPERTORY,
BIBLIOGRAPHY,
AND INDEX

Notes

All the pieces in this collection have been lightly edited. In the form in which they first appeared, many contained typographical errors and abounded in incorrect or inconsistent spelling, punctuation, and capitalization. This is not surprising: McAlmon's indifference to such matters is well known, and few of the little magazines of the twenties could afford trained proofreaders and copyeditors. In the case of books and magazines published in France, there was the further complication of compositors unfamiliar with English. Moreover, in a day when eccentricities of typography and punctuation characterized much avant-garde writing, it could not have been easy for editors and proofreaders to determine what was erroneous and what was experimental. In the present volume except for correcting obvious typographical errors, the editing has been confined almost entirely to regularizing punctuation where its presence (or absence) might be confusing, and to correcting the spelling of proper names and places. The aim has been simply to correct faults which might inconvenience or annoy the reader; there has been no attempt at over-all stylistic consistency. The various pieces were written over a span of something like twenty years, and they reflect the changes in McAlmon's way of writing. To impose on them conformity to a rigid standard of style would impair to some extent their special qualities and their historical interest; it would also be in complete contradiction to all that McAlmon stood for.

Bibliographical information about the various selections in each section is given in the paragraph immediately following the section title; a complete bibliography of McAlmon's published work begins on page 383. Persons mentioned in the text and commentary are identified in the Biographical Repertory, beginning on page 367. The reader concerned with more detailed documentation may consult my *Robert McAlmon: Expatriate Publisher and Writer* (Lincoln: University of Nebraska Press, 1957; Nebraska Paperback ed., with index and foreword by William Carlos Williams, 1959).

PROLOGUE

1. The work of "Quatre Jeunes Etats-Uniens" appeared in *Le Navire d'Argent* (March 1926), published by Adrienne Monnier. According to Sylvia Beach in *Shakespeare and Company* (New York: Harcourt, Brace and Com-

359

pany, 1959): "Included was an extract from Williams' *The Great American Novel* (*Le Grand Roman américain*), translated by Auguste Morel, the translator of *Ulysses;* Hemingway's story 'The Undefeated' (*'Invincible'*); an extract from Cummings' *The Enormous Room* entitled 'Sipliss,' translated by George Duplaix; and a story by McAlmon, 'The Publicity Agent,' (*Agence de Publicité*), translated by Adrienne and myself" (pp. 127–128). Reprinted by permission of Harcourt, Brace & World, Inc.

2. Personal conversation with Ezra Pound, 28 December 1956.

3. *transition*, No. 14 (Fall 1928), 98.

4. Ernest Walsh in *This Quarter*, I, 2 (1925–1926), 332.

I   ALL-AMERICAN BOYHOOD (1896–1919)

1. The Plains

"**The Jack Rabbit Drive**" and "**Potato Picking,**" the first and third of these "tales from childhood," were first printed in *transition*, No. 15 (February 1929), 84–93, 93–101, the literary monthly edited by Eugene Jolas and published in Paris (1927–1930). Joyce, Hemingway, Cummings, Stein, and others whose names have become twentieth-century literary fixtures were among the contributors. "Potato Picking," which was included in Edward J. O'Brien's *Best Short Stories of 1929*, is given here in a version discovered among McAlmon's posthumous papers. "**Wisdom Garnered by Day,**" the second story, appeared in the distinguished British periodical *Life and Letters*, XI, 59 (November 1934), 157–165, alongside pieces by Richard Garnett and Bertrand Russell.

1. The quotations all are from McAlmon's autobiography, *Being Geniuses Together* (London: Secker and Warburg, 1938). The first may be found on page 157; the second and third on page 159.

2. The Middle West and California

"**Blithe Insecurities**" originally was published in two parts in *Pagany*, I, 4 (Fall 1930), 32–52; II, 1 (Winter 1931), 60–81, a short-lived avant-garde quarterly over which William Carlos Williams presided as guardian angel. A shorter version, "Summer," had been included in *A Hasty Bunch* (1922), McAlmon's first collection of stories which was given its title by James Joyce. (Although *A Hasty Bunch* carries no bibliographical information, it was published in Paris by the Contact Publishing Company.) "**Three Generations of the Same**" first appeared in *A Companion Volume* (1923), McAlmon's second Paris collection, also put out by Contact Publishing Company. The following year the story was reprinted in *The Little Review*, X, 1 (Spring 1924), 43–57. Under Margaret Anderson's editorship, and with Ezra Pound as foreign editor, *The Little Review* (1914–1929) provided an outlet for some of the best and most promising new writers of the period. It attracted little attention from the general public, however, until it was stigmatized as a purveyor of obscene literature for publishing sequences of James Joyce's *Ulysses*. A revised version of "Three Generations of the Same," found among McAlmon's posthumous papers, is given here.

1. *Being Geniuses Together,* pp. 225–226.
2. "Essentials," *The Little Review,* VII, 3 (September–December 1920), 69.

II POST-ADOLESCENCE (1920–1921)

1. Greenwich Village

All the selections in this section are excerpted from *Post-Adolescence* (Paris: Contact Publishing Co., n.d.), the novel McAlmon wrote in 1920 and published in 1923. (It carries the notation: "Written previously to A Hasty Bunch in 1920.") The sequence called **"The Studio"** appears on pages 6–21; **"The Dream"** on pages 39–48; **"The Party"** on pages 48–59; and **"The Talks"** on pages 104–119. The titles were supplied by the editor. McAlmon rewrote a part of *Post-Adolescence* and it came out as "New York Sleepwalking (The final chapters of a U.S. transcontinental novel)" in two issues of *Pagany,* II, 4 (Fall 1931), 22–37; III, 1 (Winter 1932), 87–100. The earlier version, reprinted here, is much superior.

1. William Carlos Williams, *Autobiography* (New York: Random House, 1951), pp. 175–176.
2. Williams, *Autobiography,* p. 176.
3. *The transatlantic review,* II, 2 (1924), 216–217.

2. Contact

"Essentials" appeared in *The Little Review,* VII, 3 (September–December 1920), 69.
1. Williams, *Autobiography,* pp. 175–176.
2. Williams, *Autobiography,* p. 148.
3. Williams, *Autobiography,* p. 146.
4. The four issues of *Contact* put out by McAlmon and Williams (December 1920; January 1921; Spring 1921; Summer 1921) were mimeographed on brief-sized paper, except the third which was printed and contained a number of pictures. McAlmon printed a fifth and final issue in Paris, June 1923. Williams revived the name for a quarterly, three issues of which appeared in 1932, which he and Nathanael West edited and published in New York. It printed "such writing as could not be sold for profit," and its contributors included Erskine Caldwell, Nancy Cunard, Parker Tyler, E. E. Cummings, West, McAlmon, and Williams. Although McAlmon's name appeared as associate editor, he had no part in founding or running the magazine. The present incarnation of *Contact,* incorporating the *Western Review,* was so named in deference to Williams, who is listed on the masthead as a contributing editor. The San Francisco group which publishes *Contact* also has reactivated the name *Contact Editions* for their books, and their advertising manifestos quote McAlmon's original announcement: "These books seem to us to have individuality, intelligence, talent, and a live sense of literature" (see page 137).
5. The letter, which is undated, presumably was written in the summer or fall of 1921. It was called to my attention by Professor John C. Thirlwall, and is quoted with the kind permission of Miss Victoria McAlmon.

6. Knoll, *Robert McAlmon, Expatriate Publisher and Writer,* p. viii.
7. 12 March 1921, 11:4.

III BEING GENIUSES TOGETHER (1921–1927)

1. The "Right People" and the Left Bank
   The three selections in this section are taken from *Being Geniuses Together,* pp. 1–9, 10–27, 41–56. **"Wealth Breeds Complication"** and **"Don't Be Common"** are the first two chapters in the book; **"The Nightinghoul's Crying"** is the fourth, with the addition of the first four pages of Chapter Five. McAlmon's chapter titles have been retained.
   1. The Ellermans' kindness extended to other members of the family. Although they rarely entertained, when McAlmon's sister Victoria visited England early in the 1920's, they invited her to stay with them.
   2. Sylvia Beach, *Shakespeare and Company.* The lines preceding the ellipsis appear on page 25; those following it on page 102.

2. Contact Editions: Paris
   The first three selections in this section are from *Being Geniuses Together.* **"Not What the 'Public' Wants"** (title supplied by the editor) is excerpted from Chapters Five and Seven, pp. 57–58, 90–92. **"All Men Are Musicians"** (original chapter title) is excerpted from Chapter Eight, pp. 93–99, 104–106. **"Genius All Too Simple"** (original chapter title) is Chapter Nine, pp. 133–142. The fourth selection, the short story **"In-Between Ladies,"** was published in *Pagany,* II, 2 (Spring 1931), 41–49.
   1. Questionnaire in *The Little Review,* XII (May 1929), 52–53.
   2. *Letters of James Joyce,* ed. Stuart Gilbert (New York: The Viking Press, 1957), p. 173. The quotation ending this paragraph is from the same source, pp. 180–181.
   3. Donald C. Gallup, "The Making of *The Making of Americans,"* *The New Colophon: A Book-Collectors' Miscellany,* III (1950), 71.
   4. McAlmon's Contact Publishing Company announcement appeared on the inside back cover of the first issue of one of the most impressive little magazines of the twenties. Ford Madox Ford hoped to do with *the transatlantic review* in Paris what he had done twenty years earlier in London with the *English Review.* Exercising an editor's prerogative, he featured Joseph Conrad and himself; but he also was the first to sponsor Ernest Hemingway, and he found room for James Joyce, Ezra Pound, E. E. Cummings, Gertrude Stein, and McAlmon. The *transatlantic* lasted one year: January 1924–January 1925.
   5. Quoted in Will Ransom, *Private Presses and Their Books* (New York: R. R. Bowker Company, 1929), p. 432.
   6. Williams, *Autobiography,* p. 186.
   7. Beach, *Shakespeare and Company,* p. 130.
   8. Williams, *Autobiography,* p. 189.
   9. William Bird to Robert E. Knoll, 5 May 1956. In the same letter Bird tells of the disposition of unsold stock: "About 1929 I moved my office and was wondering what to do with the hundreds of unsold books, when along

came an American named Schwartz who offered me $100 for the lot (perhaps 400 or 500 volumes). I told him I did not need $100 but DID need $150, and the deal was made at that figure. What he did with them I don't know." According to Bird, Three Mountains Press never had a backer: "I financed it myself. It did not cost much more than some men spend on golf."

10. Richard Ellmann, *James Joyce* (New York: Oxford University Press, 1959), p. 528.

11. Ellmann, *James Joyce*, p. 528; see also *Letters of James Joyce*, pp. 172, 175–176.

12. Beach, *Shakespeare and Company*, p. 151.

13. *Letters of James Joyce*, p. 228.

14. Gallup, "The Making of *The Making of Americans*," p. 56.

15. Gertrude Stein, *The Autobiography of Alice B. Toklas* (New York: Harcourt, Brace and Co., 1933), p. 264.

16. Stein, *The Autobiography of Alice B. Toklas*, p. 276.

17. Gallup, "The Making of *The Making of Americans*," p. 73. The quotation directly following is from the same source, p. 74.

18. *Being Geniuses Together*, p. 224.

19. Beach, *Shakespeare and Company*, p. 102.

20. Kay Boyle, "Brighter than Most," *Prairie Schooner*, XXXIV, 1 (Spring 1960), 1–2. Reprinted by permission of Kay Boyle.

IV MIGRATIONS (1924–1930)

1. Europe at Large

The three stories discussed in "A Note on the Berlin Stories," were collected in *Distinguished Air (Grim Fairy Tales)* (Paris: Contact Editions, Three Mountains Press, 1925). The excerpts from "Distinguished Air" appear on pages 15, 26, 37–39, 50, and 48. (Citations in the order in which the quotations appear in the text.) The excerpt from "Miss Knight" appears on pages 73–74. *Being Geniuses Together* is the source of **"Let's Be Shadow-Boxers"** (original chapter title), Chapter Thirteen, pages 155–166, and Chapter Eighteen ("The Duty to Be Brave"), pages 212–219; and also of **"Williams"** (title supplied by the editor), extracted from Chapter Fifteen, pages 178–184. **"Evening on the Riviera, the Playground of the World"** was first published in 1923 in *A Companion Volume*, pp. 161–182, and was reprinted in another McAlmon collection, *The Indefinite Huntress and Other Stories* (Paris: Crosby Continental Editions, The Black Sun Press: 1932). **"The Highly Prized Pajamas"** appeared in *The New Review*, I, 4 (Winter 1931–1932), 371–382, "an international notebook for art," published in Paris.

1. Knoll, *Robert McAlmon, Expatriate Publisher and Writer*, p. viii.

2. *This Quarter*, I, 2 (1925–1926), 332.

3. *Being Geniuses Together*, p. 148.

4. Harold Loeb, *The Way It Was* (New York: Criterion Books, 1959), p. 61.

5. Letter from William Bird to Robert E. Knoll, 23 May 1958.

6. Beach, *Shakespeare and Company*, p. 77.

7. Harold Loeb, *The Way It Was*, p. 61.
8. Kay Boyle, "Brighter than Most," p. 3.
9. Beach, *Shakespeare and Company*, p. 25.
10. Kay Boyle, "I Can't Get Drunk" in *The First Lover and Other Stories* (New York: Harrison Smith and Robert Haas, 1933), pp. 207–210. © 1933, 1960 by Kay Boyle.

2. Between Two Worlds

"A Romance at Sea" came out first in *Pagany*, I, 3 (Summer 1930), 28–33; it is this version which appears here. A revised version titled "Machine-Age Romance" was included in *The Indefinite Huntress and Other Stories*. "Mexican Interval," the second selection, also was included in *The Indefinite Huntress*; Parts I, V, and VI, which are reprinted here, are found on pages 74–89 and 134–149. Extracts from this long story appeared, much butchered, in the revived *Contact*, I, 2 (May 1932), 40–51.

1. "Deracinated Encounters," *This Quarter*, I, 3 (1927), 204–221. It was labeled "Extract from Work in Progress," but no more appeared in print.
2. *Being Geniuses Together*, p. 305.
3. *Being Geniuses Together*, p. 316.
4. "Mexican Interval," *The Indefinite Huntress and Other Stories*, p. 144.
5. Questionnaire in *The Little Review*, XII (May 1929), 52–53.

V FULL CIRCLE (1930–1956)

1. Return to Paris

"Return to Paris" is comprised of the closing pages (371–373) of *Being Geniuses Together*. The title was supplied by the editor.

1. *Being Geniuses Together*, p. 318.
2. *Being Geniuses Together*, p. 320.
3. *Being Geniuses Together*, p. 223.
4. *The Letters of Ezra Pound, 1907–1941*, ed. D. D. Paige (New York: Harcourt, Brace and Co., 1950), p. 266.
5. Ellmann, *James Joyce*, p. 684.
6. *Letters of James Joyce*, p. 340.

2. Return to the Plains

Both "Green Grow the Grasses" and "The Indefinite Huntress" appeared in *The Indefinite Huntress and Other Stories*, pp. 53–73 and 5–52, respectively. This volume, published by Caresse Crosby, was number ten in a series called Modern Masterpieces in English. Also in the series were two volumes by Hemingway, *in our time* and *The Torrents of Spring*; a collection of stories by Kay Boyle; William Faulkner's *Sanctuary; Laments for the Living* by Dorothy Parker; and translations of Antoine de Saint-Exupéry's *Night Flight* by Stuart Gilbert; of Alain-Fournier's *Big Meaulnes* by François Delisle; of Charles-Louis Philippe's *Bubu of Montparnasse* by Laurence Vail, with a preface by T. S. Eliot; and Kay Boyle's translation of Raymond Radiguet's *Devil in the Flesh*, with an introduction by Aldous Huxley. "Green Grow the Grasses" previously had appeared in *Front*, I, 2 (February 1931), 97–107.

1. *Post-Adolescence*, p. 48 and p. 21.

2. Readers interested in myth can see in "The Indefinite Huntress" the retelling of an ancient tale. Dionisio is such an odd name for a Midwest farm boy that the reader is led to suspect a mythic connection. The name is of course a variant of Dionysus, the god of revel and drama. One of the well-known stories about him involves the goddess Artemis, the maiden huntress, and Orion, the hunter. In the Greek myth, Orion, deprived of his sight because of unfortunate love adventures, is aided by Dionysus, who takes him to live with Artemis. After a time Orion dies, some say by the will of the goddess. McAlmon's story echoes this myth. When we first meet Lily she is represented as coming from the fields; she is resolutely independent of men. Red, like Orion, is a hunter. After misadventures with "other Janes," through Dionisio Red comes to Lily as Orion comes to Artemis. Though Lily and Red marry, Lily like Artemis is never really "conquered by love"; Red, like the god, finds protection under the aegis of a virgin huntress and in the end he too dies.

Although the parallels are insistent, given the author's unclassical temperament one suspects that his domestication of the myth is a kind of leg-pulling. In *Being Geniuses Together* (written just after the publication of "The Indefinite Huntress"), he speaks disparagingly of things classical; the passage appears in this book on page 342. McAlmon may have started a satiric story and in the course of the writing got caught by his own fired imagination. The classic symbolism of the story, though insistent, is in this view only a fillip.

EPILOGUE

1. Kay Boyle, "Brighter than Most," p. 4.

2. The first part of this quotation is from a personal conversation with Ezra Pound, 28 December 1956. The second part appears in a letter, Ezra Pound to Robert E. Knoll, 6 July [1956].

3. Katherine Anne Porter is an exception. "He and that whole crowd who wanted to write by instinct were an anathema to me and all I worked for," she said recently. "But yes, I liked him. I liked him very much" (Conversation, Lincoln, Nebraska, 5 November 1956).

Biographical Repertory

ALDINGTON, Richard (b. 1892), British poet, novelist, and essayist. He and his American wife H.D. (Hilda Doolittle) (q.v.) were associated with Ezra Pound (q.v.) and the Imagist group in London in 1914–1915. Subsequently he made a considerable reputation as a prolific (and expert) translator. His *Life for Life's Sake* (1941) contains judgments of persons and books which are both persuasive and unfashionable.

ANDERSON, Margaret, founded and edited the influential *Little Review* (1914–1929), which reflected both her volatile personality and the rapidly shifting tastes of the period. The magazine and its editor moved from Chicago to New York to Paris with the writers it published. If, as has been said, Miss Anderson substituted impressionism for taste, she supported her enthusiasms with courage: for the publication of Joyce's *Ulysses* as a serial she was tried and convicted for obscenity in 1921. Her autobiography, *My Thirty Years War*, appeared in 1930.

ANDERSON, Sherwood (1876–1941) belonged to an older generation than the Paris expatriates, but he befriended them and was their frequent associate. He assisted Hemingway in his early days, and when Hemingway left Chicago for Paris, provided him with letters of introduction.

ANTHEIL, George (1900–1959), American composer championed by Ezra Pound. His *Ballet-Mécanique* (1925) created a sensation in Paris and almost caused a riot in New York. His autobiography, *Bad Boy of Music*, appeared in 1945.

APOLLINAIRE, Guillaume (1880–1918) was a kind of literary impresario. A polyglot, born in Rome of Polish parents, he chose French as his literary language. He was associated with advanced literary and artistic movements whose work was marked with exoticism, irony, and sometimes buffoonery.

BAUM, Vicki (1888–1960), a popular German novelist and scenarist, whose best-known book, *Grand Hotel*, was an international stage and screen success. She settled in Los Angeles in 1931.

BARNES, Djuna, American novelist. In Greenwich Village she was an original member of the Washington Square Players, later the Theatre Guild, and the Provincetown Players. Her celebrated *roman à clef, Nightwood*, which records

367

certain aspects of Paris life in the twenties, appeared in the United States in 1936 with a foreword by T. S. Eliot.

BARNEY, Natalie, bilingual poet and novelist, was born in America but migrated to Paris in the early years of this century. Because of her skill as a horsewoman Rémy de Gourmont nicknamed her "Amazone." Her salon on Rue Jacob was a meeting place for society and literature. She is said to have suggested the character "Valerie" in *The Well of Loneliness,* a novel by Radclyffe Hall which was banned in England in 1928 and temporarily suppressed in the United States.

BAYES, Nora (1880–1928), stage name of Dora Goldberg, American vaudeville and musical comedy star. Introduced such songs as "Take Me Out to the Ball Game" (written by her partner, Jack Norworth), "Over There" (*the* song of World War I; introduced in her own show at the special request of the composer George M. Cohan), and "Japanese Sandman," a great hit of 1921.

BEACH, Sylvia, was the American proprietor of the famous Left Bank bookstore, Shakespeare and Company. Here in the twenties everybody who was anybody, and some who were nobody, bought and borrowed books, left messages, and collected mail.

BEASLEY, Gertrude, was born in Texas. After attending Simmons College in Abilene, Texas, and teaching, she went first to the University of Chicago and then to Paris. Her "naturalistic" autobiography, which McAlmon published in 1925, did not create the *succès de scandale* she had hoped for.

BEERBOHM, Mary, because of her family connections and her charm, was well known in London's literary and theatrical circles and to the expatriates on the Left Bank. She and Nina Hamnett (q.v.) were often seen together.

BELL, Clive (b. 1881), British critic of contemporary art and literature. A prominent member of the Bloomsbury group, he married Vanessa Stephen, daughter of the critic Sir Leslie Stephen, and sister of Virginia Woolf.

BENDA, Julien (1867–1956), French intellectual who regarded himself as a cleric in a Religion of Intelligence. In *The Treason of the Intellectuals* (English translation 1928) he mourns the defeatist surrender of the intellectuals and their withdrawal from temporal affairs.

BIDDLE, George, American artist. One of the Philadelphia Biddles, he was educated at Groton and Harvard, and lived in Paris from 1923 to 1926. He had much more spacious quarters than most of the American expatriates, and many of *les personnalités marquantes* assembled there. His reminiscences, *An American Artist's Story,* appeared in 1939.

BIRD, William (b. 1888), American journalist, was raised in Buffalo, N.Y., where two of his schoolmates were David Lawrence and H. R. Baukhage. With Lawrence he started an international news syndicate in 1920 and has lived abroad ever since. A man of considerable charm, he appears prominently in many memoirs of the twenties, but has not yet written his own. He has lived in Tangier since 1945.

BODENHEIM, Maxwell (1893–1954) is the prototype of one kind of Bohemian. Born in Mississippi, he early moved to Greenwich Village and spent his entire adult life there. He is remembered principally as a poet. In his novels, some of which were exceedingly frank, he showed himself an impassioned, bitter critic of current institutions. The keynote of his fiction is hatred. His memoirs, *My Life and Loves in Greenwich Village* (1954), came out the same year that he and his third wife were found murdered in their dingy fifth-floor room on the lower East Side. In his later years Bodenheim had been reduced to begging on the streets and selling his poems in bars.

BONI, Albert (b. 1892), American publisher. Before World War I, Boni and his brother Charles were proprietors of the Washington Square Bookshop, later (1917) founded the publishing firm of Boni and Liveright in partnership with Horace Liveright. In 1923 the Bonis established an independent publishing house. Albert Boni helped organize the Washington Square Players which became the Theatre Guild, and was generally associated with the advanced literary and artistic movements of the twenties.

BOYLE, Kay (b. 1903) is one of the most distinguished of contemporary novelists and short-story writers. Born in St. Paul, Minnesota, she studied music in Cincinnati, and in 1921 went to France with her first husband, a Frenchman. She was encouraged in her writing by Eugene Jolas (q.v.) and Ernest Walsh (q.v.), and in spite of economic and personal difficulties earned an enviable critical reputation within a relatively short time. After living in many parts of Europe, she returned to the United States in 1941, bringing her six children with her.

BRANCUSI, Constantin (1876–1960), Roumanian sculptor whose elegant abstract forms are familiar to a wide public. In the twenties Brancusi was to sculpture what Picasso was to painting and Joyce to prose. He lived in Paris from 1904 until his death.

BRYHER (b. 1894) was christened Annie Winifred Ellerman, the daughter of the British shipping magnate Sir John Ellerman (q.v.), and took the name of one of the Scilly Isles for her professional name. Her historical novels have had substantial critical success. She was married to Robert McAlmon from 1921 to 1927. A person who has always disliked publicity, Bryher has lived in Switzerland for many years.

BUCK, Pearl (b. 1892) was awarded the Nobel Prize for Literature in 1938. Previously (1932) she had received the Pulitzer Prize for her novel *The Good Earth*.

BURKE, Kenneth (b. 1897) is an American critic and literary theorist whose books have become increasingly opaque with the years. His reputation is massive, especially among the New Critics.

BUTTS, Mary (1891–1937) belonged to a distinguished British family, whose ancestral portraits hang in the National Gallery, and she herself was drawn by Cocteau. At one time Mary Butts's books were praised, but according to Sylvia Beach "her life was tragic and her work, which was so promising, was interrupted suddenly by death." She published a kind of autobiography, *Crystal Cabinet,* in 1937.

CALLAGHAN, Morley (b. 1903), after his return to Canada, where he was born, made a considerable reputation as a novelist and man of letters.

CARNEVALI, Emanuel, was a young Italian poet who came to America before 1920 and quickly adopted American ways, or thought he did. Carnevali, who died in Italy in the mid-twenties, was generally liked by the expatriate group. He was supported for a time by Robert McAlmon.

COATES, Robert M. (b. 1897), a New Englander and a Yale man, wrote "the first Dada novel in English," *The Eater of Darkness,* which McAlmon published in 1926. It was Coates who introduced Ernest Hemingway to Gertrude Stein. Since 1928 he has been on *The New Yorker* staff, drawn there by his friendship with the late James Thurber.

COCTEAU, Jean (b. 1891), French man of letters, genius, eccentric, and expert in public relations. Gifted in promoting not only himself but also new styles and fashions, he is responsible for many innovations in painting, motion pictures, poetry, and criticism.

COWLEY, Malcolm (b. 1898) has been regarded as the quasi-official historian of the Paris expatriates since the publication of *Exile's Return* (1934, revised edition 1951), originally titled *The Lost Generation.* Cowley returned to America in the summer of 1923 and has lived in and around New York ever since. In 1948 he became literary adviser of the Viking Press.

CRANE, Hart (1899–1932) began writing verse in his early teens and by 1930 had produced *The Bridge,* a mystical interpretation of the past, present, and future of America. In his personal life, Crane was undisciplined and beset by emotional and economic problems. Returning by ship from Mexico, where he had gone as a Guggenheim scholar, he threw himself overboard. His life is sometimes regarded as the great tragedy of modern American literature.

CROSBY, Caresse, was born Polly Jacob of a prominent New York family. Her first husband was Richard Rogers Peabody of the Boston Peabodys, and her second Harry Crosby (q.v.). In Paris the Crosbys founded the Black Sun Press (1927). After Harry Crosby's death, Mrs. Crosby carried on the work of the Press, bringing out significant avant-garde works, many for the first time in English translation.

CROSBY, Harry, is in some respects the representative expatriate of the twenties, according to Malcolm Cowley. The nephew of J. P. Morgan, he cut himself loose from traditional values and experimented with a variety of esoteric philosophies; at the last he claimed to be a sun-worshiper. His death in what appears to have been a suicide pact was violent and symbolic. Caresse Crosby has described their life together in *The Passionate Years* (1953).

CUMMINGS, E. E. (b. 1894), like Hemingway, Cowley, and Dos Passos, served in the ambulance corps during World War I. He wrote of his experiences in a French concentration camp in *The Enormous Room* (1922). His poetry is marked by romantic emotions and typographical pyrotechnics.

CUNARD, Nancy, of the British shipowning family, was a great friend of George Moore's and founder of the Hours Press in Paris (1928). One of the "Bright Young People," she shocked society on both sides of the Atlantic by living in an all-Negro rooming house in Harlem—she befriended Henry Crowder, a handsome Afro-American who was a promising musician. Her mother, Lady "Emerald" Cunard (born Maude Burke of San Francisco), Yeats's patroness, was a celebrated London hostess and lion-hunter. Mother and daughter signally failed to get along, and at one time Nancy made Lady Cunard the target of a stinging magazine article.

DAVIDSON, Jo (b. 1883), American sculptor, best known for his busts of such personages as Woodrow Wilson, Anatole France, and later figures of political and literary importance.

DIAGHILEV, Sergei Pavlovich (1872–1929), a Russian aristocrat who introduced the Russian ballet to Europe and America. Diaghilev commissioned work by the greatest composers and artists of the day, and many of his ballets have become part of the standard repertory.

DOBSON, Frank (b. 1888), professor of sculpture in the Royal College of Art, London. He founded the X group of English sculptors. Some of his work is in the Tate Gallery.

H.D. (Hilda Doolittle) (1888–1961), Imagist poet and novelist. According to her husband Richard Aldington (q.v.), when Ezra Pound first read some of her poems he became "so much worked up . . . that he removed his pince-nez and informed us that we were imagists." Pound insisted that she sign her work "H.D. Imagist," and there are some critics who hold that the Imagist movement and H.D. are synonymous. Her autobiographical novel, *Bid Me to Love* (1960), is concerned with the dissolution of her marriage. For many years before her death H.D.'s home was in Switzerland.

DOS PASSOS, John (b. 1896), in his early work was stubbornly experimental in form and rebellious in subject matter. His novel *Three Soldiers* (1921) drew on his wartime experiences in the ambulance corps; *Manhattan Transfer* (1925) attempted to picture New York life through myriad impressionistic descriptive passages and through the simultaneous unfolding of the stories of several characters on different social levels. He later used this same technique to greater advantage in his trilogy *U.S.A.* (1930–1936). What is so significant about Dos Passos's work, according to Alfred Kazin, is that "though he is a direct link between the post-war decade and the crisis novel of the depression period, the defeatism of the lost generation has been slowly and subtly transferred by him from persons to society itself." At one time influenced by Marxian doctrines, Dos Passos as he has grown older has moved progressively to the right.

Douglas, Norman (1868–1951), Austrian-born Scottish novelist and essayist, lived a life which "was a negation of many of the rules for propriety on the so-called haughty level." He was best known for his sophisticated novel *South Wind* (1917) and for his brilliant and unconventional travel books. *Looking Back: An Autobiographical Excursion* appeared in 1933.

Dreiser, Theodore (1871–1945) unwittingly gave impetus to the establishment of private presses such as McAlmon's. The failure of *Sister Carrie* (1900) because of the squeamishness of publishers and their nice-nellie wives was a *cause célèbre* and explanation enough for the private publication of frank works of fiction.

Duchamp, Marcel (b. 1887), French painter, pioneer Dadaist, and (according to Sir Herbert Read) the forerunner of surrealism. His "Nude Descending the Stairs"—referred to in the popular press as "Cyclone in a Shingle Factory"— was a star attraction at the famous Armory Show of 1913. At one time Duchamp was adviser to Peggy Guggenheim (q.v.), and assisted her in building up her collection of modern art.

Earp, Thomas W., was an Oxford contemporary and friend of Aldous Huxley and Robert Graves. During World War I, in which he did not serve, Earp, according to Graves, "had set himself the task of keeping the Oxford tradition alive . . . as president and sole member, he said, of some seventeen undergraduate social and literary societies." A man of independent wealth, Earp frequently fed his hungry Bohemian friends. His essays appeared occasionally in English literary periodicals.

Ellerman, Sir John (d. 1933) was a self-made shipping magnate, accustomed to taking risks, and equally accustomed to coming out on top. A difficult man, he was extremely devoted to his wife, who was deaf and temperamental, and dominated his two children, Bryher (q.v.) and her much younger brother John (b. 1910). Ellerman fancied himself a patron of the arts, but was morbidly afraid of being cheated. He owned several literary magazines and a large block of shares in the *Times*. At his death he left an estate valued at forty million pounds.

Epstein, Sir Jacob (1880–1959) was born on New York's lower East Side, but settled in London in 1905. He survived critical abuse and the snickers of the general public, was knighted, and became the Grand Old Man of British sculpture. His autobiography, *Let There Be Sculpture*, appeared in 1940.

Fellowes, Daisy, daughter of the fourth Duc Decazes, was married to Prince Jean de Broglie in 1910. After his death in 1918 she married the Hon. Reginald Fellowes. She is the author of several books, all in French except one about cats on the Isle of Man (1929). She has contributed comment to American and British magazines, and lives in England.

FIRBANK, Ronald (1886–1926), whose literary reputation is currently booming, was the son of Sir Thomas Firbank, M.P., and a doting mother. As a Cambridge undergraduate he was famous for his preciosity and his fin-de-siècle tastes, and in the twenties he was a much-pointed-out figure in literary London. He detested "the mob" and females, was both shy and exhibitionistic, and became the subject of many legends.

FITZGERALD, F. Scott (1896–1940) in much of his later writing seems to be trapped in the age which brought him early celebrity. His brilliant and witty narrative accounts of life in American cities, on the Riviera, and in Paris echo many overtones of the twenties.

FLETCHER, John Gould (1896–1950) was one of the Imagists. An Arkansan, educated privately and at Harvard, he lived in Europe before and after World War I. In addition to his poetry he wrote several books of criticism and an autobiography, *Life Is My Song* (1937). He drowned himself in 1950.

FORD, Ford Madox (Hueffer) (1873–1939) during his editorship of the *English Review* (1909) published some of the best contemporary writing, thanks in part to his friendship with Conrad, Hardy, James, Eliot, Norman Douglas, and other literary grandees. He attempted to repeat his success in Paris with *the transatlantic review* (1924), but the magazine lasted only a year. Ford's novels recently have attracted new attention. His memoirs are not always factually reliable.

FOURNIER, ALAIN- (1886–1914), whose real name was Henri Fournier, completed only one book, *Le Grand Meaulnes*. The story of adolescents caught in love and adventure, its principal charm lies in its constant suggestion of deeper significance. Alain-Fournier was killed in action early in World War I.

GALANTIÈRE, Lewis, Chicago-born belle-lettrist, translator, and editor, worked for the American section of the International Chamber of Commerce in Paris early in the twenties. He was a friend of Sherwood Anderson, and took Hemingway around when he came to Paris in 1921. Galantière and the Hemingways lived at the Hotel Jacob on the Left Bank.

GILBERT, Stuart, arrived in Paris from Burma (1927), where he had been a British civil servant. Quickly caught up in the Joyce–Sylvia Beach circle, he assisted in translating *Ulysses* into French. His book on *Ulysses* was written with Joyce's help, and in 1957 he edited Joyce's letters. Because of his wit and precision, he has made a reputation as translator of Camus, Malraux, and others.

GOULD, Wallace, who claimed he had Indian blood, was born in Maine. When he brought his poems to New York, he found the city so frightening that he fled to Virginia and there spent the rest of his life. A great mountain of a man, Gould had many talents. He was a superb cook and for a time supported himself by baking three kinds of pound cake which he sold by mail. In Farmville, Virginia, he lived with Miss Mary Jackson, a middle-aged lady of Knickerbocker stock, whom he eventually wed. She found him dead one morning lying on his face by the woodpile, clad in his old brown wrapper. A few months later Miss Mary herself died, still a virgin, so it was said.

GUGGENHEIM, Peggy (Marguerite), belongs to a family celebrated for its philanthropies. She began collecting contemporary art relatively late in the course of her international peregrinations, and made a splash in New York championing modern (for the most part, nonobjective) painting. Nothing like so rich as some of her relatives, at the present time she houses her collections in Venice where they are on public display. Her two volumes of memoirs discourse on her life and loves. *Out of This Century* (1946) is filled with international gossip; *Confessions of an Art Addict* (1956) is more concerned with artistic matters. McAlmon was one of her particular friends when she lived in London in the twenties.

HAMNET, Nina, an English artist, was a friend of Sickert, Epstein, and Henri Gaudier-Brzeska in pre-World War I London days. In 1920 she went to Paris where she was one of the international set of the glittering postwar period. Although she was more Bohemian than most, her family connections gave her the entrée into salons closed to all but the well-born. She is the author of an uninhibited volume of reminiscences, *Laughing Torso* (1932).

HARTLEY, Marsden (1877–1943), American expressionist painter. Although he lived in Greenwich Village, Paris, Berlin, and elsewhere in Europe, Hartley had some of his greatest success painting the landscape of his native Maine. His poems appeared in little magazines during the twenties, and were collected after his death.

HEAP, Jane, was the associate editor and later editor of *The Little Review*. An outspoken woman who looked—according to William Carlos Williams— like "a heavy-set Eskimo," she fancied herself as something of an executive type and was skeptical of much that then passed for art and poetry. She was prosecuted (with Margaret Anderson) for obscenity when *The Little Review* published *Ulysses*.

HEMINGWAY, Ernest (1898–1961) quoted Gertrude Stein's pronouncement, "You are all a lost generation," as an epigraph in *The Sun Also Rises* (1926), and thus gave it world-wide currency. *The Sun Also Rises* is the best narrative picture of the period; its account of an artistic-literary society continues to influence young writers, often adversely. Most of the characters were suggested by people well known in expatriate circles.

HEMINGWAY, Hadley Richardson, was Ernest Hemingway's first wife. They met in the spring of 1921 when he was working on a magazine in Chicago, and were married that September.

HERRMANN, John, was one of the group of writers surrounding Eugene Jolas and *transition*. Herrmann's only book, *What Happens*, concerns a jewelry salesman in the Middle West. In 1925 he married the novelist Josephine Herbst.

HUDDLESTON, Sisley, British "author, journalist, critic and Bohemian," collected celebrities, but unlike most Paris expatriates had a wide acquaintance among the French as well as among English and Americans. His review of *Ulysses*—in the London *Observer*, 5 March 1923—was the first to appear; while acknowledging the work's genius, it deplored its vulgarity and materialism. Huddleston's *Paris Salons, Cafés, Studios* (1928) is filled with anecdotes about personalities of the time and place.

HUEBSCH, Ben W., was one of the most enterprising and colorful of the publishers active in the first quarter of this century. Without the flair of Horace Liveright, he had good business judgment and recognized a number of important writers early. In 1925 his house merged with the Viking Press.

JOHN, Augustus (1878–1961), British painter and etcher, usually identified with the impressionist school. He was already eminent by the twenties, and sometimes defended the art work of such avant-gardists as Wyndham Lewis (q.v.).

JOLAS, Eugene (1894–1952), whose parents were from the province of Lorraine, was born in the United States but spent his first fifteen years in Lorraine. Fluent in English, German, and French, he founded *transition*, "An International Quarterly for Creative Experiment," which was to be devoted to "The Revolution of the Word." Jolas was an admirer of James Joyce, and published his *Work in Progress* (*Finnegans Wake*) seriatim. Jolas's tall, good-looking wife was a Kentuckian.

JOYCE, James (1882–1941) was the dominant figure on the literary scene of the twenties.

KIKI of Montparnasse was a well-known artist's model.

KREYMBORG, Alfred (b. 1883) was the sage of Greenwich Village; founder of *Others* (the *others* who were not published in Harriet Monroe's *Poetry*) in 1915; co-founder with Harold Loeb of the expatriate magazine *Broom*; an experimental playwright; and in the early twenties regarded by some critics as the white hope of American poetry. His rather self-conscious memoirs, *Troubadour*, appeared in 1925.

LANHAM, Edwin M. (b. 1904), a Texan who attended Williams College, was a young sailor when McAlmon knew him. His book *Sailors Don't Care*, written with McAlmon's encouragement, received some critical attention. Subsequently a newspaperman, a novelist, and a Guggenheim fellow, in recent years he has written first-rate, literate mystery stories.

LARBAUD, Valéry (b. 1881), widely traveled, multilingual French man of letters, sees it as his mission to introduce the literature of one language to the people of another. His own books are said to be "a sort of continuous veiled autobiography."

LARDNER, Ring (1885–1933), columnist, humorist, sportswriter, whose short stories dealing with the sports and entertainment world are little classics of their kind. Generally cynical treatments of conventional subjects, they are notable for their exploitation of colloquial speech.

LEWIS, Grace Hegger, first wife of the novelist Sinclair Lewis (q.v.), has written of their marriage in *With Love from Gracie: Sinclair Lewis: 1912–1925* (1955).

LEWIS, Sinclair (1885–1951) was the first American to be awarded the Nobel Prize in Literature (1930). While it is generally agreed that his best work was done in the twenties, *It Can't Happen Here* (1935) has continuing interest.

LEWIS, (Percy) Wyndham (1886–1957) regarded himself as one of "the men of 1914," the others being Eliot, Pound, and Joyce. A painter, poet, novelist, and polemicist, he said that he was "like one of those portmanteau-men of the Italian Renaissance." His work is marked by anger and invective, and he was as controversial in political matters as in artistic.

LOEB, Harold, a cousin of Peggy Guggenheim (q.v.) and related to the founders of both the Wall Street firm of Kuhn-Loeb and the Loeb Classical Library, published *Broom,* the first expatriate literary quarterly. He was the original of "Robert Cohn" in *The Sun Also Rises.* His memoirs appeared in 1959.

LOWELL, Amy (1874–1925), of the famous Boston family, captured Imagism from Ezra Pound, whereupon he renamed it Amygism. Her flamboyant personality and important connections helped to publicize the experimental verse forms in which she was interested.

LOY, Mina, a beautiful English poet, mother of two equally beautiful daughters. In Greenwich Village she was a contributor to Kreymborg's anthologies, *Others,* and in Paris her cerebral poems appeared in McAlmon's *Lunar Baedecker* (sic). She was also an artist—at one time in the twenties she supported herself by decorating lamp shades—and after many years out of the spotlight had an art exhibit in New York. In 1958 Jonathan Williams published, or republished, her *Lunar Baedeker and Time-Tables.* Still beautiful, Mina Loy now lives in Colorado near her daughters.

LUHAN, Mabel Dodge (b. 1879) has shared her *Intimate Memories* in a four-volume work (1933–1937), the third of which tells of the years her New York salon was frequented by the leading lights of Greenwich Village. Malcolm Cowley has said that "she collected people in exactly the same spirit as she collects china dogs for her mantelpiece." Among them were John Reed, Max Eastman, Carl Van Vechten, and—perhaps the prize catch—D. H. Lawrence, to whom she devoted another book, *Lorenzo in Taos* (1932). Since 1923 she has lived in Taos, New Mexico, with her fourth husband, a Pueblo Indian.

MCALMON, Victoria, elder sister of Robert, appears under various pseudonyms in his fiction. In 1923 she visited her brother and the Ellermans in England. Because she was vice-president of the Farmer-Labor Party in Minnesota (Floyd Olson was its moving spirit), she became well acquainted with the Sidney Webbs, the Snowdons, and leaders of the English Labor Party. In 1930, after being fired from the Minnesota Public School system for her political activities, Miss McAlmon joined the faculty of Los Angeles City College. She lives in Los Angeles.

MENCKEN, H. L. (1880–1956) was literary critic and all-around iconoclast on *The Smart Set* (1908–1923), of which he became co-editor with George Jean Nathan in 1914. Subsequently he and Nathan edited the *American Mercury* (1924–1933), which they founded and which, it is said, had a liberating effect on American tastes. The Paris expatriates did not generally regard Mencken as one of their own, considering him a member of his own "booboisie."

MILLAY, Edna St. Vincent (1892–1951) "was a song and a flame, more daring and light-hearted about love than any woman had ever been in English verse," Carl Van Doren wrote, recalling the early twenties in his memoirs *Three Worlds* (1936). Edmund Wilson has described hearing her recite her poems at a Greenwich Village gathering— "She was dressed in some bright batik, and her face lit up with a flush that seemed to burn also in the bronze reflections of her not yet bobbed reddish hair"—and has stressed "her intoxicating effect on people . . . the spell that she exercised on many, of the most various professions and temperaments, of all ages and both sexes." As well as being cherished by her contemporaries, Edna Millay symbolized to the postwar younger generation the romantic appeal of Bohemian life—an appetizing Murgeresque Bohemia as opposed to the tawdriness and violence of that inhabited by Maxwell Bodenheim (q.v). Her poetry received the Pulitzer Prize in 1923.

MONNIER, Adrienne, published *Le Navire d'Argent,* which introduced Hemingway, Williams, Cummings, and McAlmon to French readers (see page 3). Her bookshop, La Maison des Amis des Livre, was just across Rue de l'Odéon from that run by Sylvia Beach, whose friend and adviser she was. Mlle. Monnier adopted a distinctive style of dress—a long, full skirt, tight velvet waistcoat, and a cloak—and was an impressive figure on the Left Bank scene. She liked Americans, and Americans liked her.

MONROE, Harriet (1860–1936) in 1912 founded *Poetry: A Magazine of Verse,* one of the first and most influential of the little magazines, which is still being published in Chicago. Miss Monroe printed—and paid for—the work of both new and already established poets. Although it was her work as an editor rather than her writing which was of consequence in American letters, she titled her autobiography *A Poet's Life* (1938).

Moore, Marianne (b. 1887) has gone her own way from her earliest years. Regardless of where the literati have chosen to congregate, she has remained in Brooklyn writing her own kind of witty, intellectual poetry, going to the zoo, and rooting for the Dodgers (while they were in Brooklyn to be rooted for). A red-headed lady given to large hats, Miss Moore is anything but Bohemian. Her friends range from Ezra Pound and William Carlos Williams to an executive of the Ford Motor Company who invited her to suggest a name for a new line of automobiles.

Moss, Arthur, who once characterized the early twenties as "days of drab realism, freudian frightmares, cabellaisian subtleties, and general literary license," edited *The Quill* in Greenwich Village (1917–1921) and *Gargoyle* in Paris (1922). The latter ran reproductions of paintings by Isaac Grunewald, Georges Braque, and others of the avant-garde. Moss was associated with William Carlos Williams on the revived *Contact* of 1932.

Munson, Gorham (b. 1896), American economist and critic, was founder and editor of *Secession* (1922–1924), a "group review" which has been described as "a queer mixture of juvenilia, arrogance, and good sense." Its contributors included E. E. Cummings and Waldo Frank. Munson was one of Hart Crane's earliest acquaintances in Greenwich Village; in Paris he was introduced to the Left Bank literati by the painter-photographer Man Ray (q.v.). Munson's memoirs, "The Fledgling Years, 1916–1924," appeared in the *Sewanee Review* (Spring 1932).

Porter, Katherine Anne (b. 1894) has published a comparatively small body of work, but she is generally recognized as one of the most gifted prose writers and finest literary craftsmen of our time. Miss Porter, who now lives in Connecticut, was born in Texas and in the twenties and thirties lived for extended periods in Mexico and Paris.

Pound, Ezra (b. 1885), the most influential teacher of his generation, has aided or helped to shape the careers of Robert Frost, T. S. Eliot, Hart Crane, and Archibald MacLeish, among others. Born in Idaho and educated at Hamilton College and the University of Pennsylvania, he traveled on the continent before settling in London (1909–1919). At the beginning of the twenties he spent a few years in Paris, then moved on to Rapallo (1924) where he remained until after World War II. From 1946 until 1958, Pound was held in St. Elizabeths hospital in Washington, D.C. Since then he has lived in Italy.

Putnam, Samuel, now well known as the translator of Rabelais and Cervantes, has recalled the expatriate years in *Paris Was Our Mistress* (1947). He came to Paris in the twenties, thanks to the help of his publisher, Pascal Covici, and remained to found a magazine of his own, *The New Review* (1931–1932).

Radiguet, Raymond (1903–1923) was a French prodigy, a protégé of Jean Cocteau, whose novel of adolescent passion, *The Devil in the Flesh* (1923; English translation 1932) caused a stir. It continues to be highly regarded, and has been made into a successful motion picture.

RIDGE, Lola (1871–1941), a Greenwich Village personage, was born in Ireland and reached New York in 1907 by way of Australia. She wrote poems on the beauty and brutality of New York life, and her consistent theme was the martyrdom of the downtrodden. Miss Ridge had a critical success during the twenties but no financial success whatever at any time.

RODKER, John, was at one time a protégé of Ezra Pound, who placed his poems in leading periodicals. When a second edition of *Ulysses* was called for in 1922, Rodker hired a room in Paris and acted as agent of the Egoist Press which brought it out. Before 1920 he had begun to print books on a small hand press, and he published a good deal of erotica on his own.

ROSENFELD, Paul (1890–1946) was the music critic on *The Dial* (1920–1927) and from 1927 to 1936 co-editor (with Van Wyck Brooks, Alfred Kreymborg, and Lewis Mumford) of *The American Caravan,* an annual which sought to provide "a medium able to accommodate a progressively broader expression of American life." His work and personality are the subject of an appreciative sketch, "Paul Rosenfeld: Three Phases," in Edmund Wilson's *Classics and Commercials* (1950).

SCHIFF, Sydney, was a late-blooming English novelist—he did not begin to write until he was fifty—with a passion for privacy. Under the pseudonym Stephen Hudson he wrote *Richard Kurt* (1919), *Myrtle* (1925), and *Richard, Myrtle, and I* (1926). He was a close friend of Katherine Mansfield and of Marcel Proust, one volume of whose work he translated.

SHORTER, Clement (1857–1926), English editor and critic, founded *The Sketch* (1893) and *The Tatler* (1903). A bibliophile, he had four enthusiasms: the Brontës, George Borrow, Samuel Johnson, and Napoleon.

SLOCOMBE, George (b. 1894) is an English journalist of wide interests—he has written books on Polish history, Henry of Navarre, and the French impressionists. He was foreign correspondent for a number of newspapers, and during the twenties reviewed some of the books by his friend James Joyce. His autobiography appeared in 1936.

SOUPAULT, Philippe (b. 1897), like Cocteau and a few other Frenchmen, "had gone in for cultivating Americans," according to McAlmon. Influenced by Rimbaud and Apollinaire, Soupault played a prominent part in the Dadaist movement and, like Gertrude Stein, experimented with automatic writing. By 1927, when he wrote his autobiography, he had turned to the study of politics. He was imprisoned by the Vichy government in 1942, and subsequently spent two years in the United States before returning to France.

STEIN, Gertrude (1874–1946) moved to Paris in 1902 and except for an American lecture tour in 1935 stayed in France until its fall in World War II. Her salon on the Rue de Fleurus was renowned both for the persons who gathered there and for the paintings on its walls—"the oldest permanent collection of modern French art in Paris," according to Janet Flanner. While critics are by no means agreed as to the value of Miss Stein's writing or her place in American letters (she herself was in no doubt about either), her style has left its mark and she was a force to be reckoned with. She has told her story in *The Autobiography of Alice B. Toklas* (1933), her first popular success.

STEIN, Leo (1872–1947), art critic and brother of Gertrude Stein, was regarded by some as the real genius in the family. He himself said that the famous collection of paintings reflected *his* judgment; and it is true that Gertrude Stein discovered no new painters of consequence after she and her brother quarreled. Leo Stein's journals were published in 1950.

STEWART, Donald Ogden (b. 1894), an Ohioan and a Yale man, served in the navy during World War I. His immensely successful *Parody Outline of History* (1921) and *Perfect Behavior* (1922) spoofed current best-sellers by H. G. Wells and Emily Post; *Mr. and Mrs. Haddock Abroad* (1924) and *Mr. and Mrs. Haddock in Paris* (1926) were comic commentaries on American tourists in Europe. His play *Rebound* was a Broadway hit of 1930.

STRANGE, Michael (*née* Blanche Marie Louise Oelrichs) wrote fashionable poetry in the twenties. One of her books was illustrated with drawings by John Barrymore, her first husband. *Who Tells Me True*, her autobiography, appeared in 1940.

SULLIVAN, J. W. N. (1886–1937) wrote on scientific subjects for the general reader. *Aspects of Science* (1923) was his most successful book; he later tried to popularize Einstein's theory in *Three Men Discuss Relativity* (1926). He also contributed to literary periodicals, and wrote an interesting study of Beethoven (1927).

THOMSON, Virgil (b. 1896), American composer, wrote the score for *Four Saints in Three Acts* (1934), the opera by Gertrude Stein, first performed in Hartford, Connecticut, under the auspices of the Friends and Enemies of Modern Music. In the twenties Thomson studied in Paris with Nadia Boulanger. Later he became music critic of the New York *Herald Tribune* (1940–1954), and very powerful.

TOKLAS, Alice B. (b. 1877), for many years the friend and companion of Gertrude Stein. After Miss Stein's death, Miss Toklas published a fascinating cookbook (1954) illustrated by Sir Francis Rose, her friend's last "discovery."

TREE, Iris, British actress, daughter of Sir Herbert Beerbohm Tree and favorite niece of Max Beerbohm. With Lady Diana Manners she toured America in the Morris Gest–Max Reinhardt production of *The Miracle* (1924).

TZARA, Tristan (b. 1896), a Roumanian poet who has lived most of his life in Paris. One of the founders of Dadaism, he edited the magazine *Dada* (1916–1920) and later was identified with the surrealists.

VAIL, Laurence, "knew all the American writers and painters and a lot of French ones too," according to his former wife, Peggy Guggenheim (q.v.), who saw him as a "king of Bohemia." At the time they were married, Vail, although an American citizen, had lived all his life abroad; he was the son of a rich New England mother and a French-American father who painted. His sister CLOTILDE VAIL is a singer. Vail's second wife was Kay Boyle (q.v.).

VALÉRY, Paul (1871–1945), French poet and man of letters, was associated with the symbolists and a member of the Mallarmé circle. (He was married to Mallarmé's daughter.) On his election to the French Academy in 1925, succeeding Anatole France, he delivered a slighting address about his predecessor instead of paying him tribute as was customary. During the twenties Valéry was a major influence in both French and English literature.

VAN VECHTEN, Carl (b. 1880), after some years as a music and drama critic on various New York papers, wrote a succession of novels, immensely popular in the twenties, alike in their agility, Gallic sophistication, and watered aesthetics. A friend of Gertrude Stein, he was her self-appointed agent in America.

WALSH, Ernest, went to Paris knowing that he was soon to die of tuberculosis. With funds supplied by his patroness, Ethel Moorhead, he founded a literary review, *This Quarter* (1925–1926), and put together three brilliant issues before his death. Accepting freedom as the *sine qua non* for the artist, Walsh allowed the contributors' work to appear wholly unedited. Ethel Moorhead wrote of him that he was "an irreverent man, without standards, without tracks. . . . A hard-witted man. A fiery-hearted man . . . A NEW MAN."

WEAVER, Harriet, edited *The Egoist: an individualist review* (1914–1919), published in London. Joyce's *Portrait of the Artist as a Young Man* appeared in its pages. Miss Weaver, who had never met Joyce, sent him money anonymously so that he might be spared some of his financial worries while working on *Ulysses;* and she converted *The Egoist* into the Egoist Press to bring out his books. Because of the English censorship laws, she was unable to publish *Ulysses*. On her death in 1961, T. S. Eliot wrote her obituary in *Encounter*, 99 (1962), 101.

WESCOTT, Glenway (b. 1901) drew on his life in Wisconsin for much of his early fiction. Only since 1940 has he worked with subject matter unrelated to pioneer midwestern families.

WEST, Nathanael (1903–1940) was the pseudonym chosen by Nathan Weinstein —in response, he said, to Horace Greeley's time-hallowed injunction. After graduating from Brown, he went to Paris (1925–1926), where he was exposed to Dadaism, surrealism, Joyce, and psychoanalysis, all of which left their traces on his first novel, *The Dream World of Balso Snell* (1931). In 1932 he was co-editor with William Carlos Williams of the revived *Contact*. During his few remaining years he wrote *Miss Lonelyhearts* (1933) and *The Day of the Locust* (1939) and worked in Hollywood as a scenarist. Shortly after his marriage to Eileen McKenny (title figure of Ruth McKenny's *My Sister Eileen),* he and his wife were killed in an automobile accident on their way back from a deer hunt in Mexico. His *Complete Works* came out in 1957.

WINDELER, B. Cyril, is the pseudonym of one of Ezra Pound's protégés of the twenties. Windeler's first book of verse was published by William Bird, and subsequent volumes were brought out by Oxford University Press. His verse play *King Minos of Knossos* (1935) received good notices.

WILLIAMS, William Carlos (b. 1883), poet and novelist, has spent his whole life as a family doctor in Rutherford, New Jersey. Cataloging his likes and dislikes, he once wrote: "I like flowers, plants, trees, and would have a private hothouse for my amusement if I could afford it. I like nearly all children, especially when they are in misfortune. I like women as contrasted with men. I dislike almost everyone between the ages of eleven and fifty-eight. I like old people. I detest the triumphant stupidity of American critics. I like Ezra Pound. I like oranges."

ZUKOVSKY, Louis, was associated with William Carlos Williams in the Objectivist movement. Together they published a few books, including an Objectivist Anthology and Williams's *Collected Poems*.

Bibliography of Robert
Mcalmon's Published Works

I. BOOKS

Explorations. London: The Egoist Press, 1921.

A Hasty Bunch. Paris: Contact Publishing Co., n.d. (1922).

A Companion Volume. Paris: Contact Publishing Co., n.d. (1923).

Post-Adolescence. Paris: Contact Publishing Co., n.d. (1923).

Village: as it happened through a fifteen year period. Paris: Contact Publishing Co., 1924.

Distinguished Air (Grim Fairy Tales). Paris: Contact Editions at the Three Mountains Press, 1925.

The Portrait of a Generation. Paris: Contact Editions, Three Mountains Press, 1926.

North America, Continent of Conjecture. Paris: Contact Editions, 1929.

The Indefinite Huntress and Other Stories. Paris: Crosby Continental Editions, The Black Sun Press, 1932.

Not Alone Lost. Norfolk, Conn.: New Directions, 1937.

Being Geniuses Together. London: Secker and Warburg, 1938.

II. CONTRIBUTIONS TO PERIODICALS AND COLLECTIONS

1919

"Flying: Aero-Laughter, Aero-Metre, Consecration, Consummation, Volplanetor, Perspicuity," *Poetry,* XIII (March 1919), 317–321. "Aero-Metre" and "Aero-Laughter" reprinted in *The Literary Digest,* 61 (5 April 1919), 40; "Aero-Laughter" reprinted in *The Independent,* 98 (26 April 1919), 125.

1920

"Essentials," *The Little Review,* VII, 3 (September–December 1920), 69–71.

"[Credo]," *Contact,* 1 (December 1920), 1.

"The Via Dolorosa of Art: White Males, Today's Music, Form Destructionist-Sculptor," *Poetry,* XVII (December 1920), 117–129.

1921

"Modern Antiques," *Contact,* 2 (January 1921), 9–10.

"Superwoman," *Contact*, 2 (January 1921), 8.
"The Blue Mandrill," *Contact*, 2 (January 1921), 8.
"Contact and Genius," *Contact*, 4 (Summer 1921), 16–17.
"White Males"; "The Wild Boar," *The Tyro*, I, 1 (1921), 6, 12 (back cover).

1922
"Blackbird," *The Bookman* [New York], 54 (February 1922), 587.

1923
"What Is Left Undone," *The Little Review*, IX, 4 (Spring 1923), 32–43.

1924
"Elsie," *the transatlantic review*, I, 1 (January 1924), 59–64.
"Three Generations: The Same," *The Little Review*, X, 1 (Spring 1924), 43–57.
"Away," *The Bookman* [New York], 59 (July 1924), 532.
"Joseph Conrad," *the transatlantic review*, II, 3 (Conrad Supplement), (September 1924), 343–344.
"[Extract from] Village," *the transatlantic review*, II, 6 (December 1924), 655–661.
"Three Poems: How variously in France . . . ; Brothers; The black cat loops . . . ," *The Little Review*, X, 2 (Autumn–Winter 1924, 1925), 3–9.

1925
"Extract from Spring Leaves Again to Consider," *Contact Collection of Contemporary Writers* [Paris: Contact Publishing Co.], 195–213.
"Extract from Work in Progress [Benny at the Revival Meeting]," *This Quarter*, I, i (Spring 1925), 167–172.
"Contributions: Completion, For Instance, Query," *Poetry*, XXVII (October 1925), 12–15; "Completion" reprinted in *The Literary Digest*, 87 (31 October 1925), 32.
"The Bullfight," *The New Coterie*, 1 (November 1925), 49–51.
"Extract from 'Transcontinental,' " *This Quarter*, I, 2 (Winter 1925–1926), 124–155.

1926
"New American Literature," (London) *Outlook*, 58 (28 August 1926), 191–192.

1927
"Deracinated Encounters," *This Quarter*, I, 3 (Spring 1927), 204–241.
"Extract from a Novel [Ni in the Desert]," *transition*, 5 (August 1927), 66–73.
"Truer than Most Accounts," *The Exile*, 2 (Autumn 1927), 40–86.

1928
"The Revolving Mirror," *larus*, I, 5, 6, 7 (April, May, June 1928) [one number], 10–39.
"Why Do Americans Live in Europe? [a symposium]," *transition*, 14 (Fall 1928), 98–100.
"Gertrude Stein," *The Exile*, 4 (Autumn 1928), 70–74.

1929

"Tales from Childhood: Potato Picking, The Jack Rabbit Drive," *transition*, 15 (February 1929), 84–101.

"Mr. Joyce Directs an Irish Prose Ballet," *transition*, 15 (February 1929), 126–134; reprinted as "Mr. Joyce Directs an Irish Word Ballet" in *An Examination of James Joyce*, [by McAlmon and others], Paris: Shakespeare and Co.; Norfolk, Conn.: New Directions; London: Faber & Faber, 105–116.

[Answer to Questionnaire], *The Little Review*, 12 (May 1929), 52–53. (With photograph of McAlmon).

"Potato Picking." *The Best Short Stories of 1929*, ed. Edward J. O'Brien. New York: Dodd, Mead Co., pp. 159–168.

"An Illiterate but Interesting Woman." *The New American Caravan, A Yearbook of American Literature*, ed. Alfred Kreymborg, Lewis Mumford, Paul Rosenfeld. New York: The Macaulay Company, pp. 161–164.

1930

"New England Victorian Episodes: Pennythinker," *Pagany*, I, 1 (Winter 1930), 25–30.

"The Crow Becomes Discursive," *The Hound and Horn*, III, 2 (January–March 1930), 212.

"A Romance at Sea," *Pagany*, I, 3 (Summer 1930), 28–33.

"Blithe Insecurities," *Pagany*, I, 4 (Fall 1930), 32–52.

"New York Harbour," *The Morada*, 5 [December 1930], 8–12.

1931

"Blithe Insecurities," *Pagany*, II, 1 (Winter 1931), 60–81.

"Fortuno Carraccioli," *Poetry*, XXXVII (February 1931), 247–251.

"Green Grow the Grasses," *Front*, I, 2 (February 1931), 97–107.

"In-Between Ladies," *Pagany*, II, 2 (Spring 1931), 41–49.

"[Excerpts from] Fortuno Carraccioli," *The Literary Digest*, 109 (9 May 1931), 24.

"New York Sleepwalking (The final chapters of a U.S. transcontinental novel)," *Pagany*, II, 4 (Fall 1931), 22–37.

1932

"The Highly Prized Pajamas," *The New Review*, I, 4 (Winter 1931–1932), 371–382.

"New York Sleepwalking," *Pagany*, III, 1 (Winter 1932), 87–100.

"It's All Very Complicated," *Contact*, I, 1 (February 1932), 64–79.

"Mexican Interval (An Excerpt)," *Contact*, I, 2 (May 1932), 40–51.

"Farewell to Alamos," *Contact*, I, 3 (October 1932), 88–91.

"Leavetaking." *Americans Abroad, An Anthology*, ed. Peter Neagoe. The Hague: The Servire Press, pp. 251–262. (With photograph of McAlmon).

"Child-Blithely." *An "Objectivists" Anthology*, ed. Louis Zukofsky. Le Beausset, Var, France & New York: TO, Publishers, p. 162.

"Historical Reminiscence." *An "Objectivists" Anthology*, ed. Louis Zukofsky. Le Beausset, Var, France & New York: TO, Publishers, pp. 41–42.

1934

"Tales of the Open Plains: The Crow Becomes Discursive, The Race, The Blackbird, The Silver Bull, The City, Threshing Season, The White Wolf, The Mother, The Frost in the Corn, The Wild Boar," *The New English Weekly*, V, 10 (21 June 1934), 228–230.

"The Mother," *The Literary Digest*, 118 (28 July 1934), 28.

"Wisdom Garnered by Day," *Life and Letters*, XI, 59 (November 1934), 157–165.

1935

"Gertrude Stein," *The New English Weekly*, VI, 21 (7 March 1935), 431.

"[Excerpts from] North America: Continent of Conjecture," *The New English Weekly*, VII, 6 (23 May 1935), 110; VII, 9 (13 June 1935), 170; VIII, 1 (17 October 1935), 31.

Index

Acknowledgments

I should like to thank the following persons for the help they have given me: Professors Norman Holmes Pearson and John C. Thirlwall, William Carlos Williams, William Bird, Kay Boyle, Ezra Pound, Robert M. Coates, Katherine Anne Porter (for a conversation which she has no doubt forgotten), and most especially Miss Victoria McAlmon. Their help has considerably lightened my labors. I am grateful also to Berenice Abbott for her friendly cooperation during the assembling of photographs for the picture section, and to Richard Greene, Assistant Art Editor, Collier's Encyclopedia, for his valuable assistance in locating news pictures.

Finally, I should like to thank the following publishers for permission to use copyrighted material: Harcourt, Brace & World, Inc. for permission to quote from *Shakespeare and Company* © 1956, 1959, by Sylvia Beach, and Random House Inc. for permission to quote from *The Autobiography of William Carlos Williams* © 1951 by William Carlos Williams.

R.E.K.

A Note on the Editor

Robert E. Knoll, a native Nebraskan, was educated at the University of Nebraska (B.A., 1943) and the University of Minnesota (M.A., Ph.D., 1947, 1950). Since 1950 he has been a member of the faculty of the University of Nebraska where he is an associate professor of English. He has edited an anthology, *Contrasts*, and is the author of *Robert McAlmon: Expatriate Publisher and Writer*, the first study on McAlmon to appear anywhere. Professor Knoll also has contributed articles to *College English* (on which he is a book review editor), *American Speech, Western Humanities Review*, and other scholarly publications.

79
83
85
89